BRADSHAW'S

GUIDE THROUGH LONDON

AND ITS ENVIRONS:

EXHIBITING IN A NOVEL AND COMPREHENSIVE FORM ALL THAT CAN BE SEEN

IN

THE METROPOLIS AND ITS VICINITY,

FOR THIRTY MILES ROUND,

FORMING A COMPLETE AND INDISPENSABLE COMPANION

TO THE RESIDENT AND STRANGER.

BY E. L. BLANCHARD.

AUTHOR OF ADAMS'S DESCRIPTIVE GUIDES TO THE "ENVIRONS OF LONDON,"
"THE WATERING PLACES OF LONDON," ETC. ETC.

CORRECTED AND REVISED UP TO THE LATEST PERIOD
BY H. KAINS JACKSON.

LONDON
W. J. ADAMS (BRADSHAW'S GUIDE OFFICE);
59, FLEET STREET.
MANCHESTER:—BRADSHAW AND BLACKLOCK
AND ALL BOOKSELLERS.
AND AT EVERY RAILWAY STATION THROUGHOUT GREAT BRITAIN AND IRELAND.

First published in Great Britain in 1861.

This edition published by in 2012 by
Conway
An imprint of Anova Books Ltd
10 Southcombe Street
London W14 0RA
www.anovabooks.com
www.conwaypublishing.com

A CIP catalogue record for this book is available from the British Library.

ISBN 9781844861828

Typeset by Mission Productions Ltd, Hong Kong
Printed and bound by CPI Group (UK) Ltd, Croydon, CR0 4YY

Publisher's Note:
In this new edition, typographical errors in the original have been corrected, with the
exception of instances where the common spelling of Victorian words would seem to differ
to their modern-day equivalents. Examples include visiters, Magna Charta and Shakespere (although these do occasionally take the modern form). The two maps titled Map of
London and Map of the Environs of London (25 miles round), which originally appeared
opposite the Title and at the end of the book cannot be reproduced in this edition due to
the limitations of size.

ABOUT THE AUTHOR.

George Bradshaw (1801–1853) was an English cartographer, printer and publisher. He is most famous for developing a series of railway timetables and guides, recently popularised by Michael Portillo in his TV series *Great Railway Journeys*. These became synonymous with their publisher so that, for Victorians and Edwardians, a railway timetable was 'a Bradshaw'. After his death Punch magazine said of Bradshaw's labours: 'seldom has the gigantic intellect of man been employed upon a work of greater utility'.

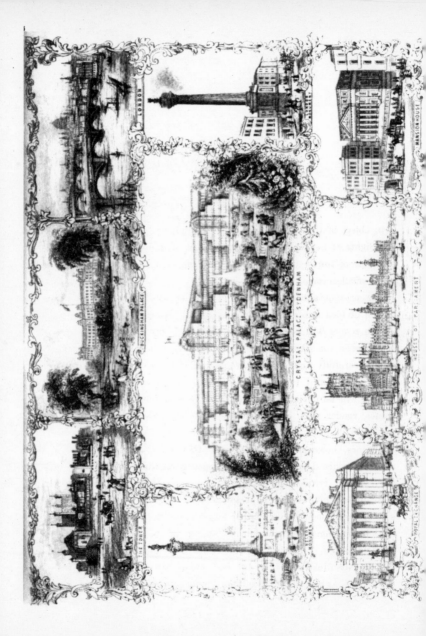

PREFACE.

THE object of this work is to supply a compact yet compendious Guide to the Sights of London, and the chief places of interest and attraction within a circuit of thirty miles, so as to give the greatest amount of information in the smallest compass.

The present edition has been remodelled in the form of an Itinerary, and is divided into such portions or routes through each district of London as the reader will be able to visit in a given time. Every object worthy of attention in the great metropolis is distinctly noticed, and each day's routes are so carefully and clearly arranged that the confusion and unnecessary fatigue incidental to an irregular and discursive wandering hither and thither will be obviated, while each day's walks are varied to diversify the scenes, render them entertaining, and thus enhance the pleasure of a visit to London.

Visitors, however, must be aware that their enjoyments of the most alluring scenes depend, in a great measure, on the frame of mind in which they admire, criticise, or satirise the various objects and peculiarities that come under their notice. A person in good humour always sees the sunny side of every cloud, while another is too prone to be prejudiced by unfavourable impressions. An anecdote is related of the impressions received by two old ladies, who went to receive their dividends at the Bank, which humorously illustrates how different minds are affected by the same circumstances, as noticed by dispositions of a diametrically opposite character.

A

A gentleman having called upon those ladies, on their return from the city, he was addressed as follows :—

"Well, Mr. H.," said Mrs. P. to him on entering the room, "we had a most agreeable ride to the Bank on Thursday, everything looked so lively; and, though we were tossed about over the rough stones, it was amusing to see the variety of people and the numerous carriages; such faces full of business, such evidences of a brilliant commerce—I was quite sorry when we got home again." Mrs. L., the sister, then entered the room, and, not having heard a syllable of the above, approached Mr. H. with an air as if expecting condolence. "I suppose," she remarked, "my sister has told you that we were almost jolted to death in that rumbling coach the other day; and it was so hot with the sun shining on it, and we were such a long time, drawl, drawl, through Fleet Street and Ludgate Hill, that I thought we should never have reached the end of our journey! I wish we could be saved the trouble of going for our money another time."

The grumbler was by much the most robust of the two; it was simply, then, the contrast between a mind disposed to receive pleasure wherever it was possible to extract it, and one attentive only to inconveniences, that caused these opposite remarks.

After three or four days' visit to the sights of the metropolis, the reader may wish to take an excursion for a day or two to some of the places of attraction in the vicinity of London, to recruit his energies and spirits, and complete his walks in the metropolis.

Among the most attractive of these excursions are those to the Crystal Palace, at Sydenham, one of the greatest treats imaginable, surpassing all conception; those to Windsor Castle, Hampton Court, Richmond, &c., &c., particulars of which will be found in the Appendix, with the necessary information as to conveyance to and from each of these places.

CONTENTS.

	Page
London as it was	8
London as it is	14

PART I.——THE CITY.

DISTRICT I.

The City, Ancient and Modern—The City Companies—St. Paul's Cathedral—Its Early History—The Present Structure—Charges of Admission—The Monuments—The Library—The Medal Room—The Great Bell—The Clock—The Whispering Gallery—The Outer Galleries—The Ball and Cross—The Crypt—St. Paul's School—The General Post-Office—Statistics of Letters—Goldsmiths' Hall—Cheapside—Bow Church—City of London School—The Guildhall—Bucklersbury, &c. 24

DISTRICT II.

The Mansion House—St. Stephen's, Walbrook—The Bank of England—The New Royal Exchange—Lloyd's—The Stock Exchange—Lothbury—Cornhill—The East India House—The Museum—Crosby Hall—The South Sea House—Modern Improvements and Antiquities 37

DISTRICT III.

Doctors Commons—Herald's College—Southwark Bridge—Queenhithe—Vintry—Whittington's Tomb—London Stone—Merchant Tailors' School—King William Street—The Monument—London Bridge—Thames Street—The New Coal Exchange—Billingsgate—The Custom House—The Tower—The Armouries—The Jewel Office—The Batteries and the Parade—Tower Hill—The Trinity House—The Mint............................ 43

DISTRICT IV.

Stationers' Hall—Warwick Lane—Newgate Market—Christ's Hospital—Newgate—The Old Bailey—Central Criminal Court—St. Sepulchre's—The Compter—Smithfield Market—Bartholomew's Hospital—St. John's Gate—The Charter House—Aldersgate Street—Whitecross Street—Panyer Alley—Holborn Hill—The Fleet—St. Andrew's Church—Ely Place—Ancient Law Courts—Holborn Bars................................. 54

DISTRICT V.

The "Times" Printing Office—Apothecaries' Hall—Blackfriars Bridge—Bridewell—St. Bride's Church—Fleet Street—St. Dunstan's—Chancery Lane—The Rolls—Temple Bar—The Temple—The Inner Temple—The Middle Temple—The Temple Church—The Temple Gardens 59

PART II.——THE EAST.

DISTRICT I.

St. Katherine's Docks—The London Docks—The Tobacco Warehouses—The Wine Vaults—
Wapping—The Thames Tunnel—Shadwell—Limehouse—The West India Docks—
Blackwell—The East India Docks—The London and Blackwall Railway............ 67

DISTRICT II.

Aldgate—Houndsditch—The Minories—Goodman's Fields—Whitechapel—Whitechapel
Road—Jews' Burial Ground—The London Hospital—Mile End Road—Bancroft's Alms-
Houses—Bethnal Green—Bonner's Fields—Victoria Park—Shoreditch—Norton Fol-
gate—Bishopsgate Without—Finsbury Circus—London Institution—Roman Catholic
Chapel, Moorfields 72

PART III.——THE WEST.

DISTRICT I.

Temple Bar to Charing Cross—St. Clement's Church—Clement's Inn—Strand Lane—The
New Church—Somerset House—King's College—Waterloo Bridge—The Savoy—
Exeter Hall—Hungerford Bridge and Market—Charing Cross Hospital—West Strand—
Trafalgar Square—Nelson Column—Jenner Monument—National Gallery—Royal
Academy, &c., &c. 76

DISTRICT II.

Charing Cross—The Admiralty—Horse Guards—Whitehall—The Treasury—Government
Offices—Westminster Bridge—Palace Yard—Westminster Hall—St. Margaret's—
Westminster Abbey—Poet's Corner—The Chapels—Dean's Yard—The Cloisters—The
Chapter House—Westminster School—The Old House of Commons—The New Houses
of Parliament—The Royal Entrance—The Victoria Tower—The House of Lords—The
House of Commons—Milbank—Chelsea New Bridge—The Penitentiary—Vauxhall
Bridge—Pimlico 83

DISTRICT III.

Charing Cross—Pall Mall East—The Haymarket—The Club Houses—Pall Mall— St. James's
Palace—St. James's Street—St. James's Park—The Green Park—Buckingham Palace—
Hyde Park Corner—Apsley House—Hyde Park—Kensington Gardens— Holland House
—Piccadilly—Albemarle Street—The Royal Institution—Mansions of the Nobility 101

DISTRICT IV.

Charing Cross to Leicester Square—Regent Street—St. James's Hall—Hanover Square—
Oxford Street—Princess's Theatre—Pantheon—London Crystal Palace—Langham Place
—Polytechnic Institution—Portland Place—Soho Square—New Oxford Street—St.
Giles's-in-the-Fields—Interesting Monuments—Seven Dials—Drury Lane—Long Acre
—Covent Garden Market—Bow Street—Theatres—Lincoln's Inn Fields—Sir John
Soane's Museum—The New Lincoln's Inn Hall—Royal College of Surgeons—Museum
of the College—Gray's Inn, Holborn—Bedford Row—Red Lion Square, &c 114

PART IV.——THE NORTH.

DISTRICT I.

Tottenham Court Road—Great Russell Street—The British Museum—The Natural History
Department—The Egyptian Antiquities—The Elgin Marbles—The Nimrod Marbles,
&c.—The Reading-Room and Library—London University College—The New Road—
Regent's Park—Botanic Gardens—Zoological Gardens—Villas—St. John's Wood—Pad-
dington—Marylebone—Fitzroy Square—Euston Square—Terminus of the North-
Western Railway—St. Pancras New Church—Burton Crescent—Guildford Street—
The Foundling Hospital, &c 132

DISTRICT II.

Gray's Inn Lane—King's Cross—Coldbath Fields—House of Correction—Sadler's Wells—The New River—Pentonville—Model Prison—Caledonian Asylum—Copenhagen Fields—Islington—Canonbury—Highbury—City Road—Old Street Road—St. Luke's—Bunhill Row—Artillery Ground—Clerkenwell, &c., &c................................ 151

PART V.——THE SOUTH.

London Bridge—The Borough—St. Saviour's Church—St. Olave's—Railway Stations—St. Thomas's Hospital—Guy's Hospital—Bermondsey—Old Inns—St. George the Martyr—The Mint—Prisons—Newington Causeway—Surrey Zoological Gardens—London Road—The Blind School—St. George's Cathedral—Bethlehem Hospital—Blackfriars' Road—Waterloo Road—Kennington Road—Vauxhall Gardens—Old Lambeth Church—Lambeth Palace—The Lollard's Tower—Astley's Theatre—Stamford Street—Bankside—Barclay's Brewery—Borough Market—Conclusion.. 156

THE TOUR OF THE THAMES

PART I.

Up the River—From London Bridge to Hampton Court, &c......................... 170

PART II.

Down the River—From London Bridge to the Nore................................ 179

GREENWICH.

Billingsgate—The Custom House—The Tower—St. Katharine's Docks—London Docks—Wapping—Rotherhithe—The Tunnel—West India Docks—Deptford—Greenwich—The Hospital—The Painted Hall—The Royal Observatory—The Park—Blackheath—Lee—Shooter's Hill—Eltham—Eltham Palace—Woolwich—The Artillery Barracks—The Royal Arsenal—The "Repository" and "Rotunda" —The "Military College" —The Dockyard—Arrangements of Admission—Return to Town................................ 185

GRAVESEND.

Erith—Purfleet—Dartford—Greenhithe—Northfleet—Rosherville—Gravesend—Windmill Hill—Tilbury Fort—Springhead—Cobham—Cobham Church—Cobham Hall—Cobham Wood—Return to Gravesend 193

WINDSOR.

Great Western Railway—Slough—Windsor—Windsor Castle—Saint George's Chapel—The Round Tower—Arrangements of Admission—The State Apartments—The Slopes—Windsor Park—The Long Walk—Equestrian Statue of George III.—Virginia Water—Belvidere—The Cascade—Fishing Temple—The Grecian Ruin—Bishopsgate—Shelley—Stoke Pogis—Gray—Burnham Beeches 202

Richmond 208
Hampton Court 211
Epsom 214
Crystal Palace, Sydenham.. 215

ILLUSTRATIONS.

	PAGE.
ARMY AND NAVY CLUB HOUSE	217
BRITISH MUSEUM	81
BUCKINGHAM PALACE	(Opposite Preface)
CHELSEA HOSPITAL	217
COVENT GARDEN MARKET	81
CRYSTAL PALACE, SYDENHAM	(Opposite Preface)
EAST INDIA HOUSE, LEADENHALL STREET	81
LONDON DOCKS, ENTRANCE TO THE, EAST SMITHFIELD	67
FLEET STREET AND ST. DUNSTAN'S WEST—MID-DAY	59
GREENWICH HOSPITAL	217
HAMPTON COURT	217
HORSE GUARDS, WHITEHALL	81
HOUSES OF PARLIAMENT	(Opposite Preface)
KEW GARDENS	217
LONDON (1590) IN THE REIGN OF QUEEN ELIZABETH	9
LONDON (1851) IN THE REIGN OF QUEEN VICTORIA	16
LONDON MONUMENT	(Opposite Preface)
LONDON, VIEW OF	,,
MANSION HOUSE	,,
NATIONAL GALLERY, TRAFALGAR SQUARE	81
NELSON MONUMENT	(Opposite Preface)
REGENT STREET AND ALL SOULS' CHURCH, LANGHAM PLACE	121
REGENT STREET FROM THE QUADRANT	81
ROYAL EXCHANGE	(Opposite Preface)
STATUE OF ACHILLES, HYDE PARK	81
STATUE OF THE DUKE OF BEDFORD, RUSSELL SQUARE	81
TEMPLE BAR	217
THE TOWER	(Opposite Preface)
WATERLOO PLACE AND PART OF REGENT STREET	81
WESTMINSTER ABBEY	217
WHITEHALL	217

LONDON (1590) IN THE REIGN OF QUEEN ELIZABETH.

THE STRAND, FLEET STREET, AND ST. PAUL'S (LOOKING EASTWARD),

With Old London Bridge and the Church of St. Mary Overy, Southwark, in the distance.

BRADSHAW'S LONDON GUIDE BOOK.

LONDON AS IT WAS:

It would be at once tedious and unsatisfactory, within the limited space to which we are necessarily restricted, if we attempted to follow through the successive reigns the different changes by which the metropolis was affected. The massacre of the Jews in the reign of Richard I.; the election of Henry Fitz-Alwyn as Mayor in the reign of King John; the rebellion of Wat Tyler in the fifth year of the reign of Richard II.; the continuous wars, alternating with the ravages of famine and pestilence, and the institution of various offices which arose out of the granting of additional privileges, are all amply recorded in the larger histories of the metropolis, but can here be little more than referred to. It will be a far pleasanter task to the reader than wading through the dry details of antiquity—which would be little more than a mere string of dates as we should be compelled to present them—if we glance instead at the City under its more graphic aspects, and by that means contrive to invest the information we are able to afford with a few points of acknowledged general interest.

We have some curious evidence in the old maps about the time of Elizabeth to show what London really was prior to the change effected by the great fire of 1666. It would be a singular contrast to conjure up before the mental vision of the omnibus passenger of the present day the appearance of the unpaved, unbuilt-on high-road of the Strand, even as it existed so late as the reign of the second Charles. The line, now unbroken, between London and West-minster, was then only conspicuous for a few scattered houses, and a village which afterwards gave a name to the whole. The church of St. Martin's literally stood "in the Fields," and all the houses on the south side had large gardens down to the river's edge, which were all distinguished by the names of the owners, and have since given rise to the various names of streets built on their site. At the end of these gardens were stairs for the convenience of taking boats, a customary conveyance then from the City to the Court. The north side of the Strand was a straight line of houses from Charing Cross to Temple Bar, and all beyond was country. The convent gardens, which then occupied part of the site of Covent Garden, were then bounded by open fields, and St. Giles's was a little distant country village. The carriage ways were left unpaved, and in wet weather the soft mire therein was left to accu-mulate until it became several feet deep. Westminster had only a few detached houses on each side of Tothill Street, some having large gardens stretching towards the Park, and some on the other side with gardens extending to Orchard Street. The Gate House (demolished in 1777) at the entrance of Tothill Street, was used as a prison for state, ecclesiastical, and parliamentary offenders, as well as for debtors and felons. The latter were brought hither through Thieving Lane and Union Street, to prevent the possibility of the culprit escaping from justice by entering the hallowed liberties of the sanctuary. Here was imprisoned the illustrious Raleigh im-mediately previous to his execution in Palace Yard. Even so late as 1763, Buckingham House enjoyed an uninterrupted prospect south and west to the river, there being only a few scattered cottages and the Stag Brewery between it and the Thames. There were none of those filthy courts between Petty France and the Park, nor any buildings in Palmer's Village or Tothill Fields, or by the Artillery Ground. There were a few pretty villas about Pye Street and Duck Lane, and these were surrounded with gardens on the banks of a pleasant stream of water; but beyond these there were no other buildings whatever.

In the reign of James I., the chief part of London was along Newgate

Street, Cheapside, the Poultry, and Cornhill, and the various streets and alleys leading from them to the banks of the Thames. Except in Coleman Street, and a few scattered houses in Lothbury and Bishopsgate, all the way lower down was garden-ground or fields. There was an irregular street from Bishopsgate to Shoreditch Church, with open fields behind the houses; and Houndsditch was a single row of houses looking on the City walls, with open fields behind them. What is now Goswell Street was then called the St. Albans Road, with a few houses. Clerkenwell consisted chiefly of the monastery, the gardens and buildings which had belonged to the church, and thence to Gray's Inn Lane was an open field, with a few gardens. From Holborn Bridge to Red Lion Street there were houses on both sides, but they ceased there, and the road to the small village of St. Giles had hedges on both sides. On the Surrey side there were not ten houses between Lambeth and where now is the west foot of Blackfriars Bridge; but from that point a row of houses was continued to the Borough. Where Christchurch now stands was a place of amusement called "Paris Gardens," and on these boards it is said that Ben Jonson was an actor. Below this was a large circular building for bull and bear baiting, a spectacle which Queen Elizabeth frequently attended. Southwark then extended but a short distance along the High Street, and there were only a few small houses scattered between Tooley Street and Horsleydown. From this sketch, derived from the maps of the period, some faint idea may be possibly presented to the reader of the rapid strides that have taken place within the last three centuries. Among the other causes that have contributed to its increasing importance may be mentioned the first formation of an American settlement, the opening of a trade with the Muscovite merchants, the establishment of the East India Company, and the trade that arose with Turkey and the Levant.

From the time of the reconstruction of the metropolis, its growth in extent and prosperity was very rapid. The revocation of the Edict of Nantes brought over a considerable number of French Protestants, who introduced the manufacture of silk, and peopled Spitalfields, and of others who, being ornamental jewellers and goldsmiths, were first established in Long Acre, Seven

Dials, and Soho. About the time of George I. the extension of building was visible in every direction. In 1718, several streets north of Tyburn Road ware laid out, and when the rows of houses were finished in 1792, it was called Oxford Street. The fifty new churches required for the increasing population were in progress, and Berkeley Square and its vicinity began to appear. At this time the Fleet River had wharves on each side for landing goods from the barges, which came up as far as Holborn Bridge. About the year 1733, the arching over the channel of the Fleet was commenced, and subsequently was extended to the Thames, forming even now one of the main sewers which falls into the Thames at Blackfriars Bridge. Fleet Market was next built, and the Fleet Prison, where a jail had stood since the twelfth century, was rebuilt, but the market has since been removed, and the prison pulled down. In 1728, the City conduits were destroyed, for the alleged reason that the public should be compelled to have the New River water laid on to their houses. In 1756, the New road was commenced, to lead from Paddington to the Bank. It is curious enough that this undertaking was vehemently opposed by the Duke of Bedford, who objected on the ground that he would be annoyed by the dust at his house, half a mile off, and that buildings might be erected which would destroy his prospect. Half a century ago, the Duke's house, that stood on the site of Bedford Place, was levelled to the ground, and now the fields beyond it are covered with mansions that enlarge the income of the Bedford family to the extent of two hundred thousand pounds a-year.

In 1747 the last beheading took place on Tower Hill, which had been a place of execution since the reign of Richard II., and in 1760 the houses and buildings were removed from London Bridge. In 1770 the City gates were removed, with the exception of Temple Bar, built a century before; and in 1783, the execution of criminals, that had previously taken place at Tyburn, was removed to the spot in front of the prison of Newgate. Of the old signs that swung over the shops till 1750, the barber's pole is about the only one that has descended to the present day. The shop fronts were not enclosed and glazed till nearly 1710, and each was open like those of the butchers at present. Maypoles stood in the Strand until 1718, and the heads of traitors frowned in terrible rows over Temple Bar until 1746.

For journeying between Westminster and the Tower, and between the Tower and Greenwich, the Thames was especially the royal road. The first Lord Mayor who went to Westminster by water was John Norman in 1454, and the pageant has been since kept up for more than four centuries, having been continued until 1857; in 1858 the aquatic portion of the ceremonial was discontinued. Stow computes that in his time there were 40,000 watermen upon the rolls of the company, and that they could furnish 20,000 men for the fleet. Great quantities of fruit were formerly brought to the London market, through the agency of the boats that then plied upon its "liquid way." Steele pleasantly describes a boat trip from Bichmond on an early summer morning, when he "fell in with a fleet of gardeners," and "landed with ten sail of apricock boats at Strand Bridge (stairs), after having put in at Nine Elms and taken in Melons." Such an arrival now would create no ordinary sensation at Covent Garden Market. Probably the last relic of going by water to places of amusement on the banks of the Thames was the voyage in small boats to Vauxhall Gardens, which to the present day have their "watergate." In 1737, this favourite mode of locomotion was thus graphically referred to:—

> "Lolling in state with one on either side
> And gently pulling with the wind and tide
> Last night, the evening of a sultry day,
> We sail'd triumphant on the liquid way,
> To hear the fiddlers of Spring Gardens play."

Till late in the reign of Elizabeth, London had no coaches; and they can scarcely be said to have come into general use until the accession of James I. Those who were called by business or pleasure to travel long distances from London, which could not easily be reached by water conveyance, rode on horses. For several centuries the rich citizens and the courtiers were equestrians. The coach first appeared in 1504. Some thirty or forty years after this date, a bill was brought into Parliament "to restrain the excessive use of coaches;" but this act of legislation was in vain. Coaches came soon to be hired. They were to be found in the suburban districts, and in inns within the town. In 1634 the first hackney-coach stand was established in London, by Captain Bailey, a naval officer. He had four hackney coaches; he put his men in livery, and appointed them to stand at the Maypole, near where Somerset House is now situated, and gave them instructions at what rates to carry passengers into several parts of the town. In 1634, also, was used the first sedan chair. Cabriolets were introduced in 1820. The omnibus was tried about 1800, with four horses and six wheels; but we refused to accept it in any shape, till we imported the fashion from Paris in 1830. There are now about 720 omnibuses for London, and upwards of 200 for the environs, the whole carrying upwards of 70,000 passengers each day, at fares varying between threepence and a shilling. It has been calculated, on the lowest average, that £2,980 per day, or £1,087,700 per annum, is expended in this mode of progression in and around London; the official weekly returns of one company alone (the London General Omnibus) showing an income of between £500,000 and £600,000 per annum, independent of all other associated or private conveyances.

Our retrospective glance at "London as it Was" would be incomplete without taking some notice of the localities where our forefathers sought their amusement, and which the reader may profitably and pleasantly contrast with the different opportunities afforded at the present day. The north side of London was famous for suburban houses of entertainment. Show-booths were erected in this immediate neighbourhood for merry-andrews and morris-dancers. The London Spa, in Exmouth-street, Clerkenwell, originally built in 1206; Phillip's new Wells; the Mulberry-gardens; the new Tunbridge-wells, a fashionable resort of the nobility and gentry during the early part of the eighteenth century; the Sir Hugh Middleton's Head; and Sadler's Music-house, now better known as Sadler's-wells, were all in this vicinity. Bagnigge-wells, once the reputed residence of Nell Gwynne, and White Conduit House, are both no more; the latter was finally demolished in 1849, the name only being retained by an ordinary tavern erected near the spot where stood the old and long-celebrated house, the spacious gardens of which have all been covered over with some hundred or two of modern residences. Canonbury-house, where Goldsmith lodged, and Highbury-barn, where he so often dined, are still in existence; but the rest have long since changed their attractions, and the very sites of many are forgotten. As population increased, the houses of entertainment spread south, east, and west. The Apollo-gardens, St. George's-fields; the "Dog and Duck," adjoining; Cumberland-gardens, Vauxhall; and the more celebrated Ranelagh and Marylebone-gardens, are all extinct; but the amusements now provided in their place are, if less distinguished by boisterous hilarity, infinitely better calculated to please a more refined taste.

With these preliminary observations, we will now proceed to consider London under its present aspect.

BRADSHAW'S LONDON GUIDE BOOK.

LONDON AS IT IS:

WITH A FEW SUGGESTIONS TO STRANGERS ON THEIR ARRIVAL.

WITHIN the last fifty years, London has more than doubled in extent; and, even as we write, is rapidly increasing in every direction. It was happily observed by Herschel, that London occupies nearly the centre of the terrestrial hemisphere—a fact not a little interesting to Englishmen; and, combined with our insular situation in that great highway of nations, not a little explanatory of our commercial eminence. No situation could have been more happily chosen. Though forty-five miles from the sea, it enjoys all the advantages of an excellent seaport, from its position on the Thames. Had it been built lower down the river, it would have been less healthy, and more exposed to hostile attacks; and, had it been placed higher up, it would have been deprived of all the advantages of a deep water harbour. It extends a length of nearly eighteen miles, calculating east and west from beyond Bow to Kew Bridge; and north to south, from Holloway to Clapham, may be estimated at a breadth of eight miles. The entire area is computed at thirty-five square miles. The number of houses is upwards of 298,000; and the rental derived from them is so enormous, that only an approximate guess can be made as to the real amount. The money expended by the inhabitants in one year is estimated at £70,000,000. Including the parliamentary boroughs created by the Reform Bill, the metropolis sends eighteen representatives to the Legislature. Of these, four are sent by the City, and two each from Finsbury, Tower Hamlets, Westminster, Marylebone, Southwark, Lambeth, and Greenwich. According to the latest returns, 28,734 vessels have been known in one year to enter the port of London; and the total average value of the property shipped annually on the Thames, is said to exceed one hundred million pounds sterling. The payments into the Exchequer, by the Custom house of London alone, amounts to as much as the net receipts of the other custom-houses in Great Britain and Ireland added together.

So vast is the population and magnitude of this metropolis of the world, that if the population of fifty of the principal cities and towns of England were added together, they would not make another London. So rapid is the growth of this queen of cities, that a population equal to that of Exeter is added to its number every eight months; but so overwhelmingly large is the capacity of this leviathan of towns, that, great as this progressive increase is, it is scarcely perceived. It is almost like throwing a bucket of water into the ocean.

The mean annual temperature is 52°, and the extremes 81° and 20°; the former generally occurring in August, and the latter in January. A smaller quantity of rain is said to fall in the vicinity of London than elsewhere in the kingdom. The prevailing wind is the south-west. It may easily be imagined that the vast town, with its dense and busy population accumulated within a circle of twelve miles in diameter, has some palpable influence upon the atmosphere over it. Such is the case. The artificially heated air sends up far more humidity in a state of vapour than the cold air above is capable of receiving, and this moisture being returned, mixed with particles of charcoal and various other infinitesimal ingredients, constitutes that terror of asthmatic country gentlemen called a London Fog. It is curious, however, that its action is found to be beneficial rather than the reverse; for, during its continuance, the fever wards of the hospitals are in great part cleared. Though there has been some diversity of opinion on the subject, it is now pretty generally acknowledged that the healthiest parts of London are the northern and north-western. On the elevated ground in Marylebone parish, says Dr. Arnott (no mean authority), the air is as pure as at Hampstead. The most unhealthy districts include the parishes in the neighbourhood of Whitechapel and Lambeth, whilst—though some allowance ought to be made for its better class of residents—the healthiest parish is St. George's, Hanover Square. In Whitechapel, 39 in 1,000 die annually; in St. George's, only 17 in 1,000—being a forcible illustration of the advantages of a more salubrious locality.

The latest returns of the Registrar-General give the average annual mortality of the City as 1 in 40, and that of the East and West London Unions, 1 in 36, (Cripplegate 1 in 32). The mortality of districts adjoining the City, is, for St. Leonard's, Shoreditch, 1 in 32; Whitecross Street, 1 in 33; City Road, 1 in 31: whilst the mortality of the healthier districts of the metropolis, is, for St. George's, Bloomsbury, 1 in 48; for St. John's, Paddington, 1 in 56; Stamford Hill, 1 in 63; and Dulwich, 1 in 91. Talent and ability are now not lacking to give to London all the benefit of its salubrious situation, and make it in reality, what it is comparatively, the healthiest city in the world.

In the midst of the 10,000 acres of bricks and mortar that, according to the latest computation, compose the modern Babylon, there is a plentiful supply of everything that can be required by its 2,336,060 inhabitants. There are 796 board and lodging houses, and for those who dine and breakfast abroad there is a choice of 330 dining-rooms, and 883 coffee-shops; besides, for the more affluent, who do not patronise the clubs, 398 hotels and taverns. There are 126 brewers and 66 distillers, and the channels through which their productions flow are amazingly numerous, including 4,340 publicans, 802 beer-shop keepers, eighty-eight ale and porter agents, and 770 wine-merchants, besides twenty makers of British wines. For the more intellectual wants, there are 858 private academies, 132 district and parochial schools, 62 British and Foreign, 17 national, and 50 collegiate institutions for granting degrees. Literature is disseminated by 452 printers, 780 publishers and booksellers, and 285 newsvendors. To those who are curious in names it may be worth while to observe that the not uncommon patronymic of "Smith" is borne by no less than 1,412 shopkeepers alone. The annual consumption is estimated at 190,000 bullocks; 776,000 sheep; 250,000 lambs; 270,000 pigs; 120,000 tons of fish; 11,000 tons of butter; 13,000 tons of cheese; 12,000,000 quarters of wheat, besides vast quantities of flour imported; 10,000,000 gallons of milk; 65,000 pipes of wine; 2,000,000 gallons of spirits; 2,000,000 barrels of ale and porter; and 3,000,000 tons of coal.

LOOKING EASTWARD FROM FLEET STREET.

Having thus prepared the visitor with these astounding statistics to antici-
pate the magnitude of a place having such marvellous capacities for absorption,
we now proceed to supply him with a few suggestions that may contribute to
his accommodation and enjoyment during his stay. On arriving by the train,
immediately after seeing to the disposal of his luggage, he should order the
driver of the vehicle to convey him at once to the hotel, inn, or boarding-
house that choice or private recommendation has rendered preferable.
Tables of the fares are to be found in the pages of "Bradshaw's Railway
Guide," which valuable little work, published monthly, price sixpence,
gives an immensity of information to travellers. As soon as he has commenced his noviciate in London, wonders begin to accumulate around
him.

An observant writer, recording his early impressions of the metropolis, says,
—"How pregnant with instruction to the mind seeking wisdom are the very
streets! How curious, recollecting that in fifty years these jostling crowds
will, with few exceptions, be mingled with the silent dust, to observe the eagerness with which, as if life and death depended upon a moment, they hurry hither
and thither, scarce taking time to see whether they can with safety pass across."
The first and strongest impression received by a stranger entering London, is
an idea of its illimitability. It is to him not only a world, but a world without
end, spreading its gigantic arms on every side. Miles of narrow dingy streets,
that, crammed to repletion with wagons, threaten to crush him between their
ponderous wheels and the contiguous walls, indicate the City, whose enormous
wealth and splendour are but poorly evidenced by dingy warehouses, dark
alleys, and retired counting-houses. Of late years the tradesmen in the leading
thoroughfares have vied with each other in generous rivalry, as to the style
of their shops and the display of their merchandise and many of the shops of
London glitter with plate-glass and valuable merchandise, almost realising
the fabled magnificence of Aladdin's palace. Hence, as from a fountain, the
stream of enterprise flows forth, inundating all lands, and returning only to flow
forth and fertilise again. Let him advance towards the West-end, and a
splendour less real than he has left behind, but more apparent, breaks upon

his astonished view. The shops of the goldsmiths, piled from floor to roof with the richest treasures of their art; the shawl-shops, through whose crystal fronts you catch the gorgeousness of their commodities within; the emporiums of art and *vertu*, where lessons of taste may be had for looking; the vast repositories of learning, appealing eloquently to the eye of the mind;—these, and a thousand other evidences of diffusive wealth, lead involuntarily to the belief that all the riches and splendour of the world must be gathered here for show. Whether we take the chaotic multitude that throng the City thoroughfares, all bustle and confusion, the subdued repose of patrician squares, the obscure alley, the princely terrace, the buildings, bridges, churches, halls, markets, theatres, hospitals, or shops, all is alike pregnant with matter meet for reflection and for wonderment, abounding in variety, contrast, novelty, and change.

About nine in the morning, the City streets begin to present an animated scene, for by that hour they are seen thronging with living beings, pouring in from every suburban radius to the great City centre like a walking torrent, until, so numerous appears the mass, London seems to be almost wholly populated by clerks. An hour afterwards, in cab and omnibus, a different class becomes visible, each looking as if the affairs of the universe rested on his individual shoulders; the compressed lip, the steady eye, the furrowed forehead, and the anxiety riding triumphant in every muscle, sufficiently denote them to be the employers. About this time the City may be considered to have received its full complement, and the bustle of the day is fairly commenced.

The whole of the metropolitan police consists of 5,504 men, of whom about only two-thirds can be on duty at one time—and these men have to traverse the extrordinary length of 3,626 miles of streets during the night, and have further to watch over and guard in the aggregate, 348,907 inhabited houses, 13,305 uninhabited houses, and 5,731 which are being built, with a population of 2,336,060 in an area of 700½ square miles. During the period of the Exhibition 8,000 extra police-officers added to the safety of property and persons in the metropolis and its environs.

Beneficent London teems with charitable institutions, hospitals, asylums, refuges for the destitute, the sick, and the lame, and the blind. Yet though there is scarcely a calamity that miserable humanity is liable to for which Pity in her affluence has not provided a palliative, the streets seem to he thronged with beggars. Without wishing to check the impulse of benevolence, we would recommend the stranger to be cautious in bestowing his indiscriminate charity as he walks along. This beggary is often a mere profession: and for those who happily have the means to spare, it is by far the best plan to make the magistrates of the public police-offices the almoners of their bounty.

In a city of such colossal proportions, it is not wonderful that fires should be numerous—sometimes as many as five or six occurring in one night. To guard as far as possible against the loss of life from these outbreaks, the Royal Society for the Preservation of Life from Fire have been most active, during the last few years, in establishing stations, where fire escapes, with conductors, are placed during the night, ready to be called upon the first alarm of fire. Upwards of 50 such stations are now established in London and its vicinity. No society more richly deserves encouragement, and it would be well if its stations were largely extended. Upwards of 400 lives have been saved by its instrumentality during the last few years. The annual cost of maintaining a station, with its Fire Escape, is £80, in addition to a first outlay of £10, for the machine, &c. The visitor to London will observe, as the dusk of evening approaches, the various Fire Escapes being wheeled to their appointed stations by the conductors. The Institution, like many others of a benevolent character in London, is chiefly supported by voluntary contributions.

An impartial French writer gives the following account of his impressions of London:—

"I warned you," he writes to a friend, "not to pay too much attention to my first impressions. I told you that I hated London, and afterwards, that the more I saw of it, the more I hated it. But now that I have seen still more of it, I begin to think it a very fine place. The general aspect of London is quite inferior to that of Paris. London has all the faults of great cities, in a greater degree, perhaps, than any other; and yet it seems to want almost all their redeeming virtues. From its immense extent, there is no consistency, completeness of effect, as the public buildings are so scattered about as to lose all power of producing an impression, except one by one. Yet, notwithstanding all this, London contains in detail much to interest and be admired. I have passed days in wandering about in the vicinity of the parks—though these can scarce be considered as part of London, though they are situated in, and enclosed by it on all sides. London contains also not less than four-and-twenty squares, which are greatly superior to anything else of the kind seen in great cities. None of them are smaller than the Place Vendome, and many of them are nearly as large as the Place de Louis XV."

The noise, the incessant din, the everlasting rumble that is at first so discordant to the ears of one coming from a quiet country place, soon becomes familiar; and it is only in the great thoroughfares, where the murmurs of myriad tongues blend with the hollow roll of the carriages, that it is ever troublesome. Not so the London mud, which, proverbial for the peculiarity of its attributes, stands unrivalled by any plebeian mud yet known. Gluey, well-kneaded, and at once sloppy and slippy, it requires a practised foot to maintain undisturbed the proud distinction of man over the lower animals—erectness of body. In crossing the streets after rain, the greatest care should be taken to avoid a fall.

The difficulty of selecting points of view whence we may form a correct estimate of the grandeur of London, is great. Views of the bird's-eye kind, like those from the Monument, St. Paul's, and the Duke of York's column, are by no means satisfactory, save in giving an idea of the vastness of its extent and the quantity of ground it covers. What with the smoke contending with haze and fog, and the great height by which the streets are narrowed into alleys, the passengers appear to be diminished to the size of ants, and seem merely to crawl along the surface of a spreading brick-red desert of tiles and chimney-pots. Instead of this, or if he will in addition to it, we recommend the individual who wants to see London under its best and most comprehensive aspect, to wend his way to Waterloo Bridge early, in a clear sunshiny morning, and there, leaning upon the parapet of the third arch from the Middlesex side, he shall behold a sight to which no other city in the world can afford a parallel.

The thickly clustered houses on every side proclaim the vast population, and the numerous towers and steeples, more than fifty of which, together with five, bridges, are visible from this spot, testify to its enormous wealth. One of the best of the suburban views is that from the archway at Highgate. The rural appearance of the road beneath, with the overhanging trees in the shrubbery on the side, and the glad chirp of birds, make a striking contrast with the world of brick and mortar that stretches forward before the eye, evidently fast encroaching upon the few remaining fields in the foreground, and apparently determined to exterminate all that is green and rural. The spires of several modern churches relieve the monotony of the mass of houses, which, at this end of London, are destitute even of the charm of antiquity to render them interesting; and, right before the eye in the distance, St. Paul's rears its well-known colossal form: a misty line beyond denotes the course of the river, and the range of the Surrey hills forms the background.

We account it needless to caution strangers against the pretended smugglers, the mock auctions, the gambling-houses, and the other nefarious places with which London, like all great cities, abounds. If he be a man of sense, his own discretion will prove his best Mentor; and, if the reverse, all the cautions in the world would never prevent his occasionally getting entangled in some one or other of the lures set in the metropolis to catch the unwary. We would have him, however, by all means avoid a crowd, which proves such a fertile source of emolument to the pickpockets. The directions of the main streets follow the course of the river Thames from east to west, and the cross streets run for the most part in a direction from north to south. This remembered, will facilitate the stranger in his progress from one point to another.

The plan we have adopted for description will be found, we believe, at once novel and advantageous. We take St. Paul's and the City as the starting point, and then divide London into its four divisions of East, West, North, and South. By this arrangement the visitor will find his task of observation much simplified, and a facility for reference given that has never been before imparted to works of a similar description.

Some new features, which the changes of the last two or three years have given the metropolis, may here be briefly noted. Upwards of 100 drinking fountains now exist, from which flow a continual stream of water, where three years since not a single one was known; and, although little artistic taste in their erection has, as yet been displayed, they must be highly useful, in a sanitary point of view. The fountains at the British Museum, at Adelaide Place, London Bridge, the Broadway, Camden Town, and in the Strand, are amongst those most generally approved. Street Railways are the latest, and are likely soon to become marked features of "London as it is;" the first two lines laid down, and now being worked at 2*d.* fares, are in each case only about a mile in length, and are along the Bayswater Road, and down the New Victoria Street, Westminster. In both places the roadways are of ample width, affording space for carriages to pass each other on one side of the tramway, which is not quite in the centre of the road. The rails are only half-an-inch raised above the surface, and the guage but 4ft. 8in.: they are kept clean by manual sweeping. The appearance of the tram carriages might be much improved, as it reminds one of a child's Noah's Ark; inside, however, there is little to be desired, they being both roomy and comfortable, and the mode of transit has many advantages which recommend its general adoption, as the obstacles, which in many of the crowded, narrow, and tortuous London streets, must prevent the introduction of a horse railway, will not arise on a hundred routes where there is a large passenger traffic to be accommodated at low fares. The system of communication introduced by the LONDON DISTRICT TELEGRAPH COMPANY is another novelty which deserves notice, adding as many nerves as there are wires to the great body of the metropolis, of which the energy was inert and cumbrous compared to what it may be, with

> "The words of fire
> Now breathed along the electric wire."

We can now whisper in any ear to which we desire to make a communication, whether the physical ear of our friend, man of business, or physician, be in his villa or counting-house, at law court, House of Commons, or railway station. The few particulars which follow are interesting:—At the Central Offices, in Cannon Street, City, nearly a hundred lines are collected, and then distributed to as many different telegraphic machines, before which sit rows of young ladies watching, or working their instruments, of which the principal use is to receive and transmit messages sent from the branch to this, the chief office, from and to the several localities in connection. These young ladies make the most expert and intelligent manipulators (their labours perhaps being lightened by enjoying the privilege dear to the fair sex, that of knowing other people's secrets, and which no one better than a woman can keep). Boys are employed to carry the messages where addressed, and are paid 1*d.* for each message, a method which makes them diligent and expeditious, whilst they earn more than the weekly wages at first paid them. Where the distances, as in the suburbs, is greater than in London, the company charge a minimum sum, being fully aware the universal adoption of their system depends on a low scale of charges. We need not indicate the messages, whether commercial or domestic, for which occasions daily occur to thousands, as they suggest themselves to every sensible person, and which, to send at once, would save both parties much trouble, anxiety, and expense. Messages by means of the London District Telegraphs can now be forwarded for 6*d.* and upwards, whilst for people of secret habits and cautious withal in conversation, such as be the merchants who most do congregrate about Mart and Stock Exchange; there are *special and private* agencies offered for some five pounds per annum, by which they may communicate, on a simple method, with all secrecy, the whispers too important for the ears of ordinary mortals (including the before-mentioned young ladies), an arrangement which city firms and the heads of departments divided from their bodies by distance will know how to value and support. A list of stations in operation may be obtained at the chief and branch offices, gratis.

We may appropriately conclude this introduction upon London Street Architecture, as it cannot fail, in its recent style of coloured bricks and ornamented fronts to attract the visitor's observation, promising to give our thoroughfares something of the picturesque appearance of many gabled old London. Amongst the most noteworthy of new buildings, are, the Crown Life Office, Bridge Street; an Insurance Office, near *Bradshaw's Guide Office*, Fleet Street; Sotheby and Wilkinson's Auction Offices, Wellington Street, Strand; Lavers and Barrand's Manufactory, Endel Street; St. Giles's National School, Broad Street, Bloomsbury; a Diamond Merchant's Shop, in Brook Street, opposite Messrs. Saunders and Otley, and some shops in Cheapside; these, and those magnificent piles of buildings erected and managed by hotel companies, such as the Grosvenor Hotel, at the Victoria Station; and the Victoria Hotel, Westminster Abbey, give a character to the localities in which they have been erected.

Having thus premised, we proceed with our systematic survey.

PART I.— THE CITY.

FIRST DAY'S ROUTE.

DISTRICT I.

THE CITY, ANCIENT AND MODERN—THE CITY COMPANIES—ST. PAUL'S CATHEDRAL
—ITS EARLY HISTORY—THE PRESENT STRUCTURE—CHARGES OF ADMISSION
—THE MONUMENTS—THE LIBRARY—THE MODEL ROOM—THE GREAT BELL—
THE CLOCK—THE WHISPERING GALLERY—THE OUTER GALLERIES—THE BALL
AND CROSS—THE CRYPT—ST. PAUL'S SCHOOL—THE GENERAL POST-OFFICE
—STATISTICS OF LETTERS—GOLDSMITHS' HALL—CHEAPSIDE—BOW CHURCH
—CITY OF LONDON SCHOOL—THE GUILDHALL—BUCKLERSBURY, &c.

THE centre of our great commercial transactions—the *heart*, as it were, of London—is that place of mighty import, the CITY, which has been not inaptly termed the Bank for the whole world. Here are situated the banking-houses, the counting-houses of the bullion, bill, and discount brokers, the offices of stock and share brokers, and the huge establishments of those wealthy individuals, who under the title of "merchants," without any other specific designation, carry on those extensive operations which give vitality to the most remote region where the foot of man has ever penetrated. There are 336 stockbroking establishments, many of them firms with two or more partners; 37 bullion, bill, and discount brokers, 248 ship and insurance brokers, and about 1,500 "merchants,"—all of whom have their places of business concentrated within a five minutes' walk of the Royal Exchange. And this is without reckoning the bankers, the general and commercial agents, the colonial, cotton, silk, and wool brokers, the corn and coal factors, the solicitors and notaries, the tradesmen and shopkeepers, and the great insurance, railway, and steam-packet companies, who have all located themselves within the same neighbourhood. Truly may we point out this thickly populated section of the metropolis as one having no parallel on the globe, and the immense amount of wealth here concentrated as equal to the entire revenue of many European States.

Since the time of the Great Fire of 1666, London has not been so greatly changed as it has been during the last quarter of a century; and it is gratifying to note that these changes distinctly show the onward progress of the nation, both in taste and wealth. It is curious to compare in an architectural point the places of business, such as banks, insurance offices, shops, taverns, &c., of the times to which we refer, and the structures intended for similar uses at the present day. The new squares, streets, and warehouses look like palaces by the contrast. This beneficial change is most visible in the City, in Threadneedle Street and Cornhill, for instance, where several noble buildings have been erected by the side of old ones, which render the contrast most notable.

So far back as the reign of Edward I. the City was divided into twenty-four wards, to each of which an alderman, chosen by the livery, was assigned, to be assisted in his duties by the common councilmen, who were chosen as at present, by the freemen of the City. The livery is a numerous body, elected by their respective guilds from amongst the freemen. These guilds, or companies, are known to have existed in this country very soon after the Norman Conquest; but the date of the charter of the Goldsmiths' and Skinners' Companies, the oldest now extant, only reaches as far as the year 1327. We need hardly say that their original object was to preserve their respective arts, trades, or mysteries, from the exercise of non-freemen. The City is now divided into twenty-six wards, the aldermen representing which constitute, with the Lord Mayor and 236 elected members, the court of common council, and have the

privilege of making bye-laws, and disposing of the funds of the corporation. The Lord Mayor is chosen from the aldermen, generally by seniority, on the 29th of September, and enters upon his office on the 9th of November following. He is assisted in the legal duties of his office by two sheriffs similarly chosen. The Recorder is appointed for life, and is the first law-officer to the City. The Aldermen are also perpetual justices of the peace for the City. The revenue of the corporation, which is derived from sundry dues, rents, interests of bequests, and other sources, may be averaged at about £200,000 annually, which is generally met by an equal expenditure. Within the last few years vast alterations have been made in this quarter of the metropolis, and the old crumbling warehouses in which the citizens of the last century amassed their well-earned wealth are rapidly giving place to handsome structures of proportionate magnitude, and the spirit of improvement that has at last penetrated these haunts of commercial enterprise has gone hand in hand with taste and liberality. There are yet, however, vestiges of those closely-built neighbourhoods that form the prominent characteristics of the City, which would convince the most sceptical, that every inch of available ground has here its corresponding value. In many places the houses still appear to shoot up in gaunt and gloomy rivalry of each other, screening the cheerful sunlight from their narrow pathways, and flinging a dusky obscurity over the bustling thoroughfare, as though the outspread wings of Mammon has enveloped its votaries in eternal shadow. The establishment of omnibuses has gone far to accelerate these alterations; for the citizen is now enabled to study his health as well as his pocket, and, whilst enjoying the fresher air of his cottage in the suburbs, can as conveniently present himself at his counting-house in the City at the accustomed early hour.

The City companies are eighty-three in number, and forty-one of these are without halls. Some exist merely for the sake of the charities at their disposal, and for the annual dinners on the 9th of November, which the bequests of members, anterior perhaps to the Reformation, enable them to discuss. Others exist but nominally, like the Bowyers, Fletchers, and Long Bowstring-makers, and some, like the Patten-makers, owing to the smallness of the fees which they exact from those who are obliged to take up the freedom of the City. Of the twelve great companies, as they are called, upwards of two-thirds are rich, not from what they make, but from what they possess. The acting companies are really very few in number. The Goldsmiths' is regarded as the chief, and the Stationers', though not one of the most ancient, (for printing was a late invention), is certainly one of the most important.

The plan we have proposed to follow out for the convenience of the stranger, will enable us, under a description of the City, to commence with an account of its principal buildings, and of these St. Paul's will form an appropriate subject with which to inaugurate our survey. Thence we shall take the reader with us along that busy thoroughfare, leading eastward from the Cathedral, and having terminated our gossiping companionship with a summary of all that claims mention in this quarter, proceed to a description of the other portions of the metropolis. For the bodily as well as the mental refreshment of the sightseeker, nearly every street provides the means of gratification; and it should not be forgotten that the City dining-rooms enjoy almost a world-wide celebrity for the excellence of their fare, and the recognised reasonableness of their charges. The chief inconvenience experienced by a countryman in threading the streets of London, arises from the constant jostling of the crowd of passengers, who may sometimes seem to have unanimously entered into a league to impede his movements. This is easily obviated by observing the rule adopted by the experienced Londoners, who maintain along their crowded pavements two distinct streams of passengers flowing in opposite directions;

and it is unwise for a stranger to deviate, even for an instant, from the course pursued by the throng with which he finds himself identified. A little tact and good temper will enable the pedestrian to discover that he can move as comfortably through the most frequented thoroughfares as with the same essentials he can make his way in the world, where the occasional jostlings encountered involve a more extensive area for their exercise. This premised —and such seeming trifles will be found in reality matters of no minor importance—we assume our privilege of companionship, and invite a pause before the solemn dome and massive grandeur of that majestic building, which, centred in the very heart of London's traffic, is consecrated to the national worship as the largest Protestant Church in the world.

St. Paul's Cathedral—Among those who do not wholly repudiate the spirit of poetry and romance which associates itself with the musty records of antiquity it has been long a favourite opinion that here stood the ancient Temple of Diana, probably as early as the second century. Situated just where the Hermin Way led the hunter forth from the northern gate immediately upon the surrounding forest, and which was plentifully stocked with wild animals, it is natural to imagine that here the ancient votary of the chase made his oblation to Diana on going forth, and that, on returning, he here offered up his spoils as a tribute in sacrifice to the tutelary deity of his pursuits. It is a singular fact, as if the custom itself had outlived the memory of its origin, that for centuries afterwards, the offering of a fat doe in winter, and a buck in summer, was annually made at the high altar on the day of the saint's commemoration, and was solemnly received by the dean and chapter, attired in their sacred vestments, and crowned with garlands of roses. As late as the reign of Elizabeth, this offering was made in lieu of twenty-two acres of land in Essex, belonging to the canons of the Church. Long before the Reformation, Old St. Paul's was renowned for its embellishments; and massive basins of gold, silver candlesticks, silver crosses, gold cups, and other ornaments of the most costly and sumptuous description, sparkled on its altar, which displayed the most extravagant workmanship, and was inlaid with precious jewels. In front of the cathedral stood the famous Paul's cross, a wooden pulpit, in which the most eminent divines preached every Sunday forenoon. For many years the old cathedral was a place of common resort, and converted into a general thoroughfare. The chapels and chantries were turned into workshops for mechanics, who pursued their business during Divine service; the vaults were made wine-cellars; shops and houses were built against the outer wall of the cathedral, and even "a playhouse" is said to have been among the erections with which the exterior was disfigured. At last the great fire took place, and put a stop to these abominations, entirely consuming in a few hours that splendid pile that had cost, for so many centuries, so much money and labour in its erection and adornment.

The important task of rebuilding the cathedral was confided to Sir Christopher Wren, who found the preliminary removal of the gigantic walls, in many places standing eighty feet in height, and five in thickness, a colossal undertaking. His skill and perseverance, however, surmounted all difficulties; and on the 21st of June, 1675, the first stone of the new cathedral was laid. Divine service was performed here for the first time after the fire on the 5th of December, 1697; but it was not until the year 1710, when Wren had arrived at his 78th year, that his son placed the highest stone of the lantern on the cupola. Notwithstanding it was thirty-five years building, it was finished by one architect and under one prelate, Henry Compton, Bishop of London. The expense of the building was £736,752, but the entire cost has been estimated at a million and a half. It stands upon two acres and sixteen perches of ground. Its entire length from east to west, within the walls, is 500 feet; its breadth from north to south, 286 feet; the circuit of the entire building, 2,292 feet; and the height to the summit of the cross, 404 feet. A beautiful view of the upper portion of the Cathedral is obtained from the new street, now in course of construction, leading from Clerkenwell to Farringdon Street, to be called Victoria Street. The entrance to the body of the cathedral, in which are the monuments of departed greatness, is now entirely free. The charges for viewing the various parts of the building are –

	s.	d.
Whispering and two outside Galleries	0	6
Ball	1	6
Library, Geometrical Staircase, Great Bell, and Model Room . . .	0	6
Clock	0	2
Crypt and Vault	0	6
	3	2

At a quarter before 10 A.M., and at a quarter past 3 P.M., the choral service is performed, and there is also divine service every week-day morning at 8 o'clock. On these occasions the body of the cathedral is of course open gratuitously to the public. On Sundays, and on every Wednesday and Friday, during Lent, sermons are preached by the dean and canons residentiary. In May and July, the anniversaries of the "sons of the clergy," and "the charity schools," generally take place; and being celebrated with much care and splendour, present the cathedral under additionally attractive aspects.

The Count de Soligny, in his "Letters on England," expresses his admiration of St. Paul's Cathedral in the following manner:—"I have just come from seeing St. Paul's Cathedral. I had been reading something about it last night, and this morning I by accident found myself on the bridge of Blackfriars, from which, as I have learned since, there is the best view of it that can be had any where, though even from that point it is seen to great disadvantage, as the whole of its lower order is concealed by the surrounding buildings. I have not, of late, been apt to be surprised; but I was so, and to a very fine effect, by the first unexpected view of this most stupendous temple. I had passed half over the bridge before I saw the cathedral, or knew that it was in sight; but turning on the left hand to look at the scenery on the banks of the Thames it stood before me with a look of grandeur and beauty of which I had formed no previous idea. After having passed all the rest of the day in examining it from every point of view, I do not hesitate to tell you that, as a whole which can be taken in by the eye at once, I think the cathedral of the city of London must be the finest thing in the world! Perhaps the finest that ever has been in the world. In saying this, I do not forget that the Parthenon once existed, and that St. Peter's still does exist. I am disposed to rank the cathedral of London before the latter, for St. Peter's is too large for all its parts to conduce to one general effect.

"St. Paul's, I repeat, is perhaps a finer work, with reference to itself, than the Parthenon was. I should think the latter was looked at with one single feeling of intense, but tranquil pleasure—a full, total unmixed delight. St. Paul's calls up feelings of a more elevated, a more impressive, and a more lasting character. These feelings vary from time to time as you continue looking, till at last they resolve themselves into a lofty but indefinite admiration, which lifts you above yourself and the earth, and inspires you with the moral assurance of the possibility of something infinitely greater, better, and happier. I cannot help being amused at fancying what the Londoners would say to my praises of their cathedral. I am sure they would *think* them quite extravagant, if they did not say so. They do not seem to have any idea even of its comparative size. I dare say, not ten among the tens of thousands who pass by it every day, have ever looked at it at all; and those who have, seem to want either taste to perceive its beauties or enthusiasm to admire them. They go to Paris and stare at everything in stupid wonder, and then come back and pass by their own magnificent cathedral, without seeming to know it stands there, though Paris contains nothing of the same kind that can approach to a comparison with it. There is, to be sure, one excuse for this. St. Paul's is so hideously clogged up on all sides with houses, that it may be passed by without being observed, if it is not looked for. It would certainly be worth while to establish a despotic monarchy in this country for one twelvemonth, if one could be sure the holder of it would have taste enough to employ part of the time in battering down all the buildings that stand within a few hundred yards of St. Paul's on every side. I cannot think of any mischief he would be able to do in the rest of the time, for which this would not compensate."

Having bestowed a glance of recognition on the statue of Queen Anne, which is seen in front of the portico facing Ludgate Hill, and obtained an entrance by the door of the northern portico, now freely open to all visitors, we are permitted to enjoy the feelings of veneration and delight which the striking and impressive view of the building is sure to induce. Eight immense piers, each of them forty feet at the base, support the great dome of the central area, exhibiting a spacious concave, embellished by Sir James Thornhill. Through some fine open screenwork may be obtained a view of the place where the usual services are performed, and which is highly decorated with dark oaken carved work. Around are the monuments of the illustrious dead, who have left to this country the legacy of names with which worth, honour, learning, and patriotism have been associated. We should probably save some misapprehension if we first inform the reader, that but few persons are buried here whose monuments have been erected in the cathedral; and, to show how recent is their introduction, the first statue erected in St. Paul's was that of the burly lexicographer, Dr. Johnson. There are about fifty monuments altogether, the finest as a work of art being generally admitted to be that by Westmacott, to the memory of Sir Ralph Abercrombie. The monuments to Nelson and Howe by Flaxman, and those to various generals by Chantrey, are also finely wrought. From these the eye will naturally be raised to an inscription more emphatic than any of the rest, which is seen on a plain marble slab over the entrance to the choir. The Latin, by frequent quotation, has become almost as familiar as the vulgar tongue, but we give the translation in preference:— "Beneath lies Sir Christopher Wren, the builder of this Church and City, who lived upwards of ninety years, not for himself but for the public good. Reader, seekest thou his monument? Look around!" Lately, the organ built by Schmidt, in 1694, at a cost of £20,000, has been removed to the north side of the choir, and the magnificent instrument, which created a sensation at the ill-starred Panopticon, has now found its right position in the cathedral; it contains sixty sounding stops, and four rows of keys; and the performance on this noble instrument most be heard to be appreciated. The stall for the bishop may be recognised by the pelican and the mitre, and the Lord Mayor's stall opposite, by the City sword and mace.

On leaving the monuments we proceed from the entrance across the cathedral to a door in the south aisle, which leads us to the outer galleries. Here a person supplies tickets, which are obtained by paying sixpence each. We may therefore appropriately remind the visitor of what he will have to accomplish. There are 280 steps to the whispering gallery round the bottom of the dome; 251 more to the gallery at the top of the dome; and 82 from that gallery into the ball. The total number is thus 616, which will forcibly impress the truth of Beattie's line—

"Ah! Who can tell how hard it is to climb?"—upon the mind of the ambitious traveller towards the top. When half-way to the whispering gallery, the visiter will see on the right the door leading to the *Library*, which is attained by passing through a long gallery. It is a handsome room about fifty feet by forty, having shelves crammed with about 7,000 goodly volumes, among which are some Latin manuscripts beautifully written by the monks 800 years ago, and an illuminated English manuscript, 600 years old, containing rules for the government of a convent. The portrait of Bishop Compton is seen over the fireplace. The most curious object is, however, the oaken floor, curiously inlaid with 2,376 small square pieces, without a nail or peg to secure their adhesion.

We are next introduced to the geometrical staircase, originally intended as a private way to the library, and which appears to be suspended without visible support. Passing the great western window we enter the *Model Room*, in which is preserved Wren's original model of the cathedral. Admirably designed as it was, this model was rejected on the absurd ground, that it differed too much from the preconceived notion of cathedrals; and, to the great chagrin of the architect, he was compelled to complete his plan in the form we now see it. Near the library door are the stairs leading to the *great bell*, and in the turret at the top, the great bell itself is seen suspended nearly forty feet from the floor. It is ten feet in diameter, ten inches thick, and weighs 11,470 pounds. The hammer of the clock strikes the hours on this bell, the deep sonorous tones of which may be heard at a great distance. This mighty tocsin is only tolled on the demise of any members of the royal family, the Archbishop of Canterbury, Bishop of

London, or the Dean of St. Paul's. It is advisable to visit this part of the cathedral between twelve and one, at which time any further explanations required can be given by the man in attendance, who superintends the gigantic machinery of the clock. There are two dial-plates, each of them fifty-seven feet in circumference; the minute hands are nine feet eight inches in length, and weigh seventy-five pounds; and the figures are two feet two and a half inches long. The fineness of the workmanship, and the unfaltering accuracy of its stupendous movements, combine to render this clock one of the greatest curiosities in the world. The visiter is next introduced to the *Whispering Gallery*, 140 yards in circumference, situated just below the dome. A stone seat extends round the gallery in front of the wall. On the side directly opposite the door by which visitors enter, several yards of the seat are covered with matting, on which the visiter being seated, the man who shows the gallery whispers with his mouth near to the wall, when, though uttered 140 feet distant, the voice is heard in a louder tone, and as if close to the listener's ear. The effect is by no means so perfect if the visiter sits down half-way between the door and matted seat, and is still less so if he stands near the man who speaks, but on the other side of the door, the mere shutting of which produces a sound like a peal of thunder rattling and rolling among the mountains. From this gallery the marble pavement of the church looks extremely beautiful, and the paintings by Sir James Thornhill, illustrative of the life of St. Paul, are here viewed to the most advantage.

Hence we go to the *Outer Gallery*, from which the immense extent of the metropolis and the circling panorama of the environs form a prospect of peculiar interest and variety. The vast lines of buildings spreading out in every direction, the busy aspect of the diminished streets immediately below, the mapped-out city looking like a fairy toy in which the world is shown in mocking miniature, and the sinuous path of the Thames, crossed by its numerous bridges, and winding between banks on which the noblest of British worthies have lived, flourished, and died, make this a scene which engrosses the attention of the mind, as much as it enchains and enchants the wandering gaze. Poets, painters, and philosophers, statesmen, and politicians, novelists, dramatists, and gallant patriots, have given a deep and enduring interest to nearly every street and alley we survey; and the eye can scarcely fix itself upon a spot that is not hallowed by some association of the past, or contemplate an object that is not identified with some glorious triumph of human learning or noble generosity.

After leaving the gallery, the payment of one shilling and sixpence will procure admission to the ball and cross. The ball is capable of holding twelve persons, and is thirty feet below the summit of the cross. It was from this spot that the ordnance survey of 1849 was made, a scaffolding being thrown around the cross for the purpose. Returning to the basement of the cathedral, those who feel disposed may obtain access to the *Crypt*, or vaults beneath for which a charge of sixpence is made. These dreary silent mansions of the dead are lighted at intervals by grated windows, which afford partial gleams of light, with broad intervals of shade between. The vaults are divided into three avenues by immense arches and pillars, some of them forty feet square. The middle one under the dome is perfectly dark, and a portion of the north aisle at the east end is dedicated to St. Faith, where are preserved the few monumental statues that escaped the ravages of the fire. Shrouded by a flat stone sunk into the pavement, lies the body of Sir Christopher Wren; and here also repose the remains of Lord Nelson, Collingwood, and the Duke of Wellington, in close proximity; and the eminent painters, Reynolds, Barry, Opie, Fuseli, West, and others who have earned the tribute of those funeral honours that a grateful country could bestow.

The open area in which the cathedral stands is called St. Paul's Churchyard, and the names of the streets and lanes branching therefrom, give token of their former connexion with the religious structure and its clerical attendants. On the south side an open arched passage leads to DOCTORS' COMMONS, and the offices attached to the ecclesiastical courts, and on the northern side the courts communicate with PATER-NOSTER Row, the great literary market, where booksellers and publishers have established themselves from a very early period, and in tall and sombre houses that little indicate the constant busy traffic going on within. Upwards of 20,000 new volumes are hence distributed annually over all parts of the world.

At the eastern end of the cathedral is St. PAUL'S SCHOOL, founded by Dean Colet in 1510, for the gratuitous education of 153 boys, several of whom are transferred afterwards to the universities. The Mercers' Company have the management of the school. The rules are very minute, and were drawn up by the founder.

The Post-Office, in St. Martin's-le-Grand, reached by turning to the left from the cathedral, next demands our notice and admiration, not only as a fine specimen of architecture, but also for the important object that it serves in receiving and distributing the epistolary intercourse of the world. It was built under the superintendence of Sir Robert Smirke, and was first opened for public business on the 23rd of September, 1829. The whole edifice is of stone, and measures 390 feet in length. Beneath the central portico is the entrance to the great hall, which is eighty feet long, sixty feet wide, and fifty-two feet high, and is supported by six Ionic columns of Portland stone. On the north side are the newspaper, inland, and foreign offices, and on the opposite is the London post department Against the walls on the western side will be found boards giving a list of persons whose address cannot be ascertained, from either erroneous or imperfect superscriptions. Beneath the hall is a tunnel uniting the two grand divisions of the building, and furnished with some ingenious machinery to facilitate the conveyance of letters from one department to another. Machinery is also employed for supplying water and fuel to the upper parts of the building, as well as for other purposes. Immediately under the portico are two large gasometers, that feed the many gas-burners required by the establishment. The entire business of the MONEY ORDER OFFICE is transacted in a building erected for the purpose in Aldersgate Street, a little above the Post-Office, and on the opposite side the way. For the attainment of exact and rapid delivery in the metropolis, London and its environs are divided into Ten Districts, each treated in many respects as a separate town, and to render this arrangement effectual correspondents are requested to add after the address the initials of the district for which the letter is intended. Books at the various post offices are sold at 1d. each, containing a list of the several streets, with the proper initial appended after them; and to give some idea of the enormous amount of business regularly transacted here, with a rapidity and accuracy almost incredible, it may be mentioned that on the 14th of February, 1850, the letters thus passed through the office for the district post alone, amounted to 187,037, exclusive of those for the provinces and places beyond sea. The increase of correspondence that has taken place since the adoption of the cheap and uniform rate of postage is as gratifying as it is remarkable. Under the old system, in 1839, the number of letters that passed through the post was 76,000,000; in 1840, when the present rate came into operation, the number was enlarged to 162,000,000. Although the business is now exactly four times and a half more than it was in 1839, the expenses of management have only doubled. In the former year the cost was about £690,000; in 1849, it was

£1,400,000. The number of news-papers passing through the Post-Office is estimated at not less than 70,000,000 per annum. Of late years the broad-sheet has materially increased in size and weight, each paper now averag-ing five ounces; so that 9,765 tons weight of papers annually, or 187 tons weekly, are thence scattered to the uttermost ends of the earth. The posting of the newspapers here at 6 P.M., the latest period at which they can be posted without fee, is one of the sights of London, and cannot fail to astonish the visitor.

In Foster Lane, at the back of the Post Office, is GOLDSMITHS' HALL, a spacious structure in the Italian style, built on the site of the old hall, which it has replaced. The principal front, which is almost screened from observa-vation by the surrounding buildings, consists of six handsome Corinthian columns, surmounted by a Corinthian entablature of great beauty. Here are assayed and examined the gold and silver articles manufactured in London, which have then the "hall mark" im-pressed upon them as a guarantee of their being genuine. The interior of the building can only be viewed by an order obtained from a member of the court.

Deviating into CHEAPSIDE, which originally received its name from *Chepe*, a market, as being the first great street of splendid shops, we shall find how well its present condition justifies its former repute. The fine statue of Sir Robert Peel is erected on the site of the ancient cross and conduit. On the south side, easily distinguished by its projecting clock, is the ancient Church of St. MARY-LE-BOW, erected by Sir Christopher Wren in 1673, and consi-dered one of his great masterpieces. The steeple, which is of Portland stone, is much admired. Some few years since the church underwent considerable alterations, the tower and spire were rebuilt after the original design; and when the dragon which forms the vane was elevated to its accustomed lofty station, one of the workmen bestrode its back, to the astonishment of an ad-miring multitude. Connected with this famous heraldic monster there is a curious story afloat. An ancient pro-phecy announced, that when the Bow Dragon and the Gresham Grasshopper should meet, on England's throne no king should sit. The prophecy was singularly verified; the late Royal Ex-change and Bow Church being under repair at the same time, and their re-spective vanes being sent to the same artificer for regilding, they were ac-tually placed side by side, in the first year of her present Majesty's reign. In this Church the Boyle Lectures are annually delivered, and the Bishops of London consecrated. Here, too, are the "Bow bells" that recalled Whit-tington, and those born within the sound are still avouched to have just claim to the epithet of "Cockney."

The City of London School lies at the back of the houses facing Bow Church, and was first opened in 1837. John Carpenter, its original founder, was town clerk of London in the reigns of Henry V. and VI. The present clear annual value of the estates he left for this purpose is not less than £900. It is a fine building of the Elizabethan style, and comprises nine class-rooms and a library, rooms for the masters, a theatre for lecturers, and other apartments. Besides the four boys who are on the foundation, and who are maintained, educated, and endowed with £100 each towards their advancement in life, the sons of freemen are admitted under certain regulations. Four scholarships have been founded in accordance with the will of the founder, and the education imparted is of an acknowledged high character.

The Guildhall is seen at the end of King Street, which runs northward from Cheapside. This is the civic palace, where the principal business of the corporation is conducted, and the magnificent banquets given that have made the City Feasts famous in history. The building was erected at different periods, an irregularity which it betrays in its architecture. The Gothic front, with the City arms in the centre, was finished in 1789, but it has been since frequently repaired. The hall, which is accessible without charge, contains some fine monuments, the principal ones being those erected in memory of the Earl of Chatham, William Pitt, and the illustrious Duke of Wellington (recently finished), and at the western end, raised on pedestals, are the two colossal figures of Gog and Magog, said to represent an ancient Briton and Saxon. This is one of the largest rooms in London, and can accommodate about 3,500 at dinner. It is 153 feet long, 48 feet broad, and 55 feet high. On the windows at each end, beautifully represented on stained glass, are the Royal arms, the insignia of the Bath, St. Patrick, the Garter, and the City arms. The other apartments are decorated with various paintings and monuments of historical interest, to view which a small fee to the official in waiting will generally be all the introduction required. In the east wing are the City Courts of law, and opposite is the Guildhall police-office, where an alderman attends daily to hear and decide cases. The Church of St. LAWRENCE, close by, was built from the designs of Wren, in 1671. Here lies Bishop Wilkins, who endeavoured to explain the art of attaching wings to the shoulders of mankind; and the register records the marriage of Archbishop Tillotson with Elizabeth French, niece to Oliver Cromwell, on the 23rd of February, 1663, and his death and burial here in 1694.

In Cheapside is SADDLERS' HALL,

rebuilt 1823, and a little farther on towards the Poultry is MERCERS' HALL, distinguished by a richly sculptured front, adorned with emblematic figures of Faith, Hope, and Charity, and containing some curious relics of Whittington, thrice Lord Mayor of London. Not fewer than 62 mayors were of this Company, from 1214 to 1702. The narrow street called the OLD JEWRY took its name from the great synagogue which stood there till the persecuted race were expelled the kingdom in 1291.

The GROCERS' HALL stands nearly on the site of the original Jewish temple. Diverging southwards from Cheapside, at this point, is Bucklersbury, that took its name from one Buckle, who had there a manor-house. In Stow's time it was the chief residence of grocers and apothecaries; but it is now chiefly occupied by the proprietors of dining-rooms. Here an excellent repast can be made for one shilling, and a positively luxurious one for double the amount.

DISTRICT II.

THE MANSION HOUSE—ST. STEPHEN'S, WALBROOK—THE BANK OF ENGLAND—THE NEW ROYAL EXCHANGE—LLOYD'S—THE STOCK EXCHANGE—LOTHBURY—CORNHILL —THE EAST INDIA HOUSE—THE MUSEUM—CROSBY HALL—THE SOUTH SEA HOUSE —MODERN IMPROVEMENTS AND ANTIQUITIES.

THE widening of the streets and the other architectural improvements recently added, where no less than seven great thoroughfares converge towards one central point, have made the present aspect of the busy region in front of the Royal Exchange worthy of the grandeur and importance of the first city in the world. The cluster of public buildings here surrounding us renders a detailed description necessary of each.

The Mansion House, the official residence of the Lord Mayor during his year of civic sovereignty, is a building of Portland stone, with a Corinthian portico of six columns in front, resting on a low basement. This edifice, which has some emblematic sculpture on the pediment, stands on the site of what was anciently called Stocks-market, the great market of the city during many centuries. A flight of steps leads to the door beneath the portico, which is the grand entrance, and to the left is the office where the police charges arc taken and adjudicated. Besides an extensive suite of domestic apartments, it contains a number of State-rooms for the reception and entertainment of company, and these when lit up present a magnificent appearance. The principal is the Egyptian-hall, a lofty room of considerable splendour. The Lord

Mayor has an allowance of £8,000 for his year of Mayoralty, but this income is often considerably exceeded by the expenditure. The use of a State coach and a superb collection of plate is also a privilege which is extended to the period of his official occupation of the Mansion House. Adjacent to the Mansion House is seen the Church of St. Stephen's, Walbrook, acknowledged to be the masterpiece of Sir Christopher Wren, for the beauty of proportion his architectural skill has imparted to the interior. It was erected in 1675. The altar-piece, by West, represents the interment of St. Stephen, and was placed there in 1776. The roof of the church is supported by Corinthian columns so disposed as to produce a grander effect than the dimensions of the church seemed to promise. Deacon's Coffee-house, close by, is worthy of mention for the quantity of newspapers, metropolitan, foreign, and provincial, provided for the visitors. The files of newspapers here kept can all be examined for a small gratuity.

The Bank of England is seen nearly opposite, bounded by Princes Street on the west, Lothbury on the north, and the new Royal Exchange on the south. It is screened by a long stone wall, handsomely ornamented; but the windows being blank, the principal front presents by no means a lively appearance. The structure was first commenced by Mr. George Sampson, in 1733, afterwards embellished by Sir Robert Taylor, and finally brought to its present unity of design by the late Sir John Soane. It occupies an irregular area of eight acres; and, as there are no windows in the exterior, the light is admitted to the various departments by nine open courts. The chief entrance is in Threadneedle Street, and leads direct to the Rotunda, a spacious circular chamber with a lofty dome, fifty-seven feet in diameter, crowned by a lantern, the divisions of which are formed by the architectural figures called caryatides. This dome is, of its class, one of the most striking works of art in the metropolis. Herein are paid half-yearly the dividends or annual interest of the national debt. The recipients frequently attend in person, ladies as well as gentlemen, acting as their own agents in the pleasant business of receiving money. In each week certain days are appointed for the transfer of stock, which is mostly effected by brokers. When an actual bargain has been made, the parties go into the bank, and the particular clerk, on whom the duty devolves, examines the books to see if the seller actually has the stock which he proposes to sell. When all is ascertained to be correct, the transfer is made out, the books are signed, and the business being completed, the purchaser is, from thenceforth, until he parts with his right, in possession of "money in the funds;"

that is, he is entitled to receive certain half-yearly sums of money called "dividends," and may attend at the Rotunda himself to have them paid to him. Should the visitor select a "dividend day" for his visit, he will be much interested in the animated scene presented, and the dexterous celerity with which the business we have indicated is carried on. The "telling-room" presents an appearance of extraordinary activity; clerks counting up and weighing gold coins, porters passing constantly to and fro, and crowds of tradesmen and others negotiating business at the counters. There is an ingeniously constructed clock in a building over the drawing-office, which indicates the time on sixteen different dials, striking the quarters as well as the hours. The other and more private portions of the bank can only be seen by an order from one of the directors, and chiefly consist of the bullion-office, in a vaulted chamber beneath, an armoury, library, treasury, and the apartments in which the notes of the bank are manufactured. The bulk of the note is printed from a steel plate, the identity of which is secured by the process of transferring. The paper is moistened for printing by water driven through its pores by the pressure of the air-pump. In this way 30,000 double notes are moistened in an hour. The printing-ink is made from linseed oil, and the charred husks and vines of Rhenish grapes. The numbering and cipher-printing are executed by the ordinary press. The tenacity of the paper used in the manufacture has been satisfactorily proved by experiment; for in its water leaf, or unsized condition, a bank note will support 36lbs., and when one grain of size has been diffused through it, it will sustain 56lbs. There are above 800 clerks employed, and the salaries and pensions amount to about £220,000 annually. Except on holidays, the Bank is open every day from nine till five, and during these hours it is accessible to strangers. This great national establishment was first incorporated in 1694. It is governed by a court of twenty-four Directors, eight of whom go out of office every year, when eight others are elected.

The New Royal Exchange is now before us, and the splendour of the architecture, and its adaptation to the purpose designed cannot fail to arrest the attention of the observer. In the open space opposite the western front is a fine equestrian statue, in bronze, of the late Duke of Wellington. It was cast, by Chantrey, from the metal of guns taken in the various victories gained by the hero of Waterloo, and cost £9,000, exclusive of the material, valued at £1,500 more. The former building which occupied its site was destroyed by fire on the night of the 10th of January, 1838. On the 17th of January, 1842, the foundation stone was laid by Prince Albert, and on the 28th of October, 1844, the Exchange was opened with great ceremony by Her Majesty in person. The extreme length of the building, which stands east and west, is 309 feet; the inner quadrangle is 170 feet by 112 feet, and the height of the tower to the top of the vane 177 feet. It is scarcely necessary to remind the intelligent reader that, in 1564, the first building on this spot owed its origin to Sir Thomas Gresham; and the gilt grasshopper, the crest of the Gresham family, is still observed to perpetuate his memory. This is literally the place where "merchants most do congregate." The area appropriated to them is very spacious, and highly ornamented with emblazoned decorations. About three o'clock is the time to see the place to advantage, as at that hour, among the concourse assembled, will be found the most eminent men in the mercantile world, who here provide the sinews of that commerce which has proved to us the foster-mother of literature and the arts, and the dispenser of luxuries, comforts, and enjoyments, to all classes of the community. In the centre of the open space is a statue of Queen Victoria, but it is hardly worthy the place in which it has been deposited. Several shops of showy exterior, and some public offices connected with the assurance companies are arranged round the building. A conspicuous part of the building is assigned to LLOYD'S, familiar abbreviation of the important society of underwriters meeting at Lloyd's Subscription Coffee-house. There are two suites of rooms, one open to the public, and the other specially reserved for subscribers. Signal service has been rendered to the maritime world by the establishment of insurances at Lloyd's. The society has agents in all the principal ports of the world, and through their means the commercial and shipping intelligence is published daily, and received with a confidence which for more than a century nothing has ever occurred to destroy. Communications respecting the arrival and departure of ships, of the existence and fate of vessels in every part of the globe, reports from consuls and commissioners resident abroad, newspapers and gazettes from every country, and other publications connected with the shipping interest, are here arranged in such perfect and convenient order, that the actual machinery by which the movements of the commercial world are regulated, seems to be placed within the hands of the directors of Lloyd's.

The Stock Exchange will be found opposite the east end of the Bank, and at the upper extremity of a narrow passage called Capel Court. It is a kind of commercial *sanctum sanctorum*, open only to its members, who are elected by ballot, and who are compelled to find sureties for honourable conduct in the discharge of their monetary obligations. Should they be unable to meet their engagements, or be proved guilty of any nefarious transaction, they are publicly posted as defaulters and excluded, and then, in the peculiar language of the Stock Exchange, they are denominated "lame ducks." The Stock Exchange is governed by a committee of twenty-four members, who are also elected annually by ballot; but the business of stock-jobbing is not entirely confined to the members, there being hosts of persons called "outsiders," who, being inadmissible to the Exchange, assemble in Bartholomew Lane, immediately in front of it, and, though in many instances of very questionable means, they talk as coolly of hundreds and thousands of pounds as though the whole wealth of the neighbouring edifice, the Bank of England, was at their command. To the uninitiated the business here carried on is as unintelligible as the jobbers themselves. Their transactions chiefly consist in the purchase and sale of government securities, railway and mining shares, and other properties of the same nature. Time-bargains form a very considerable part of the business, and are thus effected: One broker will agree to purchase of another a certain quantity of any particular stock, at a given price, on a certain day. These days, which occur at stated intervals, are called settling days. In the meanwhile, the stocks either rise or fall in value, and when the period for completing the bargain arrives, a settlement is made without the transfer of stock, the losing party paying merely the difference, or, if mutually agreed on, the affair may be carried over to the next settling-day. The sellers of time-bargains are technically termed *bears*, the buyers *bulls*, the object of the former of course being to depreciate the value of the stock sold—of the buyer, to increase it. To effect this object the most ingenious tricks are devised, false reports likely to affect their price are invented and spread abroad, and every possible *ruse* which cunning can devise is brought into play. We may here mention, for the benefit of those unversed in such subjects, that the national debt is divided into various classes under different names, bearing different rates of interest. The largest class is that termed the "Three per Cent. Consols," the latter word being a contraction of consolidated, the fund having been formed by the union of three funds, which had been kept separate. The rate of interest is indicated by its name. There are probably more than 2,000,000 persons directly concerned in the receipt of this annual interest; for though the debt stands in the names of only about 280,000 individuals., most of these are merely trustees or managers acting for societies and institutions. In Lothbury, that great banking region, is situated the central office of the ELECTRIC TELEGRAPH COMPANY, whence the wires, that have a subterranean communication with all the railway termini in London, receive and diffuse intelligence with astounding rapidity.

CORNHILL, where the glitter of the jewellers' shops, and the prosperous look of those having quieter attractions, will be sure to attract the passenger's eye with terrible provocations to become a purchaser, leads us direct to LEADENHALL STREET, where the fine massive building of the **East India House** appears upon our right. This stately-looking edifice, with its projecting portico, supported by six lofty Ionic columns, was originally built in 1726, and enlarged in 1799. The front, composed of stone, is 200 feet in length. On the apex of the pediment is a statue of Britannia, at the east corner a figure of Asia seated on a dromedary, and at the west another of Europe on a horse. The associations now belong to the past which connected this building with British enterprise, commerce, and power. Under the direct government of the crown the change of offices has been considered de-sirable, and in September last the staff and all the official papers were removed to the west portion of the Victoria Hotel, situated conveniently near the other government offices. Here, until a new home for the Indian Department has been erected, the executive will be conducted. The present offices are leased only for three years, with option of continuing them for two years more. The splendid library, containing an extensive collection of oriental MSS., Chinese printed books, drawings, and copies of almost every work relating to Asia that has been published, and a fine copy of the Koran, formerly belonging to Tippoo Saib, is, at present, well lodged in Cannon Row, Westminster; whilst the museum, which always proved attractive as one of the sights in London, is permanently deposited at Fife House, Middle Scotland Yard, near the United Service Institution, where it will be re-opened free to the public as soon as an entirely fresh arrangement of its treasures can be completed. The old House, in Leadenhall Street, has been sold, and its valuable space will probably form an appropriate site for the offices of many city commercial princes. Leadenhall Market, the City market for meat, poultry, leather, hides, &c., lies to the right of the great thoroughfare from which it takes its name. Turning into Bishopsgate, the first building that deserves mention is CROSBY HALL, now chiefly appropriated to purposes of public entertainment as a lecture and concert room; but, among other illustrious characters, it once belonged to Richard, Duke of Gloucester, afterwards King Richard III. After being the abode of many wealthy citizens and noblemen, it was subsequently converted into a Dissenters' meeting-house, and ultimately into a packer's warehouse. From this state of degradation it has been rescued within the last few years, and by means of a public subscription a great deal has been done towards restoring it towards its original beauty. Near here will be found the London Tavern, and other well-known hotels, of City reputation. In Threadneedle Street is the SOUTH SEA HOUSE, where the official business of the South Sea Company was conducted, but more recently the office of the notorious British Bank. Returning through Lothbury, we enter Gresham Street, which in 1846 swallowed up the ancient thoroughfare of Lad Lane. The "Swan with two necks," that used to be the great booking office for coaches to the north, is still a most comfortable hotel. In Milk Street, close at hand, was born Sir Thomas More, and in the Old Jewry is held the Lord Mayor's Court. Here also died the celebrated Professor Porson, in 1808, in a room of the London Institution, of which he was the Librarian. In Wood Street, Cheapside, should be noticed the fine old elm tree and decayed rookery which stands just without the main thoroughfare, in a little enclosed churchyard. This neighbourhood will be found the great emporium of the wholesale woollen and drapery establishments. A fine building at the corner of Wood Street, at its junction with Gresham Street, was erected in 1849, for the Messrs. Morley, hosiers, and glovers. It stands upon an area of 8,270 feet, and is one of the most extensive establishments of the kind in the metropolis. Hence we return to our starting-point, St. Paul's.

SECOND DAY'S ROUTE.

DISTRICT III.

DOCTORS' COMMONS—HERALDS' COLLEGE—SOUTHWARK BRIDGE—QUEENHITHE—VINTRY—WHITTINGTON'S TOMB—LONDON STONE—MERCHANT TAILORS' SCHOOL—KING WILLIAM STREET—THE MONUMENT—LONDON BRIDGE—THAMES STREET—THE NEW COAL EXCHANGE—BILLINGSGATE—THE CUSTOM HOUSE—THE TOWER—THE ARMOURIES—THE JEWEL OFFICE—THE BATTERIES AND THE PARADE—TOWER HILL—THE TRINITY HOUSE—THE MINT.

WE again start from St. Paul's, taking a south-easterly direction through Cannon Street, leading therefrom towards King William Street and London Bridge. The money provided for these new City improvements (£200,000) was raised on bonds at interest, on the credit of the City revenues and estates. The relief afforded by this new artery to the crowded thoroughfare of Cheapside is most acceptable and beneficial; and it contains some of the finest warehouses in London.

Doctors' Commons, a nest of brick buildings, entered by the archway on the right of St. Paul's Churchyard, derived its name from the civilians commoning together as in other colleges. Here are the offices where wills are registered and deposited, and marriage licences granted. The maritime and ecclesiastical courts held here, consist chiefly of the Admiralty, the Arches, the Probate, and the Consistory Courts, in all of which the business is principally carried on in writing by the doctors and proctors. At the Prerogative Office searches for wills are made, chargeable at one shilling each, and copies, which are always stamped, are to be had on application. They are registered from the year 1383.

THE COLLEGE OF ARMS, or Herald's College, is on Bennett's Hill, on the east side of Doctors' Commons. The corporation, founded in 1484, is under the control of the Duke of Norfolk, as Hereditary Earl Marshal; the present building, a plain brick structure, with Ionic pilasters, was erected in the reign of Charles II. Their office is to keep records of the genealogical descent of all noble families in the kingdom, and to search for coats of arms, &c. Strangers may view the court on application. The fees are generally moderate. Knight-rider Street was so called from the gallant train of knights who used to pass this way from the Tower Royal to the gay tournaments at Smithfield.

Southwark Bridge—Passing down Watling Street, which was the ancient Roman road, we come to Queen Street, which gives a direct communication between Cheapside and Southwark Bridge, immortalised by Charles Dickens, in "Little Dorrit." This bridge was first opened at midnight in April, 1819, having occupied five years in construction, at an expense of £800,000. Its centre arch has a span of 240 feet, and the two side ones measure 210. If we except the abutments and piers, the whole of the bridge is of cast iron, and the height of the centre arch above low water mark is 55 feet, whilst the weight of the cast-iron used for the bridge is computed at about 5,780 tons. There is a toll of one penny to foot passengers, but those who disembark from the steamboats that call at the bridge-pier pass over without charge.

The cross streets about here, with their narrow causeways and long lines of lofty warehouses and dark offices, are worth turning into for the signs of busy traffic they present, and the picturesque old-mansion appearance which many of the houses still retain. The venerable churches and churchyards, coming upon us unexpectedly in the very heart of a dense cluster of buildings, and the palpable struggling after vegetation of some smoke-blackened tree, putting forth a few withered green leaves at yearly intervals about the spot, tend to invest this region with some noticeable characteristics peculiarly its own. That the visitor may know something of the objects that lie around him, we here group together a few of the more interesting, that will furnish him with an excuse for deviating a little from his direct course.

Queenhithe, at the bottom of Queen Street, and to the right of the bridge, was formerly one of the most generally used landing-places on the banks of the river. The term *hithe* (signifying a wharf or landing-place) takes back its history to Saxon times, and shows its early origin. It was first called Queen's hithe in the reign of King John, out of compliment to his consort. Opposite is the Church of ST. MICHAEL'S, built in 1677 by Wren.

Vintners' Hall, distinguished by the figure of Bacchus striding his tun, is close by in Upper Thames Street. In the great hall is a good picture of St. Martin dividing his cloak with a supposed beggar; but why the saint was selected as a patron of the company is unknown, except that the good wine he imbibed might have produced good thoughts, and thus caused good works to become the natural consequence. The vintners were first incorporated in the reign of Edward III., when the best red wine was sold at fourpence a gallon!

Thames Street is about a mile in length, and extends from Blackfriars to the Tower, along the river bank. That part of the street below London Bridge, is called Lower Thames Street, and that part of it above the bridge, Upper Thames Street. In the middle of the 18th century it was remarkable for the number of Cheesemongers' shops in it. In the part of the vintry known as GARLIC-HITHE will be seen St. James's Church, built in 1676, and admitted to be the worst specimen of Wren's architectural abilities in London. Over the clock is a figure of the saint. The place derives its name from the quantity of garlic that used to be sold near the church. On College Hill, the next turning past Queen Street, stands St. Michael's Paternoster Royal, which was made a collegiate church (hence the name) by the executors of Sir Richard Whittington, the renowned Lord Mayor. The almshouses he founded stood on the north side of the church, but they were removed a few years ago to Highgate. This church was also one of those rebuilt by Wren after the great fire. The altar-piece was presented to the church by the directors of the British Institution in 1820, and represents Mary Magdalene anointing the feet of our Saviour. It is curious that Whittington, who was thrice Mayor, was in this church thrice buried—first, by his executors, who erected a handsome monument to his memory; then in the reign of Edward IV., when it was taken up by one Mountain, the incumbent, who supposed that great wealth had been buried with him; and finally, by the parishioners, in the next reign, who were compelled to take up the body to re-encase it in lead, of which it had been despoiled on the former occasion. In this neighbourhood was the Tower Royal, a large building of considerable strength, wherein at one time the Kings of England resided, and which, with many another palatial structure, graced the banks of the river in days gone by.

Returning to Cannon Street, by way of Dowgate Hill, we shall emerge nearly opposite ST. SWITHIN'S, another of Wren's churches, but more remarkable for having preserved on its outer wall, all that remains of the famed "London Stone," concerning the original purpose of which there has been so much speculation. There is evidence of a thousand years having passed away since it was first set up; but we must still say with Stowe, "the cause why this stone was there set, the very time when, or memory thereof is there none." Whether it was an ancient British relic, whether it marked the spot where proclamations were published, or whether it was a Roman *milliarium* whence distances were measured, is still uncertain, and probably will remain so. At the time when Stowe wrote, it stood on the south side of Cannon Street, then called Candlewick Street. In December, 1742, it was removed to the curb-stones on the north side of the street; and in 1798, it was enclosed within a modern case of an altar form, and placed in its present position, the better to preserve it. In the adjacent thoroughfare of Suffolk Lane, and on the eastern side, is the celebrated seminary of "Merchant Tailors' School," founded by that company in 1561. The present building, which is a plain massive structure, was rebuilt immediately after the great fire, and comprises a spacious school-room, a house for the head-master, a library, and a chapel. About 250 scholars are here educated, many of whom are sent to St. John's College, Oxford.

We now approach King William Street, at the northern extremity of which is the statue, by Nixon, of William IV., placed there in 1844. It is of granite, and stands, with the pedestal, 40 feet in height. The MONUMENT is now seen to raise its lofty head above us, rising from an open area on Fish Street Hill. It is almost superfluous to tell the reader it was erected in 1677, in commemoration of the Great

Fire of London, which began at the distance of 202 feet eastward from the spot, and its height has on that account been made 202 feet. It is a fluted Doric column built of Portland Stone, designed by Wren, and executed under his superintendence, at a cost of £15,000. The pediment is 40 feet high and 21 feet square, and the column is surmounted by a blazing urn of gilt brass 42 feet in height. The north and south sides of the pedestal have each a Latin inscription, one descriptive of the destruction of the city, and the other of its restoration. Within is a spiral staircase of black marble, having 345 steps by which the visiter may ascend to the summit, enclosed by an iron railing, and obtain an extensive view of the mighty city, with its suburbs stretching miles away beyond. It is open every day from nine till dusk, except Sundays, at a charge of sixpence each person.

In Great Eastcheap, on the site now occupied by the statue of William IV., stood the Boar's Head Tavern, the scene of Falstaff's memorable vagaries, as recorded by Shakespere. The original tavern was destroyed in the great fire, rebuilt immediately afterwards, and finally demolished to allow of the new London Bridge approaches in 1831. The church seen nearer the bridge is St. Magnus, erected by Wren between 1616 and 1705. The cupola and lantern has been much admired. Miles Coverdale, who lies here buried, was the rector, and under his direction, in 1635, was published the first complete English version of the Bible.

On the western side of the bridge is FISHMONGERS' HALL, a handsome structure of Portland stone, erected in 1833. On the right of the grand staircase leading to the interior is the statue of Sir William Walworth, whose hand grasps the identical dagger with which he slew Wat Tyler. The fishmongers were once the most powerful, and perhaps the wealthiest, of the City companies. The widening of the approaches to London Bridge considerably improved the value of the ground in this locality, and seven guineas per foot has been paid for frontage in King William Street. At the eastern foot of the bridge is the Government Emigration Office. So great is the traffic at this point, that on a careful inquiry, in April, 1850, it was found that in one day there passed along King William Street, from eight in the morning till eight in the evening, 11,022 vehicles, being at an average of 971 an hour, or sixteen a minute; and on the same day it was calculated that within the same space of time there passed 54,432 foot passengers, giving an average of nearly eighty a minute.

LONDON BRIDGE, with its approaches, cost about two millions, and was seven years building, being commenced in 1824, and finally opened by King William IV. and Queen Adelaide on the 1st of August, 1831. It has five elliptical arches, and presents to the eye not only a substantial and solid specimen of architecture, but a scene of bustle and traffic unsurpassed by any bridge probably in the world. It connects the heart of the City, where the mercantile world is so busily occupied and so densely concentrated, with the almost equally thickly populated Borough. A century ago, old London Bridge afforded the sole passage from one bank of the Thames to the other, and it formed the only entrance into town from the south, as it had done for eight centuries before. The first bridge was a wooden one, built between the years 993 and 1016. The first stone bridge was constructed in the reign of King John (1209), and an old tradition asserts that the foundation was laid upon woolpacks—a report manifestly arising from a tax on wool having contributed towards its expense. It was much injured by a fire in the Borough that broke out four years afterwards, when 3,000 persons perished. It had a drawbridge for the passage of ships to Queenhithe, and until the middle of the last century was crowded with houses, at one time mostly tenanted by booksellers, and at another, by pin and needle makers. There was a chapel on the bridge, and a tower whereon the heads of all unfortunate offenders were placed. An old map of the city, in 1597, represents a terrible cluster. The wharfs along the Middlesex side are chiefly devoted to the embarkation and disembarkation of passengers for Greenwich, Woolwich, and Gravesend.

Pursuing our course eastward along Lower Thames Street, we next reach the **New Coal Exchange**, built at the comer of St. Mary at Hill, and opened in November, 1849. It includes a circular area for the meeting of the merchants, 60 feet in diameter, with three galleries running round it, and the area is covered by a glazed dome 74 feet from the floor. At the angle of the two fronts is a circular tower 100 feet high, and forming a conspicuous abject from the river. The entire cost of the structure was £40,000.

Billingsgate, the great fish-market of London, is nearly opposite. It was established in 1699, and is held every day except Sunday, when mackerel are, however, vended by permission within its precincts. In November, 1849, was laid the foundation of a new market, to include an architectural frontage of 172 feet, extending from the Customhouse Quay to Nicholson's Wharf.

The Custom-House is next, presenting an extensive and rather handsome river frontage 484 feet in length, and 100 in breadth. Besides the warehouses and cellars there are nearly 180 distinct apartments in which the various officials transact their business. The interior may be visited daily from nine till three. On the first floor is the long room, which is 190 feet in length, 66 feet wide, and 50 feet high. There is a good promenade before the building, which affords a lively view of the constant traffic or the Thames. The present building was erected in 1817. On St. Dunstan's Hill adjoining is the church of St. Dunstan's in the East, noticeable for the peculiarity of its construction. From the square tower springs a lantern of singular form, having arches that support the spire, and of this flying steeple, Wren, the architect, was extremely proud.

In Mark Lane, a thoroughfare diverging northward into Fenchurch Street, is the CORK EXCHANGE, a large plain building in which the greater part of the sales of corn take place. Monday is the principal market day, when the greatest bustle prevails. Close by is the London Terminus of the Blackwall Railway.

We now approach the **Tower**, with its memories and associations of early times and struggles—its varying history as a fortress, a palace, and a prison, and its deeply stirring records of the wise, the virtuous, the daring, and the unfortunate, who have found a lodging within its walls and a death-place within its shadow. The earliest associations of this spot carry us back to the remote period where our annals merge into the twilight region of mythic fable and obscure tradition. A host of names rush into the memory; but our task is rather to describe the present than chronicle the past, else might we dwell upon the recollections here up-called of the patriot Wallace, the adventurous Raleigh, the revengeful Richard, with his helpless nephews, Clarence drowned in the Malmsey butt, the good Sir Thomas More and the chivalrous Earl of Surrey, Lady Jane Grey and her young husband, the ruthless Mary and the "Virgin Queen," besides a host of innocent victims, sacrificed in the dark days of despotism and tyranny, that "pass like veiled phantoms on before the mind." The very streets that introduce us to the spot, remind us of the city in its olden days, before gaslights and the new police had made the ways clear and the paths safe—when each house had its sign dangling in the palpable obscure of after-dark, their outlines ever and anon rendered more distinctly by the smoky glare of the linkboy's light as he piloted some bibbing citizen to his domicile, or the sudden assemblage of the swinging lanterns of horn, at the familiar cry of Watch.

The Tower is now known to have originated with the Romans, but the principal foundations were laid by William the Conqueror, to maintain his authority over the city. Subsequent monarchs built, enlarged, and re-constructed the various buildings from time to time, and the fire that consumed the grand storehouse, or small armoury, on the night of October 30, 1841, has caused some portions of the interior to assume a modern aspect. Within the outer wall the buildings cover a surface of twelve acres, surrounded by a ditch, which, though now drained and exhibiting a grassy slope, was not many years since the repulsive receptacle of stagnant water and filthy mud. The entrance is through four successive gateways, which are opened at daylight every morning, with all the forms and ceremonies of a garrisoned fortress. The appearance of the warders and yeomen, in their beefeater costume, with their large sleeves and flowing skirts ornamented with gold lace, the official badge, and their flat round caps tied about with bands of parti-coloured ribands, give a characteristic interest to the place directly we enter. At the Armoury Ticket Office within the entrance gate, a warden is in attendance to conduct parties through, from 10 till 4. A fee of one shilling is paid for viewing the Regalia and the Armoury. To the left is the Bell Tower, said to have been the prison of Queen Elizabeth and now

containing the alarm-bell of the garrison. Near where that sentry's bright bayonet glitters in the sunhine, you may see a stone arch under the esplanade. That is the water-way to the celebrated Traitor's Gate, through which offenders were conveyed, seldom to these unfortunates being other than a gate of death. A boat, securely guarded, almost unnoticed, and beyond the reach of mob or rescue, bore the prisoner swiftly down the stream. Once under the shadow of that arch, the huge gates opened to receive the victim, and as they closed again upon him, the world and hope were alike shut out. Beyond the gate a flight of stone steps was washed by the tide, and stepping ashore, the offender was within the fortress and readily consigned to any of its numerous dungeons. The last prisoner taken through Traitor's Gate was Arthur Thistlewood, afterwards hanged for the Cato Street conspiracy. Passing beneath the gateway of the "Bloody Tower," so called from it being the supposed scene of the murder of the two infant princes by their uncle Richard III., we find ourselves under the walls of the White Tower, and in front of the spot where the grand storehouse, or small armoury, stood, which was destroyed by the fire before mentioned. On this site the Waterloo Barracks have been erected. To the left is the Tower Chapel, or

Church of ST. PETER AD VINCULA. In front of the altar are buried Anne Boleyn and Catharine Howard, the ill-fated wives of Henry VIII.; in the same grave with his turbulent and ambitious brother, Lord Seymour, and side by side, with his powerful rival Dudley, the proud Duke of Northumberland, was interred the protector Somerset. Here also lie the remains of Thomas Cromwell, the rival of Wolsey; Devereux, Earl of Essex, Elizabeth's favourite; Lady Jane Grey; her husband, Lord Guildford Dudley; and under the communion table, James, the unfortunate Duke of Monmouth. Besides all these and other bygone celebrities, whose names are handed down by history, and occasionally revived in the pages of romance, here will be found many of those devoted adherents who lost their lives in the cause of the Stuarts. In one grave were interred the Lords Balmerino, Kilmarnock, and Simon Lord Lovat.

The White Tower presents a large square irregular outline, and exhibits architecture as ancient as any now remaining among us. It consists of three lofty stories, under which are spacious vaults. At the south-west corner is the entrance to the HORSE ARMOURY, which is comprised in a single apartment, 150 feet by 33. The floor is lined by a series of equestrian figures, twenty-five in number, and clothed in the armour of various reigns, ranging from that of Edward I. to James II. The figures in this romantic collection are arranged in chronological order; each is mounted in the fall field costume of its respective era, and placed beneath an arch, in the left column of which is affixed a banner displaying in letters of gold the name, rank, and period of the illustrious personages beneath, who look like animated portraits borrowed from some Illustrated History of England. A small room to the right contains in addition specimens of the various kinds of fire-arms that have been in use since the invention of gunnery. Here will be noticed, among other trophies, three swords, a helmet, and a girdle, once belonging to Tippoo Saib, and some curious Chinese dresses and accoutrements captured in one of our recent victories at Chusan. Nor should we omit to direct attention to Henry the Eighth's walking-staff, with three matchlock pistols in it, and a short bayonet in the centre of the barrels, with which trusty companion the portly monarch is said to have perambulated the streets of London in disguise after nightfall.

At the north-east corner of the Horse Armoury is the staircase leading to Queen Elizabeth's Armoury, which contains specimens of those weapons in use before the introduction of fire-arms. Here figure the partisan, the pike, the boar-spear, the bill, the glaive, the ranseur, the spontoon, the battle-axe, and other formidable arguments of a like description, with which our ancestors were wont to settle disputed questions. Here, too, are sundry instruments of torture, the thumb-screw, and the "scavenger's daughter," which make the blood run cold to look at. At the entrance the attendant will point out the apartment which was the prison of the gallant Raleigh. The lower portions of the White Tower are occupied as store-rooms tor the Ordnance Department, and the upper portion as a repository for the national records.

THE JEWEL OFFICE is generally the next place visited. The crown jewels were formerly kept in the Martin Tower, but in 1841 the present building was prepared for their reception. Here will be seen the gorgeous regalia with which our monarchs have been invested at their coronation. The most conspicuous among them is the Imperial Crown, modelled for George IV., and said to be the richest diadem in Europe. It is made of rich velvet, enclosed with silver hoops, and covered with diamonds. In the front is a large Jerusalem cross entirely frosted with brilliants, having in the centre a beautiful sapphire of the purest and deepest azure; at the back is another cross, similarly frosted, and enclosing the rock ruby worn by Edward the Black Prince, and by Henry V., at the battle of Agincourt. These matchless jewels are separated by four large diamond flowers, set between the arches, and the whole rests upon a double fillet of large pearls, enclosing several diamonds, emeralds, rubies, and amethysts of surpassing brilliancy. Besides the crown there are shown about forty other objects of curious interest, some remarkable for the amazing splendour of their ornaments, and others uniting great antiquity to dazzling lustre. They are all displayed within enclosures lined with white cloth, and fronted with large squares of plate glass. The jewels are valued collectively at nearly three millions sterling, notwithstanding the recent decision in our law courts with respect to the crown jewels of Hanover, which has had the effect of removing a portion of them to that kingdom.

Opposite the church, and on the south-west corner of the Tower Green, the ancient place of execution, is the Governor's residence, in which is the COUNCIL CHAMBER, where there is a record kept of the Gunpowder Plot, the conspirators having been examined here. The BEAUCHAMP TOWER stands half-way between the Governor's residence and the church. It was the ancient state prison, and consisted of two stories, the walls of which, with their carved memorials, bear sad testimony to the dismal thoughts of those who were here imprisoned. North of the Beauchamp Tower is the DEVELIN TOWER, and to the eastward are the remains of the BOWYER TOWER, the reputed scene of Clarence's death in the Malmsey butt, the FLINT and the BRICK TOWER, where Lady Jane Grey underwent her imprisonment. The upper story of the WAKEFIELD TOWER is pointed out as the spot where Henry VI. was murdered. Before leaving these venerable precincts, the visiter should ascend the parade, look at the old batteries, where the cannons are happily rusting away in peaceful inaction, and having explored the short streets and court-yards, which give this remarkable spot the appearance of a little fortified town, let him make his exit by the postern, on the eastern side, and contrast the advantages of our present happier condition with the evidence that has been afforded him of the brutal tastes and sanguinary pursuits of the nation, when kings upheld their thrones by the tyranny of bloodshed, and the people were taught to regard their brethren across the Channel as their natural enemies. Let him stand by the lofty dock-walls of St. Katharine, and view the thronging herd of ships that crowd upon the Pool, and he will behold a scene of true glory which the world cannot equal—a sight which is alone and unparalleled in the history of nations, a spectacle which neither Greece in her refined enlightenment, nor Rome in her imperial power, could boast. A channel left in mid-stream is lined on each side with shipping, the hulls lying dark and solid upon the water, the rigging mingling into one long-continued web, a mesh of interlacing ropes and spars. Ten thousand masts stretch tapering to the sky in token of England's commerce with each corner of the globe; the flags of all countries spread their colours to the breeze, the tongues of all nations mingle in one busy clamour, which still tells that every clime sends to this chosen haven the choicest products of their several lands, giving wealth almost beyond calculation, to be centred in the Pool, the docks, and the tall warehouses around. Such is a visible sign of the wonders wrought by popular progress, and a brilliant contrast in its picture of peaceful industry to the dark evidence of the horrors of the past, shrouded within the venerable walls of the Tower.

Before quitting the neighbourhood, there are two buildings by Tower Hill which should not escape observation. The one on the north side is the TRINITY HOUSE, a handsome structure of Portland stone, which is the seat of the Trinity Corporation, founded in 1512. Here are examined the masters of ships, and besides appointing pilots to the Thames, the government of lighthouse, harbour-dues, buoys, &c., all falls under their cognizance. To the eastern side of the hill is the MINT, a fine stone building erected from the designs of Smirke, and possessing vast mechanical aids within for executing the coinage of the United Kingdom, which is all issued from this great money manufactory. The buildings in which the coining is carried on are a series of neat workshops situated in the courts behind. The machinery is exceedingly interesting, and the whole is a model of ingenuity and exactness. Strangers can only be admitted by the special introduction of some superior officer connected with the establishment.

DISTRICT IV.

STATIONERS' HALL—WARWICK LANE—NEWGATE MARKET—CHRIST'S HOSPITAL—NEW-GATE—THE OLD BAILEY—CENTRAL CRIMINAL COURT—ST. SEPULCHRE'S—THE COMPTER—SMITHFIELD MARKET—BARTHOLOMEW'S HOSPITAL—ST. JOHN'S GATE—THE CHARTER HOUSE—ALDERSGATE STREET—WHITECROSS STREET—PANYER ALLEY—HOLBORN HILL—THE FLEET—ST. ANDREW'S CHURCH—ELY PLACE—ANCIENT LAW COURTS—HOLBORN BARS.

PROCEEDING northward from St. Paul's towards Newgate Street, we again traverse the great bookselling district, in the heart of which, standing back from a passage leading from Ludgate Hill to Paternoster Row, is STATIONERS' HALL, where the works of all authors are entered to secure their copyright. The gross amount of magazines and other periodicals, sold on the last day of the month, in Paternoster Row, has been estimated at 500,000 copies. The annual returns of periodical works alone are rated at 300,000, and this, notwithstanding the wonderful cheap-ness of price at which they are issued, so that some idea may be formed of the extensive nature of the business here transacted. Threading the tortu-ous thoroughfare of WARWICK LANE, which derived its name from the man-sion of the Earls of Warwick having been there situated in the days of yore, we pass on our left the COLLEGE OF PHYSICIANS, where the golden globe on the dome "seems to the distant sight a gilded pill." The business of the college is now removed to a much finer build-ing in Pall Mall East; and the ground floor of the old College is occupied by the butchers, who could not find room in the confused space of Newgate Market. Other manufactures are carried on in the upper floors of the building. At the back of this building, and in the midst of a densely-populated area, is NEWGATE MARKET, which is productive of considerable inconvenience to the public, from its ill-chosen situation. On market-days it frequently happens that the streets in the vicinity are completely blocked up by the butchers' carts. In thirteen slaughter houses here, there are as many as 600 sheep, and from 50 to 110 bullocks slaughtered every day. It will, certainly, be a great public convenience, if Old Smithfield, which is close at hand, as suggested, be converted into a dead meat market.

In Newgate Street, nearly opposite the entrance to the market, and standing back a little from the main thoroughfare, is seen the south front of CHRIST'S HOSPITAL, familiarly called the "Blue Coat School," from the peculiar costume worn by the boys. This noble institution, founded by Edward VI., occupies the site of an ancient monastery of Grey Friars, and was first opened for the reception and education of boys in 1552. The present annual revenue is about £50,000. About a third part of the children are educated at an auxiliary branch of the institution, at Hertford, whence they are transferred to town. Besides other endowments, Charles II. founded a ma-

thematical school for forty boys, and another, by Mr. Travers, provides a mathematical education for thirty-six more. Four boys are annually sent to Oxford and Cambridge, and there are likewise two scholarships of £80 each, one founded by the Pitt club, and the other by the proprietors of the *Times* newspaper. The buildings of the institution embrace several structures of large dimensions, chiefly ranged round open courts with cloisters beneath. The Great Hall, which occupies the first floor, is 187 feet long, 51 feet broad, and 47 feet high. In this magnificent apartment the boys take their meals, and on the eight Sunday evenings preceding Easter Sunday, the public suppers that take place, at 6 P.M., constitute one of the most interesting sights in London. Strangers are admissible by tickets, which can only be obtained from those connected with the school. The management of the institution is vested in a body of governors, composed of the Lord Mayor and Corporation, together with all benefactors to the amount of £400 and upwards. A presentation is extremely valuable. In the year ending 1849, there were 199 boys placed out, 1,409 remaining at Hertford and London, and 198 waiting to be admitted on presentations granted to that time; so that the average number of boys here educated and supported may be taken at 1,610. It is worth mentioning, as the subject has recently attracted attention, that the dress of the boys first admitted was a sort of russet, but this was soon changed for the dress they now wear, and which is the most complete representation of the monkish habit we have left. What is now called the coat, was the ancient tunic, and the petticoat or "yellow," as it is technically termed, the sleeveless or under tunic of the monastery. The girdle round the waist was also of monastic origin, but the breeches are a more recent addition. Many a bright name on England's muster-roll of celebrities has been first recorded in the books of this truly valuable institution. At the end of Newgate Street, and forming a sombre angular junction with the Old Bailey, will be seen the prison of NEWGATE, the name of which occurs so frequently in the chronicles of crime. It is a gloomy massive structure, of a quadrangular form, built in 1777, and being considerably injured by the riots in 1780, was afterwards efficiently strengthened and repaired. Within the last few years many improvements have been made; and it is a cheering reflection that in the present prison, with its clean, well-whitewashed, and well-ventilated wards, its airy courts, its infirmary, its humane regulations, and its strict but intelligent officers, the myriad miseries of the old jail have been utterly abolished. The condemned cells are at the north-east corner next to Newgate Street, and those doomed to expiate their offences on the scaffold are consequently not more than a few feet from the bustling tide of population ever streaming past, These dark and narrow dungeons have but a small grated aperture in each, letting in light from the court-yard on the other side. The executions take place in front of the debtors' door. Those desirous of inspecting the arrangements of the prison, must obtain an order from the Sheriffs, or one of the other competent City authorities.

Further on, down the Old Bailey, is the CENTRAL CRIMINAL COURT, for the trial of criminal offences. There are two court-rooms called the "Old" and the "New Courts," and to these a third has been recently added. In the Old Court, the Crown judges sit during the Sessions, and here the more serious cases are tried. In the New Court, the lighter kind of offences are disposed of by the Recorder and the Common Sergeant. A fee, ranging from one to five shillings, according to circumstances, will enable a stranger to procure admission into the gallery to hear the trials.

St. Sepulchre's Church, the solemn tolling of which is so associated with the knell of the murderer, stands on the north side of Snow Hill, nearly opposite Newgate. It was from this spot that a solemn exhortation was generally given to the prisoners appointed to die at Tyburn.

St. Bartholomew's Hospital presents a handsome stone front on the south-east side of Smithfield, and has a fine entrance under an arched gateway, which leads into a spacious square court beyond, where the principal buildings connected with the institution are situated. It was originally a priory, founded in 1102 by Rahere, minstrel or jester to Henry I., and who became the first prior of his own foundation. The present building was erected in 1729, and the great staircase was embellished by Hogarth gratuitously with such appropriate subjects as the "Good Samaritan," the "Pool of Bethesda," "Rahere laying the Foundation Stone," and "A Sick Man carried on a Bier, attended by Monks." At the head of the staircase is the hall, a very large room, ornamented with a full length of Henry VIII., and some other portraits of benefactors. Tradition asserts, and from recent discoveries, not without reason, that a subterranean passage led from the crypts below to the house of the priors situated at Canonbury. The arrangements of the wards, and the professional attendance, merit the highest commendation. All indigent persons, maimed by accident, are received at all hours of the day and night, without charge or ceremony; and, as a practical school of surgery for medical students, this hospital ranks among the highest. Lectures by eminent professors are delivered at stated periods. The annual expenditure is about £32,000. Crossing Smithfield, and passing up St. John's Street, we may direct the stranger's attention to a fine old vestige of ancient London, seen at the extremity of a narrow lane on the left, leading to St. John's Square. This is ST. JOHN'S GATE, consisting of a large pointed arch, with a Gothic window over it, and a large tower on each side. This is all that remains of a magnificent structure erected in 1110, and which was the sumptuous priory of St. John of Jerusalem, belonging to the warlike order of the Knights Hospitallers, instituted by Godfrey of Boulogne. The buildings covered a vast extent of ground, and are now occupied by St. John's Square. Adjoining the gate was the residence of Cave, the publisher of the "Gentleman's Magazine," and the spot is further rendered interesting by its association with Dr. Johnson, and other literary celebrities of the past century, who either habitually visited the spot, or took up their abode in this locality. Aylesbury Street, beyond, covers the site of the grounds formerly attached to the mansion of the Earls of Aylesbury.

Retracing our steps to St. John's Street, Charter House Lane will bring us to the CHARTER HOUSE, founded by Sir Walter Manny in 1370 as a Carthusian Monastery, from which it derives its name. After the dissolution it was, in 1611, sold for £13,000 to

Thomas Sutton, who converted it into a magnificent hospital, comprising a master, a preacher, head schoolmaster, and second master, with forty-four boys, and eighty decayed gentlemen, to defray which he endowed it with lands at that time worth £5,000. The pensioners, many of whom have distinguished themselves in the world by their talents, if they have failed in securing a stronger claim upon the favours of fortune, are allowed £14 per annum each, besides chambers, provisions, fire, and a cloak. The arrangements, though sometimes savouring of monastic quaintness, still display the charitable intentions of the founder, and effectually minister to the comfort of the unfortunate, who find here a peaceful retreat for their declining age. The School in connection with this foundation is an admirable one, and contributes to our universities some of the finest scholars. The privileges and scholastic perquisites enjoyed are very extensive.

Turning into Aldersgate Street, we may notice a fair specimen of ornamental street architecture, in the façade of the former City of London Literary and Scientific Institution, which was rebuilt at a cost of £5,000, in 1839. The institution, now the home of the Young Men's Christian Association, was founded in 1825, and has enabled many to acquire intellectual improvement at a small expense. The library contains many thousand volumes. Jewin Street will lead the curious explorer into that region familiar to the debtors, under the name of Whitecross Street. THE DEBTORS' PRISON is a substantial structure, built in 1815, for the reception of those debtors who had been previously incarcerated indiscriminately with criminals in Newgate and the Compter. There is accommodation for about 400 prisoners, access to whom is readily granted every day, at stated hours, varying according to the season.

If we again make our way into Newgate Street, the visitor should not pass Panyer Alley, the width of three streets from St. Paul's, without noticing a flat stone placed against the wall of a house there, on which is sculptured a naked child sitting upon a pannier or basket, with the following doggerel inscription, which had more truth when placed there than it has now:—"When you have sought the city round, yet still this is the highest ground. August the 27th, 1688."

Continuing our way along Skinner Street, we shall come to the foot of Holborn Hill, where the old Fleet River, that now forms the sewer underground, was once spanned by a bridge, and bore upon its surface the broad barges of the merchants. It was filled up in 1733, and finally built over. Here will be noticed a new street, communicating with the northern suburbs, and advantageously substituting a commodious thorough-

FLEET STREET AND ST. DUNSTAN'S, WEST—MID-DAY.

fare for the nests of vice and crime that until very lately occupied its site. FARRINGDON MARKET lies a little to the west of the street so called, and occupies a space of an acre and a half. There is a roofed avenue with shops all round, but vegetables form the chief commodity sold within its precincts. The Market itself having proved an utter failure, this spot, with other waste spaces in the same neighbourhood, are spoken of as likely to form the terminus of the Metropolitan Railway, an Act for which has been passed.

On the left, as we ascend Holborn Hill, is St. Andrew's Church, which was rebuilt by Wren in 1686, and is further noticeable for a fine painted window over the altar, representing the Lord's Supper and the Ascension. In the register of burials, under the date August the 28th, 1770, is recorded the name of Chatterton, the most wonderfully gifted youth the world has ever known. Here was interred another suicidal poet, Henry Neele, the young and imaginative author of the "Romance of English History," &c.

ELY PLACE, nearly opposite, was for many years the residence of the Bishops of Ely; and Hatton Garden marks the spot where the Lords Hatton had their dwelling from the time of the renowned Sir Christopher, who, as some historians assert, danced himself into the favour of the capricious Queen Elizabeth. THAVIES INN was a residence for students as long back as the days of Edward III., and was granted in fee to the Benchers of Lincoln's Inn. STAPLE'S INN was so called from its being the place where the wool-staplers used to assemble, but it gave shelter to law students possibly before the reign of Henry V. FURNIVAL'S INN, the chief now of a formidable array of law-courts that once flanked Holborn, was in old times the town abode of the Lords Furnival, a title that became extinct in the reign of Richard II.

At Holborn Bars the City boundary terminates, and hence, by Fetter Lane and Fleet Street, we may retrace our steps to St. Paul's.

DISTRICT V.

THE "TIMES" PRINTING OFFICE—APOTHECARIES' HALL—BLACKFRIAR'S BRIDGE—BRIDEWELL—ST. BRIDE'S CHURCH—FLEET STREET—ST. DUNSTAN'S—CHANCERY LANE—THE ROLLS—TEMPLE BAR—THE TEMPLE—THE INNER TEMPLE—THE MIDDLE TEMPLE—THE TEMPLE CHURCH—THE TEMPLE GARDENS.

WE now proceed from St. Paul's westward, and, to vary the route a little, we may suggest a digression towards the "TIMES" PRINTING OFFICE, situated in Printing-House Square—a small quadrangle at the back of Apothecaries' Hall, and easily reached by taking one of the tortuous thoroughfares leading southward from Ludgate Hill towards the water-side. A visit to the office during the time the huge machine is at work, casting off its impressions at the rate of 170 copies a minute, will present a sight not easily to be forgotten. From five till nine in the morning this stupendous establishment, employing nearly 300 people daily on its premises, is to be seen in active operation. The average daily circulation is 32,000; and the value of the advertisments is estimated at £110 per page of six columns. The first number of the *Times* appeared on the 1st of January 1788. The duties paid to Government for paper, advertisements, and stamps, alone, amount to £95,000 annually. A system of judicious outlay, conjoined with the tact and spirited enterprise of the late Mr. John Walter, and the indefatigable exertions and well-directed talents of those engaged in the various departments, have raised this great property to the pinnacle of newspaper prosperity; and it well deserves its recognised title of the leading organ of the world. Besides an extensive corps of editors, contributors, and reporters, for the collection and arrangement of local intelligence, correspondents at a liberal salary are stationed at all the principal places on the globe; and scarcely an event can occur any where, of which its emissaries are not prepared to supply the earliest and the fullest account.

APOTHECARIES' HALL, built in 1670, is next encountered on our way from Printing-House Square to Bridge Street, Blackfriars. Those who desire to have drugs unadulterated, may place the most implicit reliance on the articles here sold. The famous botanic garden at Chelsea, founded by Sir Hans Sloane, belongs to the Apothecaries' Company, who have the privilege of granting certificates to those desirous of vending chemicals, and for which they must pass a previous examination.

We now emerge upon Bridge Street, at the end of which is BLACKFRIARS' BRIDGE, forming an important link of communication with the opposite side of the river. Blackfriars' Bridge was commenced in 1760, and completed in November, 1769. The immense sums necessary for its construction were raised by loan, the City guaranteeing their payment by tolls to be levied on the bridge; but Government ultimately bought the tolls, and rendered it free. The entire expenditure was not less than £300,000; but it has been repaired since, at a cost nearly equal to the original amount. The bridge consists of nine arches, and, from wharf to wharf, is 995 feet in length and 42 in width. The removal of the balustrades, and the substitution of a plain parapet, somewhat spoiled its architectural beauty. The steamboat-pier on the eastern side is the most important accommodation of its class; it has no pretension to ornament, but considerably promotes the convenience of the many thousand passengers who daily embark and land at this point. From the fourth arch of the bridge, one of the best views of St. Paul's Cathedral can be obtained.

BRIDEWELL, a City house of correction, has its entrance on the western aide of Bridge Street. The building consists of a large quadrangle, one side of which is occupied by a spacious hall. The prison affords accommodation for seventy male and thirty female prisoners, who are incarcerated in single cells. The sentences vary from three days to three months. The treadmill is kept in active operation. In 1849, there was here received, under the commitments by the Lord Mayor and the Aldermen, 812 disorderly persons who had been subjected to hard labour; twenty-five apprentices sent by the Chamberlain for confinement; and 287 vagrants who had been found begging about the streets of the City; making a total of 1,124.

Near here, now represented by a plain and unpretending pump, was one of the "holy wells" with which London anciently abounded, and which were supposed to possess peculiar properties and virtues if taken at certain specified times. It was named, after the saint to whom the neighbouring church was dedicated, St. Bride's Well, and gave its name to the adjacent hospital founded by Edward VI., and which we have above described under its modern aspect as a house of correction. The churchyard at the east end of the church, or at the end of Bride Lane, is considerably elevated above the road, and the iron pump visible in the niche beneath, indicates the spot where the trusting dames of yore came to quaff the blessed waters of St. Bridget. "Cogers' Hall," a well-known debating tavern, is situated in Bride Lane; the society was first founded in 1756. The London house of the Bishop of Salisbury was near the church, and the name is retained by the adjoining square. Near to the end of Dorset Street, leading from Salisbury Square towards the Thames, was situated the "Whitefriars' Theatre;" probably one of the earliest buildings erected in the metropolis for dramatic entertainments. It was destroyed in 1580, re-erected in 1629, and finally suppressed by the Puritans in 1648. The ancient sanctuary of Whitefriars, the Alsatia of James the First's day, and repeopled by Scott in his "Fortunes of Nigel," was about the spot now occupied by the City Gas-Works, which, with their gigantic gasometer, will be noticed on the west side of the bridge stretching along the river bank.

ST. BRIDE'S CHURCH was originally destroyed by the same fire, in 1666, that consumed so many other public buildings, and was rebuilt by Wren in 1680, at a cost of £11,430. The steeple was then 234 feet in height; in consequence of which great elevation, coupled with the want of proper precautions, it was twice seriously injured by lightning. On the first of these occurrences, in June 1764, so much damage was done that it was found requisite to take down eighty-five feet of the spire. A more recent opening of the paved court affords a fine view of the church on its northern side. A house in the little quadrangle overlooking the churchyard, was one of Milton's London residences. It may be appropriately mentioned in this place, that the two obelisks at the Farringdon Street end of Fleet Street, are respectively memorials of the notorious politician John Wilks, once alderman of Farringdon Without, and Alderman Waithman.

Passing up FLEET STREET towards Temple Bar, we shall find the courts and narrow outlets of this busy thoroughfare replete with interesting associations of the past. To the left are numerous avenues leading to the Temple; and on the right or north side will be noticed BOLT COURT, where Dr. Johnson died (in the back room of the first floor of No. 8); JOHNSON'S COURTS, where he lived for some time, though it was not named after him; and CRANE COURT, where the SCOTTISH HOSPITAL is situated. This benevolent institution originated from a society formed a short time after the accession of James I., and materially contributes to the relief of distressed natives of Scotland who apply to it for assistance. The number of applicants is about 300 monthly. A few paces in advance of Anderton's Hotel (No. 164), a fine view of the western front of St. Paul's is to be obtained; nearly opposite (No. 59) is the metropolitan depot and publishing office of Bradshaw's railway publications.

ST. DUNSTAN'S-IN-THE-WEST will be observed on the right hand side. The demolition of the old church that stood here took place in 1880, and the present one, built by Mr. Shaw, was consecrated July, 1833. The curious figures that struck the quarters on the projecting clock of the old church were bought by the Marquis of Hertford, and are now at the villa in Regent's Park. The tower rises 130 feet above the base. The interior is remarkably light and elegant, with some handsome stained windows. On the eastern side is a statue of Queen Elizabeth, placed in a niche, and which was brought from the western side of Ludgate, when that gate was taken down in 1760. The height of the figure is seven feet, with the same width between the pilasters. These and the other architectural accessories are in the style of the time of James I., and form a very pleasing composition, harmonizing with the embellished house to the west. It was at this point that the Great Fire of London ceased its ravages westward. Two taverns in Fleet Street, "The Cock" and "The Rainbow," are worth mentioning on account of the reputation they have enjoyed under the same name for more than two centuries; the latter was the first coffee-house in London, and was established in 1657.

CHANCERY LANE, the well-known thoroughfare of legal repute, contains the official abode of the Law Society, founded in 1827 and incorporated 1845, at which time the present substantial structure was erected. Attorneys and solicitors are here registered. In Southampton Buildings, at the Holborn end of Chancery Lane, is the Mechanics' Institution, founded by Dr. Birkback in 1823. The ROLLS liberty is a parish of itself. The Rolls, or records of the Court of Chancery, from the reign of Richard III. to the present time, are here deposited, under the control of the Master of the Rolls. The Chapel dates back to the time of Edward III., but there is nothing now suggestive of antiquity in the appearance of the building. CLIFFORD'S INN, at the back of St. Dunstan's Church, is an inn of Chancery appertaining to the Inner Temple. An old oak case in the hall, of antique workmanship, contains the ancient records of the society. It may give additional interest to a saunter through the courts about here to mention, that in GOUGH SQUARE, No. 17, on the north-west corner, Dr. Johnson and his six amanuenses compiled the dictionary that bears his name. The whole of this neighbourhood is studded with large printing establishments.

Temple Bar, the western boundary of the City, was built from Wren's design in 1670. Statues of Queen Elizabeth and James I. are placed in niches on the eastern side, and on the western are those of Charles I. and Charles II. The interior is leased from the City by Messrs. Child, the oldest bankers in London, as a repository for their ledgers and cash-books. The heads of persons executed for high treason were formerly placed on this gate, and many a mangled trunk has been here exhibited as a sacrifice to the cause which conscience had recommended the unfortunate victim to defend. The last heads exposed here belonged to the ill-fated participators in the rising of 1745, and one remained even as late as 1773. To show the power of the Lord Mayor, the ponderous gates of the civic barrier are shut upon all occasions of royal visits to the City. The herald then sounds a trumpet, and the mayor and corporation within demand by their marshal to know the monarch's pleasure, which, being communicated, the City sword is presented, the barrier flies open, and the cavalcade proceeds to its destination.

The Inner Temple Gate was erected in the fifth year of the reign of James I., the house above the entrance being decorated with the Prince of Wales' feather, the symbol of the promising Prince Henry. It is now a hairdresser's, with an erroneous inscription alleging it to have been formerly a palace belonging to Henry VIII. and Cardinal Wolsey. The history of the Temple, which is perhaps more rife with interest and richer in old associations than any other locality in the metropolis, may be thus briefly condensed within our limits :—

The Temple owes its designation to the "Knights Templars," who used to dwell within the precincts of the place, and who removed from their former residence in Holborn to the Temple in 1184, in the reign of Henry II., when it was called the "New Temple." In 1313, at the downfall of the Templars, Edward II. gave it to Aymer de Valence, Earl of Pembroke, after whose demise it passed into the hands of the Knights of St. John, from whom the premises of the Inner Temple were soon after leased by the common law students, while those of the outer were leased by Walter Stapleton, Bishop of Exeter. On the dissolution of religious houses, the Temple became the property of the Crown, and remained so until, in 1608, King James granted it to the students of law, who have ever since retained it in undisputed possession. Their government is vested in the benchers, who comprise the most eminent members of the bar. Before any person can be admitted as a student, he must furnish a written statement giving his age, residence, and condition in life, with a certificate of his respectability, signed by himself and a bencher of the society or two barristers. No person in priest's or deacon's orders can be called to the bar. The cost is for the Middle Temple, £34; and £100 must be deposited as security with the treasurer, to be returned without interest on being called to the bar. The hall attendances, including the dinners, cost about £1, 10s. each term, or £6 per annum. You must eat, or at least sit down to, three dinners in each term, and you must pay for fourteen, whether you eat them or not. The call to the bar costs £86. Attorneys and attorneys' clerks are inadmissible as such, which of course is a virtual prohibition of any emolument being derived from the law while a student. The buildings are chiefly laid out in courts and terraces, and every floor forms one or more sets of chambers, occupied by different tenants, and in every worm-eaten rafter and crumbling brick there is a volume of bygone romance, rich in antique association, and teeming with historic lore.

There is in the tranquil retirement of these buildings, more especially such as look down upon a patch of greensward or strip of garden, embowered by shadowing trees, and enlivened by the cool melodious plash of the well-known sparkling fountain, an appearance of the most delicious quietness and study-inviting solitude, contrasting all the stronger with the noisy region which we have just quitted. The very names of "Elm" and "Fig-Tree" Courts bring evidence of their origin along with them; and the gardens, apart from all recollection of the wars of the White and Red Roses, have something pleasing and venerable in their aspect. The soot-encrusted windows above the courts seem to have a story graven upon every pane. How many portly folios and quartos brimmed with legal learning, and running over with the quirks and quiddities of many a lawyer's brain, have emanated from these cobwebbed chambers! How many gallons of the midnight oil those smoky pannels have seen consumed to perplex the minds and lighten the pockets of her Majesty's lieges ! What dignified footsteps have creaked up those dark and rambling staircases—what broken hearts and wasted fortunes may not those time-rusted ceilings have looked down upon! Here have we in sooth the true materials of novel-writing.

The Middle Temple entrance from Fleet Street is by a plain building with stone facings, built by Wren in 1684, in place of the old gate-house, which was built by Sir Amias Paulet, who put Wolsey, when a lad, into the stocks for drunkenness and riot at a fair. Wolsey curiously revenged himself afterwards, by shutting Sir Amias up for several years in the same place. Here he reedified his prison, and sumptuously garnished the outside with cardinals' hats, and arms, and sundry devices.

The Middle Temple Hall was built in the year 1572, when Plowden, the great jurist, was treasurer. The roof of the hall is said to be the finest piece of architecture extant in London. The screen is an early and elaborate specimen of the transition style, quite out of keeping with the roof and every thing around it, but well deserving notice. There is a general impression to the effect that this screen was formed from the spoils of the Spanish Armada; but the records of the Society show that it was set up thirteen years previously to the Armada putting to sea. In taking up the floor of the hall in 1764, nearly one hundred pair of dice were found, which on different occasions had dropped through the crevices in the flooring.

The whole arm of the Temple is consecrated to the recollection of some of our greatest men who here took up their residence. It was here that the stern and uncompromising Hampden studied. Glance yonder at the dark winding staircase on the south-east angle of Hare Court, and you will be gazing on the very spot where, some two centuries bygone, the ambitious Oliver Cromwell occupied a dull and gloomy chamber at the summit. In the quiet nooks about the Middle Temple the brilliant old Chaucer wrote, and the wise and valiant Sir Walter Raleigh enriched his capacious mind; whilst in later days we find Congreve, and afterwards Oliver Goldsmith, occupying the same abode, No.2, Brick Court, on the right, up two pair of stairs, and where he died, April 4, 1774. Coke and Selden, Christopher Hatton, Beaumont the poet, Edmund Burke, Dr. Johnson, Cowper, Charles Lamb, and many other distinguished ornaments to their country's literature, were likewise inhabitants of this ancient seat of learning.

The Temple Church is the place of worship for both the Inner and Middle Temple; but though the original round church was built in the year 1185, the beautiful proportions of the building alone remain, and no era save the present is represented. A few years since the exterior and interior underwent a complete repair, at a cost of £70,000, and the old monuments of the Knights Templers were so redecorated and shorn of their ancient and interesting appearance, that the dust of time no longer remains on those figures. The fine old organ, made by Father Schmidt, on which Blow and Purcell played in long-contested rivalry, has vanished. The choral services, however, are now extremely well conducted every Sunday, and the visiter to London should not fail to be present on one of these occasions at least. The round of the church is open to all, but the choir is reserved for the benchers and students.

The Temple Gardens, a large green parterre by the river side, surrounded by gravelled walks, trees, shrubs, and flowers, are historically commemorated by Shakspere in his Henry VI. (Part I.); for here were plucked the two emblems under which the houses of York and Lancaster depopulated half the country. The rose has long since failed to put forth a bud in this locality. The range of Elizabethan structures on the eastern side, is called "Paper buildings," and occupies the site of a more ancient row, destroyed a few years back by fire. Fronting the garden-gate, which is open in the summer evenings, at 6 P.M., to the public, there is the Hall of the

ENTRANCE TO THE LONDON DOCKS, EAST SMITHFIELD.

Inner Temple, possessing no features worthy of detailed notice. Its foundations were laid in the reign of Edward III.

The Temple is a thoroughfare by day, but the gates are closed at night, and admission is only granted to those passing to the chambers within.

With this we may appropriately close our walks round the City and extend our next excursion to the busy maritime districts lying eastward of St. Paul's.

PART II.——THE EAST.

THIRD DAY'S ROUTE.

DISTRICT I.

ST. KATHARINE'S DOCKS—THE LONDON DOCKS—THE TOBACCO WAREHOUSES—THE WINE VAULTS—WAPPING—THE THAMES TUNNEL—SHADWELL—LIMEHOUSE—THE WEST INDIA DOCKS—BLACKWALL—THE EAST INDIA DOCKS—THE LONDON AND BLACKWALL RAILWAY.

THE eastern division of London will be found to present a marked contrast to the other portions of the metropolis, and will amply repay the stranger for any inconvenience he may experience in his visit to this thronged and busy region. Either by boat or omnibus he may accelerate his progress towards the Docks; and, presuming that they will constitute his principal attraction, we shall commence our description with an account of these vast repositories of our commercial wealth.

St. Katharine's Docks, as the nearest, claim priority of notice. The most direct way is to pass at the back of the Tower, and through the entrance by the Mint. These docks, which include a space of twenty-five acres, ten of which are occupied by the water, were opened October 25th, 1828, the cost of construction having been £1,700,000. In the warehouses, vaults, sheds, and covered ways, there is accommodation for 110,000 tons of goods. There is the East and West Dock, a basin, and a connecting lock canal, which communicates with the river, and is so capacious that vessels of 700 tons burthen may enter at any time of the tide. A portion of the frontage is used as a steam-packet wharf. In clearing the ground to obtain the requisite space, 1,250 houses were bought and pulled down, including the ancient Hospital of St. Katharine, to which it owes its apellation, and a population of 11,300 persons had to find "a local habitation" in another locality. The capital thus employed was £1,360,000; but it has proved a highly profitable investment. Upwards of a thousand merchant vessels can be here congregated at one time. It is impossible to witness this scene of busy activity without being forcibly reminded that it is to commerce that England owes her pre-eminence in the scale of nations.

The London Docks, to which the entrance at the opposite end of St. Katharine's will conduct us, were commenced in 1802, and opened 1805. The docks comprise an area of ninety acres, and cost upwards of four millions of money. The outer walls alone cost £65,000. In 1845 some new tea-warehouses were erected, capacious enough to contain 120,000 chests. An excellent description by Henry Mayhew, as the *Morning Chronicle* Commissioner, supplies us with the following graphic details, which cannot fail to interest the visiter:—" As you enter the dock, the sight of the forest of masts in the distance, and the tall chimneys vomiting clouds of black smoke, and the many-coloured flags flying in the air, has a most peculiar effect; whilst the sheds with the monster wheels arching through the roofs, look like the paddle-boxes of huge steamers. Along the quay you see, now men with

their faces blue with indigo, and now gaugers with their long brass-tipped rule dripping with spirit from the cask they have been probing; then will come a group of flaxen-haired sailors, chattering German, and next a black sailor with a cotton handkerchief twisted turban-like round his head. Presently, a blue-smocked butcher, with fresh meat and a bunch of cabbages in the tray on his shoulder; and, shortly afterwards, a mate with green parroquets in a wooden cage. Here you will see sitting on a bench a sorrowful-looking woman with new bright cooking-tins at her side, telling you she is an emigrant preparing for her voyage. As you pass along this quay, the air is pungent with tobacco; at that, it overpowers you with the fumes of rum. Then you are nearly sickened with the stench of hides and huge bins of horns; and, shortly afterwards, the atmosphere is fragrant with coffee and spice. Nearly every where you meet stacks of cork, or else yellow bins of sulphur, or lead-coloured ore. As you enter this warehouse, the flooring is sticky, as if it had been newly tarred, with the sugar that has leaked through the casks; and, as you descend into the dark vaults, you see long lines of lights hanging from the black arches, and lamps flitting about midway. Here you sniff the fumes of the wine, and there the peculiar fungous smell of dry rot. Then the jumble of sounds as you pass along the dock, blends in any thing but sweet concord. The sailors are singing boisterous negro songs from the Yankee ship just entering—the cooper is hammering at the casks on the quay—the chains of the cranes loosed from their weight rattle as they fly up again—the ropes splash in the water—some captain shouts his orders through his hands—a goat bleats from some ship in the basin, and empty casks roll along the stones with a dull drum-like sound. Here the heavy-laden ships are down far below the quay, and you descend to them by ladders; whilst in another basin they are high up and out of the water, so that their green copper sheathing is almost level with the eye of the passenger; while above his head a long line of bowsprits stretches far over the quay, and from them hang spars and planks as a gangway to each ship." This immense establishment is worked by from one to three thousand hands, according to the "brisk" or "slack" nature of the business. One of the most extraordinary and least-known scencs of London life is presented at the dock-gates at half-past seven in the morning. Congregated within the principal entrance are masses of men of all grades, looks, and kinds—a motley group of all who want a loaf and are willing to work for it; for the London Dock is one of the few places in the metropolis where men can get employ-ment without either character or recommendation. The Tobacco Warehouses, rented by Government at £14,000 a-year, are situated close to a dock of above an acre in extent, called the Tobacco Dock, and contain accommodation for 24,000 hogsheads of the Indian weed, each hogshead averaging 1,200lbs. Near the north-east corner is a door inscribed "To the Kiln." Here the damaged tobacco is burned, the long chimney which carries off the smoke being facetiously denominated the Queen's pipe. The vaults beneath are appropriated to the reception of wines, and present in their long, dark, winding passages all the appearance of a subterranean town. The vast cellarage is arched with brick, and extends about a mile in one continuous line, with diverging branches of even greater length. There is stowage for nearly 70,000 pipes of wine and spirits. To furnish some idea of the quantity usually deposited here, we may mention that in June, 1849, these vaults contained 14,783 pipes of port, 13,107 hogsheads of sherry, 64 pipes of French wine, 796 pipes of Cape wine, 7,607 cues of wins containing 19,140 dozen, 10,113 hogsheads of brandy, and 3,642 pipes of rum. A tasting order may be procured from a wine merchant who has pipes in bond, or from the secretary at the London Dock House, in New Bank Buildings. Ladies are not admitted after

1 P.M.; and it is generally considered advisable for the uninitiated to preface their visit with a repast of a substantial character, the very atmosphere of this vinous region having an intoxicating property. The entrances to the Docks from the Thames are three, viz., Huemitage, forty five wide; Wapping, forty feet wide; and Shadwell, forty-five feet in width.

We can leave the Docks either by Pennington Street or Wapping. If the former, it should not be forgotten that in the Swedish Church, Prince Square, Ratcliffe Highway, Baron Swedenborg founder of the well-known sect which, bears his name, was buried in 1772. WAPPING presents to all the characteristics of a seaport, the inhabitants being generally connected with the shipping interests; shipbuilders, sailors, and shopkeepers dealing in commodities for the supply of seafaring men, give a lovely aspect to the place. Wapping was nothing more than a marsh till the time of Elizabeth. Execution Dock was the place where pirates were formerly hung in chains.

The Thames Tunnel, two miles below London Bridge, connects Wapping with Rotherhithe on the opposite side the river. Cylindrical shafts, of 100 steps each, give the means of descent and ascent, and each boat-passenger pays a toll of one penny. This stupendous work is 1,300 feet long, and was completed in 1842 at a total cost of £614,000, having been commenced in 1825, and executed, after various delays, in about nine years of active labour. It is a magnificent monument of the skilful engineering of Sir Isambart Brunel, the original projector. The principal apparatus was the shield, a series of cells, in which, as the miners worked at one end, the bricklayers built at the other, the top, sides, and bottom of the tunnel. With all the perils of the engineering, but seven lives were lost in the work, whereas forty men were killed in building the present London Bridge. The two arched passenger are each sixteen feet four inches in width, with a path of three foot for pedestrians, and the whole is brilliantly illuminated with gas. The annual amount of tolls is averaged at £5,000, not sufficient to more than defray the expenditure for repairs. As an exhibition, the Tunnel is deservedly one of the most popular; and during the Fancy Fair that was held here under the Thames, in the week before Easter, 1850, it was visited by no less than 59,251 persons in, five days.

Shadwell is next, and between the houses and the river-bank there are numerous small docks and building yards; so that the passenger is often surprised by seeing the prow of a ship, rising over the street, and the skeleton framework of new ones appearing at the openings. The Church of St. Paul's, Shadwell, was erected in 1821. LIME-HOUSE, where there is a pier at which the river steamboats call, had the interior of its fine old church destroyed on the morning of Good Friday, March 29th, 1850. At Limehouse begins the REGENT'S CANAL, which, after several windings and tunnels through the northern part of London, joins the Paddington Canal. This Canal is the last link near London of the chain connecting that city with Liverpool. It has two tunnels; one at Maida Hill, 370 yards long; and the other under Islington, 900 yards long. The entire length is about nine miles, and it has a fall of ninety feet by twelve locks. It is now chiefly used for supplying coal to the northern districts. What is called the Pool terminates at Limehouse Beach.

The West India Docks extend along the banks of the Thames from Limehouse to Blackwall, and cover 295 acres. They were commenced in 1800, and partially opened in 1802. Warehouses of enormous extent are ranged along the four quays. There are two docks and a canal; the northern one, for unloading vessels, having accommodation for 800 West Indiamen; and the southern one, for loading outward-board ships, receiving 200. They are now less exclusive than formerly, and ships from all parts of the world will be found together. The capital employed in construction was £1,380,000. At the highest tides the water is twenty-four feet deep, so that vessels of 1,200 tons burthen can enter. The whole space is enclosed on every side; all the buildings are fireproof, and the premises are well guarded by watchmen, so that the system of pilfering, formerly carried on to a great extent in this part of the river, is completely abolished. The carts or waggons which convey goods to town, are loaded from the backs of the warehouses without entering the dock-gates. Some admirable contrivances recently adopted, preserve the purity of the great body of water in the docks, and prevent the accumulation of mud; so that, whilst salubrity is studied and cleanliness promoted, the bed of the river is freed from obstruction, and the free transit of vessels encored without inconvenience.

Blackwall, with its fine view of the reach of the river and the pleasant uplands towards Shooter's Hill, is an agreeable termination to a progress eastward. To the large taverns here, epicures flock from May till August to eat whitebait, caught in glittering shoals about this part of the river, and turned within an hour out of the Thames into the frying-pan. With the usual accompaniments of cayenne and lemon juice, brown bread and butter, and the equally important beverage of iced punch, they make a delicious refection. A vast amount of iron shipbuilding is carried on in this district, being an art of not more than twenty years' growth. Here will be seen the clanking boiler works, the cyclopean founderies and en-gineering workshops, in which steam is the principal motive power. The Brunswick Wharf was opened July 6, 1840, and the constant arrivals and departures of the Gravesend steamboats make it a very animated promenade. This is also the terminus of the LONDON AND BLACKWALL RAILWAY. Great improvements have rerently been made at the Fenchurch Street Station. Some idea of the immense outlay upon this line which is only four and a half miles long, may be formed from the circumstance, that the portion between the Minories and Fenchurch Street (450 yards) cost £250,000. The EAST INDIA DOCKS are situated at Blackwall, covering a space of thirty-two acres. They were opened in 1806. The dock for loading outward-bound Indiamen is 780 feet in length, and 520 in width. The gates are closed at 3 P.M. in winter, and 4 P.M. in summer. It is proposed to construct docks of vast extent, nearly three miles long, on the margin of the Thames, from a point a little below the Blackwall steamboat pier down to the Eastern Counties sta-tion, opposite Woolwich. The land is already in the possession of the pro-moters. The cost of the docks is es-timated with the projected warehouses, at £1,500,000. Those who desire a more extensive acquaintance with the scenery of the river below Blackwall, should consult "Adams's Pocket De-scriptive Guide to the Environs of London," in which, within a circuit of thirty miles, every thing worth seeing will be found detailed graphically and accurately.

DISTRICT II.

ALDGATE—HOUNDSDITCH—THE MINORIES—GOODMAN'S FIELDS—WHITECHAPEL—WHITECHAPEL ROAD—JEWS' BURIAL-GROUND—THE LONDON HOSPITAL—MILE END ROAD—BANCROFT'S ALMS-HOUSES—BETHNAL GREEN—BONNER'S FIELDS—VICTORIA PARK—SHOREDITCH—NORTON FOLGATE—BISHOPSGATE WITHOUT—FINSBURY CIRCUS—LONDON INSTITUTION—ROMAN CATHOLIC CHAPEL, MOOR-FIELDS.

ALDGATE, to which an omnibus from any of the main thoroughfares will serve as a conveyance, may be taken as a suitable point at which to renew our pilgrimage in this direction. The place derives its name from the "old gate" that here guarded the entrance to the City, and which was taken down in 1606. The fictitious bank recognised as Aldgate Pump will be seen at the commencement of Aldgate High Street. Beneath the pavement is a curious chapel or crypt, presumed to have been a part of the Church of St. Michael, and built in 1108. The whole addition of soil since its commencement is supposed to have been twenty-six feet. The inn on the left, called the "Three Nuns," is as old as the days of De Foe, and is mentioned by him in his history of the Plague. Northward from Aldgate Church are HOUNDSDITCH, BEVIS MARKS, and DUKE'S PLACE, the great quarter of the Jews, and here they have settled in large numbers ever since the days of Oliver Cromwell. The MINORIES, a communication with Tower Hill, derived its name from nuns of the order of St. Clare, or minoresses who had been invited into England by Blanche, Queen of Navarre, who here founded a convent for their reception. There are now several spacious shops; amongst which, the showy finery of Moses and Sons' establishment appears conspicuous. GOODMAN'S FIELDS, now a thickly populated region, are at the back of the Minories. Stow, in his quaint fashion, tells us that, in his time, one Trollop, and afterwards Goodman, were the farmers there, and "that the fields were a farm belonging to the said

nunnery; at which farm I myself," he says, "have fetched many a halfpenny worth of milk, and never had less than three ale pints for a halfpenny in the summer, nor less than one ale quart for a halfpenny in the winter, always hot from the kine." The theatre in Goodman's Fields was where Garrick first appeared, October 19, 1741; and here he drew such audiences of gentry and nobility, that their carriages filled up the road from Temple Bar to Whitechapel. The theatre in which Garrick appeared was burned down in 1746; but in another theatre, erected on the same spot, Braham, the celebrated vocalist, made his *debût* as a boy in 1787. This was likewise burned down in 1802, and it was never afterwards rebuilt.

Whitechapel has nothing but the butcher's shambles to boast of as a characteristic feature. The church has no features of either architectural or historical interest. In the JEWS' BURIAL-GROUND in Whitechapel Road, Rothschild, the great millionaire, lies buried.

The London Hospital, seen on the right of the road, was instituted in 1740 for the relief of maimed and invalided persons who are, from the nature of their avocations, subject to casualties. The patients are chiefly those employed about the docks and the shipping. In Beaumont Square, Mile End Road, is the "Beaumont

Literary and Philosophical Institution," founded by Barber Beaumont, who died in 1841, and endowed it with £13,500.

Bancroft's Almshouses are on the north side of the Mile End Road, and were erected in 1735, for twenty-four poor men of the Drapers' Company, and a school for 100 boys. Bancroft was an officer of the Lord Mayor's court, and is said to have acquired his fortune by acts of extortion. He ordered in his will his body to be embalmed, and placed "in a coffin made of oak, lined with lead; and that the top or lid thereof be hung with hinges, neither to be nailed, screwed, locked down, or fastened in any way, but to open freely and without trouble, like the top of a trunk."

Bethnal Green. Passing up Globe Lane we can reach Bethnal Green, a large district chiefly populated by the silk-weavers of Spitalfields. Ten churches have been erected here within the last ten years; and model lodging-houses have materially contributed to the comfort of the poorer denizens. The houses generally are miserably small and densely inhabited. The line of the Eastern Counties Railway traverses the very heart of this squalid region. Bonner's Fields derived their name from the hall of Bishop Bonner, close by, and which was removed in 1845, to make way for the new Victoria Park. This episcopal palace of the sixteenth century had been divided into five separate dwellings, but its general character was that of a substantial old English hall. Underneath the east wing was a small cell, where it was said that certain of Bonner's guests, whose theological tenets were not in harmony with his own, were wont to experience unwelcome hospitality. More probably, however, this cell was a cellar, containing the wherewithal to cheer the spirits of those who sat at the board above stairs.

Victoria Park is a most desirable and ornamental addition to this quarter, and presents a prettily-planted pleasure ground of 290 acres. It is bounded on the north by fields, on the south by the Lea Union Canal, on the west by the Regent's Canal, and on the east by Old Ford Lane, leading to Hackney Wick. A handsome Elizabethan lodge has been built at the entrance, and an iron bridge of light and elegant construction adds to the general effect. A vote of £100,000 was granted by Parliament to defray its expenses. We can hence make a circuit round by the Hackney Road towards Shoreditch, or thread the mazy thoroughfares of Bethnel Green.

Shoreditch, notwithstanding its present uninviting appearance, was once a genteel district, much inhabited by the players of the court and those connected with the "Curtain" and the "Blackfriars" theatres. The parish church of St. Leonard's, built by Dance, the City architect, in 1740, presents nothing exteriorly remarkable; but in the burial-ground several distinguished personages are interred. Here the parochial register records the interment of Will Somers, Henry VIII.'s famous jester; Tarlton, the celebrated clown of Shakspere's days; Burbage the actor, and many other original personators of our great bard's creations. In Shereditch is the spacious terminus of the EASTERN COUNTIES RAILWAY. NORTON FOLGATE, a continuation of Bishopsgate Street Without, has nothing requiring notice but the City of London Theatre, built in 1838; and in Bishopsgate Street we need only direct the observer's eye to a tavern called the "Sir Paul Pindar," and which was formerly the house of a generous merchant of that name, who gave largely towards the restoration of St. Paul's. The Church of ST. BOTOLPH, close by, contains a monument to his memory. The church was built in 1728; and the living, in the gift of the Bishop of London, is more valuable than any other in the City.

In London Wall was opened, in, January 1850, the new GREEK CHURCH, the first ecclesiastical structure erected by the Greek residents in London. The exterior is plain, except at the north or entrance front, which is divided into two stories by a bold and enriched moulding, the lower story having an arcade of three arches, whence admission into the church is obtained. The interior is very lofty, and in its general form differs widely from the usual arrangements. The cost was £10,000 —evidence of great liberality on the part of the Greek residents, as there are not more than thirty families residing in the metropolis. There is one service every Sunday, commencing at eleven o'clock.

Finsbury Square, built in 1789, and reached by London Wall, a vestige, in name at least, of olden London, brings to recollection its original appellation of Fens-bury, from the marshy nature of the soil before it was drained. FINSBURY CIRCUS has on its northern side the London Institution, originally established in the Old Jewry in 1806. The present building was erected in 1819. The library, which contains upwards of 56,000 volumes, is open from 10 in the morning till 11 at night, except on Saturdays, when it closes at 3 P.M. At the corner, by East Street, is the Moorfields Roman Catholic Chapel. Here was buried Weber, the composer; but in 1844 his remains were removed to Dresden. The service in this cathedral is of a remarkably impressive character. Hence we may pursue our way by the Pavement again into the City, and recruit ourselves for further expeditions in an opposite direction.

PART III.——THE WEST.

DISTRICT I.

TEMPLE BAR TO CHARING CROSS—ST. CLEMENT'S CHURCH—CLEMENT'S INN—STRAND
LANE—THE NEW CHURCH—SOMERSET HOUSE—KING'S COLLEGE—WATERLOO BRIDGE
—THE SAVOY—EXETER HALL—HUNGERFORD BRIDGE AND MARKET—CHARING
CROSS HOSPITAL—WEST STRAND—TRAFALGAR SQUARE—THE NELSON COLUMN, AND
OTHER MONUMENTS—THE NATIONAL GALLERY—THE ROYAL ACADEMY, &C. &C.

WE now proceed from Temple Bar westward, and enter the Strand. Before us is the Church of ST. CLEMENT'S DANES, rebuilt in 1682 by William Pierce, who received the design from Wren. There was a church here before the arrival of the Danes, who destroyed it by fire. The poets Otway and Lee are buried here. On the right, by the pillars, is the entrance to CLEMENT'S INN, an inn of Chancery belonging to the Inner Temple. The hall was built in 1715. It was a residence for students in the reign of Henry IV., if not before; and Shakspere makes Falstaff say, "I do remember him at Clement's Inn, like a man made after supper of a cheese-paring." The inn is chiefly inhabited by professional persons not engaged in the law, and the rents of chambers are moderate, varying according to the altitude of the location. The kneeling figure of the negro in the garden was presented by Holles, Earl of Clare. Holywell Street is chiefly tenanted by newsvenders, second-hand booksellers, and renovators of faded garments.

Essex Street, leading down to the river, where there is a pier at which the steamboats call, stands partly upon the site of Essex House, which the talented but rash and unfortunate Earl of Essex fortified against the authorities when he fell under the shadow of Queen Elizabeth's displeasure. The story of his favour, his imprisonment, and death upon the scaffold, it is unnecessary to repeat. A little beyond on the left hand side, is the STRAND THEATRE, a small establishment devoted principally to the production of burlettas and burlesques. The Whittington Club, which formerly occupied the premises originally known as the Crown and Anchor Tavern, being destroyed by fire a few years since, has been rebuilt upon the same spot, but the chief entrance is in Arundel Street. Adjoining is the entrance to Strand Lane, into which it is worth while deviating to see the Old Roman Bath, a genuine work of the Romans, built up for many years, and only opened at a recent period, when it was found exactly as it now appears. The sides are formed of layers of brick placed edgeways, and the bottom is paved with flat bricks, having over them a thin coating of stucco, and a thick basis of cement and rubble. The spring which supplies the bath, flows up directly from the earth at the upper end, and the action of the water having worn a deep hole there, a section of the pavement is visible. The water is pure and cold, and no doubt flows from the ancient "Holy Well" of the opposite side of the Strand. The chamber which contains this remarkable piece of antiquity is one of a series of large vaulted apartments, of Roman structure, indicating considerable antiquity, notwithstanding the alterations since made.

The Church of ST. MARY-LE-STRAND, or the "New Church," as it is sometimes called, though the present one was built by Gibbs in 1717, stands on the site of the ancient maypole. Although of small dimensions, it is elegantly constructed, and possesses architectural features of much merit. At the back of the church, in Wych Street, stands the OLYMPIC THEATRE, originally built by Astley in 1805, out of the timbers of an old man-of-war, burnt down in March 1849, and rebuilt and re-opened in the December following. The new theatre has the form of an elongated horse-shoe, with but few projections, so as not to present any interruptions to either sight or sound. The height from the pit floor to the highest part of the ceiling is 37 feet. The stalls contain 38 sittings; the pit will hold about 850 persons, the boxes about 200, and the gallery 750. The total cost of reconstruction was estimated at £10,000. In Newcastle Street is LYON'S INN, so called from an old inn called the "Lion," which stood here, and was purchased by the law students in the time of Henry VIII.

Somerset House, which is now devoted to the business of Government, was the successor of a palace which was commenced by the Protector Somerset in 1546, and fell, after his death, into the hands of the Crown. The present building was erected by Sir William Chambers, and was completed in 1786. It is built in the form of a quadrangle, with wings, and has a fine entrance archway from the Strand. Opposite will be noticed Bacon's bronze allegorical sculpture of Father Thames, which with the statue of George III. cost £2,000. The Venetian front, towards the river, is of striking magnificence, and its balustraded terrace affords a fine view of the river. This portion of the building is seen to the greatest advantage from Waterloo Bridge. Here are the Offices of Stamps and Taxes, the Audit Office, the office of the Duchy of Cornwall for managing the estates of the Prince of Wales, the Admiralty, and the General Registrer's Office. Nearly a thousand Government officials are employed at Somerset House, from 10 till 4 every day, at an aggregate annual cost of about £280,000. Under the open arches, at the principal entrance, are on the left the apartments of the Royal Society and the Society of Antiquaries; and on the right, those of the London University. The Government School of Design, which was originally held here, has been amalgamated with the South Kensington Museum.

King's College, established in 1833, is on the eastern side of Somerset House, and is an institution similar in its nature to the London University College, in Gower Street, but stricter in its theological character. Every pupil must produce, before admission into the school, a certificate of good conduct, attested by his last instructor. The age is from nine till sixteen. In the Museum of the College is placed the celebrated calculating machine, invented by Mr. Babbage.

Waterloo Bridge, next seen, at the end of Wellington Street, is deserving a detailed notice, as a bridge which has been justly called the noblest in the world. It was built at the enormous cost of above one million of pounds, raised by a company incorporated in 1809, under the title of "The Strand Bridge Company." It was planned by the famous John Rennie, and opened on the anniversary of the battle of Waterloo, June 18, 1817. The bridge, formed of granite, has nine elliptical arches of 120 feet span and 85 feet high. The entire length is 2,456 feet, and its breadth within the balustrades 42 feet. The roadway on the summit of the arches is level on a line with the Strand, carried on by a gentle declivity on the opposite side. Foot-passengers pay a toll of one halfpenny. The increase in the number of vehicles passing over to the terminus of the South Western Railway, on the opposite side, has materially benefited the company's revenue. The view of London from this bridge is remarkably fine and strikingly suggestive. The features of the south bank of the river are comparatively flat and uninteresting, there being little else besides coal and timber wharfs and tall chimneys, that pour forth their volumes of smoke by night and day. But on the north shore numberless objects of interest attract the wandering eye. In the foreground Somerset House stretches magnificently along the river bank. Further on, the Temple Gardens, with their trees and verdure down to the water's edge, contrast refreshingly with the masses of brick and stone around. Glancing over the elegant steeple of St. Bride's, the huge cupola of St. Paul's is seen towering with majestic dignity above the angles of surrounding buildings; and behind these, among a cluster of spires and towers, rises the Monument, and further on the Tower, whilst the extreme distance shows us a bristling forest of masts dwindling into the hazy perspective of the Pool. Turning westward there is soon, on the Lambeth shore, the Shot Tower and Goding's lion-surmounted brewery, with the sombre dome of Bethlehem Hospital behind. On the opposite side is the Savoy, the beautiful chapel of which still remains, the graceful suspension bridge, the aristocratic-looking Whitehall Gardens, and the summit of the Nelson Column and the venerable towers of Wesminister Abbey; whilst in a favourable state of the atmosphere, a misty line of hills may be traced onward, reaching to the very heart of the most picturesque and pastoral portion of Surrey. Waterloo Bridge affords, in fact, a complete panorama for the sight-seeker, which is only not appreciated as it ought to be on account of the trifling cost that places it before him.

On the north side of the Strand, in Upper Wellington Street, is the LYCEUM THEATRE, built by Beazley on the site of an older one, and first opened in July, 1834. The portico forms the entrance to the boxes; the pit entrance is in the Strand. The interior is very handsomely decorated. The shops which we now pass on our progress westward, are generally devoted to the exposition of some one of the multifarious shapes of art. To give some idea of the valuable nature of the objects placed in this way before the gaze of the street-lounger, we may mention that, in one establishment for the sale of pictures, near Exeter Hall, works of the old masters are frequently exhibited in the shop window, estimated to be worth £30,000. Mr. Barratt, the proprietor, is, we believe, insured in one of the offices to more than double that amount. Savoy Street, on the opposite side, indicates the site of the Savoy, alternately a palace, hospital, and prison. The chapel of St. Mary-le-Savoy was originally built in 1505, but it has since been frequently altered and embellished. All that remained of the other portion of the Savoy was cleared away when Waterloo Bridge was created.

Exeter Hall, where the May Meetings are generally held, and some of our best concerts given, was built in 1831. The large hall will accommodate about 4,000 persons. A little further, towards Charing Cross, is the ADELPHI THEATRE, recently re-built, under the direction of Benjamin Webster, Esq., its present proprietor. At the back of the Theatre is Maiden Lane, with a noted place of late-hour entertainment, called the

"Cider Cellars," originally opened as a concert-room, underground, in 1730.

On the opposite side the Strand is John Street, leading to the ADELPHI TERRACE, a large pile of buildings, built by the brothers Adam in 1768, on the site of old Durham House, and the "New Exchange." The terrace front is a conspicuous object from the river, and the spacious subterranean vaults and arcades beneath, give evidence of the extreme depth of the Foundations. In John Street is the SOCIETY OF ARTS, first established in 1754, and removed here in 1774. There is gratuituous admission to see the pictures any day but Wednesday, between 10 and 4. The object of the Society is to promote the arts, manufactures, and commerce of the kingdom, by the judicious distribution of honorary or pecuniary rewards. The prizes are generally awarded at the end of May. BUCKINGHAM STREET has an old water gate at the end, built by Inigo Jones, the only remnant left of a princely mansion, built for George Villiers, the second and last duke of that family, whose name will be found perpetuated in the neighbouring streets, and an alley called "Of," to make this streetological title complete.

Hungerford Market, opened in July, 1833, occupies the site of an older market of the same name. Fruit and vegetables are sold in the avenues above, and the lower portion next the river is appropriated to the sale of fish. This is the direct entrance to HUNGERFORD SUSPENSION BRIDGE, which crosses to the Belvidere Road, on the Lambeth side. The steamboat-pier at this point is the great focus of the smaller steamboat navigation; upwards of a million passengers embarking and disembarking annually.

Hungerford Suspension Bridge was constructed under Brunel's direction, and was first opened April 18, 1845. It consists of three arches, the span of the middle one being 676 feet, 6 inches, and in the centre is 32 feet above high-water. It is only second to the suspension bridge at Fribourg, in Switzerland; and the total cost, including the purchase of property, law, parliamentary, and other expenses, was £110,000. The quantity of iron employed is estimated at 11,000 tons. A toll of one halfpenny is paid on crossing the bridge. The length of the footway is 1,440 feet.

Lowther Arcade—Nearly opposite the entrance to the Market is the Lowther Arcade, a bazaar-like avenue, where the shops seem to be turned inside out, and the stalls are crammed with French and German goods, interspersed with a prodigal display of Mosaic finery. It is 245 feet in length, and 35 feet in height, and was built in 1831. The improvements that took

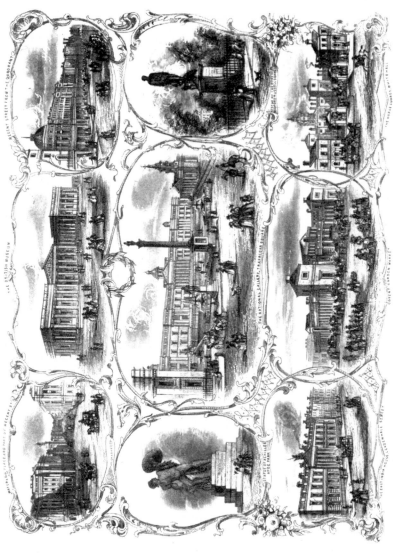

SIGHTS IN LONDON

place at the same time in this part of the West Strand, have given a modern aspect of magnificence to the adjacent thoroughfares. CHARING CROSS HOSPITAL, at the corner of King William Street, was built in 1833 by Decimus Burton. The annual revenue is about £2,500; and in 1849, 9,000 necessitous patients were relieved through its agency.

Trafalgar square.—We now arrive at Trafalgar Square, occupying the site of the old Royal Mews, and a nest of wretched courts, that were all cleared away in 1829. The fine portico and Church of St. Martin's forms a conspicuous object on the eastern side. The original Church of St. Martin's—no longer meriting its parochial addition of "in-the-Fields"—was erected in 1535. The first stone of the existing building was laid down in 1721, and it was completed by Gibbs in 1726, at the cost of £36,891, 10s. 4d. The portico has eight Corinthian columns, and supports a pediment in which are the royal arms. The interior is richly decorated. The present burial-ground is at Pratt Street, Camden Town; but in the old burying-ground, now covered by the pavement along the side of the church, was interred, among many celebrated personages, the notorious housebreaker Jack Sheppard.

Northumberland House, seen at the south-west corner, by Charing Cross, was built in the reign of James I., and is the town residence of the Duke of Northumberland. The front is surmounted by a lion, the crest of the Percys; and in the magnificent apartments within are many valuable paintings by the old masters. The grounds at the back reach to the very verge of the river.

The Nelson Column, designed by Mr. William Railton, afforded an opportunity to both architect and sculptor to combine their efforts in perpetuating the memory of Trafalgar's hero. Baily's statue on the summit is eighteen feet high, and was set up November 4, 1843. The column is built on clay; the granite was brought from the coast of Devon; the figure is of Craigleith stone; and the entire cost of the monument was £28,000. The height is nearly 177 feet, and the pedestal alone has an altitude of thirty-six feet. On the four sides of the pedestal, represented in bronze *bas relief*, are sculptures of "The Death of Nelson," by Carew; "The Battle of the Nile," by Woodington; "St. Vincent," by Watson; and "Copenhagen," by Ternouth. The *relievo* was cast in five pieces, and the thickness of the metal is about three-eighths of an inch.

The equestrian statue of George IV., at the angle of the square, is by Chantrey, and was originally intended to surmount the marble arch in front of

Buckingham Palace. The cost was 9,000 guineas. Monuments in memory of the celebrated warrior, Sir CHARLES NAPIER, of JENNER, the discoverer of vaccination, and of the hero SIR HENRY HAVELOCK, are likewise erected on this spot. The fountains, with their granite basins, have been made the subject of much ridicule. They are supplied by an artesian well, sunk to a great depth at the back of the National Gallery.

The National Gallery extends along the whole of the north side of the square, and originated in the purchase by Government of the Angerstein collection of pictures for the sum of £40,000. The present structure was designed by Wilkins, and finished in 1838. The length is 461 feet, and the greatest width is 56 feet. The central portico is the main feature of the building, and the Corinthian columns are the same which used to support the portico of old Carlton House. The Gallery is open without charge to the public every Monday, Tuesday, Wednesday, and Thursday, and on Friday and Saturday to artists. The hours are from ten till five. During the last two weeks of September and the month of October the Gallery is wholly closed. Although inferior to the great continental galleries, this is still a highly valuable collection. There are many works of the ancient masters, with some fine specimens of our own Hogarth, Wilkie, Gainsborough, Reynolds, and Lawrence. As there are so many cheap catalogues, from one penny upwards, to be had at the doors, we consider an elaborate enumeration of the pictures to be quite unnecessary. We must call the visitor's attention, however, as he passes through the hall, to the fine colossal Waterloo vase, by Sir Richard Westmacott, the material for which was captured from a French vessel that was taking it to France to be converted into a vase to celebrate the victories of Napoleon.

The Royal Academy occupies the eastern end. It was constituted, December, 1768; opened its first exhibition in Somerset House, May, 1780; and removed from Somerset House, and opened its first exhibition in Trafalgar Square, May, 1838. Its principal objects are set forth as being the establishment of a well-regulated school of design for students in the arts, and of an exhibition open to all artists of distinguished merit, where they might offer their performances to public inspection, and acquire that degree of reputation and encouragement which they should be deemed to deserve. The Society consists of forty royal academicians, including a president, twenty associates, and six associate engravers. The whole of the funds are derived from the produce of its annual exhibition, which always opens on the first Monday in May. The receipts amount now to nearly £6,000. The average number of paintings and pieces of sculpture is 1,500.

FOURTH DAY'S ROUTE.

DISTRICT II.

CHARING CROSS—THE ADMIRALTY—HORSE GUARDS—WHITEHALL—THE TREA-
SURY—GOVERNMENT OFFICES—WESTMINSTER BRIDGE—PALACE YARD—
WESTMINSTER HALL—ST. MARGARET'S—WESTMINSTER ABBEY—POET'S COR-
NER—THE CHAPELS—DEAN'S YARD—THE CLOISTERS—THE CHAPTER HOUSE—
WESTMINSTER SCHOOL—THE OLD HOUSE OF COMMONS—THE NEW HOUSES OF
PARLIAMENT—THE ROYAL ENTRANCE—THE VICTORIA TOWER—THE HOUSE
OF LORDS—THE HOUSE OF COMMONS—MILBANK—THE PENITENTIARY—VAUX-
HALL BRIDGE—CHELSEA NEW BRIDGE—PIMLICO.

Charing Cross, though now one of the busiest scenes in the metropolis, was, not more than two centuries and a half ago, within bowshot of the open country, all the way to Hampstead and Highgate. The Haymarket was a country road, with hedges on each side, running between pastures; and from old St. Martin's Church there was a quiet country lane, leading to St. Giles's, then a pleasant village sheltered by clumps of fine trees. The place exhibits at the present time far different features. On the site now occupied by the statue stood one of the numerous memorials of the affection of Edward I. for his beloved Queen Eleanor, the cross pointing out the last spot on which her body rested. It was destroyed by the Puritans in 1647. The equestrian statue of Charles I. was cast by Hubert le Sœur in 1633, but it was not placed in its present situation until 1674. The pedestal is the work of Grinling Gibbons. Every body remem-bers the story, how the statue was condemned by Parliament to be sold, and how John Rivet, the brazier, bought it and buried it under ground, making for his own profit a vast number of handles of knives and forks in brass, which he sold as made of the supposed broken statue, and which were eagerly bought by the Royalists from affection to their monarch, and by the Round-heads as a mark of triumph. It is not, however, so well known that the horse is without a girth, and that the king's sword was stolen by some felonious madcap when Queen Victoria went to open the Royal Exchange in 1844.

At the entrance to Craig's Court is Cox and Greenwood's, the largest army agency office in Great Britain. At the back of the buildings at this part is SCOTLAND YARD, so called from the kings of Scotland having been for-merly lodged here. It is the head-quarters of the metropolitan police and was also the site of the PALACE

COURT, removed here from the Marshalsea in 1801, and finally abolished on the 1st of January, 1850. On the opposite side is a range of public buildings of considerable importance, which we shall notice successively.

The Admiralty, built in 1726, contains the house and offices of those who superintend the marine department, and here a vast amount of correspondence connected with our naval affairs is received and directed. The two telegraphs that stood at the summit of the building, one communicating with Deal, and the other with Portsmouth, have been quite superseded by the quicker agency of the electric telegraph. Adjoining are the offices of the Paymaster-General.

The Horse Guards, a fine spacious stone building, with an arched opening into St. James's Park, is easily recognised by the two mounted sentinels that do duty in the small recesses on the side. Here are the offices of the Commander-in-Chief, the Military Secretary, the Quarter-Master-General, and the Secretary of War. The War Office is also here situated, and from this source all army intelligence can be obtained. (*For St. James's Park, see next district*).

Whitehall, nearly opposite the Horse Guardls is merely the vestige of a royal palace, in existence from the days of Henry VIII. to William III., and of which the present building was the banqueting hall, built by Inigo Jones in 1622. It was on the scaffold erected in front of Whitehall, facing the park, that Charles I. was executed. In the reign of George I. it was converted into a chapel, which it still is, though never consecrated; and on every Maunday-Thursday the distribution of the Queen's bounty-money to poor aged men and women furnishes an additional temptation to visit the interior. The ceiling is lined with pictures on canvas, painted by Rubens in 1635, and representing the apotheosis of James I. There is a fine organ at the end over the entrance door, and lofty galleries are on each side. At the back of the building is a fine statue in bronze of James II., the work of Grinling Gibbons. In Privy Gardens adjoining was the mansion of Sir Robert Peel, whose untimely death, July 2, 1850, the nation had to deplore. In Whitehall Yard is the UNITED SERVICE MUSEUM, which may be gratuitously inspected every day by an order from a member of the institution.

The Treasury, with its fine massive exterior, built by Barry in 1847, is a spacious building reaching from the Horse Guards to Downing Street. Here are the offices of the BOARD OF TRADE, the HOME OFFICE, and the PRIVY COUNCIL. The COLONIAL OFFICE and the FOREIGN OFFICE are both in Downing Street. Sixty-five millions of pounds sterling are annually received and paid in this focus of government influence. Hence are fulminated decrees that sway the fortunes of countries afar off; and in its vast and busy chambers are projected the influential plans that affect the Legislature of our own. A voice from Downing Street has its echo at the Antipodes.

At the end of PARLIAMENT STREET is an opening to WESTMINSTER BRIDGE, built in 1750, and now in course of removal to give place to the new iron bridge, the southern half of which, alongside, was opened on the 1st of March, 1860, for heavy traffic. Besides the great advantage it possesses over the old bridge in being very nearly level with the approaches on both sides, a tramway for omibuses and wagons has been laid down, and must, doubtless, afford great relief to the heavily loaded draught horses. A portion macadamised, is reserved for light carriages and saddle horses, whilst foot passengers, for the present, use the serviceable portion of the old bridge yet standing.

This bridge, when completed, will equally deserve a critical visit, after one to Waterloo, as both bridges will be remarkable for their level surface, and as points interesting to visitors for the views they afford.

The old bridge was 44 feet wide, the present one, inclusive of the parapets, will be 85 feet; the span of the centre arch is 120 feet. Each arch, complete, will contain 15 ribs, besides the decorative facing.

The space occupied by the numerous houses and buildings that have been and that remain to be pulled down, will render the approaches of ample and unusual width to display this latest work of engineering skill, and afford a point of view whence the Houses of Parliament, and especially the clock tower, will be displayed to the greatest advantage.

The stranger should observe that the completed portion of the new bridge is lighted by the lime light, lately introduced. Ten lights, about one-third of the number of the old gaslights, present a most brilliant appearance. It is most interesting to know that in the lime light Newton's assertions are fully corroborated. The oxy-hydrogen flame burns the constituents of water, and water is the only product of such combustion. The chief feature and improvement in these lamps is the adaptation of lime as the reflecting surface on which the jet of flame from coal gas plays, and which becomes intensified to an extraordinary degree, and makes the old gas burners, in close proximity, appear dull, as though they were burning in the day time.

New Palace Yard, the open space opposite Westminster Hall, derives its name from the ancient palace that stood here from the reign of Edward the Confessor to that of Queen Elizabeth, and of which Westminster Hall and the crypt of St. Stephen's Chapel are the only portions remaining. OLD PALACE YARD, a little further towards the Abbey, was the place of execution for Guy Fawkes and the other Gunpowder Plot conspirators. The bronze statue of Canning, by Westmacott, in the little enclosure opposite, cost £7,000. Near the Peers' Entrance, in Old Palace Yard, the statue of Richard the First, Cœur de Lion, by Marochetti, is erected.

Westminster Hall, now the focus of our superior law courts, was originally the hall of a palace built by William Rufus in 1097, and considerably altered by Richard II. in 1399. Around the hall will yet be seen on the stone moulding that king's favourite crest, the white hart couchant. The law courts have been established here since 1224. The Hall is said to be the largest unsupported by pillars in the world, and is 290 feet long, 68 feet broad, and 90 high. The roof consists of ancient oak, and has an air of solemn grandeur. Within these walls a king (Charles I.) has been tried and condemned to death, the chivalry of England assembled at the banquet-table, and the coronation fêtes celebrated of England's monarchs. To the right are the entrances to the courts of law, which are open to those who wish to witness the proceedings, and are thus to be distinguished:—The COURT OF CHANCERY, the highest court of judicature in the kingdom, next to the Parliament; the COURT OF QUEEN'S BENCH, in which are tried matters determinable at common law between the sovereign and her subjects; the COURT OF COMMON PLEAS, for causes between subject and subject; and the COURT OF EXCHEQUER, for the trial of those questions relating to the revenue.

St. Margaret's Church, opposite, and within a few yards of the north side of Westminster Abbey, was originally founded by Edward the Confessor (1061), rebuilt in the reign of Edward I., and frequently repaired since. It is the church of the House of Commons. The east window is a fine specimen of glass painting, and was a present from the magistrates of Dort, in Holland, to Henry VII., by whom it was intended for his neighbouring chapel. Having frequently changed hands, it was finally bought by the parish for the sum of 400 guineas. It represents the crucifixion, with, in the lower panels, figures of Arthur prince of Wales, eldest son of Henry VII., and his bride Catharine of Arragon. The figure of St. George, with the customary national emblems, make up an impressive and striking tableau. Caxton the printer, Skelton the poet laureate, Sir Walter Raleigh, and some other persons of note, were here buried.

Westminster Abbey is open to public inspection between 11 and 3, and in the summer months between 4 and 6 P.M. The nave, transept, and cloisters are free. The charge for admission to the rest of the abbey is sixpence. The entrance is by POET'S CORNER, at the south transept. As one of the principal features of London, and eminently deserving a most careful and elaborate examination, we devote a proportionate degree of space to its description. The general dimensions are:—length from east to west, 375 feet; breadth from north to south, 200 feet; height from the floor of the nave to the roof of the interior, 101 feet; height from the choir to the lantern, 142 feet.

A Latin cross, the favourite form in early times, marks the general outline of this wonderful structure; but the cloisters and numerous chapels added to the main building, take greatly from the original simplicity of the plan. The western front is formed of the entrance porch, stretching far inward and vaulted, and two square towers. A magnificent central window, shields, and other sculptural ornaments, invest this portion with an aspect of great splendour; but architects discover in it faults which can be defended by no rule of their art, and Sir Christopher Wren, to whom the charge of conducting its repair was entrusted by the Government, is accused of having erred in an attempt to combine the Gothic with the dissimilar style of Grecian architecture. The other portion of the architecture, with the exception of Henry the Seventh's Chapel, is early English.

The origin of this magnificent edifice is traced to a very remote period, and it is said to have been founded by Sebert, King of the East Saxons, in 616. This spot of ground was then a small insulated tract, surrounded by the Thames, and called Thorny Island. Edward the Confessor, and afterwards Henry III., enlarged and rebuilt it; and in January, 1502, Henry VII. laid the first stone of the superb chapel which bears his name, granting to the Abbey numerous estates, which increased its wealth in proportion to the growth of its importance. Henry VIII. appropriated a large portion of its revenue and converted the Abbey into a cathedral, and Westminster into a city. Wren made extensive repairs at the beginning of the eighteenth century; and, since then, a complete restoration of this ancient structure has taken place, at various times, which has preserved it to us in its existing splendour.

POET'S CORNER is usually the first place that engages the attention of the visiter, and here it is advisable to wait until a sufficient party is formed for the guide to serve as a cicerone through the building. For this purpose a verger is always in attendance, at the stated hours we have named. It is here that the choicest genius of the land has received from admiring ages the acknowledgment of its worth. Here it is that our British poets seem to be still looking upon the world which they delighted and improved by their song; and he would scarcely deserve to share in the good diffused by the elevated strains of these mighty men who could stand in the midst of this chamber of soul-breathing imagery without a deep and generous emotion of thankfulness that such men have been given to his country. We select a few of the monuments here as especially deserving notice :—

CAMDEN, the eminent antiquary (d. 1623), and for some time master of Westminster School, where Ben Jonson was one of his pupils. In his left hand is a book, and in his right hand are his gloves resting upon the altar.

GARRICK (d. 1779). Garrick is throwing aside a curtain, which reveals a medallion of Shakspere, allegorically indicating the power he possessed of unveiling the beauties of the bard of all time. Tragedy and comedy are seen personified with their appropriate emblems.

ADDISON (d. 1719). A fine sculpture by Westmacott. The statue of one great essayist appears on a circular basement, surrounded by small figures of the muses.

HANDEL (*d.* 1759). The figure of this eminent composer, by Roubiliac, is elegantly wrought, and the features bear a faithful resemblance to the original. The left arm is resting on a group of musical instruments; the attitude expresses rapt attention to the harp of a seraph in the clouds above, and the oratorio of the "Messiah" lies open at the sublime and appropriate passage, "I know that my Redeemer liveth."

GOLDSMITH (*d.* 1774). This consists simply of a bust of the poet, in profile, in high relief, in a medallion; and is placed in the area of a pointed arch, between the monuments of Gay and the Duke of Argyle. It was executed by Nollekens. Dr. Johnson wrote the epitaph, which is inscribed on a white marble tablet beneath the bust.

GAY (*d.* 1732): Rysbrach. A winged boy exhibits a medallion portrait; and masks, musical instruments, and a dagger, are grouped around as devices, showing the various styles of writing in which he excelled, from fables to satire.

THOMSON (*d.* 1748). The figure of the poet is resting the left arm on a pedestal. In basso relievo, on the pedestal, the "Seasons" are represented, a boy pointing to them, and offering as the reward of genius a wreath of laurel.

SHAKSPERE (*d.* 1616): Scheemaker.

The bard is shown leaning on a pedestal, the bust of Queen Elizabeth indicating the period in which he flourished. The glowing epitaph of Milton deserves to be read at leisure; it is a glorious sonnet, worthy of the genius of both; and as such its transcription in this place will be readily forgiven:—

" What needs my Shakspere for his honour'd bones ?
The labour of an age in piled stones
Or that his hallow'd relics should be hid
Under a starry-pointing pyramid ?
Dear son of Memory! great heir of Fame
What need'st thou such weak witness of thy name ?
Thou, in our wonder and astonishment,
Hast built thyself a livelong monument;
For whilst, to the shame of slow-endeavouring art,
Thy easy numbers flow, and that each heart
Hath from the leaves of thy unvalued book
Those Delphic lines with deep impression took,
Then thou, our fancy of itself bereaving,
Dust make us marble with too much conceiving,
And so sepulchred in such pomp dust lie
That kings, for such a tomb, would wish to die."

SOUTHEY (*d.* 1843). A monument by Weekes, deservedly commemorative of this great critic, poet, and historian.

PRIOR (*d.* 1721). On one side of the pedestal stands Thalia with a flute, on the other Clio with her book closed. Between them, on a raised altar, is a bust; and over that a pediment, with boys on each side; one with an hourglass in his hand, the sand run out; the other holding a torch reversed. Prior left £500 for the erection of this monument, which was designed by Gibbs, the architect of St. Martin's.

GRAY (*d.* 1771). This is a fine monument by Bacon. The lyric muse is exhibiting a medallion of Gray, and, at the same time, pointing to the monument of Milton immediately above.

SPENSER (*d.* 1598). This is an exact copy of the original monument, which was of Purbeck stone, and so decayed in 1778 that its removal was determined on, and the present placed there as its substitute. The inscription runs thus :— "Here lies, expecting the second coming of our Saviour Christ Jesus, the body of Edmund Spenser, the prince of poets in his time, whose divine spirit needs no other witness than the works which be left behind him."

MILTON (*d.* 1674). A bust and tablet by Rysbrach, with a lyre beneath, encircled by a serpent holding an apple. It is peculiarly suggestive of Dryden's graceful panegyric:—

> " Three poets, in three distant ages born,
> Greece, Italy, and England did adorn;
> The first in loftiness of thought surpass'd,
> The next in majesty, in both the last—
> The force of nature could no further go;
> To make the third she join'd the other two."

BEN JONSON (*d.* 1637). This monument, which was not erected until about a century after the poet's death, is a neatly sculptured tablet, by Rysbrach, with a head in relief, and emblematic devices. The expressive epitaph, "O! rare Ben Jonson," is the more forcible for its quaint brevity.

Besides those poets we have mentioned, will be found monuments to Campbell, Rowe, Anstey, Dryden, Cowley, Chaucer, Phillips, Michael Drayton, Mason, Shadwell, and Samuel Butler, the witty author of Hudibras; whilst some others who have been buried in the Abbey on account of their rank, valour, or patriotism, have their names here perpetuated by some "storied urn or monumental bust."

THE CHAPEL OF ST. BENEDICT is generally the first chapel shown. The principal tombs are those of Langham, Archbishop of Canterbury (*d.* 1376); the Countess of Hertford (*d.* 1598), sister of the Lord High Admiral Nottingham, engaged in the defeat of the Spanish Armada; and several of the Deans. Close to the gate of entrance is the ancient monument of Sebert, King of the East Saxons (*d.* 616), and of his Queen Athelgoda (*d.* 615).

THE CHAPEL OF ST. EDMUND contains twenty monuments, among which the most important are:—John of Eltham (*d.* 1334), second son of Edward II., and born in Eltham Palace; a small tomb with two alabaster figures representing William of Windsor and Blanche de la Tour, children of Edward III., who died in infancy; Lady Elizabeth Russell, of the Bedford family, traditionally alleged to have died from the prick of a needle, and Lord Russell, her father (*d.* 1584), represented in effigy within a recess formed by Corinthian columns; William de Valence (*d*. 1208), Earl of Pembroke, and half-brother to Henry III. The effigy is of oak, and was originally covered with thin plates of gilt copper, exhibiting the earliest existing instance of enamelled metal being used for the purpose. Here there is also a grave-stone to the memory of the celebrated Edward Lord Herbert, of Cherbury, who died in 1678. A fine bust of Richard Tufton, son of Sir John Tufton, and brother of the Earl of Thanet (*d*. 1631), is seen to the right as we leave the chapel.

THE CHAPEL OF ST. NICHOLAS contains monuments to Lady Cecil, (*d*. 1591), a lady of the bed-chamber to Queen Elizabeth; Duchess of Somerset (*d*. 1587), wife of the Protector Somerset; Lord Burleigh's magnificent monument to his wife Mildred and his daughter Anne; and the Marchioness of Winchester. The large alter-tomb in the centre of the chapel is to the memory of Sir George Villiers and his lady, the father and mother of the celebrated Duke of Buckingham of the time of James I.

THE CHAPEL OF HENRY VII., which is the next visited, has been called the wonder of the world, and never, perhaps, did the genius of art, combined with the power and resources of wealth, produce a nobler specimen of architectural skill. It was commenced in 1502, the first stone having been laid in the presence of this monarch, and was completed in about ten years. King Henry lived to see the building nearly completed, and was buried in the sumptuous tomb which had been prepared according to his command for the reception of his remains. The splendour of this building, when its gates were first opened to crowds of devout worshippers, forms a favourite theme with the antiquary, whose imagination might well be moved at the pictures drawn of the altars covered with gold, of the cross of the same metal, the beauteous marble pillars, and the image of the Virgin bedight with sparkling jewels. With the exception of the plinth, every part is covered by sculptural decorations, giving to stone the character of embroidery; the buttress towers are crested by ornamental domes, and enriched by niches and elegant tracery; the cross-springers are perforated into airy forms, and the very cornices and parapets are charged even to profusion with armorial cognisances and knotted foliage. How magical must have been the effect when in the days of yore the sun's rays beamed through the orient colours and imagery of its painted windows, and tinged the aërial perspective with all the gorgeous hues of the prism and the rainbow.

The entrance is by a flight of twelve steps leading through the porch, which is upwards of twenty-eight feet in width, to the brazen gates of the chapel itself. Upon the summit of the small pillars are Henry's supporters, viz., the lion, the dragon, and the greyhound; in the spandrils of the middle arch are his arms, and in those of the small arches his badges. The architecture of the nave is equally beautiful and rich in ornament. A long range of statues imparts a grace and animation to the rest of the decorative appliances; and the noble arch which extends its magnificent span over the nave from north to south, forms in itself a splendid object for the eye to contemplate. The chapel consists of a central aisle, with fine small chapels at the east end, and two side aisles, north and south. The principal object of admiration, both for its workmanship and its antiquity, is the tomb of Henry VII. and Elizabeth his queen. It stands in the body of the chapel, enclosed in a chantry of brass, admirably designed and executed, and ornamented with statues of saints. Within, on a tomb of black marble, repose the effigies of the royal pair in their state robes. At the head of the chantry rest the remains of Edward VI., who died in 1552. In the north aisle are the monuments of Queen Elizabeth; the murdered princes, Edward V. and his brother Richard; Sophia and Maria, infant daughters of James I.; and George Saville, Marquis of Halifax. In the south aisle are monuments of Mary, Queen of Scots; Catharine, Lady Walpole; Margaret Beaufort, Countess of Richmond, the mother of Henry VII.; and a monument on which lies a lady finely robed, the effigy of Margaret Douglas, the mother of Lord Darnley, husband of Mary, Queen of Scots. At the east end of the south aisle is the royal vault as it is called, in which the remains of Charles II., William III., and Mary his consort, Queen Anne, and Prince George, are all deposited. In the vault beneath the centre of the nave, King George II. and Queen Caroline, Frederick, Prince of Wales, the father of George III., and the Duke of Cumberland, of Culloden celebrity, are all interred. It will be interesting to mention that the remains of King George II. and his Queen lie mingled together, the monarch having expressly desired that a side should be taken from each coffin expressly for the purpose. In 1837, when the vault was opened for the last time, the two sides which were withdrawn were seen standing against the wall. The stalls on each side the nave are formed of oak, and are surmounted by richly carved canopies. These stalls are now appropriated to the Knights of the Bath, whose names and arms are fixed at the back on plates or gilt copper. At the grand installation which took place in 1812, silken banners were hung round the chapel, bearing the arms of the distinguished men who then belonged to the order.

THE CHAPEL OF ST. PAUL follows next in rotation. On the right as you enter, is a fine altar-tomb to Lodowick Robsart, the standard-bearer to Henry V. at the battle of Agincourt; Sir Thomas Bromley (d. 1587), who was privy counsellor to Queen Elizabeth, and sat as Lord Chancellor at the trial of Mary Queen of Scots; his hands are clasped in the attitude of prayer, and his eight children are kneeling at the base. There is also, among others, a colossal statue, by Chantrey, of James Watt (d. 1819), who is represented seated on an oblong pedestal, with compasses, and forming plans. This memorial cost £6,000, and has an inscription from the pen of Lord Brougham.

THE CHAPEL OF ST. EDWARD THE CONFESSOR is the sixth, and by many considered the most interesting. It occupies the space at the back of the high altar, at the eastern end of the choir. The screen which divides the chapel from the choir was placed there in the reign of Edward VI., and though sadly dilapidated, is justly regarded as one of the most interesting remains of ancient art. It is decorated with a frieze, divided into fourteen compartments, and representing in elaborate sculpture the traditionary events of the Confessor's life. The first three are merely historical; the fourth represents King Edward alarmed by the appearance of Satan dancing upon the money collected for the payment of Dane-gelt; and in the next we have Edward's generous admonition to the thief who was purloining his treasure. The rest of the representations are so remarkable, that the curious in historical traditions will be amply repaid by tracing the events they display. The tomb of the monarch occupies the centre of the chapel, and the translation of his remains to this superb shrine was for nearly three hundred years commemorated as a grand festival. Offerings of the richest kind, gold and jewels, were presented at the altar; and the shrine itself, constructed of the most precious materials, is said to have presented, before it was despoiled at the Reformation, a specimen of the most sumptuous art. By order of James II., the coffin which contains the saint was enclosed within another, made of planks two inches thick, and bound together with iron. Surrounding this magnificent mausoleum of the Confessor are the tombs of Edward I., Henry III., Queen Eleanor, Henry V., Queen Philippa, Edward III., and Richard II. Each of these shrines affords some proof of the luxurious taste which prevailed in the periods when they were raised, and of the pious reverence with which the remains of the great and good were regarded by their followers; but on none does the eye rest with more pleasure than on that dedicated to Queen Eleanor, the consort of the adventurous Edward I. In all the dangers of that monarch's long and valorous career, she was ever at his side; and a tradition, that we hold it heresy to disbelieve, adds, that when in the Holy Land he lay almost in the agonies of death, she saved his life by sucking away the poison that had been infused by the dagger of the Saracen. When the tomb of Edward I. was opened in 1774, the body of the king was discovered almost perfect, with a tin gilt crown upon his head, a sceptre of gilt copper in his right hand, and a sceptre and dove of the same material in his left; and in this mimic semblance of state he is now lying. The chapel containing the remains of Henry V. occupies the whole of the east end of the Confessor's, and is supposed to have been erected early in the reign of Henry VI. Several relics of the monarch's warlike achievements are preserved in this shrine, and the very helmet which it is said he wore in his boldest encounters with the enemy. In addition to the monuments, this chapel contains some other objects of curiosity. The principal of these is the ancient chair used at the coronation of the kings from the time of Edward I., and which, within its seat, has the "prophetic or fatal stone of Scone,"— so called from the belief of the Scots, to whom it originally belonged, that whenever it was lost the power of the nation would decline. In the year 1296 was fought that dreadful battle between Edward I. and John Baliol, which decided the fate of the latter; and this celebrated stone was then removed with the royal jewels to London, where it has ever since remained. The stone is twenty-six inches long, sixteen inches wide, and eleven inches thick, and is fixed in the bottom of the chair by cramps of iron. The more modern chair was fashioned for Mary, Queen of William III. The painted windows demand attention, both on account of their great age and their curiosity as works of art. The glass of which they are made is not less than the eighth of an inch thick, whilst the figures, which are nearly seven feet high, are formed out of an innumerable variety of small pieces, so cut as to compose, with proper shades of colour, the form and drapery of the characters described. In the legend of Edward the Confessor and the pilgrim, the deep and brilliant colours of the glass, the beautiful arrangement of the drapery, and the noble expression given to the countenances of the figures, well deserve the admiration with which they are viewed.

THE CHAPEL OF ST. ERASMUS is the seventh, and by this we enter the eighth chapel, dedicated to ST. JOHN THE BAPTIST. In the former must be noticed the elaborately wrought tomb of Henry Carey, Lord Hunsdon, first cousin to Queen Elizabeth; and the tomb of Cecil, Earl of Exeter, and his two countesses. In the ambulatory is a fine monument to General Wolfe (d. 1759), representing the death of the hero in his victorious expedition against Quebec. Screens formerly divided the east aisle of the north transept into the chapels of ST. JOHN, ST. MICHAEL, AND ST. ANDREW. Among the tombs especially demanding notice are Sir Humphrey Davy (d. 1829); Thomas Telford (d. 1834), a colossal figure by Bailey, in honour of the architect of the Menai Bridge; and a monument—one of Roubiliac's last and best works—to Joseph Gascoigne Nightingale and his lady. The lower portion appears throwing open its marble doors, and a shrouded skeleton as Death is seen launching his dart at the lady, who has sunk affrighted into her husband's arms. With this portion of the Abbey the guide usually ceases to attend, and the visiter pursues his way alone.

Entering the north transept, the magnificence of the interior at once strikes the beholder with reverential awe; grand masses of towering Gothic columns connect the pavement with the roof, and separate the nave from the side aisles. A screen divides the nave from the choir, which is surmounted by a noble organ. The walls are enriched with a great profusion of sepulchral monuments, and above the line of tombs there are chambers and galleries, looking dreary and solemn in their antiquity, and only relieved by the transient sunbeam glancing across the misty height of the nave. The northern window is richly ornamented with stained glass, representing the Holy Scriptures, surrounded by appropriate figures. From this window proceeds a calm ray of light, very advantageous to the display of the finely executed pieces of sculpture on which it falls, lighting up the interesting memorials of those whose exploits or exertions deserve the notice of posterity.

In the NORTH TRANSEPT are inscribed tombs covering the remains of the statesmen Pitt, Fox, Grattan, Canning, and Lord Londonderry. The latter has a fine statue of Carrara marble, placed there in June, 1850. Bacon's noble monument to the Earl of Chatham, Flaxman's portrait-statue of Lord Mansfield, the fine statue of Sir William Follett by Behnes, and a statue without an inscription, representing John Philip Kemble the tragedian, will be noticed among the other memorials of the illustrious dead. Under the organ-screen are monuments to Sir Isaac Newton and Earl Stanhope. THE NORTH AISLE introduces us to tablets commemorative of the eminent musicians Dr. Burney (*d.* 1814), Dr. Croft (*d.* 1727), Dr. Blow (*d.* 1708), Dr. Arnold (*d.* 1802), Dr. Purcell (*d.* 1697), and a fine monument to the unfortunate Major André, executed by the Americans as a spy in 1780. We cannot quit this solemn scene without recalling the exquisite reflections made by Addison, and which are as appropriate now as when they were suggested by the associations of the place more than a century ago. "When I look," says our delightful essayist, "upon the tombs of the great, every emotion of envy dies within me; when I read the epitaphs of the beautiful, every inordinate desire goes out; when I meet with the grief of parents upon a tombstone, my heart melts with compassion; when I see the tombs of the parents themselves, I consider the vanity of grieving for those whom we must quickly follow; when I see kings lying side by side, or the holy men that divided the world with their contests and disputes, I reflect with sorrow and astonishment on the little competitions, factions, and debates of mankind; when I read the several dates of the tombs, of some that died yesterday and some six hundred years ago, I consider that great day when we shall all of us be con-

temporaries, and make our appearance together."

Leaving the interior of the Abbey, we next pass through the churchyard of St. Margaret's, and enter DEAN'S YARD on the left, a small square enclosing a green, which serves as a playground for the scholars of Westminster School. Part of the north boundary of the square is formed by the outer wall of the JERUSALEM CHAMBER, in which King Henry IV. died. The CLOISTERS are almost entire, and filled with monuments. In them may still be traced the signs of monastic life. The door ways are pointed out by which the monks proceeded to the refectory and other portions of the building set apart for their retreat; and one can hardly trace these winding passages, looking so cool and sombre in the summer's sunshine, without bringing to recollection the customs that prevailed, the mode of worship, the manners, habits, and opinions that existed when the venerable walls of these cloisters bore no sign of decay. They are built in a quadrangular form, with piazzas towards the court, in which several of the prebendaries have houses.

The entrance into the CHAPTER HOUSE, built in 1250, is on one side of the cloisters, through a Gothic portal, the mouldings of which are exquisitely carved. By consent of the Abbot, in

1377, the Commons of Great Britain first held their parliaments in this place, until, in 1547, Edward VI. granted them the Chapel of St. Stephen. It is at present a repository of the public records, among which is the original Doomsday Book, now nearly 800 years old. It is comprised in two volumes; one a large folio, the other a quarto. The first, beginning with Kent and ending with Lincolnshire, is written on 382 double pages of vellum, in the same band, in a small but plain character, each page having a double column. The quarto volume is on 450 pages of vellum, in single columns, and contains the counties of Essex, Norfolk, and Suffolk. This singular record is in high preservation, the words being us legible as when first written, though the ink has been dry since 1086.

West of the Abbey stood the eleemosynary or ALMONRY, where the alms of the Abbey were distributed. It was here, in 1474, that William Caxton produced the first printed book. The house in which he is said to have lived fell down from decay in November, 1845; and, since then, the miserable dens and low lodging-houses by which it was surrounded have been all cleared away. The Sanctuary, where criminals successfully sought refuge from the consequences of their crimes, was close by. The open space in front of Westminster Hospital still perpetuates the name.

WESTMINSTER SCHOOL, in Dean's Yard, is certainly the first in point of antiquity in the metropolis, if not in rank. It is understood to have been founded towards the close of the eleventh century; but in 1569 Queen Elizabeth restored it, and provided for the education of forty boys, denominated the Queen's scholars. From this period it has been distinguished by the erudition of its masters and the shining talents of their scholars. When Camden, the renowned antiquary, was master, Ben Jonson was one of his pupils. Dryden not only studied within these monastic walls, but carved his name on one of the forms—a relic jealously preserved; and Cowley, Cowper, Southey, Wren, Locke, and Colman, may be enumerated as some few of the great men educated here, whose names the world will not willingly let die. Every Christmas a play of Terence is performed by the Queen's scholars, according to an ancient custom; and in this, many of the sons of our nobility and gentry display their elocutionary powers to advantage.

The WESTMINSTER HOSPITAL, built in 1834, in the Broad Sanctuary, at the north-west corner of the Abbey, was originally established in 1715, through the exertions of Mr. Henry Hoare, the banker in Fleet Street, and was the first hospital founded and supported by voluntary contributions. The present structure is from the designs of Mr. Inwood, and is capable of containing 220 patients.

Retracing our steps to Old Palace Yard, we pass the place which was the site of the Houses of Lords and Commons from the reign of Henry III. to the destruction of both by fire, October 16, 1834. In Bellamy's "Kitchen," a plain apartment, with an immense fire, meat screen, and a continuous relay of gridirons, the statesmen of England have often dined, and enjoyed an unpretending chop or steak with more apparent zest than in their own palatial residences, where luxury and splendour are visible in every part. The room latterly devoted to parliamentary proceedings was originally St. Stephen's Chapel, founded by King Stephen, and a portion of the old Westminster Palace.

ABINGDON STREET brings us to that noble edifice, the **New Houses of Parliament**, or the "New Palace at Westminster," as it has been appropriately called, being the largest Gothic edifice in the world. The architect, the late Sir Chas. Barry (who died suddenly, May 12th, 1860, and was interred in the neighbouring old abbey, on the 22nd of the same month), incorporated the entire establishment of the Houses of Parliament, the Courts of Law, and Westminster Hall, in one edifice, as being most conducive to internal convenience and economy, and to the grandeur and importance of the ex-

terior. The first stone was laid April 27, 1840. The building covers a space of nearly eight acres. The river frontage is 900 feet in length, and divided into five principal compartments, panelled with tracery, and decorated with rows of statues and shields, exhibiting the arms of the monarchs of England since the Conquest. The terrace is intended to be appropriated to the exclusive use of the Speaker and the members of both Houses for air and exercise. This terrace, built of Aberdeen granite, is 30 feet in breadth, and extends between the wings at the north and south ends of the front, a length of 680 feet. Behind, the building rises in three distinct stories; the first a basement, which is on the level of the street; the next is the story of the principal floor, upon which the Houses of Lords and Commons, the state rooms, the division lobby, conference rooms, libraries, and other principal apartments and offices are placed; and the third contains committee rooms and other apartments for the officers of the House. The central portion of the river front and the towers at each wing run up another story. The three principal towers are called the Royal or Victoria Tower, the Central Tower, and the Clock Tower. The Victoria Tower, at the south-west angle, is a stupendous work, and contains the royal entrance, 75 feet square, and approaches an altitude of 340 feet, being only 64 feet less than the height of the cross of St. Paul's. The Central Tower contains the grand central hall, and is 60 feet in diameter, and 300 feet to the top of the lantern surmounting it. The Clock Tower, nearest Westminster Bridge, is 40 feet square, and with its belfry spire, richly decorated, is 320 feet high. The smaller towers give a picturesque effect to the river front, which, with that portion of the structure, can be best seen to advantage from the opposite bank of the Thames. There are nearly 500 statues in and about the building, and the most eminent artists in every department have contributed to its embellishments.

The royal entrance is at the Victoria Tower, which communicates with the Norman porch, so designated from the fresco illustrations of the Norman kings and their historic exploits. On the right band is the robing-room, fitted up with much magnificence, and to this succeeds a spacious and sumptuously-decorated apartment 110 feet in length, 45 in width, and 45 feet in height, called the Royal Gallery, ornamented with frescoes descriptive of events in English history, and having windows filled with stained glass, and a matchless ceiling emblazoned with heraldic insignia. The Princes' Chamber, an apartment equally splendid, leads into the HOUSE OF PEERS, a noble room 45 feet wide, 45 feet high, and nearly 100 feet long. The peers assembled here for the first time, April 15, 1847. At the southern end, on a dais of three steps, and surmounted by a superb Gothic canopy, is the royal throne. The body of the house is occupied by a large oak table and the red woolsack of the Chancellor. The carpet is blue, powdered profusely with stars, and the carpet of the throne is red, variegated with roses and heraldic lions. The chamber is lighted by twelve windows glazed with stained glass, representing the kings and queens of England, and at night it is illuminated by thirty branch lights and four elaborately wrought brass candelabra. The ornamental frescoes are in six compartments, three at each end, and are the first on a large scale executed in this country. The subjects are—the Baptism of Ethelbert, by Mr. Dyce, R.A., Edward III. conferring the Order of the Garter on the Black Prince, and Henry Prince of Wales committed to prison for assaulting Judge Gascoigne, by Mr. Cope, R.A. In the central compartment, over the Strangers' Gallery, is the Spirit of Religion, by Mr. Horsley, the Spirit of Chivalry, and the Spirit of Law, by Mr. Maclise, R.A. Between the windows, niches, eighteen in number, sustain statues of the barons who enforced Magna Charta. The walls and ceilings are enriched, besides, with gorgeous decorations exhibiting the arms and escutcheons of the sovereigns and chancellors of England. The prevailing colour of the ceiling is rich blue, bordered with red and gold.

The House of Commons is 62 feet long by 45 broad, and is also 45 feet in height, being purposely as limited in dimensions as possible, that the speeches may be distinctly heard by all present. The House sat for the first time in this building May 30, 1850. It is in a direct line with the House of Lords, at the north end of the structure. The Speaker's chair is placed in such a position, that supposing all the doors open between them, the Chancellor on the woolsack and the Speaker in the chair would exactly face each other. Over the Speaker's chair is the Reporters' Gallery, and over that again is the Strangers' Gallery. It is calculated to accommodate 277 members on the floor, 133 in the side galleries, and 66 in the lower gallery over the bar; making 476 in all. The chamber is lighted by six windows of stained glass on each side, and the floor is of iron, perforated for the purposes of ventilation. The ceiling of brown oak is reticulated into a succession of quadrangles with richly carved borders, and the panel-fronts of the surrounding galleries are of the same characteristic national material. The centre window bears the emblazoned arms of the cities of London and Westminster.

How far economy has been carried out may be gathered from the fact that, although the original estimate only amounted to a million and a half, more than two millions has been already expended, and other votes of money will yet be necessary before its completion. In 1834, Sir Charles Barry prepared an estimate showing that £284,000 would be necessary for the completion of the Palace, but that sum has already grown to £304,000, and its indefinite extension is certain, while everything is incomplete, and the body of the building is already exhibiting symptoms of decay. In addition to the above, a sum of £20,000 has been expended in completing the Victoria and clock towers. There is an item of £14,000 for furniture for the Speaker's house, and other items have grown and multiplied in a surprising ratio. This expenditure has arisen more from the conduct of the house than from the errors of the achitect, for the plans have been constantly altered, and the alarming result is that the actual amount which it has cost, and will yet cost, is involved in mystery. The edifice is constructed upon a fireproof principle; there is very little wood about the building, and all communications with the private residences are shut off by iron doors set in thick party walls.

The public are admitted to view the House of Lords by an order from the Lord Chamberlain, or by the personal introduction of a peer when the House is not sitting. The orders are procurable on Wednesdays, between eleven and four. A peer's order will also admit to the Strangers' Gallery, to hear the debates. To the House of Commons a member's order will likewise procure admission. Though the stately Palace of the Parliament cannot for centuries rival in its associations the humbler structure of St. Stephen's Chapel, let us hope that it will never forfeit its highest claim to our admiration as the classical sanctuary of Britain's intellectual greatness, the chosen palladium of her proudest attributes—freedom, eloquence, and power.

Continuing our way along MILBANK, we may mention that this, in the time of Elizabeth, was a mere marsh, and Milbank was the name of a large house belonging to the Grosvenor family, that derived its name from a mill once occupying its site.

The Church of ST. JOHN THE EVANGELIST, seen on the right, was begun in 1721 and finished in 1728. To Sir John Vanbrugh this architectural eccentricity is ascribed, and its four belfries have not been inaptly compared to an inverted table with its legs in the air. Churchill, the satirist, was for some time the curate and lecturer here.

The PENITENTIARY, observed a little beyond, was designed by Jeremy Bentham, and is octagonal in form, enclosing a space of about eighteen acres. It was built in 1819, on ground bought in 1799 from the Marquis of Salisbury, and cost nearly half a million. It is devoted to the industrial reformation of prisoners, and as such is the largest prison in London. All convicts sentenced to transportation are here for three months prior to the sentence being carried into execution. On the Inspector's report to the Home Secretary, the place of transportation is then indicated. About 4,000 criminals are every year thus doomed to expiate their offences. Admission can only be obtained by an order from the Secretary of State for the Home department, or from the Resident Inspectors.

We next arrive at VAUXHALL BRIDGE, begun in 1811, and finished in June, 1816, at an expense of £300,000. It consists of nine cast-iron arches, each 78 feet in span, and is 810 feet long. The toll of one penny is demanded for each passenger; and a steamboat pier below materially contributes to increase the traffic.

Vauxhall Bridge Road will conduct us to PIMLICO and the opulent region of Belgravia, where a new town round Belgrave and Eaton Squares has arisen within the last ten years. The whole of this vast territory, now thickly inhabited by the wealthy and the titled, and having long lines of palace-like houses spreading forth in every direction, was within the memory of many living a spacious open tract, known as "The Five Fields"—a place infested by robbers, &c. Here also, very recently, the largest and grandest railway station has been opened, and will form the terminus of many important lines. Occupying the site of the Grosvenor canal basin, the VICTORIA STATION is now the busy scene of the arrival and departure trains of the West End and Crystal Palace, the Brighton and South Coast, and the Chatham and Dover lines, and before another year has passed, the trains of the Great Western Company (making a circuit and crossing the river twice, over a bridge in course of erection at Cremorne, and back over the Victoria Bridge), will bring their passengers to the magnificent hotel connected with this Belgravia terminus.

CHELSEA NEW BRIDGE, certainly one of the handsomest of the many bridges which now span the "silent highway," occupies a position near Chelsea Hospital, and leads to Battersea Park, to the formation of which the bridge is undoubtedly due. This convenient thoroughfare was opened to the public in March, 1858 :—its cost was £88,000.

Hence we can take an omnibus back to Charing Cross, or stroll leisurely through St. James's Park, by way of varying our return. For description of the park, see page 105.

FIFTH DAY'S ROUTE.

DISTRICT III.

CHARING CROSS—PALL MALL EAST—HAYMARKET—CLUB HOUSES—PALL MALL— ST. JAMES'S PALACE—ST. JAMES'S STREET—ST. JAMES'S PARK—GREEN PARK— BUCKINGHAM PALACE—HYDE PARK CORNER—APSLEY HOUSE—HYDE PARK— KENSINGTON GARDENS—SOUTH KENSINGTON MUSEUM—HOLLAND HOUSE—PICCA- DILLY—ALBEMARLE STREET—ROYAL INSTITUTION—MANSIONS OF THE NOBILITY

FROM Charing Cross we make our way across Trafalgar Square to PALL MALL EAST, at the corner of which is the "ROYAL COLLEGE OF PHYSICIANS," built by Smirke at a cost of £30,000, and opened in 1835. The portico, supported by six Ionic columns, leads to a spacious hall and staircase. In the library are some fine portraits and busts of the most eminent physicians. Admission can be obtained by orders from the members. The UNION CLUB-HOUSE adjoining, in the square, was also built from the designs of Smirke. Wyatt's equestrian statue of George III. was erected in 1836. The horse is considered a fine specimen of workmanship, and the likeness to the monarch admirable.

The HAYMARKET, so called from a market for hay having been kept here as late as 1830, introduces us to the Theatre bearing the same name, and which was built by Nash in 1821. It has a stately portico, supported by six Corinthian columns, and an interior handsomely fitted up. It is one of the best conducted in the metropolis. HER MAJESTY'S THEATRE, on the opposite side, is the largest theatre in Europe, La Scala, at Milan, excepted, and is calculated to hold 3,000 persons. The present edifice was built from a design, by Messrs. Nash and Repton, in 1818, and is surrounded on all sides by a covered colonnade, supported by Doric cast iron pillars. The interior has five tiers of boxes, which are each either private property or let to persons of rank and fashion for the season. Many of the double boxes on the grand tier have sold for as much as £8,000. Visiters to all parts of the theatre but the gallery are expected to appear in evening costume, frock-coats and coloured trousers and cravats not being admissible. The season usually begins in February and continues till August. Nights of performance—Tuesdays, Thursdays, and Saturdays.

The Club-Houses, those most magnificent buildings where the most distinguished members of the worlds of fashion, politics, and literature, meet for the purposes of lounging away their spare hours in conversation, reading, and refreshment, are now around us on every side, and merit a passing glance. For the convenience of the stranger, we group them together in that order which from this point seems moat desirable for observation. There are thirty-seven principal clubs in the metropolis, comprising nearly 30,000 members. At the corner of Suffolk Street is the UNIVERSITY CLUB-HOUSE, built by Wilkins in 1824, for members of the Universities of Oxford and Cambridge. The TRAVELLERS' CLUB, 106 Pall Mall, was rebuilt by Barry in 1832. The club is limited to 700 members, and each pays thirty guineas on admission, besides his annual subscription. The ATHENÆUM CLUB, standing partly on the site of Carlton Palace, was built by Decimus Burton in 1829, and is an elegant edifice of Grecian architecture, with a statue of Minerva over the portico. The number of members is fixed at 1,200, and they must have attained distinguished eminence in science, literature, and the arts. The CARLTON CLUB, Pall Mall, has been lately rebuilt by Sydney Smirke, with three uniform façades in the Italian style. It is exclusively frequented by the Conservative party. The UNITED SERVICE CLUB was erected by John Nash in 1826, and is esteemed one of the most commodious. It is of the Doric order, with a noble portico of eight double columns, forming the entrance. The REFORM CLUB-HOUSE, on the south side of Pall Mall, was founded in 1832, and built from Barry's designs. The exterior is remarkably fine. In the interior are portraits of the leading Reformers. The entrance fee is twenty-six guineas, and each member pays ten guineas' annual subscription. The number of members is limited to 1,400. At the corner of St James's Square is the splendid new building of the ARMY AND NAVY CLUB, built in 1849, from the designs of Messrs. Smith and Parnell. There are 1,450 members, who each pay an entrance fee of £30, and an annual subscription of six guineas.

Situated on the spot where Carlton House formerly stood, and at one of the entrances to St. James's Park, is seen the DUKE OF YORK'S COLUMN, erected by public subscription in 1833. The column, 124 feet high, was designed by Wyatt, is of Scotch granite, and is surmounted by a statue of the Duke, by Westmacott, 14 foot high. Opposite, at the bottom of Waterloo Place, the Guards' Memorial to the officers and privates who fell in the Crimea, forms a conspicuous object, and occupies one of the best sites in London. The memorial is very massive, and formed of bronze figures, and a granite pyramidal pedestal, which deserves to be enriched with bronze trophies, so as to cover its present bare appearance.

PALL MALL, so called from a game of that name, introduced into England in the reign of Charles I., is a thoroughfare full of historic interest, and the clubs, already mentioned, form a distinguishing feature of the lines of stately edifices that adorn this locality.

In the height of the London season, brilliant and well-appointed equipages, and all the appliances of wealth and distinction, are to be here seen rolling along in every variety and in every direction. One might suppose that a succession of brilliant fêtes was going forward, and that the rank, beauty, and fashion of the metropolis were wending their way to some scene of unusual gaiety. Few would imagine that the fair occupants of the carriages were intent merely on lounging in some emporium of taste, and that the bustle and excitement were things of everyday occurrence. Many stately mansions here have been gradually giving place to the warehouses and show-rooms of the trader. The large brick house where the Duke of Schomberg resided, is now devoted to trade. The late residence of the Duke of Buckingham, the saloons of which boasted the presence of a galaxy of rank and beauty unparalleled in any country, has been converted into a club-house, called "The Park Club," and a little higher up was the residence (No. 50) of Mr. Vernon, in whose house, the home and haunt of art, was stored the magnificent collection of pictures which the owner bequeathed to the nation. It is now also a club-house. THE SOCIETY OF PAINTERS IN WATER COLOURS (No. 53), where many distinguished artists annually exhibit their pictures, and the

BRITISH INSTITUTION next door, where two exhibitions are annually given of living artists in the spring, and the old masters in the summer, add the attractions of art to the associations of opulence. The latter exhibition, opened in 1806, was the celebrated Shakspere Gallery of Alderman Boydell; on the front of the building may still be noticed a fine bas-relief of Shakspere between Poetry and Painting, executed by Thomas Banks, at a cost of 500 guineas. MARLBOROUGH HOUSE, on the south side, was built in 1710, for *the* Duke of Marlborough, by Sir Christopher Wren, and became the property of the Crown by purchase in 1817, when it was appropriated as the residence of the Princess Charlotte and Prince Leopold, who will now have a royal successor in the, Prince of Wales. Here remains, in a dismantled state, Wellington's Funeral Car, which is not now exhibited. Probably it will shortly be removed, and being renovated, become one of the sights of Chelsea Hospital. **St. James's Palace** was originally an hospital, founded by some pious citizens even before the Conquest, and was seized by Henry VIII. in 1531, when he converted it into a palace, enclosed the park, and made it an appurtenance to Whitehall. The ancient brick gate-way, by which we enter, is the oldest portion of the building remaining. The palace is still used for the levees and drawing-

rooms of the court, for which its arrangements are better adapted than for a royal residence. In the courtyard adjoining, the bands of the foot-guards play every morning at eleven, and their able performance of the most lively pieces of music should be heard. The apartments in the several courts are chiefly occupied by those attached to the court. The CHAPEL ROYAL is on the right, between the colour-court, where the bands perform, and the Ambassadors' court. The building is oblong, and is divided into compartments with armorial bearings. Among the memorable marriages that have taken place in this chapel may be mentioned, that of George IV. and Queen Caroline, her present Majesty and Prince Albert, and the Prince Frederick William of Prussia and our Princess Royal, which took place in 1858. The Duke of Wellington, when in town, was a constant attendant of the morning service in this chapel, and the seats are nearly all appropriated to the nobility, who may here feel that the mightiest monarch and the meanest serf must bow at the same footstool. The service is performed at 8 A.M., and 12 noon; a fee of two shillings is usually paid for admission. The choral service is chanted by the boys of the Chapel Royal, who are maintained and taught out of the revenues. The Royal Family no longer attend, the Queen having had a chapel attached to Buckingham Palace.

ST. JAMES'S STREET, a direct thoroughfare, leading from the Palace into Piccadilly, has some buildings worthy of notice. WHITE'S CLUB-HOUSE (Nos. 37 and 38) was established as a chocolate house in 1699. The club is limited to 550 members, and in its bygone days has been famous for the immense amount of gaming here carried on. BOODLE'S, another club-house, is No. 28. BROOKES'S, a handsome building, and the former haunt of the Whig party, is No. 60; it was established in 1764. ARTHUR'S (No. 69) derived its name from the original proprietor, Mr. Arthur, and is of equally long standing. THE NEW CONSERVATIVE CLUB-HOUSE, on the west side, occupies the site of the Old Thatched House Tavern, and was built in 1845, from the designs of Sydney Smirke. The interior is magnificently decorated, and the apartments at once convenient and surpassingly elegant in their arrangements. A little further towards Piccadilly is the MILITARY, NAVAL, AND COUNTY SERVICE CLUB, occupying the house that until 1849 was Crockford's celebrated club-house, where a man a day was ruined, according to the boast of that notorious gamester. KING STREET, leading from the eastern side of St. James's Street to ST. JAMES'S SQUARE,

the most fashionable in London, contains the ST. JAMES'S THEATRE, now under the popular management of Mr. Wigan; and WILLIS'S ROOMS, where the renowned assemblies take place, under the world-famous distinction of ALMACK'S.

Entering St. James's Park by the old palace gateway, we pass on our right STAFFORD HOUSE, the town mansion of the Sutherland family. It was originally built for the Duke of York; but in 1841 it was sold to the present possessor for the sum of £72,000, and the Crown devoted the purchase-money to the establishment of Victoria Park. The Sutherland Gallery contains a magnificent collection of pictures; and in size, taste, and decorations, the interior of the mansion is unequalled.

St. James's Park covers an area of eighty-seven acres, and from its oblong form is about two miles in circuit. It was first formed and planted by Henry VIII., considerably improved by Charles II., and by a succession of judicious alterations and embellishments, made during the reigns of George IV. and Queen Victoria, has reached the present highly ornamental condition in which we now view it. The fine gravelled avenue, planted with long rows of stately trees, is called the MALL. The south side the Park, ranging from Storey's Gate to Buckingham Gate, is still known as the "Bird-Cage Walk," from the aviary established there by James I. The Wellington Barracks, occupying a large frontage on this side, were erected in 1834. The open space in front of the Horse Guards, is called the Parade, and here regiments are frequently reviewed. Here, also, are two curious pieces of ordnance; one a Turkish piece, brought by our troops from Alexandria in 1798, and the other a large mortar, taken in 1816 at the siege of Cadiz. It was cast at Seville by order of Napoleon, and left behind in the retreat, by Soult. Its extreme range was said to be 6,220 yards, and its weight is recorded at 16 tons. The inclosure, with its serpentine walks through parterres and shrubberies, and its ornamental lake, with islands thickly planted in the midst, is a favourite promenade with all who can avail themselves of its privileges, and on a Sunday afternoon is crowded with the inhabitants of the dusty city, who are athirst for the sight of green leaves and opening blossoms. Owing to a recent admirable arrangement, by which the trees and shrubs are labelled with their respective English and botanical appellations, an attentive observer may gain a few agreeable lessons in botany during his stroll through the grounds. In the year 1837, the Ornithological Society was formed in the metropolis, having, as the original prospectus modestly averred, "no privileges to claim or offer, excepting those of rendering services to science, and contributing to the amusement and information of the public." Their object was, to include within their collection every species of hardy aquatic birds, waders, swimmers, and divers, and this idea has been most successfully carried out. The Society's cottage occupies the eastern extremity of the island in the park, and is nearly opposite to the State Paper Office and the Treasury. The design, by John Burgess Watson, Esq., presents a pleasing specimen of the Swiss style. It contains a council-room, with apartments for the resident keeper, a facetious duodecimo volume of humanity, bound in green cloth, and lettered with brass buttons; a room for the culinary department; and, finally, a large lobby fitted up with steam apparatus for hatching eggs. Within the grounds attached to the cottage are places for rearing the young birds, and the various aquatic fowl likewise breed on the island, making their own nests among the shrubs and grasses, and appearing a happy and contented feathered colony in their new abode. The collection comprises about three hundred birds, including twenty-one species and fifty-one distinct varieties. From different openings in the park some fine views may be gained of the surrounding buildings, and the massive towers of Westminster Abbey look nowhere so well as from the northern side of the inclosure. Seats are placed at convenient distances for the use of the public, and the time of closing the gates is notified at the several entrances.

The Green Park, which extends towards Piccadilly from St. James's Park, has been much improved of late years, and now presents a delightful grassy surface, with undulating slopes, of more than fifty-six acres in extent. From the highest ground there is a pleasing prospect of St· James's Park and Buckingham Palace, beyond which may be noticed the distant range of the Surrey hills. The eastern side is bounded by many of the finest mansions of the nobility, among which may be successively pointed out STAFFORD HOUSE, the residence of the Sutherland family, BRIDGEWATER HOUSE, the residence of the Earl of Ellesmere, built in 1849 by Barry, and having a fine collection of pictures; SPENCER HOUSE, the residence of the Earl Spencer; and a fine old-fashioned house, distinguished by its bow window and pink blind, where Rogers, the poet and banker, resided, since 1808, up to the time of his death, and forming No. 22, St. James's Place. The road leading from Buckingham Palace to Hyde Park Corner is called Constitution Hill.

Buckingham Palace, the town residence of Her Majesty, having cost millions of money, was finally completed by the architectural additions and alterations made in the year 1850. It was first built by Nash, on the site of Old Buckingham House, in the reign of George IV., and first occupied by her present Majesty in 1837. The marble arch, which cost £80,000, and gave rise to such a diversity of opinions as to where it should be placed, no longer forms the portal to the palace. The metal gates cost three thousand guineas. The state apartments look out upon the spacious and diversified gardens at the back; the throne-room is sixty-four feet in length, and elegantly hung with striped crimson satin. The ceiling is richly emblazoned, and beneath runs a frieze of white marble representing the wars of the Roses, designed by Stothard, and executed by Baily. The centre of the eastern front is occupied by the Green Drawing-Room, and is fifty feet in length, and more than thirty in height, with hangings of green satin. The Grand Staircase, the Library, and the Sculpture Gallery, have been newly constructed and decorated, on a scale of great magnificence. In the State-rooms are pictures by ancient and modern masters, of the highest order of excellence. On the south side is the chapel, originally a conservatory; it was consecrated by the Archbishop of Canterbury in 1843. There is a small Pavilion in the Gardens which contains eight fresco paintings from Comus, exquisitely executed by Eastlake, Stanfield, Dyce, Landseer, Maclise, Ross, Ewins, and Leslie, with an ornamental border by Gruner. The

Royal Mews has an entrance in Queen's Row; here are kept the state horses and carriages. The Royal Standard floating from the top of the palace indicates the presence of her Majesty within its walls. Admission to view the interior can only be gained in the absence of the royal family, and then only by special favour of the Lord Chamberlain.

By traversing the broad Avenue of Constitution Hill, or, which is far preferable, taking an angular direction across the sloping uplands of the Green Park, we shall arrive at HYDE PARK CORNER, where the busy traffic of Piccadilly, streaming westward to the suburbs of Chelsea, Fulham, Brompton, Kensington and Hammersmith, gives a lively and animated aspect to the thoroughfare at this point. Before entering Hyde Park, we must pause to take cognizance of a few notable features that surround this locality.

The triumphal arch at the left of Piccadilly was designed by Decimus Burton, and erected in 1828. It is surmounted by Wyatt's equestrian statue of the Duke of Wellington, erected by a public subscription of £30,000 in 1846, and upwards of twenty-seven feet high. Opposite there is another archway with three avenues for carriages, two smaller ones for pedestrians, and a fine screen of fluted Ionic columns, extending 107 feet, and forming a grand entrance to Hyde Park. ST. GEORGE'S HOSPITAL was built by Wilkins, and has a spacious frontage 180 feet in length, with a vestibule in the centre 30 feet high, and surmounted by lofty pilasters. There is a theatre for the delivery of lectures, a museum, and about 340 beds for patients, divided into 16 wards. The present building was erected about 20 years since; but the existence of the hospital dates from 1733. APSLEY HOUSE, the town residence of the Duke of Wellington since 1820, was considerably altered and improved by Wyatt in 1828, and now ranks as a fine addition to this part of the metropolis. The ornamental architecture of the building is of the Corinthian order, and the whole is enclosed by a rich bronze palisade. The interior is magnificently decorated, and there is a fine collection of paintings by old and modern masters, the latter chiefly referring to the memorable day of Waterloo and its associations.

Hyde Park was originally a manor belonging to Westminster Abbey; but in the reign of Henry VIII. it was acquired by the Crown, and fenced in for the preservation of deer. The open iron railing was placed round it in the time of George IV. The park covers about 400 acres, and in the height of the season presents every fine afternoon a lively appearance, from the number of splendid equipages and fashionable visitors that throng the drives and promenades. At the south-east corner by the archway we have just described is a colossal statue of Achilles, cast by Westmacott from cannon taken in the victories of Salamanca, Vittoria, Toulouse, and Waterloo. It stands on a granite pedestal, is twenty feet high, thirty tons in weight, and the cost was defrayed by a subscription of £10,000 raised among the ladies. It is inscribed, "By the Women of England to Arthur Duke of Wellington, and his brave Companions in Arms," and was here erected 18th of June, 1822. From the extent and convenient situation of the park, it has often been chosen for reviews of troops; but its selection as the arena for the grand National Exposition of 1851 will not only show the dawning of a brighter era, but convince the world that it is still better adapted for exhibiting the blessings of peace than developing the arts of war. The scenery of the park is varied, and enriched by several fine plantations and a winding stream of water called the Serpentine, fifty acres in extent. It was formed in 1733 by Caroline, Queen of George II., who caused the bed of a stream to be enlarged that flowed through the park from Bayswater, and fell into the Thames at Ranelagh. This stream was cut off in 1834, and the Chelsea Water-works Company now supply the deficiency. The depth varies from two to forty feet. At the east end is a waterfall made in 1820, and at its western end is a neat stone bridge by Rennie, of five arches, and built in 1826. 12,000 persons have been known to bathe here of a Sunday, and in the winter the frozen surface is a favourite resort of skaters. On the northern bank is a small but appropriate edifice built by Decimus Burton, as the receiving-house for the Royal Humane Society, who have saved many thousand lives by their gallant exertions. The Society was founded by Dr. Hawes in 1774, and is supported by the contributions of the benevolent. On the south side are the Knightsbridge Barracks. There are seven entrances open to the public from six in the morning till nine at night, viz.—Hyde Park Corner; Cumberland Gate, Oxford Street end; Victoria Gate, Bayswater; Grosvenor Gate, Park Lane; Stanhope Gate, Kensington Gate, and the new Albert Gate at Knightsbridge. The park is only accessible to private vehicles; hackney carriages and cabs being rigidly excluded. According to the hour which the visitor selects for his stroll, he can enjoy either the delights of a purely sylvan solitude, or the gaiety of the fashionable world, in which he will here be certain to behold the regnant attractions.

Kensington Gardens, so closely connected with Hyde Park that we cannot dissever their descriptions, were originally the pleasure-grounds attached to Kensington Palace, and have been much enlarged by successive sovereigns. They are now about three miles in circumference. The entrances are:—near Victoria Gate; another at Kensington Gore, adjoining the palace; a third westward of the first milestone on the Kensington Road; and a fourth near the bridge over the Serpentine. Pedestrians only are admitted; and to those who can enjoy the pleasures of a saunter through the umbrageous avenues and agreeable vistas which this place affords, there can be no resort abounding with more facilities for enjoyment. Between 5 and 6 P.M., on every Tuesday and Friday in the summer months, the fashionable *champêtre* concerts of the band of the First Life Guards may be heard in these grounds, and generally draw together a large concourse of visitors. The grounds were laid out by Kent, the renowned landscape gardener; but within the last ten years alterations, that have proved striking improvements, have been made with considerable advantage to the public. KENSINGTON PALACE, where Her present Majesty was born, and the late Duke of Sussex died, is a large brick edifice, with no exterior beauty, but within possessing some handsome apartments. It was bought by William III. from Heneage Finch, Earl of Nottingham, and Lord Chancellor, and has ever since belonged to the Crown. A small douceur will generally prevail upon the housekeeper to grant admission; but since the greater portion of the pictures has been removed, there is really very little to be seen. Those who like to emerge at the Kensington Gate, will be rewarded by extending their stroll to HOLLAND HOUSE, on the north side of the road, and about two miles from Hyde Park Corner. The mansion, which is one of the finest Elizabethan structures we have left, was erected by Thorpe, in 1607, for Sir Walter Cope. It afterwards came into the possession of Henry Rich, Earl of Holland, his son-in-law, and by whom it was first called Holland House. The earl, who was a political waverer in the troublous times of Charles I., was twice made a prisoner in this house, first by Charles, in 1633, upon the occasion of his challenging Lord Weston, and a second time, by command of the Parliament, after the unsuccessful issue of his attempt to restore the king in 1648. He lost his life upon the scaffold in the cause of monarchy in 1649, and, within four months from his death, Lambert, then general of the army, fixed his quarters at Holland House, which, however, was soon restored to the widowed countess. Its celebrity as the residence of Addison, who became possessed of it by his marriage, in 1716, with Charlotte, Countess-Dowager of Warwick, and the impressive death of the illustrious essayist here in 1719, need not be detailed. About the year 1762, the property passed by sale to the Fox family, and here the statesman, Charles James Fox, passed many of the earlier days of his life. His nephew, the late Lord Holland, distinguished for his varied proficiency in literature, and his warm patronage of genius, afterwards became the owner. The stone gateway was designed by Inigo Jones; the raised terrace in front of the house was made in 1848; and the mansion altogether, whether as a fine example of picturesque architecture, placed in a park-like domain, or as a place of historical fame and association with literature and art, is invested with the highest interest.

The South Kensington Museum has added largely to the attractions of this favourite portion of the metropolis. The School of Design, originally commenced in Somerset House, after gradually increasing in extent and usefulness, has now found a most appropriate and commodious home at South Kensington. A large collection of objects relating to education, architecture, and trade, of pictures, ornamental art, and models of patented inventions, is open to the public, daily, from 10 till 4, and from 7 till 10 in the evenings of Mondays and Thursdays, excepting holidays. The admission is perfectly free on Mondays, Tuesdays, and Saturdays; on Wednesdays, Thursdays, and Fridays, a charge of 6*d.* is made for each person. Some choice pictures are here exhibited, including the Vernon and Turner Collection, removed from Marlbro' House. The Library of Art is open daily from 11 till 9 free to the regular students. Occasional students are admitted upon payment of 6*d.*, which entitles to entrance for six days from the day or payment. The establishment of the Museum, which was brought about by the Commissioners for the Great Exhibition of 1851, bids fair to give additional interest and importance to this already-attractive locality.

We may hence, by omnibus, return through Piccadilly to Charing Cross; and those who feel an interest in the associations of a place, will feel some pleasure in tracing with us the principal features of the thoroughfare as we shall endeavour to describe them, both with reference to their former and modern condition.

Piccadilly is shown in a map of London of the time of Queen Elizabeth as a rudely defined road out of the town, with one or two houses at the angle where the road, which afterwards became Regent Street, turned off, and a windmill a little to the east of this, the recollection of which is still preserved in Windmill Street. The origin of the name seems uncertain; but it was thought by some, at the commencement of the seventeenth century, to have been given to a noted house there as being the skirt or fringe of the town—a *picardill* having been a kind of stiff collar or fringe to the skirt of a garment. At the corner of DOWN STREET is the mansion, finished in 1850, of Henry Thomas Hope, Esq., and erected under the joint superintendence of M. Dusillion a French architect, and Professor Donaldson. It has a frontage of 70 feet in Piccadilly, and 64 feet in Down Street. The total height from the level of the street to the top of the balustrade is 63 feet. The building is enclosed with a handsome iron railing, cast in Paris for the purpose. The entire cost, exclusive of the decorations, which are magnificent, was £30,000. The collection of pictures is extremely valuable. Clarges Street was built in 1717, and was so called after Sir Walter Clarges, the nephew of Anne, wife of General Monk. DEVONSHIRE HOUSE, by STRATTON STREET, is an old brick mansion, built by Kent, in 1738, for William Cavendish, third duke of Devonshire, at a cost of £25,000. The old entrance, taken down in 1840, was by a flight of steps on each side. The gardens extended northward to those of Lansdowne House, in Berkeley Square. In Stratton Street, built 1695, and called after the Baron Berkeley, of Stratton, in Cornwall, lived Mrs. Coutts, afterwards Duchess of St. Albans. The House (No.1), is now the residence of Miss Angela Burdett Contts, understood to be the wealthiest heiress in the kingdom. BERKELEY STREET leads to the aristocratic Berkeley Square, where is situated the noble mansion of the Marquis of Lansdowne. There is here a fine gallery 100 feet in length, filled with antique statues and busts. ARLINGTON STREET, on the opposite side, contains the mansions of the Duke of Beaufort (No. 22), the Marquis of Salisbury (No. 20), and the Earl of Yarborough (No. 17). Next door was the mansion (No. 16) of the Duke of Rutland, where the Duke of York died in 1827. In DOVER STREET is Ashburnham House (No. 80), the customary residence of the Russian Ambassador. ALBEMARLE STREET contains the ROYAL INSTITUTION, so famous for the weekly lectures on chemical science by Professors Faraday and Brande. It was established in 1799, and a handsome façade of fourteen fluted Corinthian columns, by Vulliamy, was added to the building in 1836. The cost of this tasteful embellishment was £1,853. An admission fee of five guineas, and an annual subscription of five guineas, entitle a member, who must be balloted for, to enjoy the privileges of the Institution. On the ground floor the principal apartments are, a newspaper room, a small library, and a cabinet of minerals. On the first floor is the apparatus room, communicating with the theatre, which will accommodate 900 persons. On the same floor is a spacious and valuable library. The laboratory on the basement story is fitted up on a scale of magnitude and completeness not before attempted in this country. In this apartment is the large galvanic apparatus with which Sir Humphrey Davy made his famous discovery of the composition of the fixed alkalies.

Burlington Arcade, a favourite lounge, and fitted up with some tasty shops, is upwards of 200 yards in length, and has a bazaar attached. It was originally built in 1819, sustained some few years back considerable injury by fire, and is now re-embellished. At night, when the shops are illuminated, the vista has a pretty effect. It is a thoroughfare into Cork Street. BURLINGTON HOUSE adjoining is almost screened from the sight of the passenger by a lofty brick wall, behind which is a spacious court-yard. The first house was built about 1650, and when Lord Burlington was asked why he built his house so far out of town, he replied, more like a peer than a prophet, "because he was determined to have no building beyond him." In 1735, when the title became extinct, the house became the property of the Dukes of Devonshire. THE ALBANY, a series of chambers on a superior scale, deserves notice for the number of eminent literary men who have been its inhabitants, and amongst whom may be mentioned Monk Lewis, Canning, Byron, and Bulwer. The man-

sion in the centre was designed by Sir W. Chambers for the first Viscount Melbourne, who afterwards exchanged it with the Duke of York and Albany—whence its name—for Melbourne House, Whitehall. THE EGYPTIAN HALL, on the opposite side the way, owes its appellation to its style of architecture, and is celebrated as the spot where Albert Smith for nearly five years, ascended Mont Blanc daily, to the delight and amusement of thousands of visitors. The entertainxsment was certainly the most unique in London.

St. James's Church was built by Wren in 1684, at the expense of Henry Jermyn, Earl of St. Alban, from whom the adjacent street derives its appellation. The interior is of exquisite workmanship, and has a fine organ intended by James II. for his popish chapel at Whitehall, and given to this church by his daughter Mary. At the east end of the chancel a new painted window, representing the crucifixion, was erected in 1846. In the churchyard adjoining lie Arbuthnot the wit, Akenside the poet, Dodsley the Bookseller, Gillray the caricaturist, and Vandervelde the painter. Here, and at St. George's, Hanover Square, most of the fashionable marriages are solemnized. Hence we pass down the Haymarket, and again reach Charing Cross.

H

SIXTH DAY'S ROUTE.

DISTRICT IV.

CHARING CROSS TO LEICESTER SQUARE—REGENT STREET—ST. JAMES'S HALL—HANOVER SQUARE—OXFORD STREET—PRINCESS'S THEATRE—PANTHEON—LONDON CRYSTAL PALACE—LANGHAM PLACE—POLYTECHNIC INSTITUTION—PORTLAND PLACE—SOHO SQUARE—NEW OXFORD STREET—ST. GILES'S-IN-THE-FIELDS—INTERESTING MONUMENTS—SEVEN DIALS—DRURY LANE—LONG ACRE—COVENT GARDEN MARKET—BOW STREET—THEATRES—LINCOLN'S INN FIELDS—SIR JOHN SOANE'S MUSEUM—THE NEW LINCOLN'S INN HALL—ROYAL COLLEGE OF SURGEONS—MUSEUM OF THE COLLEGE—GRAY'S INN, HOLBORN—BEDFORD ROW—RED LION SQUARE, ETC.

FROM Charing Cross we now pursue the opposite direction of ST. MARTIN'S LANE, noticing at the back of the National Gallery the new structure built and opened in 1849, called the ST. MARTIN'S BATHS AND WASHHOUSES, and of which, in the first six mouths, no less than 106,760 persons availed themselves. At the end is CRANBOURNE STREET, that in March 1841, was opened as a broad and commodious thoroughfare, communicating with Long Acre, and supplanting the former narrow outlet of Cranbourne Alley. Another new and wide street is now opened opposite, and connects this improving neighbourhood directly with King Street, Covent Garden. We are thus introduced to LEICESTER SQUARE, so called from the stately mansion built by Robert Sidney, Earl of Leicester, that occupied its northern side, and which was frequently tenanted by branches of the royal family until the reign of George III. The square has a dingy, dreary aspect, and will soon disappear before the onward progress of improvement. In the centre is the large building erected by Mr. Wyld for the exhibition of his gigantic model of the earth. Around the square are some popular exhibitions—the Alhambra Palace; BURFORD'S PANORAMA; and the WESTERN LITERARY AND SCIENTIFIC INSTITUTION, established in 1825, are here situated. On the south side, by St. Martin's Street, lived Sir Isaac Newton; and Hogarth and Sir Joshua Reynolds were also inhabitants of houses on the eastern and western sides of the square.

Coventry Street, to which we are now brought, leads direct to Piceadilly. To give some idea of the immense cost involved in disturbing the old thoroughfares, we may mention that when the houses were taken down here in 1844, to form the present improved avenue, no less than £71,827 was paid to the Marquis of Salisbury for his claims upon the estate, and upwards of £100,000 was distributed among the shopkeepers, for the good-will of their respective establishments. In PRINCE'S STREET will be remarked the Church of ST. ANNE'S, SOHO, the tower and spire of which, built in 1686 by Hakewell, enjoy the unenviable distinction of being the ugliest in London. The whole of this district is thickly crowded with foreigners, who, settling in this locality, have given quite a continental tone to the coffee-houses and dining-rooms of the neighbourhood.

Hence we continue along Coventry Street till we arrive at the REGENT CIRCUS, where a fine view of the splendid avenue of Regent Street becomes apparent, linking St. James Park with the Regent's Park by nearly two miles of mansion-like shops and palace-like mansions.

Regent Street was designed by Nash, and commenced under his direction in 1816. The houses in this magnificent thoroughfare are from the designs of Nash, Soane, Repton, Decimus Burton, and other architects, producjag an extent and variety of architeciural display unparalleled in Europe. The shops are of unequalled beauty, and unrivalled for the opulence of their contents. The quadrant was constructed for the purpose of avoiding the obliquity of the turning; but the shadow of the colonnade being found to interfere with the interests of the shopkeepers beneath, the 145 stately cast-iron columns that supported it were removed at the latter end of 1848, and the present architectural embellishments substituted. The building surmounted by the colossal figure of Britannia is the COUNTY FIRE OFFICE, founded by Barber Beaumont, and built in 1819. The attractions of the shop-windows, which, of course, are too varied to particularize, will be found amply sufficient to engage the attention of the stranger; but, to make our route more complete as well as more interesting, we shall notice as we proceed the places that abut on the thoroughfare, in addition to those that fall in the direct line of progress.

A new building called the LONDON CRYSTAL PALACE, to form a Bazaar, is just completed, close to the Regent Circus, mainly formed of iron and glass, for the exhibition and sale of choice specimens of manufacture. A large photographic establishment forms one of the principal features of this new lounge, and in addition to the display of wares, there is a conservatory, aquarium, and aviary attached. The principal entrance is in Oxford Street, two doors from Regent Street, the carriage entrance being in John Street, Oxford Street. The whole has been designed by the celebrated Owen Jones, the architect.

ST. JAMES'S MUSIC HALL, erected for concerts, scientific meetings, public dinners, &c., has its main entrance at 27, Piccadilly, and 78, Regent Street. It is the third, in point of size, of the Halls used for these purposes in London,

Exeter Hall, and the Surrey Gardens Music Hall being somewhat larger. This hall affords sitting accommodation for about 2,500 persons: it is about 140 feet in length, by 60.

Golden Square is a small and not particularly verdant area on the same side as WARWICK STREET, where a fine Roman Catholic chapel is situated. In the centre of the square is a dismal-looking statue of George I., brought from Canons at the Chandos sale.

On the right hand side of Regent Street is ARCHBISHOP TENNISON'S CHAPEL and SCHOOL. On the opposite side is HANOVER CHAPEL, built in 1823 by Cockerell, at the cost of £16,180. The Ionic portico has been admired for its classic proportions, but the two square turrets on the top have been not inaptly compared to churchwardens' money boxes. HANOVER SQUARE, to which HANOVER STREET leads, was built in 1718, and is one of the most fashionable of the squares of London. On the south side of the enclosure is a fine bronze statue of the statesman Pitt, executed by Chantrey at a cost of £7,000, and placed there in 1831. The statue is twelve feet high, and the granite pedestal on which it stands fifteen feet high. On the east side of the square are the HANOVER SQUARE ROOMS, where the concerts of the Philharmonic Society and of the Ancient Concerts are held. The assembly room is capable of containing 800 persons, and is handsomely decorated.

On the opposite side (No. 18) is the ORIENTAL CLUB, founded in 1824, for the friendly meeting of those gentlemen who have resided in the East. In Tenterden Street adjoining is the ROYAL ACADEMY OF MUSIC, founded in 1822 by the Earl of Westmoreland, and affording the first instruction that can be given to both resident and non-resident pupils. The terms of admission are proportionately high; the indoor pupils paying ten guineas entrance fee, and fifty guineas annually. ST. GEORGE'S CHURCH, Hanover Square, was built by John James, and finished in 1724. It has a handsome portico of six Corinthian columns, and over the altar is a curious stained-glass window brought from a convent at Mechlin, and as old as the beginning of the sixteenth century. It is generally chosen by the fashionable world as the place of matrimonial solemnization.

It will not be uninteresting to mention, that this large district, that for years has constituted the most fashionable haunt of the titled and the wealthy, was, not more than a century and a half ago, the most filthy and repulsive in the metropolis. In 1700, BOND STREET was built no further than the west end of Clifford Street, and took its name from the proprietor, a baronet of a family now extinct. NEW BOND STREET was at that time an open field, called Conduit Mead, from one of the conduits which supplied this part of the town with water, and CONDUIT STREET received its name for the same reason. Further west is GROSVENOR STREET, leading to GROSVENOR SQUARE, formed in 1715, and occupying six acres of ground. The square and the adjoining streets are on the Grosvenor estate, from which they derive their name. An equestrian statue of George I. formerly stood within the railings, but the pedestal is now vacant. It was at the Earl of Harrowby's (No. 39) where the Cato-street conspiracy was to have been carried out, and the massacre of the ministers consummated. Most of the squares about this neighbourhood, we may observe, seem to have the stamp of the last century indelibly impressed upon them. As the eye catches a vestige of bygone days in the conical extinguishers on the railings, and the recollection of the old flambeaux is restored, with the accompanying adjuncts of linkboys and sedans, one may almost picture the old nobility in the court costume of the first and second Georges, dozing away their hundred years of somniferous captivity, and doomed some day to wake up, sword, bagwig, ruffles, and all, and take a wondering survey of this modern metropolis, with its perplexing growth of buildings, and puzzling magnitude of improvements.

Crossing Oxford Street—to which we shall presently return—a continuation of Regent Street brings us to the POLYTECHNIC INSTITUTION, one of the best and most instructive of our exhibitions, and first opened in the autumn of 1838. The large hall contains a variety of most interesting models of machinery and model inventions. The largest geological model in the world, formed principally of real materials, occupies one entire side of the gallery, and shows the nature of the earth's crust above and below the surface, from the Arctic Regions to the Equator, while views of the various countries above the surface are executed in a high style of art. Silver, copper, coal, and other mines are seen in working operation, together with the beds of ponds, rivers, and oceans.

Annual exhibitions of pictures take place, one for the works of deceased, and one of living artists.

The gallery also contains original drawings by Turner, and many choice works of art. There are two theatres, one for illustrating science, and one for musical and popular entertainments. A laboratory is open for analysis and students. The long canals of water display various models of ships; the descent of a diver, 15 feet under water; the operations of the diving bell, and the thousand and one things to be seen here form a fund of occupation suitable for all classes and tastes. At the end of LANGHAM PLACE is ALL SOULS' Church, built by Nash, in 1823, at an expenditure of £16,000. The steeple, with its odd extinguisher-like shape, has been much criticised. A fine picture by Westall, R.A., is placed over the altar.

At the end of PORTLAND PLACE is a statue of the Duke of Kent, the father of her present Majesty. It was designed and cast by Gahegan. To the west are some of the finest and most aristocratically inhabited streets in the metropolis, but presenting nothing deserving especial mention. PORTMAN SQUARE, the residence of many of the nobility, was finished in 1784, on a spot of ground formerly known, from its proximity to Tyburn, as "Great Gibbet Field." At the north-west side of the square is the house occupied, till 1800, by the kind-hearted, but eccentric Mrs. Montague, who, every May-day, used here to entertain the chimney-sweepers. In Baker Street, that extends from the square northward, is situated the celebrated

Tussaud's Wax Exhibition.— Amongst the almost endless attractions here, the most imposing are the magnificent combination of figures in the centre of the room, representing the Queen's coronation, with some of its principal actors, the Royal Family at Home, &c., &c. This exhibition should not be overlooked; and at the BAKER STREET BAZAAR is held the Christmas Cattle Show, that annually attracts a large Concourse of visitors.

Returning to OXFORD STREET, and proceeding eastward, we have on our right hand, soon after passing, ARGYLL STREET, the PANTHEON, converted in 1834 into a bazaar, having been closed for many years as a theatre. The alterations and re-construction cost £40,000, and were designed by Sydney Smirke. The rooms above are for the exhibition and sale of pictures, and below is a well-arranged bazaar, with a conservatory, laid out in exquisite taste, and abundant in birds and flowers. There is an entrance to this portion of the building in GREAT MARLBOROUGH STREET.

The Princess's Theatre is on the opposite side the way, built on the site of what was formerly the Queen's Bazaar. The interior is elegantly decorated, and will contain about 1,800 to 2,000 persons. The late manager of this theatre, Mr. Charles Kean, has done more for the advancement of the drama during his eight years' occupation than any man living. Inheriting a celebrated name, he has even added to its reputation by his unblemished character and conduct. His revivals of Shakspeare's plays were on a scale of grandeur never before thought of, and Mr. Kean brought in the aid of almost every science to add to the attraction of the scene, so that the antiquary and the archaeologist were equally gratified with the mere dramatist, in witnessing the fidelity and attention to historical details in the various productions of Mr. Kean, who has also had the honour of conducting the Court theatricals at Windsor Castle, &c. The last and best act of Mr. Kean's managerial career was to preside at a public meeting of the poor players' friend (in July, 1858), for the purpose of establishing a Dramatic College, for providing homes for the poor and distressed members of the profession—the first stone of which was laid by his Royal Highness the Prince Consort, on the 1st of June, 1860, at Woking, in Surrey. On Mr. Kean's retirement he was succeeded by Mr. Harris, the present lessee, whose enterprise sustains the popularity of his theatre. Mr. Fechter, the celebrated German actor, appeared recently, and created great sensation in theatrical circles in the character of Hamlet.

Soho Square, on the right hand side of Oxford Street, and in which the short thoroughfare of CHARLES STREET will conduct us, is chiefly tenanted by music publishers and those connected with the musical profession. In the centre is a stable of Charles II, in whose reign the ground was principally built upon. The large building on the north-west aide is the SOHO BAZAAR, the largest in London, and still much frequented for the purchase of fancy articles, and as a fashionable lounge for ladies. It was established in 1815.

At the eastern extremity of Oxford Street, turning a little to the right, we enter Broad Street, a continuation of Holborn, and have before us the parish-church of St. GILES'S-IN-THE-FIELDS, a name that has long since lost its rural significance. The church was built by Henry Flitcroft on the site of an older one, in 1784, and has a tower at the west end. Over the street-entrance to the churchyard is the Lich-gate, having an elaborate and curious specimen of bronze sculpture, representing the Last Judgment, brought from Florence, and placed on the gate of the old church in 1686. The church itself contains little to demand attention on the exterior, and within, the chief monument of interest is a recumbent figure of Alice, Duchess Dudley, who died at her residence, in this parish, 1669, aged 90; she was the widow of Sir Robert Dudley, the son of Robert, Earl of Leicester. On the eastern side, is a monument erected by Inigo Jones, at his own expense, to George Chapman, the first metrical translator of Homer (d. 1634); and here, too, lie, Shirley, the dramatist (d. 1666), Sir Roger L'Estrange, the journalist (d. 1704:), and Andrew Marvel (d. 1678), the stanch-hearted poet and patriot. An altar-tomb records the interment here of Richard Penderell (d. 1671), "preserver and conduct to his sacred majesty, King Charles II., after his escape from Worcester fight." The epitaph inscribed upon his tomb is such a solemn specimen of bombastic absurdity, that it will repay for being transcribed :—

" Hold, passenger, here's shrouded in this hearse
  Unparallel'd Pendrill, through the universe,
  Like when the eastern star from heaven gave light
  To three lost kings, so he in such dark night
  To Britain's monarch, tost by adverse war.
  On earth appear'd a second eastern star;

A pole, a storm in her rebellious main,
A pilot to her royal sovereign.
Now to triumph in heaven's eternal sphere
He's hence advanced for his just steerage here;
Whilst Albion's chronicles with matchless fame
Embalms the story of great Pendrill's name."

On the very verge of the churchyard, overlooking the busy traffic of Broad Street, lies a flat stone, having upon it some faint vestiges of what was once a coat-of-arms and some appearance of an inscription; but the most expert of heralds would fail to describe the one, and, eyes, however penetrating, may be baffled to decipher the other. Yet this is a grave without its dead—a mockery of the tomb—a cheating of the sexton; for hither were brought the decapitated remains of one who was among the brightest and most popular young noblemen of his time, and hence were they afterwards disinterred and privately conveyed to Dilston, in Northumberland, where they moulder in the family vault, amid the ashes of his forefathers. Here, in fact, was first deposited the body of the amiable and unfortunate James Radcliffe, Earl of Derwentwater, whose fatal connection with the fortunes of the pretender, and untimely death on Tower Hill, are matters of history, and reveal a sad tragedy, in which he was at once the hero and the victim. The burial-ground of the parish, until the closing of all such places by a recent act of parliament, was in the Pancras Road, near the old church of St. Pancras. The ground was laid out and a chapel built in 1804, and there rest the remains of Flaxman, the eminent sculptor, and Sir John Soane, the architect. The central point in this neighbourhood, called SEVEN DIALS, and whence seven streets radiate, derived its name from a column, on the summit of which were seven dials occupying the centre. It was removed in 1773, under the absurd and erroneous impression that a large sum of money had been buried beneath. The angular direction of each street renders the spot rather embarrassing to a pedestrian who crosses this maze of buildings unexpectedly, and frequently causes him to diverge from the road that would lead him to his destination.

Drury Lane, now the most uninviting street in London for a residence, was, up to the reign of William III. rather a genteel and fashionable locality. It derived its name from Drury House, the mansion of Sir William Drury, and which afterwards passed into the possession of the Craven family. The Olympic Theatre partly occupies its site. The Marquis of Argyll and Alexander Earl of Stirling both had houses in this street between 1634 and 1637; and here, likewise, lodged Nell Gwynne. GREAT QUEEN STREET, leading to Lincoln's Inn Fields, was built in 1629, and was so called after Henrietta Maria, Queen of Charles I. The house in which Sir Godfrey Kneller lived was lately sold; the ori-

REGENT STREET, AND ALL SOULS' CHURCH, LANGHAM PLACE.

ginal houses on the south side were built by Inigo Jones. In the Baptist Chapel, in Little Wild Street, a sermon commemorative of the great storm of November, 1703, is still annually preached. The street was so called from Weld House and gardens that once occupied its site.

Long Acre, for nearly two centuries the chosen abode of coachmakers, contains a spacious building, erected in 1850 from the designs of W. Westmacott, and appropriated for lectures, concerts, &c., under the title of "ST. MARTIN'S MUSIC HALL."

Bow Street, in which the celebrated police office is situated, rife with the associations of the drama and its votaries, is said to have been built in 1637, and to have been so called from "its running in shape of a bent bow." Waller the poet, Wycherley the dramatist, and Fielding the novelist, who here wrote "Tom Jones," were all inhabitants of this street. The corner house on the western side, abutting on Russell Street, was the celebrated "Will's Coffee House," the famous resort of all the wits in the days of Dryden, and so called from one William Urwin, who first established it.

In RUSSELL STREET were two other celebrated coffee-houses, Tom's (No. 17) on the north side, and Button's on the south side exactly opposite. TOM'S COFFEE HOUSE, so memorable for its frequenters in the reign of Queen Anne, and for half a century afterwards, be-

came in 1768 the focus of the conversational talent of Dr. Johnson, Garrick, Murphy, Dr. Dodd, Goldsmith, Sir Joshua Reynolds, Foote, Sir Philip Francis, George Colman the elder, and others of rank and eminence, being then converted into a suite of rooms for the friendly reunions of the distinguished subscribers. Button's, so called after Daniel Button, servant to Lady Warwick, whom Addison married, was established in 1712, and is well remembered by all readers of the "Guardian," for the lion's head that was here set up as a letter-box to receive the correspondence. This ingenious piece of workmanship, "a proper emblem of knowledge and action, being all head and paws," after undergoing various changes of ownership, was finally purchased by the Duke of Bedford, for his mansion at Woburn, where it is still carefully preserved. Addison avowedly derived the idea from the use of the lion erected near the Doge's palace, at Venice, into the wide gaping mouth of which public and private accusations were conveyed by anonymous informers. Addison, Pope, Steele, Swift, Arbuthnot, and many others bearing great and distinguished names, were regular visitors to Button's.

We now approach COVENT GARDEN MARKET, the great metropolitan fruit and flower market, and so called from the ground on which it stands being originally the convent garden of the Abbey at Westminser. The open quadrangle was formed in 1631, at the expense of Francis, fourth Earl of Bedford; and the piazza was chiefly constructed from the designs of Inigo Jones. The original market stood in the space on which Southampton and Tavistock Streets are now built, and thence was removed further into the square, the sides of which were then surrounded with mansions of the nobility and gentry, who have long since been displaced by tavern and hotel keepers. The present market was erected at the cost of John, Duke of Bedford, in 1830, and from the design and under the direction of Mr. Fowler. The market is placed under the control of an officer called clerk of the market, and three beadles or toll collectors; and the revenue derived therefrom by the Bedford family is very considerable. The toll for potatoes, the market for which fronts Tavistock Row, is 1s. 2d. per ton; on vegetables, 1s. per waggon; the latter are pitched in the spaces, and still sold in open market to the higglers and retail dealers who principally supply the shops of the outskirts. The fruit, flower, and herb markets occupy the centre and north avenues of the market, and the central avenue, on a market-day as you enter from the church, presents, in the spring and summer, a flower show of surpassing beauty. "Few places," observes a well-known writer, "surprise a stranger more than when he emerges suddenly from that great, crowded, and noisy thoroughfare, the Strand, and finds himself all at once in this little world of flowers. In this spot are to be found the first offerings of spring; the snowdrop, that comes like an unbidden guest, violets and primroses, which have been gathered in many a far-off dell and sunny dingle, come to tell us the progress that nature is making in the green and out-of-door world. Many a sad and many a pleasing thought must have been awakened in the bosoms of thousands who have long been indwellers in this mighty city, by walking through the ranks of flowers which are here placed. They must have recalled the image of some old home far away, and probably never again to be visited by them—the porch over which the woodbine or jasmine trailed, and the garden fence along which the clustering moss roses hung many a flower is thus borne away and treasured for the old memories it awakens, and for the tender recollections it recalls. Here are purchased the cut flowers that decorate the banquet and the ball-room—the posy which the blushing bride bears with downcast look in her hand—the bouquet, which is rained down at the feet of our favourite actresses; and here also affection comes for its last tribute to place beside the pale face of the beloved dead, or plant around the grave in the cemetery. The house of mirth and the house of mourning are both supplied from the same common store, and pride, love, interest, fame, and vanity, come either to select their garlands." From each corner of the wings, facing Russell Street, are flights of steps leading to conservatories above, ornamented with a fountain, and affording a good view of the general appearance of the market and the arcade beneath. The market days are Tuesday, Thursday, and Saturday, but the latter is the principal. At a very early hour in the morning, generally by 3 o'clock, the whole of the streets which open into Covent Garden are thronged with vehicles, and buyers and sellers are astir with the dawn to effect the sales and purchases which are to apply the dinner-tables of London with vegetables. From 5 till 7, the market is one busy scene of animation, and the stranger should on no account miss an opportunity of being present. It is not generally known that this district was separated from the adjoining parish of St. Martin's-in-the-Fields, and formed into a parish during the Commonwealth, which act being considered illegal, was obliged to be confirmed by another passed in 1660. Though the resident market people do not pay directly to the parish fund, they yet indemnify the Duke of Bedford in an increased rent, and he pays no less than £4,800 for poor-rates annually, out of the revenue he derives from the market.

St. Paul's Church, at the western end, was rebuilt by Hardwick, on the plan and in the proportions of the old church by Inigo Jones, that was built in 1633, and destroyed by fire September 17th, 1795. The original clock was the first with a long pendulum made in Europe; the present has an illuminated dial. In the church yard are buried, among other eminent personages, Samuel Butler, the witty author of Hudibras, and who died in Rose Street, Long Acre (1680), of consumption accelerated by poverty. Wycherley, the dramatist (*d.* 1715); Grinling Gibbons, the sculptor (*d.* 1721); Susannah Centlivre, the lively authoress of some of our best comedies (*d.* 1723); Macklin, the actor, who died in 1797, at the great age of 107; and Dr. Walcot (*d.* 1819), the Peter Pindar of satirical memory. The hustings for the old Westminster elections were always erected on the east side of the church, and the space being then entirely open, formed the battlefield for the supporters of the different candidates. In King Street is the GARRICK CLUB, instituted in 1831 as a club for those connected with the drama, and having the finest collection of theatrical portraits extant.

The New Royal Italian Opera, Bow Street, is built on the site of the late Theatre Royal, Covent Garden, which, at the period of its destruction by fire, in March, 1856, was decidedly the most splendid theatre in Europe. The present structure is in every respect worthy of its predecessor, and is really a beautiful building, particularly well adapted for the purpose for which it was constructed, its acoustic properties being very remarkable. It was completed in a most incredibly brief period, from the design of Charles Barry, Esq., and was opened within six months from the laying the foundation-stone by the proprietor, Mr. Gye, to the astonishment of all who had watched its progress—the interior being completed in a sufficient state for opening to the public within that time, and the entire design, which embraced a concert and floral hall, has since been finished in all its details.

Drury Lane Theatre was built by Wyatt in 1812, on the site of a former one burned down in February, 1809. The present portico and colonnade were subsequent additions. The interior is light, elegant, and capacious, and will contain about 2,500 persons. The heavy expenditure of these establishments seems latterly to have been a fatal impediment in the way of their success. Nineteen out of Dryden's twenty-seven plays were produced at the old theatre that formerly occupied this spot; seven out of Nathaniel Lee's eleven; all the good ones of Wycherley; two of Congreve's; and all Farquhar's, except the "Beaux Stratagem," whilst in the building that immediately preceded the present one, Sheridan produced four of his finest plays. The recollections of the past should serve as a stimulus to the dramatic enterprise of the present; but we are afraid "Old Drury" can never be again so famous a theatre as it has been.

At the back of Drury Lane is Princes Street, leading to DUKE STREET, where there is a Roman Catholic chapel much frequented by the humbler class of foreigners and Irish who live about the neighbourhood. The first chapel on this site was destroyed during the riots of 1780. The streets leading to CLARE MARKET indicate the name of William Holles, created Baron Houghton, Earl of Clare, who had a mansion here. The market is surrounded by slaughter-houses, and of a Saturday night presents a noisy indication of the marvellous extent to which street traffic is carried on in this vicinity. PORTUGAL STREET was once famous for the LINCOLN'S INN THEATRE, afterwards converted into Copeland's china repository, and within the last seven years pulled down to enlarge the museum of the Royal College of Surgeons. Here was the "Beggar's Opera" originally produced in 1728, and hence did Lavinia Fenton, the original Polly, go to be made Duchess of Bolton. In the churchyard, which is the burying-ground to St. Clement's Danes, Joe Miller, of Jest-book celebrity, has a

headstone to his memory. KING'S COL-
LEGE HOSPITAL was instituted 1839.
In the ten years succeeding, no less
than 11,747 cases have been relieved
within its walls, and medical assistance
given to 138,448 out-patients, making
in all a sum of 150,195 cases in which
human suffering has been removed
or mitigated. The Hospital makes up
120 beds. In Portugal Street is the
INSOLVENT DEBTOR'S COURT.

Lincoln's Inn Fields form a fine
open square, said to be the dimensions
of the base of one of the pyramids of
Egypt. The western side was built by
Inigo Jones. Here, on the 21st of
July, 1683, was beheaded Lord William
Russell; he had been tried and condemned to death in Hicks's Hall. On
the north side (No. 13) is SIR JOHN
SOANE'S MUSEUM, open to the public
gratis, on Thursdays and Fridays,
during the months of April, May, and
June. Foreigners, and those unable to
attend at these stated periods, are admitted by special application, on Tuesdays, from February till August. It is
usual to call a few days before, and
leave the name and address of the party
desiring admission with the curator,
when the ticket of admission will be
granted upon personal application, or
forwarded by post. The collection is
one of great value and interest, and is
contained in no less than twenty-four
rooms, many or them, however, being
of exceedingly limited dimensions.
Architectural antiquities, curious relics, and some fine paintings by the
most eminent masters, render a visit
extremely gratifying; and the manner
in which so miscellaneous an assortment is arranged within so limited a
space, deserves notice. Here is a fine
Egyptian sarcophagus formed of alabaster, and, though nearly three inches
thick, perfectly transparent. It was
discovered by Belzoni in 1816, and
purchased by Soane for £2,000. It is
said to be the tomb of Osirei, father
of the Great Rameses, but it has an
antiquity to boast of full three thousand years. Among other interesting
objects, will be found the Napoleon
medals, Sir Christopher Wren's watch,
Peter the Great's pistol, formerly in
Napoleon's possession, Tippoo Saib's
ivory table and chairs, from the Serin-
gapatam palace, Hogarth's original
paintings of the "RAKE'S PROGRESS,"
and "The Election," paintings by Ca-
naletti, Sir Joshua Reynolds, Turner,
Sir Thomas Lawrence, with some
curious manuscripts, among which is
Tasso's original copy of the "Geru-
salemme," and some rare books, including the first folio editions of
Shakspere, bought from the Kemble
collection. The mansion was built by
Soane in 1812. LINDSEY House (No. 59)
was originally built by Inigo Jones for
the Earl of Lindsey, who was General

of the King's forces for Charles I., and fell at the battle of Edgehill. A fine masterpiece of the period is still to be seen in part of the chambers.

Those much frequented thoroughfares, GREAT and LITTLE TURNSTILE, derived their names from the turning-stiles which two centuries ago stood at their respective ends, and were so placed both for the convenience of foot passengers, and to prevent the straying of cattle, the fields being at that period used for pasturage. On the east side of the square, occupying a portion of what was, till very recently, Lincoln's Inn gardens, is the new LINCOLN'S INN HALL and library, built by Hardwick in the Tudor style, and publicly opened by her Majesty with great ceremony in October, 1845. The hall, which has a roof of oak finely carved, is 62 feet high, 45 feet wide, and 120 feet in length. The library is 80 feet long, 40 feet wide, and 44 feet high, and contains some valuable records, and a fine collection of law books. The CHAPEL, built by Inigo Jones, and consecrated in 1623, is at the back of these buildings, and is chiefly noticeable for some richly stained glass windows. It is reared on huge pillars and arches, leaving an open walk beneath the chapel, which was formerly much frequented.

On the south tide of Lincoln's Inn Fields is the ROYAL COLLEGE OF SUR-GEONS, a massive building erected from the designs of Barry, and presenting a noble colonnade and portico of the Ionic order. Admittance is obtained by tickets from any member of the college, and the days of admission are Monday, Tuesday, Wednesday, and Thursday, between twelve and four o'clock, the month of September excepted, when it is altogether closed. It should be understood that these orders are not transferable, and the name of the visiter is, for obvious reasons, written on the ticket of admission.

The magnificent MUSEUM attached to the College—the first of its kind in the world—owes its foundation to the untiring industry and well-directed talents of John Hunter, the great anatomist and physiologist. It was originally arranged by him in 1787, and having left directions in his will that the collection should be offered to government, Parliament, six years afterwards, voted £15,000 for the museum, and a building being erected here for its reception, it was first opened in 1813. This proving too small for the display and arrangement of the specimens that were afterwards added, the present noble structure was built in 1836, at the expense of the College, and at the cost of £40,000. At present the total number of specimens is about twenty-three thousand,

and of these ten thousand belonged to Hunter's original collection. It would be manifestly impossible to give even a synopsis of those specimens in the prescribed limits of this work, and indeed the majority of them would be of little interest to the general reader. We shall therefore confine ourselves to those that usually invite the curiosity of the non-professional visiter, and refer others desirous of becoming more intimately acquainted with the preparations, to the elaborate catalogues of the Museum. The view that meets the eye on entering at the chief door from the hall of the College, is particularly striking and impressive. The first large object seen on the right, is the fossil shell of a gigantic extinct armadillo from Buenos Ayres. A shell of the common armadillo is placed on this enormous specimen, to show by comparison its vast size, which was its only protection, as it had no joints to roll itself up with, like the animal of the present day. On the left is the fossil skeleton of the mylodon, a large extinct quadruped of the sloth family, also found at Buenos Ayres. It is disposed as if climbing up a tree to feed on the branches, such being the manner in which it is conjectured its subsistence was procured. Beyond this, to the left, is the skeleton of the hippopotamus, and on the extreme right, over the shell of the armadillo, are the bones of the pelvis, tail, and left hind leg of the mighty *megatherium*, an animal of antediluvian associations It seems to have been a sort of stupendous sloth, with haunches more than five feet wide, a body twelve feet long, and eight feet high, feet a yard in length, and terminated by most gigantic claws. Its tail was clad in a kind of armadillo-like armour, and was much larger than the tail of any other beast. The entire frame was an apparatus of colossal mechanism, calculated to be the vehicle of life and enjoyment to a gigantic race of quadrupeds, which, though they have ceased to be counted among the living inhabitants of our planet, have in their fossil bones left behind them imperishable monuments of the consummate skill with which they were constructed.

The cabinets on each side the centre avenue, contain various anatomical preparations of parts of the human subject, fishes, and reptiles. The large skeleton to the right of the centre is that of Charles Byrne or O'Bryan, the Irish giant, and is eight feet in height. He died in Cockspur Street in 1783, at the age of twenty-two, his death being accelerated by excessive drinking. Two ordinary skeletons, male and female, are placed on his left side, and on his right is that of Caroline Crachami, the Sicilian dwarf, who died in Bond Street in 1824, at the age of ten years. The skeleton, which is only twenty inches in height, is placed under a glass case. On the pedestal there are two plaster casts of hands—one of Mons. Louis, the French giant, who measured seven feet four inches, and the other the right hand of Patrick Cotter, whose height in 1802 was eight feet eight inches. In the glass case adjoining is preserved the glove of O'Bryan. His shoes are in the possession of a gentleman at Chertsey, and are more like huge coal-scuttles than the ordinary coverings of any human feet. Proceeding along the museum on the left, are casts in plaster of the bones of an extinct and huge bird, which must have stood at least ten feet high, and was a native of New Zealand. It is called the *Din-ornis giganteus*, and is placed, by way of contrast, at the side of a full-grown ostrich. Still further is the skeleton of the American elk, and under it that of the great penguin, from the extreme southern point that Ross touched at. This is the only specimen of the kind in England. Behind this is a specimen of the giraffe, and on the right is seen the skeleton of the gigantic extinct deer, the *Migaceros Hibernicus*, very commonly but erroneously called "the Irish elk." It was exhumed from a peat-bog near Limerick. The span of the antlers, measured in a straight line between the extreme tips, is eight feet; the length of a single antler, following the curve, seven feet three inches; height of the skeleton to the top of the skull, seven feet six inches; weight of the skull and antlers, seventy-six pounds. The large skeleton in the centre will be looked at with interest; it is that of the Elephant *Chunee*, brought to England in 1810. After being exhibited on the stage of Covent Garden Theatre, it was purchased by Mr. Cross, for his menagerie at Exeter Change, and in consequence of an in-flammation of one of the tusks, which rendered the poor animal ungovernably violent, it was shot in 1826. The com-pany of soldiers employed to shoot him discharged upwards of one hundred bullets and musket balls at him without effect; and it was only when the familiar voice of the keeper called him by name that the animal turned round, presented a vulnerable point, and was shot dead at the feet of his well-known attendant. On the platform may be seen the base of the inflamed tusk, showing the splin-ter of ivory that projected into the pulp. In the front is the plaster cast of a young negro, and a bust of John Hunter by Flaxman.

Passing through a doorway on the left hand, we enter the small museum, which contains many objects of popular interest. Immediately before us is the skeleton of a man who died at the age of twenty-five, from hydrocephalus, or water on the brain. The skull is enormous, measuring forty-eight inches in circumference, and the entire skeleton displays many peculiarities highly interesting to the anatomist. It was pretented by the late Mr. Liston, the surgeon. In the next case are the two skulls of a double-headed child, born in Bengal, and who lived to be four years old, when it was killed by the bite of a cobra di capello. The skulls are united by the crowns, and the upper head is consequently inverted. It had four eyes, which moved in different directions at the same time, and the upper eyelids were never thoroughly closed, even when the child was asleep. In the same case is a portion of the intestines of Napoleon, showing the progress of the disease which carried him off. Adjoining this singular relic of the exiled Emperor, is a very remarkable skeleton, the joints of which are anchylosed, or rendered immoveable by unnatural splints of bone growing out in all directions. Here, too, is preserved a female monstrous embryo, found in the abdomen of a boy sixteen years of age, at Sherborne, in Dorsetshire, June 16, 1814. But, perhaps, the object of the greatest interest is the preparation known as the shaft case, between the wall-cabinets on the left hand. On the 13th of June, 1812, Mr. Thomas Tipple was impaled by the shaft of a chaise, near Stratford, in Essex. The shaft entered his chest under the left arm, and came out under the right arm, being thrust through by the violence of an unruly horse, as far as the first tag hook, which also penetrated the chest, and wounded the left lung. Two veterinary surgeons, Messrs. E. and H. Lawrence, who were passing at the time, extracted the shaft; and, wonderful to relate, the patient recovered, surviving the injury eleven years. As a companion to this, is the iron pivot of a try-sail mast which was driven right through the body of a seaman, John Toyler, a Prussian by birth, of the brig Jane of Scarborough. The accident occurred in the London Docks, February 26, 1831. Whilst guiding the pivot of the try-sail mast into the main boom, the tackle gave way, and the pivot pasted obliquely through Toyler's body between the heart and left lung, and pinned him to the deck. The try-sail mast was 39 feet long, and weighed about 600 pounds. He was conveyed, apparently dead, to the London Hospital, where, under the care of Mr. J. G. Andrews, he recovered so entirely in five months as to be able to walk from the hospital to the college and back again. He at the same time sustained various other injuries; his scalp was laid open, and his lower jaw and four ribs fractured; but he ultimately returned to his duties as a seaman, and not very long ago revisited the college in a robust state of health. Here, also, is the cast in wax of the band that united the Siamese twins. There are several mummies in this room, amongst which may be observed the wife of the eccentric Martin van Butchell, and a female who died of consumption in 1775. The plan pursued, was that of injecting all the vessels with camphor and turpentine. A mummy in a sitting position, with its cheeks resting on the hands, deserves attention. It is supposed to be that of a Peruvian nobleman who immolated himself with his wife and child some centuries ago. The expression of the figure is painful. The portrait of Hunter is by Sir Joshua Reynolds. We have thus sketched the principal points or the collection, feeling that from what has been here only superficially described, there is amply sufficient to interest the non-professional visiter, as well as those for whose anatomical pursuits the specimens were originally accumulated. But unrivalled as this collection certainly is, scarcely a day passes without some addition to its stores. "Doctors on shipboard, doctors with armies, doctors in Arctic ships, or on Niger expeditions; in the far regions of Hindustan, and in the fogs and storms of Labrador, think now and then of their 'dissecting days,' and of the noble collection in Lincoln's Inn Fields, which every true student feels bound to honour, and to help to make complete. Many, when going forth into distant countries, are supplied from this place with bottles specially adapted to receive objects in request, and receive also a volume of instructions how the specimens may be best preserved. Never a week passes but something rare or curious makes its appearance in Lincoln's Inn Fields; sometimes from one quarter, sometimes from another, but there is always something coming, either by messenger or parcel-cart. Apart from these foreign sources, there are other contributaries to the general stock. Country doctors and hospital surgeons, from time to time, send in their quota; the Zoological Society likewise contribute all their dead animals. When the elephant died at the Regent's Park Gardens, a College student and an assistant were busily occupied for days dissecting the huge animal. When the rhinoceros expired at the same place, a portion of its viscera was hailed as a prize; and when the whale was cast, not long ago, upon the shores of the Thames, the watermen who claimed it as their booty, steamed off to the College to find a customer for portions of the unwieldy monster; nor were they disappointed."

Crossing Holborn, through Great Turnstile, or by the upper end of Chancery Lane, we may penetrate the shady avenues of GRAY'S INN, another inn of court, with two inns of Chancery attached (Staple Inn and Barnard's Inn), which has sufficient antiquity to date back its records to the time of Edward III. It was originally the residence of Lord Gray; the hall was built about 1560, and the gardens, to which it is said the great Lord Bacon contributed a few trees, planted about 1600. Among its more eminent students may be mentioned Hall the chronicler, the great Lord Burleigh, Bacon, Bradshaw, who sat as president at the trial of Charles I., and Robert Southey. Within Gray's Inn Gate was the shop in which Jacob Tonson, the bookseller, began his publishing career. Gray's Inn Walks used to be a favourite promenade in the time of Charles II., and in the days of the *Tatler* and *Spectator*. BEDFORD Row, adjoining, is a fine specimen of the broad thoroughfares of a century back, when all beyond this point was nearly open country to the very margin of Hampstead and Highgate. The name is derived from the benevolent purposes to which those lands and others adjacent were devoted by Sir William Harpur (Lord Mayor of London in 1561, died in 1573), who bequeathed the revenues to Bedford, his native place, there to found a free and perpetual school, and endow other charities. In this row lived Bishop Warburton, and here in 1731, in the eighty-second year of her age, died Mrs. Elizabeth Cromwell, granddaughter of Oliver Cromwell. At No. 14, John Abernethy, the celebrated surgeon, breathed his last. In RED LION SQUARE is situated the office of the MENDICITY SOCIETY, an excellent institution, and as serviceable for assisting the really necessitous poor as for the invaluable aid which it furnishes to the public in detecting the extensively ramified system of the begging letter impostor. In this square lived and died the benevolent Joseph Hanway the traveller, who was the first to venture to carry an umbrella in the streets of London, and who, after carrying one for thirty years, saw them come into general use.

Returning to Holborn, we can hence pass either to Charing Cross or Temple Bar, and having thus completed our walks through the West-end of London, prepare to take an equally interesting, and perhaps even a more excursive, ramble in a northerly direction.

PART IV.——THE NORTH.

SEVENTH DAY'S ROUTE.

DISTRICT I.

TOTTENHAM COURT ROAD—GREAT RUSSELL STREET—THE BRITISH MUSEUM—THE
NATURAL HISTORY DEPARTMENT—THE EGYPTIAN ANTIQUITIES—THE ELGIN
MARBLES—THE NIMROUD MARBLES, &c.—THE READING-ROOM AND LIBRARY —
LONDON UNIVERSITY COLLEGE—THE NEW ROAD—REGENT'S PARK—BOTANIC
GARDENS—VILLAS—ZOOLOGICAL GARDENS—ST. JOHN'S WOOD—PADDINGTON
—MARYLEBONE—FITZROY SQUARE—EUSTON SQUARE—TERMINUS OF THE
NORTH WESTERN RAILWAY—ST. PANCRAS NEW CHURCH—BURTON CRESCENT—
GUILDFORD STREET—THE FOUNDLING HOSPITAL, &c.

COMMENCING our progress northward from TOTTENHAM COURT ROAD, so called from it leading to the ancient manor of "Tottenham Court" belonging to St. Paul's, we deviate into GREAT RUSSELL STREET for the purpose of introducing the visiter to that noble institution, the BRITISH MUSEUM. This may truly be described as a spot where British enterprise has brought from every country something to attract the eye and interest the mind; where the rudest indications of barbaric skill and the highest manifestations of civilized ingenuity are alike preserved; and for which nature has surrendered its stores, art contributed its fairest creations, discovery yielded its richest treasures, and antiquity displayed its choicest relics, to bring the triumphs of the present into startling contrast with the glories of the past.

The British Museum stands upon the site of Montague House, where the collection was exhibited until the new building was completed for its reception in 1850, until which time, part of the old mansion of the Dukes of Montague was visible; but the gateway being then finally demolished, the last vestige of the ancient structure disappeared, and now the Museum, with its majestic portico, forms a striking architectural ornament to the street in which it stands.

The present building was commenced in 1823 from the designs of Sir Robert Smirke, and has been completed at an expenditure of £753,495. It is of the Grecian Ionic order of architecture.

The principal entrance has a magnificent portico, supported by eight columns, and with the wings on each side forms a frontage of 370 feet. Passing under this portico by a massive and finely carved oaken doorway, we enter the new hall, 30 feet high, and 62 feet by 51 broad. A grand staircase, 17 feet in width, and enclosed by walls of highly polished red granite, leads to the suite of rooms appropriated to the NATURAL HISTORY DEPARTMENT, and to the left is the entrance to the GALLERY OF ANTIQUITIES. For the convenience of those who can only take a rapid glance at the contents, we shall proceed to give a general indication of the most popularly interesting objects; but those who contemplate—as it deserves —devoting several days to an examination of this interesting building, should purchase the catalogues that are to be obtained about the Museum.

In the HALL will be noticed Chantrey's statue of Sir Joseph Banks, and Roubiliac's statue of Shakspere, the latter sculptured with all the skill of that celebrated artist, but, at the same time, possessing all the faults of an unnatural school. Near it is the statue of the Hon. Anne Seymour Damer, a liberal patroness of sculpture, in which she had some skill herself, as her own miniature figure of the genius of the Thames, which she holds in her arms, will testify. Passing on to the MAM-MALIA SALOON, we find ourselves in a spacious lofty apartment, around the walls of which are arranged the specimens of rapacious and hoofed beasts; whilst on the floor are placed the larger animals, among which will be observed the wild ox, from Chillingham Park, Northumberland. A miscellaneous collection of animals of the monkey tribe will be seen in a number of the cases; among these is a fine specimen of the black ourang, a native of Africa. Passing onwards will be noticed the species that have prehensile tails, with which they lay hold of branches, and thus in climbing have all the advantages of a fifth arm. The monkeys that are natives of America differ from those found in the other quarters of the globe, in having longer tails and no pouches in their cheeks. Case 18, especially, presents some beautiful varieties, amongst which the bearded ape is conspicuous, and close to it is the rib-nosed baboon, that once was a great favourite at Exeter Change, where he had been taught the questionable accomplishments of drinking grog and smoking tobacco.

The Eastern Zoological Gallery introduces us to a varied collection of birds, that are alike distinguished by the richness and brilliancy of their colours, and the beauty and elegance of their forms. The first section contains the *Rapsorial* and *Passerine* birds (birds of prey), which generally build on trees or high places, and have their young hatched blind and nearly naked, so that for a time it is necessary for them to be fed by their parents, and remain in the nest. The first family is that of the condors, chiefly inhabitants of America. The muscles in the wings of these giants of the feathered race are so powerful, that a blow from one of them has destroyed life. A magnificent specimen of the golden eagle, with the wings extended, shows the rapacity with which it devours its prey. The family of falcons (*Falconidæ*), which occupy the next cases, have their heads covered with feathers, and the eyebrows prominent, giving the eye the appearance of being deeply set in the head, and imparting a character very different from that of the vultures. The beak exhibits a remarkable conformation, having a deep notch near its roof, which enables them to wound or tear their prey with greater facility. The other varieties here are the ignoble falcons with simple, and the hawks with rather longitudinal nostrils; whilst the honey buzzard, osprey, and kites, have an oblique slit covered with a valve behind. These distinctions will readily enable the visiter to distinguish the several kinds. Amongst the hawks, the most remarkable bird is the secretary, brought from the Cape of Good Hope; where it is called the serpent-eater, from those reptiles being its prey. Next are the eagles, to describe the different varieties of which a volume might be devoted. We now approach the numerous and most solemn family of the owls (*Strigidæ*,) most of which are remarkable for the radiated circles of feathers surrounding their eyes, and for their large ears, which, as they hunt in the dark, may enable them to discover their prey by the sense of hearing when not within the range of their imperfect vision. The magnificent bird seen in Case 40 belongs to the genus *Trogon*, and is well worthy of the adjunct "resplendent," which has been appended to it. Their feet are often feathered almost to the toes, and their soft, full, lax plumage and lengthened tail, bestow upon the species a peculiar aspect. These birds abound in South America, where they conceal themselves in the central solitudes of umbrageous forests, and, except during the breeding season, dwell insulated and alone. They feed chiefly on fruits and winged insects. Their skins are of so delicate a texture, as to be with difficulty preserved in a complete or natural condition, whence they have here rather a heavy shapeless aspect. The greater portion of the plumage gleams like burnished gold. The head is ornamented with a brilliant crest of decomposed barbs, the wing coverts falling in flakes of golden green over the deep purplish black of the primary and secondary quill feathers; the rich carmine of the lower parts presenting a warmth and depth of effect which no Venetian painter ever equalled, whilst the long waving of the tail, extending about three times the length of the whole body, completes a combination of beauty almost unexampled in the feathered tribes. Case 48 presents the *Menura superba*, or lyre-tail, from New Holland, characterised, as its name implies, by the great extension and peculiar shape of its tail feathers. Pursuing our examination of the cases to the left, we find in Case 64 a magnificent specimen of the bird of paradise, about which such fabulous wonders were related and believed during our early intercourse with Eastern countries. The bill is straight, compressed, rather strong, and unnotched; the nostrils being surrounded by a close tissue of feathers of a velvet texture, sometimes resplendent with metallic lustre. They always fly against the wind, that their flowing plumage may not be discomposed. We now pass the kingfishers, remarkable for their length of bill and splendour of plumage. The *Alcedo ispida* (our common kingfisher) is the only species which we find in Europe, and it yields to few of its brethren in lustrous beauty. It is one of the rarest and certainly the handsomest of all our resident species. It

haunts the banks of lakes and rivers, building in willows near their margin, and preys chiefly on small fish, on which it darts with the rapidity of an arrow, plunging its little gem-like body for one flashing moment into the crystal and willow-hung stream, and re-appearing the next with its prey secured. In Case 72 the Indian hornbill, with its immense curved beak, will attract observation; and near it is a skeleton of the beak, enabling us better to understand and appreciate the enormous weight this bird has to carry. Notwithstanding this, the tongue is very small, and the most singular feature in their economy consists in their devouring greedily and without injury the seeds of the nux vomica, to others a deadly poison. Yonder is the woodpecker, a small but attractive bird, whose curious propensities for "tapping the hollow beech tree" have been recorded in song and story. We are next surrounded by the tribe of parrots, and the lories, parokeets, macaws, and cockatoos, belonging to the genus *Psittacus*. They have the bill curved, thick, and generally sharp-pointed, and the tongue thick, round, and fleshy, the lower larynx being furnished on each side with three peculiar muscles, which probably contribute to the facility with which these birds acquire the articular intonation of the human voice. The great scarlet macaw is one of the most gorgeous of the number. Case 104 comprises the Gallinaceous tribe. The cock of the woods is now utterly extinct as a wild British species, though once so common in these islands. The ostrich —among birds what the camelopard is among animals—is so incapacitated by its heaviness for flight, that it has recourse to its legs instead of wings for safety, and in this manner it has been known to outstrip the fleetest horse. In the same case (109) is the bustard, the largest of European birds, and the rarest with us; the peculiar conformation of the breast deserves notice. In Case 114 is the singular bird called the trumpeter, of which there are only two species, found in South America and the Brazils. It is of use there to the natives when domesticated, by its quality of making a peculiarly shrill noise, or "trumpeting," when danger is near; for this purpose it is often set to guard poultry, and feeding chiefly on serpents, its presence is much sought after. We now come to the *Waders*, or birds that seek their food in marshes along the banks and shores of rivers and lakes. The structure of their feet and legs is seen to be admirably adapted for this purpose, being so lengthened as to admit of the species wading to a considerable depth without wetting their feathers, and it is to this length of limb that they are indebted for their classical appellation of *Grallatores*, as if they went on stilts. Such species as are provided with a long, sharp, and hard-pointed bill, live chiefly on fish and reptiles, as the whole tribe of herons; where that organ is softer and more flexible, they subsist on worms and insects, whilst a limited few feed on grass. The habits of both species are migratory, and it is somewhat remarkable that the old and young birds pursue their journeys in separate assemblages. The heron, the tiger bittern, the scarlet ibis—a brilliant bird confined to tropical countries— and some interesting objects of the same kind, furnish the finest specimens. Here (Case 108) is the foot of the Dodo, a bird now supposed to be extinct, and only known by a few scanty remains, and a painting here exhibited, sketched from a living bird brought from the Mauritius. After noticing (Case D) a singularly well preserved skeleton of a swan, we pass a motley variety of the storks, so well known in Holland for their familiarity with mankind. The mandibles are broad and light and when struck together produce a sharp, short, snapping sound, which is almost the only one they utter. The gigantic stork, otherwise called the adjutant, from its peculiar mode of standing in a military position, is a native of India, where it often measures seven feet in height. The crane (Case 135) is a migratory bird well known in Britain during former ages, and still frequent in the northern and eastern countries or Europe. The beautiful Balearic crane occurs only in Africa and some of the Mediterranean islands; whilst the Demoiselle, with which it is associated, is also confined to the scorching clime of Africa. Its feminine appellation is bestowed in consequence of its peculiar, and what may be called affected, gestures. That odd-looking bird in the adjoining case is the spoonbill, deriving its name from the rounded spoon-like enlargement at the extremity of the bill. They inhabit Europe, Africa, and America, where they grope about in marshy places, in search of shellfish. The ducks, wild and common, native and foreign, are so familiar to our view that we may pass them over, to next direct the visiter's attention to those wandering sea-birds, that having a flight characterised by extreme buoyancy and rapidity combined, are met with on all parts of the ocean, and frequently at the greatest distance from land. The largest and most powerful of these is the albatross, with its full soft plumage, and long elastic wings. The gulls, of which we have a motley group, chiefly frequent the coasts and breed along the shores of unfrequented islands and headlands, laying in a hollow on the ground from two to four greyish eggs, with dusky spots. The pelican, easily recognised by its expansive pouch, is found chiefly in the tropical and warmer temperate regions of the old continent, and is common in the eastern countries of Europe. The fable, once universally believed, of the female pelican nursing its young with her own blood, arose probably from the way in which it discharges the fish contained in the pouch, as by this action the red tip of the upper mandible comes in contact with the breast. The common frigate birds, or men-of-war birds, form a ravenous tribe, chiefly incidental to the Island of Ascension and the tropical regions. The one here exhibited was captured off Jamaica, having choked itself with the bone of a flying fish which it had captured during its aërial excursions. Although for the most part deriving its subsistence at immeasurable distances from the shore, it is never seen to rest upon the surface, and for weeks it has been reported this singular bird can remain upon the wing without feeling fatigue. In each recess are small table-cases, containing the eggs of birds, arranged in the same series as the birds themselves; and along the centre, in the larger double cases, are shells systematically arranged, together with models in clay and plaster of Paris of some of the molluscous animals inhabiting the larger shells. To have attempted the preservation of the mollusc and its shell together, it is easily seen, would have been a fruitless task, not only that the soft gelatinous bodies would have been so much distorted and contracted as to have spoiled in drying, but also that in general they would have shrunk into the cells and thus become lost to observation. In consequence of this casts were procured, and the shell and its former inhabitant may now be examined in the same case together. The collection of fossils, insects, reptiles, and crustacea, is very complete and interesting; but as the inscriptions speak for themselves, it is unnecessary to occupy the time of the reader with a bare enumeration of names. We must, however, direct the visiter's attention to the mineralogical and geological collections in the northern gallery, and especially to the meteoric stones, enormous masses of iron that have fallen from the sky at different times and places. Here, also, is exhibited the famous "Show-stone" of Dr. Dee, in Case 20. In the Medal Room is a valuable assortment of ancient Greek, Roman, and British coins, chronologically and geographically arranged.

THE EGYPTIAN ROOM, that lies to the left at the extremity of the eastern gallery, contains various Egyptian curiosities, of which the most important are the mummies. The Case R R, contains the mummy of Harsontioff, priest of Ammon. The upper part is enveloped by a linen covering of blue, with figures and subjects embossed and gilded. On the head is the scarabæus or sacred beetle; round the fillets of the head are embossed lines of hieroglyphics, and on the soles of the sandal are two bearded male figures, with their hands and arms tied, short garments round the loins, and the chlamys on their shoulders emblematical of the enemies of Egypt. Its dimensions are about five feet eight inches. Case U U, is the coffin of Penamoun, the incense-bearer of Thebes. The face is of dark-polished wood, ornamented with a small square beard. The head is in a rich claft, representing the wings and body of a bird, with two side ornaments; round the neck is a pectoral plate representing a disked face in a boat. The hands are crossed on the breast, each holding a roll of papyrus, and below is the good demon. Round the sides of the chest, traced in yellow upon a black ground, is a cat grasping a snake; the mummy on its bier with the soul soaring above, an indubitable proof that the Egyptians believed in the immortality of the soul; and in addition to these, we find a temple on a mountain, above which are the symbols of east and west, a lion-headed mummied deity holding two swords, a man walking holding in each hand a star, the judgment-scene, a deity with two snaked heads, and the disc of the sun descending below the solar mountain. Next in interest may be considered the Case Z Z, containing the mummy of Mautemmen, a female attendant on the worship of Ammon, and most probably a priestess. The body is swathed in such a manner as to exhibit the whole of the form, and it is impossible to look upon the perfect preservation of this figure without emotion. Round the body, ankles, and upper parts of the arms, are broad bands similarly ornamented, others are narrower and cross from the shoulder to the belt, whilst the arms are swathed with narrow strips like the animal mummies. The back part of the head, and the extremities of the head and feet are bared, representing the hair and bones. In the centre, of the room (Case A A A) is the wooden sarcophagus of Cleopatra, daughter of Candace. On the arched part of the cover are judgment-scenes before Ra and Osiris, a train of inferior deities seated in porches and holding swords in their hands; two rows of hawks with human and animals' heads, on one side a boat with a disc attached to a snake drawn by four deities; on the other a boat with a disc of the symbolic eye attached to a snake drawn by three jackals; the good demon; the scarabæus with extended wings, and Isis and another deity paying it homage. The interior represents heaven surrounded by zodiacal signs, and at the aides of the head are four tortoises. The upper end has the hawk, and the lower the sacred cow, seated on a pedestal. On the sides are the twenty-four hours as female figures, twelve on each side, and each procession being closed by a thirteenth female as personifications of the morning and evening star. It is nearly 6 feet in length, 2 in breadth, and 2 feet in height. In Case D D, we find the mummy of part of a bull, remarkable for its perfect preservation, after a lapse of three thousand years. On the forehead is the triangular mark of Apis, to whom all cattle were sacred. In Case B B, we meet with a small coffin in a vaulted cover, containing the mummy of a Greco-Egyptian child. The body is covered with an external wrapper, having a representation of the deceased in a toga. The hair is crowned with a wreath, the feet are in shoes, and the left hand is holding a branch of laurel, whilst the other is raised. On the top of the cover is a viper between two wreaths. In Case E E are mummies of the ibis and the crocodile, embalming being as much practised by the Egyptians on animals as it was upon mankind; and, as these specimens show, even vegetables have been embalmed in a similar manner. The small bronze Egyptian deities in Case A cannot fail to repay inspection, from their singularity of design and beauty of execution. In Case F are some specimens of Coptic carving, that make it difficult to say whether the grotesque or the beautiful most predominate. Here is a small figure that seems formerly to have had a spear in its hand. The arms are jointed as if once moveable, and the cap which surmounts the head is remarkable for the singular form which it exhibits. Near it is a more grotesque figure, and, from the mechanical flexibility of the limbs, it is surmised that these statues were employed by the priests to excite the imagination of the people. Another, representing a kneeling female of benignant aspect, should be noticed for the artistic development of the form, and the exquisite finish of the drapery. The small bronze idols in the cases following are of the most exquisite workmanship. Cases I, K, and L introduce us to a series of articles of household furniture, chiefly procured from the tombs of the kings at Thebes. Closely approximating the seats with four turned legs, which, with the rails, are inlaid with ivory, is a wig of human hair, claiming for the barber's art an antiquity of which few seem to be aware. From the upper part, which is curled, depend long and tightly platted locks, the colour being black with an auburn tinge. In the next case (L), are several specimens of the cithara, corresponding to our modern guitar, and other musical instruments, among which are a pair of cymbals, green with age and rust, and of a similar construction to those in use at the present day. The glass cases round the mummy boxes are filled entirely with articles of Egyptian finery, such as rings, seals, toys, &c., and are curiously corroborative of the love of dress which has never ceased to exist among the ladies from that time to the present. The rooms leading from this are filled with vases and terra cotta, chiefly of Etruscan workmanship. The Bronze Room contains the Barberini, or Portland Vase, that in February, 1845, was wantonly injured by a supposed lunatic, who mischievously smashed it into pieces; but it has since been so cleverly restored, that the union of the fragments is scarcely perceptible. It was discovered in a sepulchral chamber about three miles from Rome, in 1643, and bought by Sir William Hamilton at the sale of the Barberini Library, where it was deposited. Though placed in the British Museum since 1810, the vase is still the property of the Duke of Portland, into whose possession it came by purchase, having been bought by the Portland family for £1,029.

We now descend to that magnificent hall on the ground floor called the EGYPTIAN SALOON, containing the most valuable collection of ancient colossal sculpture in the world, and the perspective at once impresses upon the mind an idea of extraordinary grandeur. The general characteristics of these specimens of Egyptian sculpture are extreme simplicity or uniformity in the composition of the lines, want of variety of action, and the absence of any sentiment or expression in the heads. Their statues are either standing quite upright, sitting with all their limbs at right angles to the body, or kneeling on both knees. The backs are uniformly supported by a kind of block or pilaster, which is generally covered with hieroglyphics, and the heads, when they are human, are sometimes uncovered, but more frequently they are surmounted by an emblematical head-dress, in which is distinguished the lotos, a globe, a serpent or some sacred symbol, or else the covering consists of a kind of close cap, entirely concealing the hair, and falling in broad flaps upon the shoulders. For the light or majestic drapery of the Grecians, possessing all that is beautiful in outline, admirable in effect, noble in design, and perfect in execution, we are here presented with enormous masses of granite and porphyry, with colossal fragments of gigantic statues, whose enormous dimensions, overwhelmed by the shocks of nature or the fury of the elements, have been scattered in ages past over regions at present inaccessible, or buried beneath these arid and burning sands, which have at once been their tomb and their protection. That stately figure, resting his hands upon his knees and having a grave monarchical aspect, is the statue of Bubastes, (No. 63), and of which Nos. 62 and 37 are counterparts. The pillar (No. 64) is a granite column, with six rows of shields containing hieroglyphics, among which the names of Rameses and Amenoph III. have been identified. No. 67 is the fragment of a statue belonging to the pedestal of the great Sphinx, and is presumed to be emblematical of a shepherdess or protectress of the fields. No. 70 is a broken fragment of what was once a seated male statue, holding in front of its knees a child, standing with a label on his breast, inscribed with hieroglyphics, indicative of the royal name Amyrteus. On each side are two most curiously carved figures, one representing an agricultural labourer, with an implement resembling a pickaxe in his left hand; the other being a statue of a prince of Ethiopia, holding in his hands an altar, inscribed with hieroglyphics, and having on it a ram's head to be offered as a sacrifice. We now come to a beautiful fragment of a colossal statue (No. 19), which is sure to attract attention. This is called the head of the young Memnon, but in reality it is the upper portion of a statue of Rameses the Great, brought by Belzoni in 1817 from the ruins of the Memnonium, a building dedicated to Memnon, at Thebes. This fragment is composed of one piece of granite of two colours, and the face, which is in remarkably fine preservation, is executed in a very admirable manner. It will be observed that there is a hole in the right breast, drilled, it is supposed, by the French for the purpose of blowing off with gunpowder the right shoulder, and rendering the transport of the head more easy. The height of the fragment is about nine feet. Opposite is placed another head of nearly equal dimensions, and but little inferior in beauty of workmanship, seeming as fresh and perfect as when it first left the sculptor's hand. Behind this huge head, and formerly belonging to it, is a granite arm (No. 55), which was also brought from Thebes by Belzoni. The external anatomy of the muscles is very boldly expressed, and when we consider its gigantic proportions, and the exquisite polish given to the hard granite of which it is composed, we must acknowledge it a wonderful triumph of execution. The circumference of the arm round the thickest part below the elbow, is 61 inches, and the length of the long joint of the middle finger, 14 inches. At the back of Memnon's head is a massive sculptured image of the Egyptian *scarabæus* or beetle (No. 74), brought from Constantinople, and forming part of the Elgin collection. It is cut in green granite, and is one of those symbolical figures that occur most frequently in their sculpture and paintings. The colossal ram's head (No.7) originally formed part of a sphinx, and was one of the many objects collected by the French from different parts of Egypt, and which came by the right of conquest into the possession of the English, to whom they were formally ceded by the treaty of Alexandria in September 1801, and conveyed hither in the year following. The head is made of an exceedingly soft sandstone, of an apparently dirty yellow colour. On the summit of the head, there is an irregular oblong hole, about 7 inches long and four deep. The tip of the horn is also fractured. Adjoining (No.8) is a figure of the deity Hapimoous, a personification of the Nile, and bearing an altar of libations dedicated to a king of the 22nd dynasty. We next pass several sarcophagi, or stone coffins. The one No. 23 is composed of black granite, and is covered with hieroglyphics within and without. It was brought from Grand Cairo, where it was used by the Turks as a cistern, which accounts for the large hole drilled into it at the lower end. The other sarcophagus (No. 10) was brought, from the mosque of St. Athanasius, at Alexandria, and contains no less than 21,700 characters inscribed upon it. The average thickness is 10 inches, and the whole length exceeds 10 feet. Towards the right is the Rosetta stone (No. 24), which was found at the mouth of the Rosetta branch of the Nile. It is a piece of black basalt, in its present state much mutilated, both at the top and at the right side. Its greatest length, measured on the flat face which contains the writing, is about 3 feet, and in thickness about the average of eleven inches. The great peculiarity of this object is, that on its surface are three inscriptions of the same import—viz., one in hieroglyphics, another in the ancient vernacular of Egypt, and a third in the Greek tongue. These inscriptions record the services which the fifth Ptolemy had rendered to his country, and were engraved by order of the high priests, when they were assembled at Memphis, for the purpose of investing him with the royal prerogative. It was captured from the French as they were conveying it from Egypt to the Louvre, and has thrown much light on the inscriptions of ancient Egypt. No. 43 is the sacred boat, conveying a group, of which a fragment only remains of a vulture overshadowing a female. We have only space now to direct attention to a statue of the great Rameses (No. 96), holding a tablet with offerings, under which is a vase found near Abydos. The hieroglyphics inform us, that the king is desiring success in the war he is about to undertake. The rest of the figures present the same characteristics of Egyptian sculpture, with the forehead low, the eyebrows scarcely marked, the eyes rather long and flat, not sunk deep into the head, and drawn slightly in an oblique direction. The two lions couchant in red marble (1 and 34) must not escape observation. On the base is the name of Amenoph III. (Memnon), and the amazing antiquity of the sculpture is thus shown. Near them is the fragment of a colossal foot, supposed to have been broken from some statue of Apollo; its length is 2 feet 11 inches. Fragments of this description are scattered in various portions of the hall.

We now proceed to the ELGIN SALOON, where the Elgin marbles arc deposited, and which are universally acknowledged to be the most valuable extant. They are mostly basso-relievos, and fragments of statuary that adorned the Parthenon at Athens, and were so called from the Earl of Elgin, who obtained permission to bring them from Greece, in 1801. The collection was purchased for £35,000, and thus these sculptures were rescued from destruction, and preserved among our choicest national treasures. To better understand these, the visiter should first examine the two models in the PHIGALIAN SALOON, one the restored, model of the Parthenon, the other a model of the Parthenon after the Venetian bombardment in 1687. The building of the Parthenon is recorded by Plutarch, in his life of Pericles, who also informs us that Phidias was entrusted with the control and superintendence of all the great works undertaken during his administration; and it may reasonably be inferred, that the sculpture which adorned this noble temple, was designed by that great master, and executed by the disciples of his school under his immediate direction. Particular attention should be bestowed on (98) the head of a horse from the car of night, full of vivacity and strength of expression. The red numbers are to facilitate a reference from the Museum synopsis to the marbles, and are those now in use. Two of the most celebrated features of the room are the *Ilyssus* (99), and the *Theseus* (93). The first is the personification of the small stream that ran through Athens, and although mutilated, is the very triumph of art; whilst the other presents a striking effect, from the regularity and precision with which the lineaments of the human form have been transferred to stone. Though more than two thousand years have passed away since the gifted hands which gave them being have crumbled into dust, they are still acknowledged the types of abstract beauty, and artists bow before them as the idols of artistic worship. The Metopes, or groups which adorn the frieze, are remarkably fine, but our limits forbid us dwelling upon them. The other rooms contain the *Xanthian marbles*, brought from the ruined city of Xanthus, and of an earlier date even than those of the Parthenon; the *Bodroum marbles*, brought to England in 1846, from Asia Minor; the *Nimroud marbles*, which we owe to Dr. Layard's recent researches on the site of the ancient Nineveh; and the *Townley Collection*, bequeathed by their collector, Charles Townley. All these have objects of rare and enduring interest; but as a cheap catalogue gives the enumeration of their names—and we could here do little more—we shall employ the space at our disposal for the description of the remaining portions of the Museum.

LIBRARY.—For this purpose a new building on a most magnificent scale, peculiarly adapted for the literary requirements of the age, has just been completed. The building occupies the inner quadrangle of the Museum. The details of the plan were suggested by Mr. Panizzi to the trustees; the plan was approved of, and Mr. Sydney Smirke appointed as the architect of the undertaking. The sum of £61,000 was set apart to defray the cost of the building.

THE READING-ROOM contains ample and comfortable accommodation for 300 readers. Each person has a separate table 4ft. 3in. long. He is screened from the opposite occupant by a longitudinal division, which is fitted with a hinged desk graduated on sloping racks, and a folding shelf for spare books.

The framework of each table is of iron, forming air-distributing channels, which are contrived so that the air may be delivered at the top of the longitudinal screen division, above the level of the heads of the readers, or, if desired, only at each end pedestal of the tables, all the outlets being under the control of valves. A tubular foot-rail also passes from end to end of each table, which may have a current of warm water passed through at pleasure, and be used as a foot-warmer.

The Catalogue tables, with shelves under, and air-distributing tubes between, are ranged in two concentric circles around the central superintendent's inclosure or rostrum, the latter being fitted with tables, ticket boxes, with dwarf partitions surmounted by glass screens, dividing a passage leading to the surrounding libraries. Altogether, the building is remarkable, not only for its immensity, but for the ingenuity displayed in its interior arrangements. It is calculated that the inner library shelves in galleries within the dome-room will contain 80,000 volumes. Two lifts are placed at convenient stations, for the purpose of raising the books to the level of the several gallery floors. The building contains three miles lineal of book-cases, and which in all the cases are eight feet high; assuming them all to be spaced for the averaged octavo book size, the entire ranges form twenty-five miles of shelves; assuming the shelves to be filled with books, of paper of average thickness, the leaves placed edge to edge would extend about 25,000 miles, or more than three times the diameter of the globe. The cost, about £150,000, includes the fittings and furniture.

THE BRITISH MUSEUM is open to the public on Mondays, Wednesdays, and Fridays, between 10 and 4 from the 7th of September to the 4th of May, and between 10 and 7 from the 7th of May to the 1st of September, and daily, except Saturdays, during the weeks of Easter, Whitsuntide, and Christmas.

We are again in the midst of the squares. BLOOMSBURY SQUARE, first laid out by the Earl of Southampton, about 1670, has a fine bronze statue, by Westmacott, of Charles James Fox, erected opposite Bedford Place. The church, with the peculiar steeple seen towering above the surrounding buildings, is the parish church of St. George's, Bloomsbury, built by Nicholas Hawksmoor in 1730. A statue of King George I. crowns the steeple. RUSSELL SQUARE; containing a statue, by Westmacott, of Francis, Duke of Bedford, was built in 1803. In Great Coram Street is the RUSSELL INSTITUTION, founded in 1808 as a lecture-hall and library, and possessing Haydon's celebrated picture of the Retreat of the Ten Thousand, presented in 1836 by the Duke of Bedford. QUEEN'S SQUARE, adjacent, was planted in the reign of Queen Anne, and contains a statue of that Queen. TORRINGTON and WOBURN SQUARES are also great ornaments to the neighbourhood.

In Gower Street is UNIVERSITY COLLEGE HOSPITAL, founded in 1833. The first stone of the north wing was laid by Lord Brougham in 1846. Nearly opposite is the LONDON UNIVERSITY COLLEGE, founded in 1828, and built by Wilkins, the architect of the National Gallery. It is furnished with every professional capability for prosecuting studies in science and the classics, and for the benefit of persons who, by their religious opinions, were precluded from taking degrees in the Universities of Oxford and Cambridge. In 1850, the University had on its books 546 graduates, and 810 matriculated under-graduates. The building extends a length of 420 feet, and has a richly ornamented Corinthian portico, ascended by a flight of steps.

Regent's Park.—Entering the NEW ROAD, and turning to the left, we reach the REGENT'S PARK, consisting of about 400 acres, occupying the site of Old Marylebone Fields. The park and the surrounding crescents were laid out in 1812, from a plan by Nash, and the ornamental plantations, and the broad sweeping avenues that intersect the greensward in all directions, were further improved and extended in 1833 and 1838. Around are terraces of striking architectural magnificence, and the outer road forms an agreeable drive of nearly three miles in length; whilst the enclosure, with its broad and shaded avenues, its smoothly gravelled walks, its soft green turf, its rows of stately trees, its pleasant vistas, and the zone of noble mansions by which it is engirdled, is a rare boon to the pedestrian, and of which the Londoner may well be proud. At the south end of the park is the COLOSSEUM, one of the most popular exhibitions in the metropolis, and built by Decimus Burton in 1824. From the moment the visitor enters the building, until he retires, the scene presented is the most varied and pleasing that can be imagined. The celebrated picture of London (taken from the bell of St. Paul's), and a view of Paris by moonlight, are among the chief attractions, which consist of entertainments and lectures upon the model of the Polytechnic Institution. A little further on, at the north-east corner of the park, is the Gothic structure of St. KATHERINE'S HOSPITAL, built in 1827, and containing a chapel, six residences for pensioners, and a detached residence for the master. It was originally founded near the Tower by Maude of Boulogne, the wife of King Stephen, and for centuries did the lowly turrets of St. Katharine attract the gaze and inspire the prayer of the outward-bound mariner, and through many generations was the top-sail lowered in reverence to its tutelar saint, as the well-manned vessel, laden with the precious freights of early commerce, slowly passed along. But now in St. Katharine's docks the merchant ships of London ride over the spot where the convent once stood, and, transplanted here, it affords to this day a comfortable subsistence to its lay sisters and brethren, at the nomination of the Queen's Consort of England. There are some extensive barracks in Albany Street, at the back of this portion of the Park, under the title of the Horse Guards Barracks.

The Botanic Gardens, covering a space of nearly twenty acres, form an interesting feature of the inner circle. They belong to the Royal Botanical Society, founded in 1839, and in the handsome conservatory frequently attract 2,000 visiters to behold the collection of rare plants exhibited, and the distribution of the medals for prizes. St. JOHN'S LODGE, in the immediate vicinity, is the seat of Sir Isaac Lionel Goldsmid. The mansion overlooks a beautiful lake, overhung by graceful trees, and margined by the garden and archery grounds of the Toxopholite

Society. On the line of the outer road is Holford Villa; and a little to the south of it is the splendid villa of the Marquis of Hertford, built by Decimus Burton. Altogether, the mansions of this district are among the most pleasing of all the architectural creations that serve to increase its picturesque beauty. Their structure is light and elegant, and very different from the brick and mortar monstrosities that line the southern outlets of London. They have all the freshness and quietude of rural retreats, though the wealth and fashion of the metropolis congregate in the same parish; and their gay equipages are constantly whirling along the adjacent road. The south side of the park, parallel to the New Road, is about half a mile in length; the east side, extending northward to Gloucester Gate, is nearly three-quarters of a mile.

The Zoological Gardens, on the north-eastern slope of the REGENT'S PARK, were instituted in 1826, the principal founders being Sir Stamford Raffles and Sir Humphrey Davy. On Mondays the admission is sixpence, on other days one shilling each. There are about 1,500 living specimens, and of these 152 species belong to the mammalia alone; among which, the last attractive feature is the young Hippopotamus, captured in August, 1849, at the island of Obaysch, about 1,350 miles above Cairo, and transmitted to this country as the gift of the Pasha of Egypt, in June 1850. There have been several recent improvements in the gardens, and additions to the buildings. A new entrance has been formed at the termination of the broad walk in the Regent's Park, which saves the foot visiter the trouble of going round by the road. The latest improvement has been the conversion of the building which was formerly occupied by the carnivora, into a Reptile House. This place adjoins the Museum, and externally it is fitted up in the style of a Swiss cottage. It is capacious, and well adapted for the purpose to which it has been devoted by the Society. The collection of reptiles, though not large, is probably greater than in any preceding exhibition of the live animals of this class. There are altogether twenty-one species, and of these the snakes form by far the largest number. Instead of the old plan of enclosing the creatures in a dark box, at the bottom of which they can scarcely be seen curled up, they are placed in large glass cases, in which all their movements can be watched. Branches of trees are introduced into the cases, so that the animals may indulge in their arboreal habits. Here will be seen the Fetish snake of Africa, where it is worshipped by the natives—it weighs 70lbs.; a fine specimen of the rattlesnake, with a young one, born since its arrival in this country; specimens of the puff-adder; and a few of the lizard tribe. There is also a case of green frogs. The tree frog of Europe is peculiarly interesting. Although of a bright green when exposed to the light, these creatures become almost black in the dark. In 1849, the number of visiters was 168,895. The view of Primrose Hill from this part is extremely pleasing, and the hill itself, which is now almost belted with buildings, affords in return a good opportunity for surveying to advantage the western portions of the metropolis.

West and north-west of the park is a picturesque and fashionably inhabited locality, of considerable extent, and called ST. JOHN'S WOOD, from the ground having formerly belonged to the priors of St. John of Jerusalem. The villas are of the first class; and the roads, laid out within the last ten years, are lined with the prettiest ornamental cottages and gardens imaginable. In Hamilton Terrace is ST. MARK'S CHURCH, built in 1847 at a cost of £9,830. ST. JOHN'S WOOD CHAPEL is of little architectural merit; but in the burial-ground adjoining lie not a few whose names are familiar to the ear, and among which we may make mention of JOANNA SOUTHCOTT (d. 1814), whose claims to the character of a prophetess have been long since satisfactorily examined and decided; Richard Brothers (d. 1824), another wild claimant to the inspiration of prophecy; and the clever performer Daniel Terry (*d.* 1829), who, as actor and dramatist, alike merited the favour of the public, and the friendship of Sir Walter Scott.

Lord's Cricket Ground, a famous spot for the gentlemen of the bat and ball, is near the Eyre Arms Tavern, and abutting on the St. John's Wood Road; a great match, frequently recurring through the season, is a sight worth witnessing.

In the rear of this district, stretching away to the very verge of Hyde Park and Bayswater, lies a town, or rather city, of squares, crescents, terraces, and noble streets, comprising stately mansions, and two spacious churches, all built within the last dozen years. The erection of an entire district, Portland New Town, and apparently interminable lines of Grecianized villas, extending from the Edgeware Road, have arisen with almost magical celerity, on what was, till very recently, mere waste and neglected ground. The increased value of this property may be estimated by the fact, that a plot of land which, in the early part of the last century, was let for £12 per year, now produces a rental of £12,000, and the manors of Paddington and Westbourne, which, at the dissolution, produced but a trifling sum, now return to the Bishop of London a rental of £75,000 per annum. Three guineas a foot for building-ground has been frequently paid, when a good situation was wanted by a speculator.

PADDINGTON was, but a few years back, a rural village, with a few old houses on each side of the Edgeware Road, and some rustic taverns of picturesque appearance, screened by high elms, with long troughs for horses, and straggling sign-posts. The green was a complete country retreat, and the group of elms was a study for all the landscape painters in the metropolis. The diagonal path led to the church, then a little Gothic building overspread with ivy, and was completely sequestered as any village church a hundred miles from London. It was pulled down in 1791, and the present one erected in its stead. Nollekens the sculptor, Mrs. Siddons the actress, and W. Collins the marine landscape painter, are buried in the churchyard. There are four new churches recently built in the parish—ST. JAMES'S, ST. JOHN'S, HOLY TRINITY, and ALL SOULS'; and it is now one of the busiest and most thickly populated of the London suburbs. In Praed Street is the terminus of the GREAT WESTERN RAILWAY, opened for short distances in June 1838, and to Bristol in June 1841. The basin of the Paddington Canal is in convenient proximity. The whole of this newly-created district is a wonder of architectural magnificence. All the way westward from Hyde Park Terrace, through Bayswater to Notting Hill, the road is flanked with elegant and massive mansions, and on the western verge of Kensington Gardens is a new thoroughfare to Kensington itself, on which are built several detached villas in the striking Italian style, with ornamental parapets and prospect-towers. The now happily forgotten, but once famous, agent of capital punishment, the "leafless tree" of Tyburn, stood on the spot of ground occupied by No. 49, Connaught Square. The last execution there took place in 1783.

Re-entering the New Road by Lisson Grove, we pass the MARYLEBONE BATHS AND WASH-HOUSES, erected January 1850, adjoining the District County Court. The design is in the Italian style, and the building has a frontage of 160 feet, with a depth of 230 feet. There are 107 separate baths, besides two large swimming baths, with a constant supply of tepid water. The cost was about £20,000, including the freehold site. MARYLEBONE NEW CHURCH, opposite York Gate, one of the entrances to the Regent's Park, was built in 1817, at a cost of £60,000. FITZROY SQUARE, completed 1793, and EUSTON SQUARE, of much later erection, derive their names from the Fitzroys, Dukes of Grafton, and Earls of Euston, who are the ground landlords.

An opening at the northern end leads to the stately terminus of the NORTH WESTERN RAILWAY, which was first opened to Birmingham September 17, 1838. The massive, but elegant, entrance is in the Grecian Doric style of architecture, and is 70 feet high. The great hall, opened in May 1849, is of immense size, and magnificently embellished. It is said to have cost £150,000. On the other side of Euston Square, in the New Road, is ST. PANCRAS NEW CHURCH, finished in 1822, at a cost of £76,680. The exterior is adapted from Greek models, and the entablatures of the side porticoes are supported by Caryatides, holding ewers and inverted torches. The pulpit and reading-desk are formed from the celebrated Fairlop Oak, that was blown down in 1820, after having, for some seven centuries, graced the avenues of Hainault forest. The interior of the church is elegantly constructed, and greater light and elevation are only wanted to render it faultless.

Passing at the back of the church through BURTON CRESCENT, so called after the builder, and entering HUNTER STREET, we may point out the NATIONAL SCOTTISH CHURCH in REGENT SQUARE, originally built for Irving of "unknown tongue" celebrity. It is a large Gothic structure of little architectural merit. Crossing BRUNSWICK SQUARE into Guildford Street, the FOUNDLING HOSPITAL is seen to the left, founded in 1739 by Captain Thomas Coram, as an hospital for poor illegitimate children whose mothers are known, and whose reception is regulated by a committee, who examine whether the case is such as to require the relief afforded by the institution or not. It is a handsome structure, with a good garden and commodious playground for the children. The chapel is in the centre, and the east wing is appropriated to the girls, and the west to the boys. The annual income is averaged at £10,000, and about 460 children are maintained and educated. In the interior are some excellent paintings by Hogarth and others. A visit during Divine service on a Sunday to the chapel, is a great treat to the lovers of sacred music, and the interesting and impressive scene to be there witnessed will not be readily forgotten.

LAMB'S CONDUIT STREET, deriving its name from a conduit that stood in the fields near Holborn, and which was erected, in 1577, at the expense of a benevolent clothworker of that name, will bring us to RED LION STREET, whence retracing our steps through a district already made familiar to the reader, we can regain the point of our departure.

EIGHTH DAY'S ROUTE.

DISTRICT II.

GRAY'S INN LANE—KING'S CROSS—COLDBATH FIELDS—HOUSE OF CORRECTION— SADLER'S WELLS—THE NEW RIVER—PENTONVILLE—MODEL PRISON—CALEDONIAN ASYLUM—COPENHAGEN FIELDS—ISLINGTON—CANONBURY—HIGHBURY —CITY ROAD—OLD STREET ROAD—ST. LUKE'S—BUNHILL ROW—ARTILLERY GROUND—CLERKENWELL, &c. &c.

TAKING again a northerly course, we pursue our way from Holborn up GRAY'S INN LANE, in which stands the ROYAL FREE HOSPITAL, founded in 1828, and affording, as its name implies, immediate assistance to all destitute persons requiring medical relief. From the period of its foundation till 1849, 310,547 persons have been gratuitously relieved, and of these 28,190 belonged to 1849 alone. The road leads to KING'S CROSS, so called from an execrable statue of George IV., that stood there till 1842, and which has also derived the name of Battle Bridge from a sanguinary battle fought at this spot between King Alfred and the Danes. Here is the terminus of the GREAT NORTHERN RAILWAY, for which the site was cleared in 1850. The road, close by, branches off in a north-westerly direction to CAMDEN TOWN and KENTISH TOWN, leading past the old Church of ST. PANCRAS, originally erected in 1180, and repaired and enlarged in 1848. Nearly opposite to the church is a neat and commodious range of residences known as THE MODEL BUILDINGS, and supplying all the conveniences of a metropolitan lodging-house on a better and more economical principle.

For the sake of visiting localities of greater interest, we shall, however, turn aside from Gray's Inn Lane, nearly opposite Theobald's Road, and enter COLDBATH FIELDS, a district long built over, but once famous for a cold spring that still exists in Bath Street. Here is the MIDDLESEX HOUSE OF CORRECTION, opened in 1794. There are 530 cells, and the average number of prisoners daily within the walls, and subject to penal discipline, is 1,000. Workshops on a large scale have been recently added, to furnish employment to the prisoners.

The eastern wall of the House of Correction runs parallel with the Bagnigge Wells Road, where stood Bagnigge Wells, a kind of minor Vauxhall of the day, and existing within the last half century; but of late it has been built over by the Messrs. Cubitt, who have extensive premises at the back, forming quite a little town of itself. In Exmouth Street is the SPA FIELDS CHAPEL, once a theatre, and purchased for its present purpose by the Countess of Huntingdon.

SADLER'S WELL'S THEATRE is in the immediate vicinity, its western side, till very lately, having a fine grove of trees forming an avenue to the St. John Street Road. The name originates from the discovery, in 1683, of a well on this spot, by Mr. Sadler, one of the surveyors of the highways, and who built a Music House to divert the company attracted by the mineral spring. Latterly, having enjoyed the advantages of more creditable management, it has become one of the most favourite establishments in the metropolis. A neighbouring tavern reminds us of our proximity to the NEW RIVER head and reservoir, which, after having originated with the enterprise of Sir Hugh Myddelton, who was ruined by the scheme, now brings a fortune to every shareholder. Its length from Chadwell, in Hertfordshire, where it rises, to this point, where it supplies the greater part of the metropolis on the north side the Thames, is nearly forty miles.

PENTONVILLE, a large district on the north side of the New Road, was unbuilt upon till 1773, when the fields of Mr. Henry Penton were appropriated to receive the increasing population. Of late years it has extended rapidly. Barnsbury Road and Barnsbury Park, a new and daily improving district, derive their names from Lady Juliana Berners, Abbess of St. Albans, who had a large manor in this neighbourhood.

WHITE CONDUIT HOUSE, a once favourite place of entertainment, and much resorted to in the days of Oliver Goldsmith, who was one of its frequent visiters, was demolished in 1849, and a street and a smaller tavern were erected on its grounds. The PENTONVILLE or MODEL PRISON, in the Caledonian Road, was built in 1842 at the cost of £84,169. It occupies about seven acres of ground, and contains 1,000 separate cells, which are well lit, warmed, and ventilated on an improved plan. In 1849, the total number of prisoners was 1,106; the total expenses for the same year £15,675; but from this a deduction is to be made of £2,425, earned by the prisoners, who are either taught useful trades, or pursue their original vocation within its walls. The West India Docks and Birmingham Junction Railway runs close by; and a little further on is the CALEDONIAN ASYLUM, built in 1828, "for the purpose of supporting and educating the children of soldiers, sailors, and marines, natives of Scotland, who have died or been disabled in the service of their country, and of indigent Scotch parents resident in London, not entitled to parochial relief." From Copenhagen Fields opposite, now the site of the great cattle market formerly held in Smithfield, there is a good view of northern London and the country towards Highgate, Hornsey, and Essex.

The New ROAD at "The Angel," the great focus of northern omnibus traffic, merges into the "City Road," which leads past Finsbury Square to the Bank. ISLINGTON, an immense suburb, now grown into part of the metropolis itself, lies to the north, and contains a population of little less than 60,000. In the Liverpool Road is the LONDON FEVER HOSPITAL, removed hither from King's Cross in 1849. The old Church of ST. MARY'S, in the Upper Street, was opened in May, 1754; the steeple is more curious than elegant. ST. PETER'S CHURCH was built by Barry in 1835, at a cost of £3,407. CANONBURY TOWER, 17 feet square, and about 60 feet high, is a vestige of the old Manor-House that arose out of the mansion built by Prior Bolton, of St. Bartholomew's, in Smithfield. Oliver Goldsmith lodged here in 1764, and one of the upper apartments in the tower is yet pointed out as the place where he wrote the "Vicar of Wakefield." Not far from Islington Green, in the Lower Road, is the "QUEEN'S HEAD," a tavern of modern construction, but built upon the site of a very ancient one that existed till 1829. A portion of the old wainscoted parlour still remains; whilst a tankard, with a curious, but not exactly quotable inscription, recounts the bygone celebrities of the place. A walk through HIGHBURY, noticing its picturesque little church, finished in 1848, and past the Sluice-house, and the New River, to Hornsey Wood House, will give the stranger an agreeable idea of the picturesque character of this vast appurtenance to the mammoth city. The New Islington Cattle Market is close to the New North Road.

Returning to the Angel, and proceeding eastward on the CITY ROAD, first opened in 1761, we must pause to notice the Elizabethan Almshouses, founded by Lady Owen in 1610, and recently rebuilt. They stand on the eastern side of St. John Street Road, and furnish habitations for poor old women of the parish of St. Mary, Islington, and St. James's, Clerkenwell, together with a school for poor boys of the same parishes, an equal number from each. Crossing the bridge that spans a branch of the Regent's Canal, we pass the "EAGLE" on our left, a minor, but generally well-conducted house for operatic entertainments, under the title of the "Grecian Saloon," and reach the OLD STREET ROAD, the suburbs of Hoxton and Hackney lying to the north. At the corner is ST. LUKE'S HOSPITAL, for lunatics, instituted in 1751, and built by Dance in 1784. No patient is received here who is known to be in possession of means for decent support in a private asylum. The parish church of ST. LUKE'S, seen further on, is by no means remark-

able for beauty. It was built in 1733. BUNHILL Row should be traversed, for the sake of seeing the large Burial Ground, for nearly two centuries used by the Dissenters as a place of interment. Here is buried, John Bunyan, the well-known author of the "Pilgrim's Progress" (d. 1688); George Fox, the founder of the Society of Friends (d. 1690); Daniel De Foe (d. 1731); Isaac Watts (d. 1748); and Blake (d. 1828), and Stothard (d. 1834), the painters, besides others, who, like those we have recorded, have left a reputation as well as a name behind them. In ARTILLERY WALK adjoining, Milton finished his "Paradise Lost," and here, in 1674, he died.

The ARTILLERY GROUND is now, as it has been for upwards of two centuries, the exercising ground of the Honourable Artillery Company of the City of London, the old City trained band, formed in 1585, to oppose the contemplated Spanish invasion. When the alarm subsided, the City volunteers discontinued their customary exercises, and the grounds were used by the gunners of the Tower. In 1610 a new company was formed, and the weekly exercise rigidly enforced. On the breaking out of the Civil War, they took part against the king; and though previously held in low estimation, and treated merely as "holiday" soldiers, they did good service to the Parliamentary cause, especially at the battle of Newbury. Clarendon is forced to admit that they "behaved themselves to wonder, and were in truth the preservation of that army that day." Cromwell himself acknowledged their value, and gave the command of them to Major-General Skipton. They then numbered 18,000 foot and 600 horse, divided into six regiments of trained bands, six of auxiliaries, and one of horse. Disbanded at the Restoration, a new company was formed, of which Charles II. and his brother the Duke of York became members. Since that period they have led a peaceful life; and, except in 1780, when by their promptness they saved the Bank of England, their appearances in public have been confined to festive occasions. The strength of the Company has gradually fallen off. In 1708, they numbered about 700; in 1720, about 600; and in 1844, only about 250. Prince Albert is their colonel. Now again with rifle volunteer corps forming everywhere under royal and national patronage, this ancient company will probably greatly increase in numerical and effective strength. Our younger readers will remember that Cowper tells us of John Gilpin:—

"A train-band captain eke was he
Of famous London town."

From the Artillery Ground Lunardi made his first balloon ascent in 1784.

Returning to Old Street, and crossing GOSWELL STREET, we pass through a narrow thoroughfare chiefly inhabited by brokers, and called WILDERNESS ROW, whence we may extend our perambulations to CLERKENWELL GREEN, part of a region thickly populated by watch and clock makers. Here is the SESSIONS HOUSE for Middlesex, the building dating from 1782, and near it is the Church of St. James's, Clerkenwell, built on the site of a much older church to the same saint, and originally the choir of a Benedictine nunnery founded about 1100. The present building was begun in 1788, and finished in 1792. In the vaults is preserved the tomb of Prior Weston, the last Prior of the Hospital of St. John of Jerusalem. Here also rest the remains of Bishop Burnet. North of the Green is the Clerkenwell HOUSE OF DETENTION, for receiving prisoners who have not yet had sentence passed upon them. The annual expenditure is said to be nearly £7,000, and the average number of prisoners daily 110. A chapel and school-room are attached to the premises. Hence we may return into St. John Street, and so reach Smithfield; or, by permeating the uninviting thoroughfares at the back of Saffron Hill and Hatton Garden, return by way of Holborn. Should the latter, for the sake of novelty, be chosen, the visiter will be able to gather some insight into that colony, which, for the last century, has been the chosen refuge of the lower class of emigrants, and the favourite haunt of those vagrant Savoyards who gain a precarious subsistence by grinding barrel-organs through the metropolis, from sunrise till sundown. Here, too, live the greater part of the image-venders and modellers, the sellers of cheap earthenware and Birmingham goods, the dealers in broken clocks and umbrellas, and specimens of those indescribable traders about the pavement who live by the sale of fruit or fish according to the season. This portion, indeed, is the focus of those scattered rays of itinerant life that penetrate at various periods of the day into every portion of the streets of London, giving a distinct character to its thoroughfares, and colouring, as it were, the stream of daily traffic with the motley hues of metropolitan vagabondism. As such it may, with proper precautions that suggest themselves, form with advantage one of the places visited by the stranger in London.

PART V.——THE SOUTH.

LONDON BRIDGE—THE BOROUGH—ST. SAVIOUR'S CHURCH—ST. OLAVE'S—RAILWAY STATIONS—ST. THOMAS'S HOSPITAL—GUY'S HOSPITAL—BERMONDSEY—OLD INNS—ST. GEORGE THE MARTYR—THE MINT—PRISONS—NEWINGTON CAUSEWAY—SURREY ZOOLOGICAL GARDENS—LONDON ROAD—THE BLIND SCHOOL—ST. GEORGE'S CATHEDRAL—BETHLEHEM HOSPITAL—BLACKFRIARS' ROAD—WATERLOO ROAD—KENNINGTON ROAD—VAUXHALL GARDENS—OLD LAMBETH CHURCH—LAMBETH PALACE—THE LOLLARD'S TOWER—ASTLEY'S THEATRE—STAMFORD-STREET—BANKSIDE—BARCLAY'S BREWERY—BOROUGH MARKET—CONCLUSION.

CROSSING London Bridge we now enter the BOROUGH OF SOUTHWARK, one of the most animated parts of the metropolis, from the extent of the business carried on in this extensive locality, and one of the most interesting from its antiquity. On the right is the old Church of ST. SAVIOUR'S, erected on the site of the ancient priory of St. Mary Overy, and first made the parochial church in 1540. The choir, restored in 1822, and the beautiful Ladye Chapel, renovated in 1832, form the oldest portions of the present structure. Here is a monument to Gower the poet, and contemporary of Chaucer; it was restored by the Duke of Sutherland, a descendant of the Gower family, in 1832. These fathers of English poetry followed each other closely to the grave; Chaucer died in 1400, aged 72, and Gower in 1402, blind and full of years. John Fletcher and Philip Massinger the dramatists are also interred here, but without inscriptions. On the opposite side is the Church of St. Olave's, which, by a corruption of names sufficient to puzzle a phonetic philosopher, gave the appellation of Tooley Street to the long straggling thoroughfare that hence leads to Bermondsey, Horsleydown, and the river-side districts.

The spacious terminus of the SOUTH EASTERN, LONDON AND BRIGHTON, GREENWICH, NORTH KENT, and CROYDON Railways, that all converge at this point, is seen at the end of a broad turning that leads from the main road up to the respective stations. The premises are not without some pretensions to ornament; but, what is still better, their arrangements are admirably made to give the greatest possible accommodation to the public without the slightest approach to confusion. The various additions to the original structure have been made from time to time as the increase in the traffic of the respective lines called for their extension, and beneath are spacious vaults under the arches for the stowage of heavy goods.

Close to this cluster of railway stations is ST. THOMAS'S HOSPITAL, originally founded as an Almonry, in 1213, by the Prior of Bermondsey, and opened as an hospital in 1552. The present edifice, which, since the date of its erection in 1706, has been frequently altered and repaired, consists of three courts, with colonnades between each, and containing 20 wards and 485 beds. The annual expenditure is about £15,000. To show the immense extent of the benefits conferred by these noble charities, we may mention that in 1849 there were admitted, cured, and discharged 4,737 in-patients, and 59,109 out-patients, including casualties, whilst many have been relieved with money and necessaries at their departure, to accommodate and support them in their journeys to their several habitations. In the middle of one of the courts is a bronze statue, by Scheemaker, of Edward VI.; and in another is a statue of Sir Robert Clayton, a Lord Mayor of London who gave a considerable amount towards its endowment. The statue was erected before his death, which happened in 1714.

In St. Thomas's Street, on the right hand side, is GUY'S HOSPITAL, founded by Thomas Guy, a benevolent bookseller in Lombard Street, who, by various successes in trade and speculation, succeeded at last in amassing a considerable fortune. He made liberal gifts to St. Thomas's during his lifetime, and also founded an almshouse, afterwards endowed by his will, for fourteen poor people at Tamworth, his mother's native town, which he represented in several parliaments. He left annuities to his older relatives, amounting to £870 a-year; and to the younger, extending to grandchildren of his uncles and aunts, he left stock in the funds, mostly in sums of £1,000 each, to the extent of more than £74,000, besides bequeathing land. To Christ's Hospital he gave a perpetual annuity of £400, to receive, on the nomination of his trustees, four children yearly, who must be his connexions, and there are always applicants. He left £1,000 to discharge poor prisoners in London, Middlesex, and Surrey, at £5 each; and another £1,000 to be distributed among poor housekeepers at the discretion of his executors. The erection of the hospital, the earliest part of which was built by Dance, cost nearly £19,000, and the rest of his personal property, about £219,000, was devoted to the endowment of his hospital. Though seventy-six when it was commenced, the humane founder lived to see the hospital ready to receive its patients, the first sixty of whom entered in January 1725. Guy's Hospital now occupies a site of five acres and a half. Against the stone front of the building, on entering, are the emblematic figures of Æsculapius and Hygeia. In the west wing is the chapel, and opposite, in the east wing, which is the older, is the court-room; in the former was buried Sir Astley Cooper, the eminent surgeon, who died in 1841. In the centre of the first court is the statue of the founder, in bronze, executed by Scheemaker; and in the chapel is a fine piece of sculpture by the elder Bacon, representing Guy in his livery gown holding out one hand to raise a poor invalid lying on the earth, and pointing with the other to a distressed object carried on a litter into the hospital, which is seen in the background. This cost £1,000. The buildings, which are airy and well suited to promote recovery, contain about 530 beds for in-patients, and there are 50,000 out-patients relieved annually, nine-tenths of whom are on the average cured. Eastward, towards Bermondsey, is a poverty-stricken region called the Maze, and a Roman Catholic Chapel and Convent, where the ceremony of taking the veil may be occasionally witnessed. ST. PAUL'S CHURCH, in that district, was finished in 1841.

The old inns in the Borough, with their wide, rambling staircases, and wooden galleries round the inn-yards, are pleasant reminiscences of the ancient days of coach and waggon traffic, and must not escape observation. Many of these have had an existence for centuries, and we have little occasion to remind the reader of Chaucer, that the TALBOT (No. 75) in High Street, was the Tabard "where Geoffrey Chaucer, knight, and nine-and-twenty pilgrims, lodged on their journey to Canterbury, in 1383." The sign was changed from the "Tabard," which signifies the sleeveless coat worn by the heralds, to the "Talbot," in 1677, when a great portion of the present building was erected.

A little further on, at the corner of Great Dover Street and Blackman Street, is the parochial church of ST. GEORGE THE MARTYR, built in 1737, on the site of an older one. Over the altar is a painted window, representing our Saviour preaching in the Temple. Here are entombed the remains of Edward Cocker, the author of the once famous, often-mentioned, and yet seldom-seen school-book, "Cocker's Arithmetic." It is curious that no map of this parish is known to exist; a fact not more strange and discreditable than that a resolution was passed at a vestry-meeting, held in 1776, "to sell to Mr. Samuel Carter all the parish papers and documents in a lump, at the rate of three-halfpence per pound, he being at the expense of carrying them away." Kent Street, at the back, so called from its having formed the great road to the county of Kent, is a wretched and profligate part of the Borough. In 1633, it was described as "very long and very ill-built, and inhabited chiefly by broommen and mumpers," and its present character would, if described, be found even more disreputable. On the site of a distillery opposite St. George's Church, was the palace of Charles Brandon, Duke of Suffolk, the husband of Mary, sister of Henry VIII., and widow of Louis XII. In 1545, this princely edifice was converted by Henry VIII. into a Royal Mint, subsequently taken down, and replaced by a number of mean and irregular dwellings. In 1697, the number of houses was 92; in 1830, they amounted to 1,712. Even as early as the time of Edward VI., the Mint had become an asylum for debtors, felons, rogues, and vagabonds of every description, and it was only partially put down by Act of Parliament, at the latter end of the reign of George I. Here were the cheap lodging-houses of the Borough. On an average, each house in winter sheltered 70 persons, and in summer about 30. The usual charge to each person was threepence for the 24 hours. No stranger should trust himself in this locality without an efficient protection, the utmost vigilance of the police being found insufficient to repress the acts of violence and robbery still perpetrated occasionally within its precincts, notwithstanding the improvements which have been made of late years even in this locality.

On the left, reached either through Trinity Square or by the Lane itself, is HORSEMONGER LANE JAIL, the place of imprisonment and execution for the county of Surrey. On the right, at the corner of the Borough Road, is the QUEEN'S BENCH PRISON, the sombre walls of which, fifty feet high, with the *chevaux de frize* at the top, look grimly down upon the busy thoroughfare beneath. This is a prison of great antiquity, and, for some years past, has been used exclusively for debtors. There are nearly 250 distinct rooms within, and, since the Fleet and the Marshalsea have been abolished, the vacancies have been very rare. It is here that tradition asserts Prince Henry, afterwards Henry V., was sent by the independent Judge Gascoigne, for striking him on the bench. In the Borough Road is the BRITISH AND FOREIGN SCHOOL, and the SOUTHWARK LITERARY INSTITUTION.

Resuming our progress, we arrive at the well-known tavern, called the ELEPHANT AND CASTLE, whence omnibuses are constantly arriving from, and departing to, all parts of the metropolis and its environs. The quaint old pile opposite is "The Fishmongers' Almshouses," built about 1633; latterly the company have determined on a removal of their hospital to a more open and airy site at East Hill, Wandsworth, where the first stone of a new asylum was laid in June, 1849. The New Kent Road leads to Deptford and Greenwich;

the Wallworth Road to Camberwell, and the south-westward over Kennington Common to Brixton and Clapham. In Penton Place is the entrance to the SURREY GARDENS and MUSIC HALL, which occupies the site formerly known as the Surrey Zoological Gardens. They were opened for concerts and other entertainments by a company, which not proving successful, they have only been temporarily occupied for a variety of *alfresco* entertainments. The celebrated Spurgeon lately preached in this hall to a congregation often amounting to 10,000; and he has now erected a handsome and commodious Tabernacle on the vacant space opposite the Elephant and Castle. This building, one of the largest and most imposing in the metropolis, has cost nearly £30,000, which large amount has been subscribed by the Baptist preacher's zealous and liberal friends. Seats for 3,000 persons, and standing room for 1,000 more are provided, and such an immense congregation is not unfrequently collected to hear the Rev. Mr. Spurgeon in his new chapel-temple.

Returning by the LONDON ROAD, we may notice at the end some workshops, that till recently formed part of the establishment of the PHILANTHROPIC SOCIETY, instituted in 1788 for the reformation of youthful offenders by religious and industrial training. Until the year 1850, this was the place where the operations of the Society were carried on; but the institution is now removed to Red Hill, near Reigate, and the manufactory is transformed into a farm. The farm consists of 133 acres, and has been taken on a lease of 150 years. The number of boys at school generally averages about 100, and they are all destined for emigrants to the British Colonies. Immediately adjacent is the school for the education of the INDIGENT BLIND, founded in 1799. On any day except Saturdays and Sundays, the inmates may be seen at work between 10 and 12 A.M., and 2 and 5 P.M. There are about seventy inmates, who are taught to make baskets, cradles, clothes, boots, shoes, mats, and various other articles, which are sold at the school. The present spacious Gothic structure was built in 1837, and is admirably adapted to its purpose.

In the last century St. George's Fields, the site of these palaces of philanthropy, was the scene of low dissipation; and here, on the very focus of the "No Popery" riots of 1780, has arisen the ROMAN CATHOLIC CATHEDRAL. This singular evidence of the mutations to which localities are subject, and striking proof of our advance in liberality of opinion, occupies a large plot of ground at the corner of the Lambeth Road, and nearly facing the eastern wing of Bethlehem Hospital. The building was commenced in 1840, from the designs of Pugin, and was consecrated with great pomp and ceremony on Tuesday, the 4th of July, 1848. The cathedral is dedicated to St. George, and is in the later decorated style. It is cruciform in plan, and consists of a nave and aisles, the tower, a chancel, and two chapels; one is dedicated in honour of the Holy Sacrament, and the other in honour of the Virgin, and between them is the high altar. The body of the church is allotted to the laity, and is calculated to seat about 3,000 persons. The principal entrance is in the great tower, intended to be carried up to the height of 320 feet, and over the deeply-moulded doorway is a brilliantly painted window, representing St. George, St. Michael, and other saints. The arch which opens to the nave is 40 feet high. The cross, an original work of the fifteenth century, was purchased in Belgium, and, restored, forms one of the finest examples existing, quite equal to that of Louvain, and probably executed by the same artist. The range of monastic buildings adjoining, includes a convent for Sisters of Mercy, and a school for 300 children. The expenditure has hitherto been £40,000, but when finished according to the designs, will be nearly £100,000.

Bethlehem Hospital, a noble institution, designed for the reception of those who are suffering from that most awful of human maladies, mental aberration, covers a surface of fourteen acres, and presents a fine exterior, consisting of a centre and two wings about 700 feet in length. Old "Bedlam," in

Moorfields, having been taken down in 1814, the present structure was raised in St. George's Fields, and finished soon after, on the site of a notorious tavern, called "The Dog and Duck." A new wing was added in 1839, and since then other portions of the premises have been considerably enlarged. The annual expenses reach nearly £20,000. In the vestibule are the two statues of Raving and Melancholy Madness, which were sculptured by Caius Cibber, and formerly surmounted the hospital in Moorfields. One is said to represent the tall porter of Oliver Cromwell, who was a lunatic at the time. On entering the grand hall, the eye of the visitor is first attracted by the spacious staircase, which ascends from the ground floor to the council-chamber above. On each side, passages run laterally through the building, the one to the right leading to the male, the other to the female ward. Following the former, we are inducted through a long series of galleries, ascended by stone staircases, to the apartments occupied by the patients. The sleeping-rooms contain a low truckle bedstead, with chair and table, light and air being admitted through a small barred circular window at the top. Each door opens to the gallery, affording a promenade 250 feet in length, where the patients can resort for exercise when the weather proves unfavourable. To the left of the gallery is the dining-room, capable of accommodating about 100 persons. The diet, which is of the best kind, is served on wooden bowls and platters, and is seldom unaccompanied by good appetites. These corridors are preserved at an equable temperature through every change of season, by the introduction of warm air-pipes and stoves beneath the flooring, so constructed that every patient's room has an equal degree of warmth. Each story has one of these galleries connected with it, from the last of which a stone staircase conducts to the chapel, a spacious but neat apartment, well adapted to the solemn purpose for which it has been consecrated. A curtain separates the male and female auditors, the former occupying the left, the latter the right benches, whilst the pulpit is arranged so as to give the minister a commanding view of his congregation. Not only is strict decorum here observed, but the most marked attention is paid to the preacher's exhortations, and the responses are followed with apparent heartfelt and unaffected devotion. Descending from the chapel, we partly retrace our steps, and arrive at the playground, a large open space appropriated to the recreation and exercise of the patients, where they may be seen pursuing, with considerable eagerness, the different pastimes in which their fancy leads them to indulge. There are four of these arenas appropriated to recreation, and there is evidence constantly afforded that this exercise not only conduces to their immediate health, but also to their ultimate recovery. The kitchen is a large apartment, fitted up with huge boilers, a large steam apparatus, and every accessory to the culinary art. As the authorities of the Institution grind their own corn, make their own bread, and brew their own beer, it may be readily surmised enough occupation is given to the assistants in those departments. Ascending to the council-chamber, a magnificent apartment adorned with the arms and bequests of every donor to the hospital, together with an excellent portrait of its founder, Henry VIII., by Holbein, we are conducted to the female ward, which is in nearly every respect similar to the one just described. The workshops are in another portion of the building, where those patients who, from their previous employment, are qualified for their task, may be seen working at their respective trades. A library is also at the disposal of those who may feel inclined to read and study. The freedom of ventilation, and the establishment of baths accessible to all, must not be forgotten as highly deserving commendation with the other arrangements. A proof of the general health and longevity enjoyed by the inmates may be found in the fact, that

Margaret Nicholson, who was confined in the hospital for attempting to stab George III., died here in 1828, after an imprisonment of forty-two years; and James Hatfield, who was confined for a similar offence in 1800, only died as recently as 1841. During the year 1849, there were admitted 150 males, and 194 females; discharged cured, 70 males, and 106 females. By an order from one of the Governors, visiters can be admitted on Tuesdays, Wednesdays, Thursdays, and Fridays. The ratio of cures is said to be fifty-nine in every hundred. The general aspect of the patients is that of extreme contentment, excepting, of course, those labouring under particular delusions. Not the slightest restriction is visible throughout, and there are but few whose demeanour is violent enough to require more rigid measures. Kindness is the only charm by which the attendants exert a mastery over the patients, and the influence thus possessed is most remarkable. Whilst the impression left on the mind of a visiter is that of a mournful gratification, it is yet blended with a feeling of intense satisfaction, arising from a knowledge that the comforts of his afflicted fellow-creatures are so industriously sought after, and so assiduously promoted.

At the junction of the London Road with the Blackfriars Road, is an obelisk, standing in the centre of the open ground whence six roads branch off in different directions. It is now considered merely as the indicator of various distances, for few seem to recollect that it was placed there in 1771, to commemorate the independent and patriotic spirit with which Brass Crosby, Esq., then Lord Mayor, released a printer who had been seized, contrary to law, by the House of Commons, and for committing the messenger of the House to prison, though, for this last daring achievement, he was himself incarcerated in the Tower. Nearly at the corner of the Blackfriars Road is the SURVEY THEATRE, originally opened in 1782 as a Circus, by Messrs. Hughes and Dibdin, who conducted it for some time with considerable success, as an exhibition of ballets, pantomimes, and horsemanship. It was burned down in 1805, and being rebuilt the following year, has, subsequently, proved one of the most attractive of the minor theatres. In 1848, it was considerably improved, being re-embellished, and nearly rebuilt. A short distance from it, in the Blackfriars Road, is the MAGDALEN HOSPITAL, established in 1758 for the relief and reformation of those unfortunate females, who, having strayed from the paths of virtue, and become outcasts from society, may here find a refuge and a home. Since the period of its existence, more than 6,000 poor girls who were admitted, have been restored to their friends, or placed in reputable employments. The committee meet every Thursday to receive applicants, and Divine service is performed at the chapel twice every Sunday. Few will be deterred from attendance on this last occasion, by hearing that a collection is made previously to admission, for supporting this excellent institution, and for which a small donation is expected from the visiter. The powerful and deeply interesting effect, produced by the combination of female voices— those of the Magdalens themselves— will leave an impression of the choral service not easily to be forgotten. Lower down, on the opposite side of the road, is the octagon building known as ROWLAND HILL'S CHAPEL, originally erected in 1784.

The Waterloo Road, leading to Waterloo Bridge, is a broad, but ill-built thoroughfare, much better than it used to be, but still susceptible of vast improvement. About half-way down, on the eastern side, is the VICTORIA THEATRE, a cheap place of minor dramatic entertainment, and opened as the Coburg Theatre in 1818. On the same side the way, and nearer the bridge, is ST. JOHN'S CHURCH, built in 1824. Within the narrow limits of the churchyard lie several of the sons of Thespis, who have furnished in their lifetime many mirthful hours to the public. Opposite, are the vast premises forming the London TERMINUS of the SOUTH WESTERN RAILWAY. The extension from Vauxhall to the Waterloo Road was thrown open July 11, 1848. The advantages of this metropolitan station have been very great, both to mere pleasure-seekers and men of business; and when about to undertake a journey on this most tempting and trustworthy of all the railways, it is felt to be something akin to magic, to be wafted from the very heart of London to the verge of Southampton Water, in less time than one could walk from here to Hampstead; or, enabled to enjoy the enchanting scenery of Richmond and Hampton Court for an expenditure of the same sum that would be absorbed in the most moderate indulgence at a gloomy tavern in town.

The Westminster Road, leading to Westminster Bridge, has at the angle of junction with the Kennington Road the FEMALE ORPHAN ASYLUM, an excellent institution for the reception of destitute female orphans. It was founded in 1758, and incorporated in 1800. From its foundation to the present time nearly 3,000 orphan girls have been sheltered, educated, and fitted for domestic employment. No girl is admitted under eight or above ten years of age, and none remain after they have attained the age of sixteen. The asylum, which contains about 160 inmates, is open to visitors, by special order, on Tuesdays, Wednesdays, and Fridays, between the hours of 11 and 2 P.M. Adjoining is a chapel, where Divine service is performed every Sunday.

The Kennington Road, leading to Kennington Common and the southern suburbs, is a spacious well-inhabited thoroughfare, with some neat squares and terraces adjoining. In Kennington Lane is the LICENSED VICTUALLERS' SCHOOL, and further on is the principal entrance to VAUXHALL GARDENS, a favourite place of summer resort, from the reign of Charles II. to that of Victoria. They were first opened for public amusement by Jonathan Tyers, in June, 1732, and their long career of 127 years was brought to a close only in 1859, when they were sold for building purposes.

From Bethlehem Hospital the road leads direct through Church Street to old Lambeth Church and Palace. To the left are some narrow streets, now traversed by the viaduct of the South Western Railway, and worth looking at as vestiges of the old river side habitations. They are now, for the most part, tenanted by soap-boilers, whitening manufacturers, and the proprietors of bone factories and potteries; the dense smoke vomited forth from the tall chimneys, and the noisome odours resulting from the various processes carried on, by no means contributing to increase the salubrity of the locality.

The old parish church of ST. MARY'S adjoins the Palace. The tower, built about the reign of Edward IV. (1375), has been lately restored, and other necessary repairs made, from time to time, to ensure the safety of the structure, have materially effaced the outward indications of antiquity it once possessed. Beneath these walls Mary d'Este, the Queen of James II., flying with her infant prince from the ruin impending over their House, after crossing the Thames from the abdicated Whitehall, took shelter from the inclement weather of the night of December 6th, 1688. Here she waited with aggravated misery till a common coach, procured from an adjacent inn, arrived, and conveyed her to Gravesend, whence she bade an eternal adieu to these kingdoms. The interior has no especial feature requiring notice, beyond the painting in the south-east window, which represents the full-length figure of a pedlar with his pack, staff, and dog. A pleasant tradition, repeated so often that it has come at last to be believed, relates how the parish received from this illustrious unknown, the bequest of a piece of ground, on condition that the portrait of himself and dog was preserved in one of the church windows; and, to favour its probability, the painting is jealously perpetuated, and to a recent date the Belvidere Road, as it is now called, went by the appellation of "Pedlar's Acre." A walk through the churchyard, that thickly-tenanted sepulchre of past generations, will, however, repay the observer for half an hour's meditation among the tombs. Most conspicuous amongst them is the altar-tomb of old John Tradescant, the indefatigable collector of curiosities who, with his son, rests beneath a monument somewhat incongruously embellished with pyramids, palms, death's-heads, and pelicans. He is the first person who ever formed a cabinet of curiosities in this kingdom, and is said to have been at one part of his life gardener to Charles I. We are indebted to him for the introduction into this country of many valuable fruits and flowers indigenous to the East. At his death, in 1652, his collection fell as a legacy into the possession of Elias Ashmole, who removed it afterwards to Oxford, where it is still preserved in the Ashmolean Museum. The monument, that had suffered considerably from time, was repaired in 1773, and then an inscription was added, which is too quaint and characteristic to be passed over by the student in this kind of literature. A marble slab near the vestry door, perpetuates the memory of Elias Ashmole himself. In this place also, rest the remains of Archbishops Denison, Bancroft, Hutton, and Secker, without any other remarkable monument than their good works to preserve their memory from oblivion.

Lambeth Palace has been, from a very early period, the London residence of the Archbishops of Canterbury. Close to the church is the picturesque gatehouse of red brick, built in 1500. The hall to which it leads is a spacious structure, 93 feet by 38, and was built by Archbishop Juxon, whose arms are over the door, with the date of 1663. The chapel is the oldest portion of the palace, and was built by Boniface, Archbishop of Canterbury, in 1224. The library now contains about 25,000 volumes, and was founded by Archbishop Bancroft, who died in 1610, and left all his books to his successors for ever. It has since been considerably enriched and enlarged. Here are some scarce works of ancient date, and some rare old volumes of divinity. But by far the best known, and most interesting portion of Lambeth Palace, is the LOLLARD'S TOWER at the western end, which is pointed out to later ages as the very prison in which the persecuted followers of Wickliffe were incarcerated. This tower, so fraught with the associations of history and the tales of legendary lore, was built, for £280, by Henry Chicheley, who enjoyed the primacy from 1414 to 1443. A niche, in which was once placed the image of St. Thomas, may be noticed in the front facing the river. At the summit is a small room, 13 feet by 12, and about 8 feet in height. This is called "the prison," and on the oak wainscoting, which is above an inch thick, several broken sentences and names, in curious antique characters, are inscribed. Here you read a mere record of a name, such as "Chessam Doctor," and there a prayer, more earnest in its appeal to our sympathies, such as "Jhs cyppe me out of alle el compane, amen" (Jesus keep me out of all evil company); together with the plainer memorials of "John Worth," and others. Eight large iron rings in the wall, to which the prisoners were chained before they were brought to the stake, attest the nature of the apartment, and the cruelties that were practised within it. The gardens at the back, thirty acres in extent, are laid out with great taste, and the tall old trees materially contribute to the picturesque effect of the building, as seen from the river.

Through BISHOP'S WALK, whence across the river an excellent view can be gained of the New Houses of Parliament, and Stangate, a famous spot for boat-builders, we come to the WESTMINSTER BRIDGE ROAD, at the commencement of which is ASTLEY'S AMPHITHEATRE. In 1774, Philip Astley, who is said to have enjoyed the enviable privilege of being the handsomest man in England, erected a booth on this spot for horsemanship and other amusements in the open air. The success of this enabled him to build a theatre, which was thrice destroyed by fire, and thrice rebuilt. The last fire took place in 1841, when the excellent management of Ducrow had raised the establishment to a high rank among its contemporaries; and since then a new theatre has been constructed on a larger scale. The present one will hold about 3,000 spectators, and the arena for the equestrians is 126 feet in circumference. The performances are varied, and generally well sustained.

Crossing the old district of Pedlar's Acre, and proceeding down the Belvidere Road, we shall have an excellent opportunity of noticing the extent of the artificial elevation given to the road when the approaches to Waterloo Bridge were made. Indeed, it hardly needs the occasional incursions of the river to remind the water-side inhabitants, that this now dense and widely-spreading region was once a marsh, and even within the recollection of many living, a flat swampy level, scarcely raised above the surface of the Thames. The great timber yards about here are well worthy a visit, and seem in their colossal piles to threaten exhaustion to the forests of Norway and Sweden.

Stamford Street, or the Commercial Road, leading by the water-side, will bring us to the Blackfriars Road.

CHRIST CHURCH, built in 1737, stands partly on the site of Paris Garden, one of the ancient playhouses of the metropolis. It seems to have been much frequented on Sundays for bearbaiting, a favourite sport in the time of Queen Elizabeth. Continuing our way along the BANKSIDE, once the scene of our ancestors' dissipation and debauchery, but now chiefly frequented by bargemen and those connected with the smaller river craft, we come to BARCLAY AND PERKINS' BREWERY, so associated all over the world with the celebrity of London porter. On part of the ground occupied by the adjacent premises, stood the GLOBE THEATRE, built 1594, and demolished 1644, and here many of Shakspere's plays were originally produced. The buildings belonging to the Brewery, which is the largest in the world, extend over ten acres. It was founded by Thrale, Dr. Johnson's friend, and sold by the executors of Mrs. Thrale for £135,000. Among the host of curiosities to be seen in London, this mammoth establishment is one of the most characteristic and interesting, and should be visited by all who can obtain the necessary introduction. The quantity of malt consumed here, in 1849, was 115,542 quarters; and in the busy season of the year there are about 600 quarters of malt brewed daily. Among the many vats to be seen is one containing 3,500 barrels of porter, which, at the selling price, would yield £9,000. There are 180 horses employed in the cartage department, which are a show of themselves. They are brought principally from Flanders, and cost £50 to £80 each. There are annually consumed by these horses 5,000 qrs. of oats, beans, or other grain, which is bruised; 450 tons of clover, and 170 tons of straw for litter. The manure, spent hops, and other refuse, are let yearly, and the sum paid for 1850 was £75. The lessee employs the railway company to take it from the premises to his farm. On an average, there are weekly 18 tons of stable manure, and 37 tons of refuse, chiefly spent hops, which is about 1s. 7d. per ton for the manure, and all the rest for nothing. There are now four partners in the house, who conduct every department of it in the most liberal manner, as may be judged when we state that they pay their head brewer a salary of £1,000 per year. In the by-streets between here and London Bridge, some of the walls of WINCHESTER HOUSE, the ancient palace of the Bishops of Winchester, are still visible; and the CLINK, a prison by the Bankside, of the time of James I., still perpetuates its name in one of the adjacent thoroughfares.

Hence we cross by the Borough Market back to London Bridge, and so, having effected a complete circuit of the southern portion of the metropolis, return to the point from which we originally started.

And here the Guide resigns his companionship, trusting, within that space to which he was restricted, he has succeeded in making the task assigned as agreeable to others as it has been congenial to himself. Before, however, finally relinquishing his office, he would again earnestly impress upon the stranger the necessity of once during his stay at least going to Waterloo Bridge of a clear morning to see the metropolis by sunrise. Then will he truly feel with Wordsworth:—

" Earth has not any thing to show more fair;
  Dull would he be of soul who could pass by
  A sight so touching in its majesty;
  This city now doth like a garment wear
  The beauty of the morning; silent, bare,
  Ships, towers, domes, theatres, and temples lie,
  Open unto the fields and to the sky,
  All bright and glittering in the smokeless air.
  Never did sun more beautifully steep
  In his first splendour valley, rock, or hill;
  Ne'er saw I—never felt—a calm so deep,
  The river glideth at its own sweet will
  Dear God! the very houses seem asleep,
  And all that mighty heart is lying still."

THE TOUR OF THE THAMES.

A COMPLETE STEAMBOAT COMPANION FOR SUMMER EXCURSIONS,
HAMPTON COURT TO THE NORE.

PART I.

UP THE RIVER—FROM LONDON BRIDGE TO HAMPTON COURT, ETC.

London Bridge.—From the rude wooden structure, with turrets and roofed bulwarks, that was swept away by the river in 1091, to the present substantial erection, of which the foundation stone was laid in 1825, there is a complete series of events associated with this spot, which would furnish an inexhaustible mine for the materials of history and romance. Peter, curate of St. Mary Colechurch, whose bones were found beneath the masonry of the chapel in 1832, built the first London Bridge of stone in 1209. The traitors' heads that were stuck about its battlements, the lines of houses that overhung the sides, and were taken down in 1757, the successive calamities of siege, and fire, and flood that beset it during its existence of six centuries, all invest the site of these reminiscences with a stirring and enduring interest.

The present bridge was thrown open in 1831, having cost, with its approaches, nearly a million and a half of money. It is about 100 feet higher up the river than the old one. There are five arches, the centre one being the largest of the kind ever attempted: the span is 152 feet 6 inches. The roadway is 52 feet in width. Contiguous to the bridge are the steamboat piers, that contribute largely to the animated scene this portion of the river always presents. On the Surrey side of the Thames, in the vast area now occupied by Barclay and Perkins's Brewery, was the site of the Globe Theatre, so suggestive of the days of Shakspere and his contemporaries.

Southwark Bridge was commenced in 1814, and completed in 1819. The iron used in its construction was cast at Rotherham, in Yorkshire. It is 700 feet in length, 42 in width, 53 in height, and has three arches, of which the centre has a span of 240 feet. About here may be seen the steam-dredging engines, which maintain the depth of the river, and free it from obstructions. They consist of iron frames, with buckets and cutters, made so as to scoop the bed of the river.

Blackfriars Bridge, which is the next reached, has had its architectural beauty somewhat spoiled by the removal of the balustrades, and the substitution of a plain parapet. The recent repairs cost upwards of £300,000. It was finished in 1770; is 1,000 feet in length, 42 in width, 62 in height, and has nine arches, the centre having a span of 100 feet. There is a fine view here of St. Paul's. The site of the ancient sanctuary of Whitefriars, the "Alsatia" of James I., is marked out by the huge gasometer of the City Gas Works, seen just above. The Temple Gardens, wherein the roses were plucked that served for the emblems of the York and Lancaster wars, are next observed: the roses have ceased to bloom; but the gardens have been celebrated of late years for the most extensive show of choice varieties of the chrysanthemum. The elegant new Library, in the Gothic style, of the Middle Temple, and SOMERSET HOUSE, with its fine balustraded terrace, next claims our notice.

Waterloo Bridge was commenced in 1809, and opened with great state in 1817, on the anniversary of the battle from which it takes its name. A million of money was expended in this structure, which Canova has pronounced the finest in the world. It has nine arches, each of 120 feet span, and is altogether 1,326 feet in length. Buckingham Gate, by the Adelphi Terrace, is the last vestige of the stately mansion of the Duke of Buckingham, and was the work of Inigo Jones.

Hungerford Suspension Bridge, by Brunel, is a marvel of modern mechanical ingenuity. Its centre span, alone is nearly 100 feet greater than the entire of the Menai Bridge. The weight of iron is 700,000 tons. This is the great central focus of the passenger traffic of the Thames. Passing the mansions in Whitehall Gardens, among which that of the late Sir Robert Peel is prominently distinguishable, we next pass under the arches of

Westminster Bridge.—This bridge was built in 1750. The whole superstructure, and much of the piers, are now pulled down, and a wooden gallery on tall piles is provided for foot passengers, whilst the completed portion of the iron bridge alongside is used for heavy traffic. Passing under the arches, the steamboat traveller should turn and view the new half of the iron structure.

The New Houses of Parliament here present a bold frontage to the river, upwards of 800 feet in length, and are decked with a rich display of architectural embellishments. This parliamentary palace covers an area of nine acres, and has eleven open courts. The Victoria Tower attains a height of 400 feet, and other towers of less magnitude crown other portions of the building. The interior is redundant with sculptures, paintings, and other decorative embellishments. On the opposite side of the river is

Lambeth Palace, the town residence of the Archbishops of Canterbury. The tower next to the chapel is still known as the Lollard's Tower, and there are large iron rings to which those unfortunate persons were manacled still exhibited on the walls. Adjoining is the old parish church of Lambeth, with a tower, lately repaired, of the time of Edward IV., and some curious tombs, for the lovers of antiquarian research. On the Middlesex bank is the

Penitentiary, built about thirty years ago, and designed for the punishment and reformation of prisoners who were formerly sentenced to transportation. It is an octangular building, with an outer wall, enclosing eighteen acres of ground.

Vauxhall Bridge, with a pier affording convenient facilities to passengers, is now encountered, and may be briefly described. It was commenced in 1811, and finished five years afterwards. It is 810 feet long, and has a span of 78 feet for the centre arch. The river now introduces us to various interesting objects in rapid succession. To the right lie the new streets, stretching forth towards the modern elegant region of Belgravia, and exhibiting evidence of the wealth and station of the metropolitan colonists advancing in this direction. To the left is "Nine Elms" with its steamboat pier, clipped of much lively animation since the extension of the South Western Railway to Waterloo Bridge. A little higher stood the Red House, a noted place of resort for pigeon-shooting, and a favourite haunt for Sunday-strolling citizens.

The Victoria Railway Bridge here crosses the river, and is one of the most satisfactory bridges spanning the Thames. Built on three stone piers, its noble iron arches have an appearance of strength and elegance which, with its level road, make it one of the latest triumphs of science and art, remembering that it has been completed in about twelve months. Over this important bridge run, or will run, the trains of the Brighton, Crystal Palace, Chatham and Dover, and Great Western railway companies (rails of both guages being laid down) to the new and magnificent Victoria Station, close to Buckingham Palace.

Chelsea Hospital, for invalids in the land service. It was built by Sir Christopher Wren, on the site of an old college which had been escheated to the crown, at an expenditure of £150,000, and begun in the reign of Charles II., was completed in that of William III. The principal building consists of a large quadrangle, open at the south side; in the centre is a bronze statue of Charles II. in a Roman habit. On the east and west are buildings, each 365 feet in length, that contain the apartments for the pensioners. The hall wherein the pensioners dine is situated on the opposite side of the vestibule, and is of the same dimensions as the chapel—110 feet in length. At the upper end is a picture of Charles II. on horseback, a gift of the Earl of Ranelagh. A small gratuity to the pensioners will enable the visiter to see every portion of the building open to the public.

The Botanic Gardens adjacent, belonging to the Apothecaries' Company, were founded by Sir Hans Sloane, and are noted for two venerable cedars that are prominent objects from the river. The Cadogan Pier affords easy access to Cheyne Walk, which, a century ago, was the favourite residence of many persons of distinction. At the upper end stood the palace of the Bishops of Winchester; and the tavern called Don Saltern's Coffee-House still remains, which was once a noted house of entertainment when kept by an eccentric barber named Salter, who had a museum of wondrous rarities, to which Sir Hans Sloane largely contributed. This tavern is said to have been a favourite lounge of Richard Cromwell, son of the great Oliver, and who, when he came here, is described to have been "a little and very neat old man, with a placid countenance."

Battersea Bridge, a wretched impediment of wood, has about eighty years of existence to answer for as an obstacle in the way of our river navigation.

Chelsea New Bridge, which forms so beautiful an ornament to this part of the river, connects Chelsea with Battersea Park. On the right lies Cremorne, a favourite place of amusement, with some fine grounds attached; and, across the river, the village of Battersea, with its church, assumes a picturesque effect.

Putney Bridge, built by subscription in 1729, is another wooden structure of equal inconvenience with that of Battersea. It links together the parishes of Fulham and Putney. Fulham Church has a stone tower of the fourteenth century, partially rebuilt about four years ago. All the Bishops of London, with the exception of Bishop Porteus, have been buried here since the Reformation. In the palace-garden of the Bishop of London, close by, are many fine forest trees of extreme rarity. The house itself is of brick, was built in the reign of Henry VII., and has a moat surrounding the grounds.

Hammersmith Suspension Bridge is a light and elegant structure, completed by Tierney Clarke in 1827, at a cost of about £80,000. To the left will be seen the village of BARNES, memorable, among other associations, as being the place where Sir Francis Walsingham entertained Queen Elizabeth and her retinue, at enormous expense, though the next year he died at his house in Seething-lane so poor, that his friends were obliged to bury him privately at night. The church, about a quarter of a mile from the river, is one of the most ancient in the neighbourhood of the metropolis, having been erected in the reign of Richard I. (1189). Here lived Jacob Tonson, the bookseller, the founder and secretary of the Kit-Cat Club. After passing CHISWICK, on the Middlesex bank, and the hamlet of MORTLAKE, on the Surrey side, we come to

Kew Bridge, with its seven stone arches, constructed in 1789, and which sold for £22,000 a few years since.

The Botanic Gardens at Kew are open to the public every day throughout the year from one till dusk. The entrance is from Kew Green. A volume would be required to describe its attractions thoroughly; but, among other rarities shown, may be enumerated the Egyptian Papyrus, the Bread Fruit Tree, the Cow Tree, the Cocoanut, Coffee, Banana, and a fine Weeping Willow, reared from that which overshadowed the exiled emperor's tomb at St. Helena.

Passing the straggling town of OLD BRENTFORD, we soon come within view of ZION HOUSE and grounds, the seat of the Duke of Northumberland. It was once the residence of Lady Jane Grey,

who was thence conducted to the Tower. The ivied turret of Isleworth Church looks well in the landscape. Perch, roach, and dace are to be met with here, except when the tide is flowing; but, for the purpose of preserving the fish in the Thames, angling is prohibited during March, April, and May. The promenade on the banks of the river up to Richmond Bridge is a delightful saunter of a summer's morning. The Richmond and Windsor branch of the South Western Railway crosses the Thames by a handsome iron bridge of three arches.

Richmond Bridge has five arches, of which the central arch is sixty feet wide and twenty-five high. The first stone was laid in 1774, and it was completed in 1777, at a cost of £26,000. Some picturesque snatches of scenery are caught through its arches. The aits, studding the broad stream with willows and poplars, the grounds of Twickenham Park, the hill with its crown of villas, and the terrace gardens sloping down the side, make up a beautiful picture on a sunshiny day. The view from the summit of Richmond Hill has been thus graphically described with equal force and justice: —"Of all that belongs to the beautiful in scenery nothing here is wanting. Wood and water, softly swelling hills and hazy distance, with village spires and lordly halls, are blended in beautiful harmony. From the gentle slope of the hill, a vast expanse of country stretches far away, till the distance is closed by the hills of Buckinghamshire on the north-west, and the Surrey Downs on the south-east, and all this intermediate space is one wide valley of the most luxuriant fertility, but appearing to the eye a succession of densely wooded tracts, broken and diversified by a few undulations of barren uplands, and here and there a line of white vapoury smoke, with a tower or spire marking the site of a goodly town or humble village. In the midst the broad placid river, studded with islets, and its surface alive with flocks of swans and innumerable pleasure skiffs, winds gracefully away till lost among the foliage, only to be occasionally tracked afterwards by a glittering thread of silver, seen as the sun glances suddenly upon it between the dark trunks of the trees; and something of majesty is added to the exceeding loveliness by Windsor's royal towers, which loom out so finely on the distant horizon." Richmond Park, with its fine oaks and elms, its wide glades and grassy undulations, affords some lovely glimpses of silvan scenery. On the mound within the enclosure at the end of the terrace, it is said that Henry VIII. took his stand to watch for the rocket which was to ascend as a signal of the execution of Ann Boleyn. The picturesque road that leads under the brow of the Park to Petersham is a delicious bit of rurality. On the other side of the bridge is

Twickenham, with its ait, that, from the celebrity of its fishy delicacies, has achieved a distinctive reputation as Eel-pie Island. The glories of Pope's Villa and Strawberry Hill have both gone, but a flaunting red-brick villa indicates the site of the one, and a part of the mansion still remains to identify the other. The villas that fringe the bank about here, give a pretty appearance to the windings of the river. It was at Orleans House that Louis Philippe resided when Duke of Orleans.

Teddington is now reached, noticeable chiefly for its lock, so well known to the brethren of the angle. The tide ascends above London Bridge to Teddington, a distance of nineteen miles. The high-water mark is about eighteen inches higher than at London Bridge, and the time of high water is about two hours later. Low water surface at Teddington is about 16¾ feet higher than at London Bridge. Altogether, the tide flows a distance of more than sixty miles from the sea, which is said to be a greater length than it flows into any other river in Europe. This is the first station on the Thames where trout can be taken.

Kingston comes next, with its antique church and Saxon associations.

The present bridge has five arches, and was built in 1828, but the old wooden one is said to have been built even prior to that at London Bridge. The vicinity of the railway has given rise to a new town, which is already abundant in villa residences, and has the convenience of handsome rows of shops besides.

Hampton Wick, on the Middlesex side of the bridge, is a capital point for the pedestrian to start from on his way to Hampton Court. One Timothy Bennett, a cobbler of Hampton Wick, "being unwilling to leave the world worse than he found it, by a vigorous application of the laws of his country, obtained a free passage through Bushy Park, which had long been withheld from the people." There is a print of this humble patriot extant, taken in the year 1752, when he was aged 75.

Thames Ditton is not without charms for the angler, who here finds roach, perch, dace, and chub, to reward his piscatorial exertions, as well as an occasional fine trout or jack. At Moulsey, opposite Hampton Bridge, the "sullen Mole that runneth underground" finds its way to the Thames.

Hampton Court is now gained. If its Palace does not present its best front to the Thames, it undoubtedly looks charmingly picturesque from it, backed as it is by a magnificent framework of foliage, that sets off the vener-

able ruddiness of this grand historical building to great advantage. Open every day, except Friday, to the public, it is gratifying to know that thousands of delighted visiters flock here annually; and the fine works of art and glorious scenes of nature that they behold within its precincts cannot but produce a beneficial effect, even on the minds of those least prone to appreciate them. The portion of the Palace seen from the river was built by Wren, for William III. The eight acres of ground occupied by the Palace are surrounded by exquisite combinations of wood and garden scenery. For an account of the attractions within, we must refer the reader to the other portions of our work, wherein they are fully described. The Hampton Court Branch of the South Western Railway was opened February 1st, 1849. It is one mile and a half long, and has a continuous embankment eighteen feet high. It has been estimated that 180,000 persons visit Hampton Court annually, a number, great as it may appear, now likely to be increased from the additional facilities given for railway communication.

Hampton Court Bridge is an old-fashioned wooden structure, consisting of ten arches, and was built in 1778. The view from the bridge is extremely pretty, the channel of the Thames being here narrowed by islands, and completely overhung in parts by drooping foliage.

Sunbury, on the Middlesex bank, presents another lock or weir to the river voyager. The church looks very picturesque, and in artistic contrast to the turret of Shepperton Church, seen in the distance beyond. The osier beds that now intersect the river give a varied character to the landscape, and the groups of houses, clustered among the trees, that greet the eye at intervals, furnish some nice bits for the portfolio of the sketcher.

Walton Bridge spans the river soon after. The village is on the Surrey side, just below the bridge. The church is a massive structure, built about the twelfth century, of flints and rough stones intermixed, and in some places covered with plaster. A square tower of substantial aspect rises at the west end. In the interior of the church is a large black marble slab, denoting the resting-place of William Lilly, the astrologer. A short distance above the bridge, is Coway or Causeway Stakes, ascribed by tradition to point out the ford at which Cæsar crossed the Thames in his march to encounter the Britons. This ford was subsequently destroyed by planting stakes shod with iron in a straight line across the river; the ford or causeway presenting an irregular curve, which the stakes crossed in two places and effectually blocked up. One of these stakes, too heavy or too firmly fixed to be raised, remains still imbedded in the river, and can be distinctly seen when the water is clear and the sunlight falls glancingly upon it. The Wey falls into the Thames a short distance beyond.

Chertsey Bridge next crosses the river. It is of stone, and was built in 1786. The town has been described in another part of this work. About a mile above, on the Middlesex side, is the pleasantly-secluded village of Laleham.

Staines Bridge, with its three flat granite arches, was opened in 1832, by William IV. Staines is on the Middlesex shore, and Egham on the opposite. Northward of the bridge is the city boundary stone, with this inscription:— "God preserve the City of London. A.D. 1280;" and here the jurisdiction of the Lord Mayor, as conservator of the Thames, terminates. The Coln flows into the Thames a little above. The famous RUNNIMEDE, where King John signed Magna Charta (June 15th, 1215), is on the north side of Egham, and extends a considerable distance along the bank. Opposite is CHARTER ISLAND, a place well known to pic-nic providers; and at Ankerwyke, close by, is a yew-tree, now flourishing luxuriantly, though it is said to have been in the enjoyment of a green old age when the memorable compact received the royal signature.

An abrupt curve of the river brings us to the ferry at Old Windsor, and the renowned Datchet Meads, identified so closely with the memory of Falstaff. The station of the Richmond, Windsor, and Staines Railway is at hand, and will furnish a rapid as well as pleasant means of transit back to town. The iron bridge that crosses the river here connects Eton with Windsor, and serves as a link between the counties of Buckingham and Berks. Here, as "wanders the hoary Thames along his silver winding way," we obtain a fine view of the terraced heights of

Windsor Castle. The Terrace is seen to its full extent. King John's Tower, Queen Elizabeth's Gallery, George the Fourth's Tower, the Cornwall Tower, the Brunswick Tower, 100 feet high, and the majestic Keep, soaring in its massive magnificence above all, make up a fine picture, with the verdant slopes that form the foreground. Nowhere, it has been truly said, has man been more lavish of his labour, or more ostentatious of his means; and nowhere has nature been more bountiful of her gifts.

The North Terrace, constructed by Queen Elizabeth, should, for the fine prospect it affords, be the first and last thing seen on visiting the Castle. The approach to it is down some steps; through a darkened archway under Queen Elizabeth's Library, which serves as a sort of frame to the magical view beyond. It alone repays the journey. The bird's-eye view of the town of Windsor, the little church of Datchet shooting upwards through the trees, the distant spires and antique towers of Eton, "crowning the watery glade," as Gray described them, with the white lines of silvery vapour marking the track of the railway, combine to form a landscape unrivalled for majestic beauty. A full description of the Castle is given in the excursion to Windsor that occupies a portion of the pages of our "Pocket Guide;" but it must not be forgotten that a tour through the cloisters and passages alone will furnish some picturesque combinations of form, light, and shade, and exquisite mellow tones of colour. The out-door attractions of Windsor and its neighbourhood are quite as great as those that lie inside the Castle. After such an experience of its beauties as we have indicated, the tourist will be disposed to exclaim with the poet:—

" The splendid Thames, with all the strength of life,
  Its boldest beauty and its sweetest breath,
 Peopled with such a world of love and strife,
  Upon whose borders grandeur gathereth
 Its hundred monuments of fame and pride,
  And the link'd sweetness of fair Nature's charms
 Whose lovely landscapes peep into his tide,
  And fold their sapphire beauty to his arms."

PART II.

DOWN THE RIVER—FROM LONDON BRIDGE TO THE NORE.

The Thames below Bridge—The characteristics of the river at this point are full of interest. A perfect forest of masts, belonging to ships of all sizes and all nations, looms out in the Pool. Colliers, coasters, steamboats, and river craft throng the Thames in every direction; and the fleet of merchantmen daily arriving, and the restless activity seen along the banks, give a Londoner a vast conception of the glories of that commerce which has been the cause of the riches and grandeur of his native city. From London Bridge to Deptford, a distance of four miles, with a breadth across varying from 290 to 350 yards, the Pool is narrowed to a small channel by the mass of ships ranged on each side, and which renders the navigation of this portion sometimes very intricate. The depth of the river varies considerably; the mean range of the tidal influx at London Bridge being seventeen feet. Up to Woolwich, the river is navigable for ships of any burden; to Blackwall, for those of 1,400 tons; and to St. Katharine's Docks, for those of 800 tons. The wharfs and granaries along the banks are recognised as the largest in the world.

THE TOWER—After passing Billingsgate, behind which the New Coal Exchange is situated, that was opened by Prince Albert in November, 1849, the Tower becomes the first prominent object on the northern bank of the Thames. It is a large pile of building, including an area of more than twelve acres, and owes its irregularity to having been erected and enlarged by various sovereigns at distant periods of time. Besides being the repository of the regalia, it is now used as a garrison and arsenal. The river view is very fine, and a gateway through which the state victims were conveyed, is peculiarly suggestive of historic fancies, strangely contrasting with the peaceful indications of commerce that now lie scattered around.

ST. KATHARINE'S DOCKS, adjacent to the Tower, occupy twenty-four acres, and were opened in 1828. From morning till night this vast scene of commercial action presents to the observant eye a panoramic view of the various vessels trading to all parts of the globe.

THE LONDON DOCKS come next, covering an area of thirty-four acres. In the vaults can be stowed more than 65,000 pipes of wines and spirits.

THE THAMES TUNNEL affords a convenient, as well as curious, communication between Wapping and Rother-hithe. It is 1,300 feet long, and passes underneath the river at the depth of 63 feet. The approach at each end is by a vast circular shaft with a spiral roadway. The entire work was executed in about nine years of actual operation, though the first boring commenced in 1826. The opening took place in 1843. The entire cost was about £600,000. With all the perils of the engineering, but seven lives were lost in the course of the work, whilst forty men were killed during the building of the present London Bridge. It is a glorious monument to the memory of Brunel.

THE WEST INDIA DOCKS, extending across the northern extremity of the Isle of Dogs, from Limehouse to Blackwall, were opened in 1802, and formed the first establishment of the kind in London. The chief warehouses for import goods are on the quays which bound that enclosure. They are admirably contrived for the reception, preservation, and delivery of goods, and are capable of storing away 170,000 hogsheads of sugar, besides coffee and other colonial productions. The whole space occupied by these docks extends over 295 acres. It is enclosed on every side; all the buildings are fire-proof; and the premises are well guarded by watchmen, so that the system of pilfering formerly carried on here is com-pletely abolished. The nearest end is at Limehouse, three miles from the Royal Exchange, and the other end, half a mile further, is at Blackwall; the expense of cartage was therefore considerable, until the construction of the Blackwall Railway lessened the outlay, by increasing the facility of removal. Some admirable contrivances have been lately adopted, by which the great body of water in the docks is kept always sweet, and by which the constant deposit of mud from the water of the river is carried away gradually.

THE COMMERCIAL DOCKS are on the other side of the river, and were originally intended, and principally used, for the vessels connected with the Baltic and the whale fisheries. Hemp, corn, timber, and iron, are usually stored here in great quantities. The logs of the Canadian and Norwegian forests line its immense area, affording a pleasant shelter for the perch, which securely swim beneath its sombre waters undisturbed, unless when the logs are removed for the purposes of commerce, or when the permission of the directors is obtained for a day's vocation in the "gentle craft."

DEPTFORD, with its docks, store-houses, victualling-office, and busy ship-yards, next claims our notice. It has been a place for shipbuilding since the time of Henry VIII. A short distance further, and the DREADNOUGHT, the old man-of-war that once captured a Spanish three-decker in Trafalgar Bay, is seen before us. As a marine hospital, the vessel is open for the reception of the sick or disabled seamen of all nations.

GREENWICH we have already spoken of at some length in another "Excursion," but it well deserves a few words in addition. The Observatory, that stands out so boldly picturesque from the clustering foliage of the Park, and forms so striking an object from the river, was built in 1675 from the materials of Duke Humphrey's Tower, which previously occupied its site. Precisely at 1 P.M., on every day of the year, a ball attached to a staff on the summit of the Observatory, is seen to fall: by this all the vessels within sight regulate their chronometers. The Park is rich in sylvan beauty and historical interest. A pleasant writer (Thomas Miller) has enumerated some of its associations so accurately and graphically, that the passage well deserves quotation:— "Let us pause on the brow of this hill, and recall a few of the stirring scenes which these aged hawthorns have overlooked. They are the ancient foresters of the chase, and many of them have stood through the wintry storms of past centuries, and were gnarled, and knotted, and stricken with age, long before Evelyn planned and planted those noble avenues of chestnuts and elms. Below, between the plain at the foot of the hill and the river, stood the old Palace of Greenwich, in which Henry VIII. held his revels, and where Edward VI., the boy king, died. The early chroniclers say that his death was caused by poison, which he inhaled while smelling a nosegay. That ancient palace was no doubt rich in the spoils of many a plundered abbey and ruined monastery. On this hill, Cardinal Wolsey may have meditated, with all his blushing honours thick upon him. Katharine, the broken-hearted queen, may here have reined in her palfrey, or from this aged hawthorn have torn off a spray, when it was, as now, fragrant and white with May blossoms. On yonder plain, where so many happy faces are now seen, in former days the tournament was held. In this park the crafty Cecil mused many an hour, as he plotted the return of the Princess Mary, whilst the ink was scarcely dry with which he recorded his allegiance to the Lady Jane Grey." Groups of nurserymaids and children are familiar features in the modern aspect of the place. The latter flit, climb, and leap over every broken hillock, slide into every green dell, swing, toss, and tumble round and upon each sinewy tree, as if they were the legitimate possessors of the Park, and lived entirely upon gingerbread, oranges, nuts, and lemonade—viands which, it seems proper to believe, are indispensable to the real enjoyment of these shady avenues. The whole front of the Hospital, 875 feet long, looks, with its terrace, a magnificent building from the river. The pile consists of four quadrangles, detached from each other. The principal quadrangle is 273 feet wide. West of this part is King Charles's building; on the east lies Queen Anne's building; and to the south are the structures built by Sir Christopher Wren, called, on the western side, King William's, and on the east, Queen Mary's buildings. Besides the four quadrangular piles, which, as it were, constitute the Palace, there is the infirmary, a handsome square brick building, 193 feet in length, and 75 broad, another asylum for the helpless, capable of containing 117 persons, with their attendants; a building opposite this for civil officers of the Hospital; and, finally, the Naval Asylum, where a fine model frigate may be seen planted on the grass plot. These are all perfectly arranged for the fulfilment of their designed purpose.

The Isle of Dogs, originally called the Isle of Ducks, from the quantity of wild-fowl that found a resting-place upon it, is now seen on the opposite side; and following the abrupt turn which the river takes, we come to BLACKWALL, at the back of which the East India Docks occupy a large space of ground. The Blackwall Pier, with the handsome terminus of the Blackwall Railway, is always a lively scene, from the constant passenger traffic that animates the spacious area. Wigram's shipbuilding yard is adjoining, and a little further down, the river Lea, under the name of Bow Creek, has its outlet into the Thames.

On the right, after entering Woolwich Reach, is seen Charlton, with its picturesque church; and, on the Essex bank, the new station of the Eastern Counties Railway affords a pleasant summer lounge to those who have no opportunity of proceeding farther, or who await the arrival of the Gravesend boats, that call here going and returning. A short distance above, the river Roding flows into the Thames, after a sinuous course, from Dunmow, of 38 miles.

Woolwich is a place for sight-seekers to glory in; and, in another part of this work, the Rotunda, Cannon Foundery, Arsenal, and Barracks, have been fully described. The characteristics of Woolwich, as visible from the river, have been thus neatly and graphically given:—"The long lines of walls, the closely pressed tide-gates, with the bows of many a noble vessel towering proudly over them from their docks, like sea-monarchs on their thrones, looking down in scorn on the river waves; the high heaps of timber, the huge coiled cables, the church tower in the background, the heavy lighters crowded along the shore; the light raking craft, with pennants long streaming in the wind; the well-manned boats, pulled hither and thither by sturdy hands, with an occasional portly form and cocked hat in the stern-sheets; the sun glittering with a playful brightness on the many eye-like windows that break the monotony of what, otherwise, would look like slate-roof barns, belonging to some giant farmhouse; the gloomy hulks, moored along the shore, with the water dashing sullenly against the chains that bind them—all tell us that we are sweeping by that ancient dockyard and those famous shipbuilding slips, where England stores the lightning, and forges the thunderbolts which have enabled her to acquire and keep the rule of the main." The Arsenal contains every description of missile or warlike implement now in use, and has a furnace, for the casting of cannon, in which seventeen tons of metal can be melted at once. The public are admitted free to the Arsenal, Dockyard, and Military Repository, every day, from 9 till 11, and from 1 till 4, upon inscribing their names and address in a book kept for that purpose; if a party of from two to six, or even more, (known to each other), apply for admission—the chief of such party only is required to subscribe his or her name and address, inserting the *number* of persons accom-

panying them;—upon an extraordinary pressure of work, admission is suspended, as such visits are supposed to interfere with the progress of labour. A special order is required for foreigners.

The bend of the river is here known as Gallion's Reach, and is plentifully studded with buoys, placed there by the Corporation of London, for the use of Indiamen coming into port. The little bankside tavern, half-way between London and Gravesend, is a conspicuous object on the. Kentish shore.

Erith with its pretty rural church and stately pier, comes next into sight. Nearly opposite, on the Essex coast, is PURFLEET, and its gunpowder stores. GREENHITHE, a little further on, with Ingress Abbey, the late Alderman Harmer's seat, has a picturesque look from the river. It was from this point that Sir John Franklin sailed with the Erebus and Terror, June 19, 1845. The chalky line of hills, variegated with verdure, and at the summit crested with a handsome Gothic range of almshouses, brings us to NORTHFLEET, where ROSHERVILLE GARDENS have long been familiar to the public. This popular place of recreation abounds in attractions, all of which are of the most varied and extensive character. The banqueting-hall, a room of immense dimensions, is capable of accommodating one thousand persons, and the grounds are delightfully laid out with all that can minister to the gratification of the senses.

Gravesend, with the slope of Windmill Hill rising proudly behind the town, and circled by new streets and terraces in every direction, has been amply described in the excursion appropriated to that town and the places surrounding. TILBURY FORT, with its gate or block-house of the time of Henry VIII., lies across the river, and the widening expanse of water, enlivened by the constant transit of vessels, presents to us a moving panorama of animated interest.

From hence to the Nore there is nothing on either side the river deserving of a detailed notice. SHEERNESS, standing on the extreme north-western point of the Isle of Sheppey, where the river Medway joins with the Thames, is, however, a naval station of too much importance to be lightly passed over. Within the last thirty years, the dockyard has been greatly extended and improved, at a cost of about three millions, and it is now one of the finest in Europe. It has an area of sixty acres, and is surrounded by an extremely well built brick wall, that cost £40,000 in its erection. It is sufficiently capacious to hold men-of-war, with all their guns and stores on board. The storehouse is supposed to be the largest building in this country: it is six stories high, and will contain at least 30,000 tons of stores. The chief trade in the town arises from the dockyards and other establishments connected with the Government; but there are also copperas works of considerable extent. The pyrites or copperas stones, are collected in heaps upon the beach, from the falling cliffs, and carried away in vessels. There was at one time a great scarcity of fresh water experienced here, but it is now supplied from four subscription wells, which have been sunk to a depth of 360 feet. In digging them the workmen discovered, at 200 feet below the surface, a complete prostrate forest, through which, in the prosecution of their work, they were compelled to burn their way. On the cliffs, leading from the beach towards Minster, there is a fine view to be obtained. The German Ocean on the east, the rivers Thames and Medway, bearing innumerable vessels of all kinds, with the town and harbour of Sheerness to the north and west; and the fertile valleys of Kent, with the Medway winding through them, and the towns and villages interspersed towards the south, combine in presenting a diversified landscape rarely excelled.

An excursion up the Medway, to Chatham and Rochester, should not be omitted where time and opportunity serve; but as a description of both the above places will be found in another portion of our "Guide to the Environs," recapitulation would be useless.

GREENWICH.

BILLINGSGATE.—THE CUSTOM-HOUSE—THE TOWER—SAINT KATHARINE'S DOCKS —LONDON DOCKS—WAPPING—ROTHERHITHE—THE TUNNEL—WEST INDIA DOCKS—DEPTFORD—GREENWICH—THE HOSPITAL—THE PAINTED HALL— THE ROYAL OBSERVATORY—THE PARK—BLACKHEATH—LEE—SHOOTER'S HILL—ELTHAM—ELTHAM PALACE—WOOLWICH—THE ARTILLERY BARRACKS —THE ROYAL ARSENAL—THE "REPOSITORY" AND "ROTUNDA"—THE "MILI- TARY COLLEGE"—THE DOCKYARD—ARRANGEMENTS OF ADMISSION—RETURN TO TOWN.

THERE are no less than four modes of getting to Greenwich, each of them to be severally commended as speedy, agreeable, and economical. They are, —1. By omnibus from Charing Cross down the New Kent Road. 2. By Greenwich Railway from the south side of London Bridge. 3. By Blackwall Railway, from Fenchurch Street to Blackwall, crossing the river by a steamer. And 4. By steamboats from Westminster, Waterloo, Blackfriars, and London Bridges, from which two companies keep up a constant succession of departures every twenty minutes throughout the day. For the sake of variety, we shall proceed to describe the journey by water, which, of a fine day, is not only the most agreeable, but, as furnishing an excellent opportunity of seeing the scenery of the Thames, is perhaps most desirable to strangers.

Leaving London Bridge, a perfect forest of masts, belonging to ships of all sizes and all nations, looms out in the Pool. BILLINGSGATE, situated chiefly at the back of that cluster of buildings by the Custom-House, has been since the days of William III. the most famous fishmarket in Europe. The CUSTOM-HOUSE, 480 feet in length, was begun in 1813, and finished four years afterwards, at a cost of nearly half a million. It contains nearly 200 distinct apartments, each having a range of communication with the Long Room, which is 197 feet long, and 50 feet high. One hundred clerks are engaged about this room alone, and the principal business of "clearing" is here conduct- ed. We next see the Tower, said to have been built by Julius Cæsar, and afterwards reconstructed by William the Conqueror. The last state prisoners here were Thistlewood and his associates, in 1820, for the Cato Street conspiracy. The public have free access from ten till four, sixpence being charged to view the regalia. About half a mile lower down are the warehouses of ST. KATHARINE'S DOCKS, which cost one million in construction, and were first opened in 1828. The London Docks, close by, opened in 1805, occupy a space of about thirty acres. WAPPING is a well-known resort for sailors, and those connected with maritime pursuits. At Execution Dock pirates were formerly hung in chains. ROTHERHITHE, opposite, is, in its river frontage, only distinguished by a mass of warehouses, and the glimpse we get of the old parish church, where Prince Lee Boo was buried. The TUNNEL, over which we next pass, was first commenced, to afford a subaqueous communication between the two sides of the river, in 1825, and was completed, after much difficulty and expense, in twenty years. Sir I. Brunel was the projector and engineer. The height is nearly twenty-five feet, and the length 1,300 feet. One penny toll is charged for each passenger. Entering the Lower Pool we pass LIMEHOUSE, where the Regent's Canal communicates with the Thames, and have next to notice the WEST INDIA DOCKS, opened in 1802, after an expenditure of £1,200,000, and extending over an area of 204 acres. On the

opposite side of the River are the COMMERCIAL DOCKS, after which is passed Earl's Sluice, forming the boundary between Surrey and Kent. DEPTFORD, where the dockyard and its bustling animation gives a lively appearance to the shore, reminds one of Peter the Great, who, in 1698, came to Saye's Court and studied the craft of shipbuilding at the once picturesque retreat of Evelyn, the antobiographist and author of "Sylva." But, alas for the glories of Saye's Court—its glittering hollies, long avenues, and trim hedges! That portion of the victualling yard where oxen are slaughtered, and hogs salted for the use of the navy, occupies the enchanting grounds wherein Evelyn was wont to delight, and on the site of the mansion itself is the common workhouse of the parish. Approaching Greenwich Reach, where large quantities of whitebait are caught in the season, the opening of the river discloses a pretty view of a distant country beyond, and, with a few more revolutions of the paddle-wheel, we are brought to our destination.

Greenwich presents a striking appearance from the river, its Hospital forming one of the most prominent attractions of the place. Here was the palace erected by Humphrey Duke of Gloucester, and by him called Placentia; and here were born Henry VIII. and his two daughters, Queens Mary and

Elizabeth. Charles II. began the present magnificent edifice, and William III. appropriated it to its present patriotic purpose, since which time successive sovereigns have contributed to enrich it with various additions. As the first generally seen, we shall begin our description with an account of its interior. The Chapel and Picture Gallery are open gratis on Mondays and Fridays; on other days threepence each is charged for admission. It is as well to remind the reader that the Hospital consists of four distinct piles of building, distinguished by the appellations of King Charles's, King William's, Queen Mary's, and Queen Anne's. King Charles's and Queen Anne's are those next the river, and between them is the grand square, 270 feet wide, and the terrace by the river front, 865 feet in length. Beyond the square are seen the Hall and Chapel with their noble domes, and the two colonnades, which are backed by the eminence whereon the Observatory stands throned amid a grove of trees. In the centre of the great square is Rysbrach's statue of George II., carved out of white marble, from a block taken from the French by Sir George Rooke, and which weighed eleven tons. On the west side is King Charles's building, erected chiefly of Portland stone, in the year 1684. The whole contains about 300 beds, distributed in thirteen wards. Queen Anne's building, on the east side of the square, corresponding with that on the opposite side, was begun in 1693 and completed in 1726. There are here 24 wards with 437 beds, and several of the officers' apartments. To the south-west is King William's building, comprising the great hall, vestibule, and dome, erected, between 1698 and 1703, by Sir Christopher Wren. It contains 11 wards and 554 beds. Queen Mary's building was, with the chapel, not completed till 1752. It contains 13 wards and 1,100 beds. The PAINTED HALL, a noble structure opposite the chapel, is divided into three rooms, exhibiting as you enter statues of Nelson and Duncan, with twenty-eight pictures of various sizes; the chief are Turner's large picture of "The Battle of Trafalgar," the "Relief of Gibraltar," and the "Defeat of the French Fleet under Comte de Grasse." On the opposite side is Loutherbourg's picture of Lord Howe's victory on the memorable 1st of June 1794, whilst above are suspended the flags taken in the battle. The other pictures up the steps are chronologically arranged, the most prominent being the "Death of Captain Cook," the "Battle of Camperdown," "Nelson leaping into the San Josef," and the "Bombardment of Algiers." It may not be generally known that every mariner, either in the royal navy or merchant service, pays sixpence a month towards the support of this noble institution, which has of course, besides, a handsome revenue (£130,000) derived from other sources. The pensioners, who are of every rank, from the admiral to the humblest sailor, are qualified for admission by being either maimed or disabled by age. Foreigners who have served two consecutive years in the British service are equally entitled to the privileges, and the widows of seamen are exclusively appointed nurses. The Hospital was first opened in January, 1705, and now the pensioners provided with food, clothes, lodging, and a small stipend for pocket-money, number nearly 2,500. The number of out-pensioners is about 3,000. The "Royal Naval School," for training the sons of seamen to the naval service, is a most interesting institution, administering the best instruction to now about 450 boys.

The "Royal Observatory," occupying the most elevated spot in Greenwich Park, was built on the site of the old castle, the foundation stone being laid on the 10th of August, 1675. The first superintendent of the establishment was Flamstead, and he commenced his observations in the following year. It stands about 300 feet above the level of the river. For the guidance of the shipping the round globe at its summit drops precisely at 1 P.M., to give the exact Greenwich time. The noble park is chiefly planted with elms and chestnut trees, and contains 188 acres. It was walled round with brick in the reign of James I. The views from the summit are very fine, embracing perhaps the finest prospects of London and the Thames, the forests of Hainault and Epping, the heights of Hampstead, and a survey of Kent, Surrey, and Essex, as far as the eye can reach. The flitting of the fawns through the distant glades, the venerable aspect of the trees themselves—many of them saplings in the time of Elizabeth—and the appearance of the veteran pensioners, some without a leg or arm, others hobbling on from the infirmity of wounds or age, and all clad in the old-fashioned blue coats and breeches, with cocked hats, give beauty and animation to a scene which no other country in the world can boast.

Through large gateways of open ironwork, lately substituted for a small doorway in the wall at the southern extremity of the park, near the keeper's new Gothic lodge, we pass on to Blackheath, where Wat Tyler assembled the Kentish rebels in the reign of Richard II., and where Jack Cade and his fellow insurgents are said to have held their midnight meetings in a cavern which still remains, though so choked up as to be considered nearly inaccessible. LEE is about a mile distant, crossing the Heath towards the south. In the old church was buried Halley the Astrologer. On the east of Blackheath is Morden College, founded in 1695 for decayed merchants, and now having about forty recipients of its benefits. Following the old Dover road, which, crossing the Heath, leads on to Shooter's Hill, we pass a rustic little hostelry on our left, distinguished by the peculiar title of the "Sun-in-the-Sands." Hazlitt, Hunt, and others of our essayists, were often wont to ramble over here; there is the advantage of an open balcony, from which a pleasant view may be obtained of the surrounding country. It is recorded by old Hall, the historian, that King Henry VIII. often rode "a-maying from Greenwich to the high ground of Shooter's Hill with Queen Katharine his wife, and many lords and ladies in gay attire." Several jousts and tourneys took place here in the same reign, at one of which the King himself, accompanied by the Duke of Suffolk, the Earl of Essex, and Sir George Carew, challenged all comers to tilt at the barriers. This was on the 20th of May in the eighth year of King Harry's reign: he got too crass and corpulent for such athletic pastimes afterwards. Shooter's Hill—anciently *Suiter's* hill, from the number of applicants, doubtless, that came this way to procure places about the court—is 446 feet high, and commands an expansive prospect. The "mighty mass of brick and smoke and shipping," as Byron calls the view of London from this point, is well contrasted with the foliage of the wooded country extending towards the south beyond the vale of Eltham. On the summit rises the commemorative castle of Severndroog, built in 1784 by Sir William James, to celebrate the conquest of one so called on the coast of Malabar.

For those who either have seen Woolwich, or who prefer postponing their visit thither for a distant excursion, we can especially recommend a deviation from Shooter's Hill down the inviting green lane at its base that leads to ELTHAM, a pleasant walk of hardly two miles. Here stood anciently one of the most magnificent of England's royal palaces. Anthony Bek, the "battling Bishop" of Durham, erected the first mansion about the middle of the thirteenth century, and on his death the manor with its possessions fell to the Crown, which is still the rightful owner of the property. John, son of Edward II., was born here in 1316, and was thence called John of Eltham. In the next reign the Parliament was here convened, and Edward IV., after rebuilding it, kept his Christmas here with great splendour in 1482. Henry VII. made still further additions, and in his time the Royal Palace consisted of four quadrangles enclosed within a high wall, and encircled by a moat. A garden and three parks were attached, comprising about 1,800 acres, and were well stocked with deer. The many fine old trees that still remain, show how richly wooded this district must have formerly been. All that now remains of this once stately edifice is the Hall or Banqueting Room, which has been for years converted to the plebeian uses of a barn. Nothing can be more interesting than this relic of ancient kingly grandeur. The symbol of the rose, seen on various portions of the building, identifies the Hall as that erected by Edward IV. In 1828 its neglected condition attracted the attention of antiquarians, and government undertook the work of restoration, to secure the permanence of what remained. The Hall is about 100 feet long, and 60 feet high, and it has been well said "the taste and talent of ages are concentrated in its design." The windows have been built up, but the splendid roof is nearly perfect. From the immense length of the beams, sound and straight throughout, it has been considered that a forest must have yielded its choicest timber for the supply, and it is evident the material has been wrought with amazing labour and admirable skill Some of the walls of the old garden are perceptible to the east of the palace, and there is an ancient dwelling close by worth notice. In 1834 some curious subterraneous passages were discovered. Under the ground-floor was found a trap-door opening into a room underground, ten feet wide, and communicating with Middle Park, where there were excavations sufficient to contain sixty horses. About 500 feet of this passage was entered, and 200 feet of another, which passed under the moat, and was believed, from traditions extant, to lead under Blackheath to Greenwich or the river. In the field leading from Eltham to Mottingham the archway was broken into, but the brickwork could be traced considerably further in the same direction. After leaving the Hall go and see Eltham Church; not that it is architecturally remarkable, but in the churchyard will be found a tomb to Doggett the comedian, who bequeathed the coat and badge still rowed for every 1st of August by the "jolly young watermen" of the Thames. Hence we can get back to Greenwich, and go home by railway.

Woolwich can be reached either by water, or, as forming a continuation of our present stroll down the road, we can turn off by the sixth milestone and go through Charlton, or take the road to the left at Shooter's Hill. Of course nearly all the interest connected with Woolwich is concentrated in the government establishments, which are acknowledged to be the finest in the world. These, consisting of the Dockyard, Arsenal, and Royal Military Repository, we shall describe in the rotation generally adopted when seeing them. Coming from Shooter's Hill and crossing Woolwich Common, the extensive range of buildings forming the barracks of the Royal Artillery first attracts attention. The principal front extends above 1,200 feet. In the eastern wing is the chapel, containing 1,000 sittings, and the other principal parts of the building are the library and reading-room, plentifully supplied with newspapers and periodicals. The whole establishment affords excellent accommodation for upwards of 4,000 men. The troops, when on parade, present a very animated appearance. The "Royal Arsenal" will be observed but a short distance off, composed of several buildings, wherein the manufacture of implements of warfare is carried on upon the most extensive scale. On entering the gateway the visiter will see the "Foundery" before him, provided with every thing necessary for casting the largest pieces of ordnance, for which, as in the other branches of manufacture, steam power has been lately applied. Connected with the "Pattern Room," adjoining, will be noticed several of the illuminations and devices used in St. James's Park to commemorate the peace of 1814. The "Laboratory" exhibits a busy scene, for here are made the cartridges, rockets, fireworks, and the other chemical contrivances for warfare, which,

though full of "sound and fury," are far from being considered amongst the enemy as "signifying nothing." To the north are the storehouses, where are comprised outfittings for 15,000 cavalry horses, and accoutrements for service. The area of the Arsenal includes no less than 24,000 pieces of ordnance, and 3,000,000 of cannon-ball piled up in huge pyramids. The "Repository" and "Rotunda" are on the margin of the Common, to the south of the town, and contain models of the most celebrated fortifications in Europe, with curiosities innumerable. To the southeast of the Repository is the "Royal Military Academy," for the education of the cadets in all the branches of artillery and engineering. The present building, partly in the Elizabethan style, was erected in 1805, and though 300 could be accommodated, the number of cadets at present does not exceed 160. In going from the Arsenal to the Garrison there will be noticed, on the right of the road, an extensive building forming the headquarters of the Royal Sappers and Miners. On the same side the way is the "Field Artillery Depot," where the guns are mounted and kept in readiness for instant action. The Hospital is to the left of the Garrison entrance, fitted up with 700 beds, and under the superintendence of the most skilful medical officers. From the Arsenal we proceed to the Dockyard, which, commencing at the village of New Charlton on the west, extends a mile along the banks of the river to the east. There are two large dry docks for the repair of vessels, and a spacious basin for receiving vessels of the largest size. The granite docks, and the Foundery and Boiler-making department, recently added, have been great improvements. Timber-sheds, mast-houses, storehouses, and ranges of massive anchors, give a very busy aspect to the place, which was first formed in the reign of Henry VIII., and considerably enlarged by Charles I. The "Royal Marine Barracks," designed by Mr. Crew, cost £100,000. An excellent feature is the kitchen, appropriated to every forty men, so that the meals may be taken apart from the bedroom. There is also a school attached for two hundred boys and girls. The following form the arrangements of admission to the above important buildings:— To the Arsenal, the Royal Repository, and the Dockyard, *free*; the hours being from 9 till 11 A.M., and 1 till 4 P.M. Visitors are required to leave their name at the gates. The other buildings require the escort of one of the principal officers.

Though within a short period nearly 2,000 additional houses have been built, the town presents few inducements for a prolonged visit, and has no feature of interest in itself whatever. The old church looks better at a distance than close, and there are few monuments in the churchyard bearing names familiar to the eye and ear. Perhaps, after his visit to the Arsenal, the visiter will feel most interested in that to Schalch, a Swiss, who died in 1776, at the advanced age of ninety years, sixty of which he passed as superintendent of the Foundery there. Indeed, it was to him chiefly that the establishment owed its origin, for he was the cause of its removal from Moorfields, and the improvements made in conducting the operations.

From Woolwich we have the choice of four speedy modes of transit to town:—1. By steamer direct to London Bridge and Westminster; 2. By steam ferry across to Blackwall, and so on by railway to Fenchurch Street; 3. By a similar conveyance to the new station of the Eastern Counties Railway, on the Essex banks of the river, which brings us to Shoreditch; and 4. By the North Kent line. The Woolwich station, eight miles and twenty-one chains from London, is in the close vicinity of the Barracks; the two tunnels between Woolwich and Charlton are, respectively, 120 and 100 yards in extent; and the Blackheath tunnel, near Morden College, is 1,681 yards long. The excursionist may consult his own convenience for preference of choice.

GRAVESEND.

ERITH—PURFLEET—DARTFORD—GREENHITHE—NORTHFLEET—ROSHERVILLE—
GRAVESEND—WINDMILL HILL—TILBURY FORT—SPRINGHEAD—COBHAM—
COBHAM CHURCH—COBHAM HALL—COBHAM WOOD—RETURN TO GRAVESEND.

Gravesend, despite its acknowledged character as the "Watering-Place" of Cockaigne, where Londoners diurnally resort, and place implicit faith in the salt breezes wafted by an easterly wind to its shores, is yet one of the most pleasantly situated, and most easily attained, of all the places throned upon the margin of the Thames. It is, moreover, a capital starting-point for a series of excursions through the finest parts of Kent and has besides, in its own immediate neighbourhood, some tempting allurements to the summer excursionist in the way of attractive scenery and venerable buildings. Having previously given a description of the objects passed down the river as far as Woolwich, we shall resume our details from that point, to avoid repetition.

Off Woolwich will be observed the old ships known as "The Hulks," where the convicts, working in gangs, are employed in various useful works for the benefit of that community whose laws they have violated. After passing Halfway Reach, where there is a small public-house, known as "The Halfway House," indicating that point (14¾ miles from London) to be exactly midway between London Bridge and Gravesend, we see on the Essex coast Dagenham Breach, where, in December 1707, the tide broke through the dikes and flooded upwards of 1,000 acres. ERITH next presents its picturesque church and wooded uplands to the right, and is a tempting village to loiter in when opportunity serves. A fine pier, at which the London steam-boats frequently call, has been constructed for the accommodation of those who embark or disembark here, and an "Arboretum," with extensive pleasure grounds, has been recently opened to attract visiters. Erith Church is a charming study for either artist or antiquary. The ivy which clings about the structure, and the masses of foliage that rise beyond, give it a very striking aspect. The structure consists of a nave and chancel, with a low tower and spire, and evidently has a venerable length of years; for, besides the data of some of its monuments going back as far as the year 1420, it has been identified as the spot where King John and the Barons drew up their treaty of peace. In the south chapel is an alabaster tomb, much mutilated, to the memory of Elizabeth, Countess of Shrewsbury, and her daughter Anne, Countess of Pembroke, who both died in the reign of Elizabeth. Adjacent are some fine brasses, in good preservation, though the inscriptions attached to them have been quite obliterated. They all belong to the Waldens, members of the same family. Belvidere, formerly the seat of Lord Saye and Sele, is an elegant mansion, in a very romantic situation, commanding extensive views over the country round. It was rebuilt towards the close of the last century, and contains some fine apartments of true aristocratic splendour. From Northumberland Heath, a spacious tract of fertile ground in this parish, the metropolitan markets are largely supplied with Kentish cherries; and in the neighbourhood some handsome houses and villas have been lately erected. East India vessels frequently anchor in Erith Beach, and discharge their cargoes.

Purfleet, with its romantic chalk cliffs and excavations, is next visible on the Essex shore, and is said to have been thus called from an ejaculation of Queen Elizabeth, who exclaimed, "Alas! my *Poor Fleet*," as she witnessed from this spot the departure of her little force to oppose the passage of the "Invincible" Armada. The "poor fleet" having returned victorious, the place became thus designated in memory of the event; but it seems to have been after all but a sorry royal pun, for in the time of Edward III. it was called the manor of Portflete, and then belonged to the Knights of St. John of Jerusalem. Here the Government Powder Magazine is kept, having been, in the year 1762, removed hence from Greenwich. About three million pounds of gunpowder are generally preserved in the building, which of course has been so constructed that no danger by explosion need be apprehended. Lightning conductors are affixed to the exterior, and the usual regulations are observed when entering. Across the open country, on the Kentish side, may be seen the ancient church of DARTFORD, a creek where the river Darent or Dart discharges its waters into the Thames, affording a navigable communication with the town. Dartford was an important Roman station, and is memorable in history as the scene of Wat Tyler's insurrection in 1382. There are still some remains of a nunnery founded by Edward III., and the powder mills and iron founderies of Messrs. Hall give great importance to the traffic carried on by the inhabitants.

Greenhithe, which we next pass,

has several neat residences within its limits, occupying very pleasant situations; but, beyond the pier, and a small parish church at Swanscombe, has no feature calling for special mention. The stately mansion seen from the river is "Ingress Abbey," formerly the seat of the late J. Harmer, Esq., and is chiefly composed of the stone obtained from old London Bridge when pulled down. Swanscombe Wood, at the back, is a rare spot for pic-nic parties, and has a cavern rejoicing in the appellation of "Clappernapper's Hole," with some smuggling traditions in connexion with it. Here it was that the men of Kent stopped the Norman Conqueror, and compelled him to concede the ancient privilege of Gavelkind. WEST THURROCK, on the opposite side the river, is devoid of any thing to win more than a passing glance, though Belmont Castle, a fine castellated edifice belonging to a gentleman named Webb, is in a very agreeable position. From Greenhithe to Grays—a small market-town on the Essex coast, with a new pier and numerous brick kilns—the river is called St. Clement's Reach; and we then enter Northfleet Hope, where the widened expanse shows us the approach to Gravesend, and the straggling buildings of Northfleet poised upon a range of chalk cliffs.

Northfleet has an ancient church, one of the largest in Kent, containing several monuments of interesting antiquity, among which will be found one to Dr. Brown, physician to Charles II., and some curious brasses of the fourteenth century. The extensive excavations about here, forming a sort of miniature Switzerland, not only give the scenery a wild and romantic aspect, but furnish valuable materials for the potteries. ROSHERVILLE, though a suburb of Gravesend, belongs to this parish, and its neat pier is soon seen to the right, forming an elegant communication with that extensive range of buildings erected a few years since on the estate of the late Jeremiah Rosher. The Rosherville Gardens are open daily to the public, at the moderate admission fee of sixpence, and present a combination of attractions, produced by the united agency of nature and art, that leave them almost without a rival. It is absolutely astonishing to see what a fairyland has been here created out of a chalkpit. There are gala nights throughout the summer, when fireworks, music, and illuminations are added to the other enchantments of the spot. The Clifton Baths, on what is called "The Parade," are commodiously fitted up for cold, shower, warm, and vapour bathing, and seem to have been built in grotesque mimicry of the Pavilion at Brighton.

Gravesend has from the river a varied and pleasing aspect, which is not destroyed by a more intimate acquaintance with the town. Passengers are disembarked at the Rosherville Terrace and Town Piers, according to the boat in which the passage is taken. The latter, formed of cast iron, belongs to the corporation, and leads up through the narrow High Street, studded with taverns, to the London Road. The Terrace Pier, projecting on twenty-two cast iron columns nearly 200 feet into the river, leads direct to Harmer Street and Windmill Hill, besides affording a convenient approach to the elegant suburban district of Milton. The Terrace Gardens, on each side the entrance to the pier, are really very creditably and tastefully laid out, and as a day-admission ticket can be had for twopence, expense is no obstacle to the public frequenting them. Directly you traverse the streets of Gravesend, you see at a glance for what the town is famous. Shrimps and water-cresses tempt the visiter in every possible variety of supply, and places where both are obtainable, with "Tea at ninepence a-head," are in wonderful numerical strength. Like all other resorts for London visitors, taverns and tea gardens are abundant; their name is legion, and most of them have mazes, archery grounds, and "gipsy tents" attached, where the inquisitive that way can purchase the prophecy of a magnificent

fortune for the smallest sum in silver. Apartments can be had in nearly every house, and from the recognised salubrity of the air, and the beauty of the scenery surrounding, they are rarely untenanted during the height of the summer season. There is an excellent market, held every Wednesday and Saturday; a Town Hall, built in 1836; a Literary Institution, with a library, billiard-rooms, and assembly-rooms inclusive, built in 1842; churches and chapels in abundance; numerous libraries and bazaars; water-works on the summit of Windmill Hill; baths by the river, and a commodious Custom-house near the Terrace Gardens. Those who like to bathe in something approximating to salt water, should be governed by the influx of the tide, at which time an ablution that may be called a "Sea bath" can be indulged in with more personal gratification. Windmill Hill is, however, the magnet of the multitude, and a pleasanter or more varied panorama than that to be obtained from its summit is not to be found in places of much higher pretensions. There is one of the best views of the Thames winding between the shores of Kent and Essex, and, on every side, a far-spread landscape that embraces the shipping at the Nore, Southend Pier, Knockholt Beeches, on the very verge of Sussex, and a range of country spangled with clustered cottages and distant masses of woodland, that displays around a picture of unrivalled luxuriance and fertility. The Hill is crowned by an excellent tavern called "The Belle Vue," to the proprietor of which belongs the old windmill—the first erected in England, and as old in its foundations as the days of Edward III. Here refreshments are provided on the largest and most liberal scale, and an admirable Camera, together with some pleasure-grounds, and a labyrinth of ingenious construction, offer the best and most captivating allurements to visitors. Of late years every available spot has been built upon about the hill; and on a fine day thousands of our metropolitan denizens, leaving the purlieus of the smoke environed city, may be seen here, scattered over its sloping sides, participating in the healthful enjoyment it affords, and breathing the purer and fresher atmosphere of its elevated region. Those aquatically disposed will find it worth their while to take a boat across the river to TILBURY FORT, opposite, which was built by Henry VIII., to guard this portion of the river; and visitors are permitted, on application to the resident governor, to inspect the fortifications. Returning to Gravesend, the environs will be found replete with rural walks to gratify the eye and mind of the rambler. At SPRINGHEAD, where there is a water-cress plantation of considerable extent, will be seen the Cemetery, neatly laid out, and covering an extent of about six acres. But of all the places round, none should neglect an excursion to COBHAM, four miles distant, where, in the old wood and hall, a day's enjoyment can be most fully ensured. There are several vehicles always ready to be hired, that will take the visiter at a reasonable rate by the road; but as those who can appreciate a delightful walk will not find the distance too fatiguing, we shall proceed to indicate the route for the pedestrian. The Hall and Picture Gallery are open to the public every Friday; admission is by tickets, price one shilling each, supplied at Caddel's Library, and the proceeds thus resulting are applied to the school and other free institutions of the neighbourhood.

Taking the footpath at the back of Windmill Hill, the pedestrian will find it traversing a picturesque country, now crossing the sweeping undulation to a corn-field, and anon skirting a shaded copse with bluebells and primroses starting up in prodigal luxuriance through the tangled underwood. We next pass through a hop-plantation; and in summer, when the bine has sprung up to the top of the poles, and the shoots have thrust themselves off to the next, and so joined in a leafy communion of luxuriant vegetation, the scene becomes truly Arcadian, and an excellent substitute for the vineyards of the south. Leaving the little village of Singlewell to the right, we have a finger-post to guide us, and a few minutes after reach the outskirts of this sequestered village. The first object to which the visiter will naturally direct his attention is the old church, occupying rising ground in nearly the centre of the parish, and having on the southern side an extensive view. The antiquarian may here enjoy a great treat in inspecting the ancient monuments to be found in the interior, as there are several brasses of the Cobham family, successive generations of which, from the year 1354, have lived and died in the parish, as these memorials testify. On an altar-monument, in the middle of the chancel, are two full-length effigies, with several children around them in a kneeling position. This was erected to the memory of George Lord Cobham, who had been the governor of Calais in the reign of Elizabeth, and who died in 1558. On the tomb of Maud de Cobham is a curious sculptured figure of a dog, and one similar will be found in the chancel on the tomb of Joan, wife of Reginald Braybroke. They are worthy notice, as exemplifying the attachment felt towards two faithful canine adherents to the fortunes of the family. Outside, on the southern wall, there are some elegant tablets too of the Darnley family, and around are many humbler tombs bearing quaint and curious inscriptions. In such a scene we can afford to smile at the hackneyed quotations, the recurrence of the same breaches of grammar, the inroads upon the laws of poetry and the common-sense of prose. Occasionally, however, we meet with epitaphs endowed with a keen perception of beauty, or indicative of strong natural feeling, and these cannot but excite a solemn pleasure in the heart of the rural pedestrian. At the back of the church are some almshouses for the reception of twenty poor people, who have each a quarter of an acre of land, and a monthly stipend of eighteen shillings. It was originally founded in 1362. The inmates of this ancient building, dignified with the name of a college, are nominated respectively by the proprietor of Cobham Hall, the wardens of Rochester Bridge, and the neighbouring parishes. Passing through the village, which the readers of "Pickwick" will remember to have been the scene of one of the most humorous adventures of that renowned "Club," we proceed to the old Hall, bearing the name of a family that, from the reign of King John to the accession of James I., was amongst the most eminent in the country. Before describing the building, it will not be uninteresting to glance at the history of its former owners. In the fifteenth century the Cobham estate belonged to Joan, granddaughter and heiress of John Lord Cobham. This lady had no less than five husbands, one of them being the celebrated Sir John Oldcastle, who assumed the title of Cobham. Sir John, who had been the intimate friend of Henry V. in his younger days, and in whom some have erroneously detected the original of Sir John Falstaff, was soon after charged by the clergy with favouring the Lollards, and inciting "grievous heresy" in the king's dominions. In the proclamation issued by the king, it is declared that the Lollards meant to destroy him, confiscate the possessions of the church, and appoint Sir John Oldcastle president of the Commonwealth. He was in consequence taken prisoner in 1416, and, after an obstinate resistance, was sentenced to be hanged as a traitor and burned as a heretic. The estates, however, remained in the possession of his widow, who died in 1433, and from this period till 1596 they descended in lineal succession. In that year they came into the possession of Henry Lord Cobham, who was Lord Warden of the Cinque Ports, Constable of Dover Castle, and Lord-Lieutenant of the county. In 1603 this nobleman was accused, with others, of having been concerned in Sir Walter Raleigh's conspiracy; and being brought to trial at Winchester, on account of the plague then raging in London, they were found guilty, and judgment of death recorded. The brother of Lord Cobham was executed, but in his own case the sentence was remitted, and the estate being confiscated, he was reduced to the greatest poverty, his death, in 1619, being accelerated through absolute want. Having thus fallen into possession of the Crown, the manor of Cobham was granted by James I. to James Stewart, one of his own kinsmen, who seems, with his successor, not to have exhibited very thrifty management; for the house and grounds were sold at the close of the seventeenth century to enable the owner to satisfy his creditors. The price given furnishes a curious contrast with that which would be realized in the present day. The deer park, with the paddocks, containing as by survey 830 acres, was only valued at ten shillings the acre, the timber, woods, &c., being all included. It is also incidentally mentioned that at this time the mansion, which cost £60,000 building, had fourteen acres of orchard and garden-ground attached.

The remainder of its history may be briefly told. In 1714, the Hall and estate came by marriage into the possession of an Irish family of the name of Bligh, one of whom, in 1725, was created Earl of Darnley, and the seat of the Earls of Darnley it has continued to be ever since. The Hall is a massive and stately structure, consisting of two wings and a noble centre, the work of Inigo Jones. The oldest portions are those at the two extremities, flanked with octagonal towers; but modern art, in contributing the sashed windows and brickwork facing, has increased the comfort of the mansion at the expense of the picturesque. The Picture Gallery, having a choice collection of paintings by the old masters, and the unique gilt hall, form the most prominent features of attraction in the interior; but the apartments besides are elegantly furnished, and the quadrangle and old brick passages of the outbuildings wear about them an aspect of unmistakeable antiquity. On the south side, leading up to the principal entrance, is a noble lime-tree avenue, extending upwards of 3,000 feet in length. In the park, which is nearly seven miles round, there are some noble oak and chestnut trees, many of them measuring twenty feet and upwards in circumference. It has also the reputation of producing venison of superior flavour, derived from the peculiar excellence of the herbage; and it was on this fare probably that both Queen Elizabeth and Charles II. were regaled when they visited Cobham; for the former, according to Strype, was welcomed with a "delectable banquet and great cheer." In a romantic spot, towards the south-east end of the park, on an eminence called "William's Hill," there is a spacious mausoleum, erected in 1783 by the present Lord Darnley's grandfather. It is built of Portland stone, in an octagonal form, after the Doric order, and cost £9,000, but never having been consecrated, it has not been devoted to the purpose for which it was intended.

Cobham Wood is a glorious region for the rambler, and the footpath to Rochester, through the very heart of its sylvan solitudes, a delightful tract to follow. The pedestrian can also return, through the wood and Upper Shorne, to Gravesend by way of Chalk. Either way, a day's enjoyment here is complete. The countless hordes of wild-flowers, the golden treasures of the prickly gorse, the dark green majesty of the fern—that always looks to us like a miniature resemblance to those Eastern trees spoken of in the "Arabian Nights" —and all these spangled with the heads of sunlight, flung down, through the spreading branches overhead, from the azure canopy above, and there is here enough and more than enough to drive away from the heart every sign of care and worldly grievance. It is no slight addition to the picturesque charms of the forest foliage if you can wait and watch the effect of the sunset, marking the rich gradations of light and shade, in which the quivering leaves are alternately steeped. In fact, there is many a less interesting place to loiter in than Cobham Wood; and the dreamy tone imparted to the mental faculties by such a meditative lounge is a sort of warm bath for the imagination, refreshing it with a reverie which will enable the everyday realities of life to be more vigorously grappled with, and more successfully turned to advantage.* In such a place as this we may loll upon a couch of grassy surface, and luxuriate to our heart's content in the prospect before us—see with dreamy rapture the picturesque villages peacefully folded yonder in the green bosom of the undulating hills—gaze with delight on that old grey ruin, with its ivy-mantled walls and broken arches—watch with intense pleasure the glancing of the golden sunshine through the forest foliage;—and, whilst the only sounds that lull the drowsy sense of hearing are the gentle swaying to and fro of the leafy branches, and the thrilling melody of the skylark, subdued softly into silence by the blue distance, feel how

> " —pleasant it is when woods are green,
>   And winds are soft and low,
> To lie amid some sylvan scene,
> Where the long drooping boughs between,
> Shadows dark and sunlight sheen,
>   Alternate come and go."

* For further particulars connected with Gravesend and the scenery of the coast, see "Adams's Guide to the Watering-Places of England," in which a complete description is given of all the most admired marine resorts throughout England, the Channel Islands, &c.

The whole country round here is full of temptations for the erratic rambler; and the winding green lanes and quiet footpaths, that lead away from Cobham to the secluded villages towards the south, are enough to make a staid, sober citizen, who cherishes an intrusive recollection of dismal counting-houses and their commercial concomitants, envy that reckless freedom and joyous liberty possessed by the wandering vagrants whom he will occasionally encounter on the road. It is just the region where imagination lends a ray of ideal beauty to even the most trite occurrences of such a roaming life as that of the gipsy. We feel momentarily fascinated with that glorious embodiment of the poetry of vagabondism— that sunny existence spent in by-roads and bosky dells, tented by the spreading branches of fine old oaks, and sheltered by Nature's awnings from the summer rays—that relic of the eastern clime, which serves as a picturesque inroad on the dull conventionalities of country living, and throws a dash of romantic adventure into a chance encounter with the tribe. Yet with whatever alluring colours fancy may invest the gipsy life, another moment's reflection soon dispels the illusion, by reminding us that the aspect under which they view their career is widely different to what seems apparent to an unconcerned observer; and that, although daily surrounded by landscapes of rural beauty and sublimity, a want of mental refinement disqualifies them for the thorough enjoyment of the scenes by which they are environed. But to those with an imagination properly constituted, there is an extraordinary charm about a ramble of this kind. We put off all the grating cares and petty annoyances of life when we put on our easy boots. We become ourselves the very incarnations of happiness; the pink—possibly not of perfec-tion—but of pleasantry; and in short, if the proper state of mind has been duly attained, a day's ramble in Cobham Wood will make one of those "green spots in memory's waste" on which it is so delightful afterwards to repose, and listlessly ruminate over cheerful retrospections:—

" As when in ocean sinks the orb of day,
  Long on the wave reflected lustres play;
  These once bright scenes of days left far behind,
  Glance on the darken'd mirror of the mind."

WINDSOR.

GREAT WESTERN AND SOUTH WESTERN RAILWAYS—WINDSOR—WINDSOR CASTLE—
SAINT GEORGE'S CHAPEL—THE ROUND TOWER—ARRANGEMENTS OF ADMISSION—
THE STATE APARTMENTS—THE SLOPES—WINDSOR PARK—THE LONG WALK—
EQUESTRIAN STATUE OF GEORGE III.—VIRGINIA WATER—BELVIDERE—THE
CASCADE—FISHING TEMPLE—THE GRECIAN RUIN—BISHOPSGATE—SHELLEY—
STOKE POGIS—GRAY—BURNHAM BEECHES.

FOR the accomplishment of this excursion we must resort to steam, and the locomotive powers of the Great Western or South Western Railways, which run trains frequently throughout the day (for times, &c., see BRADSHAW'S RAILWAY GUIDE). The Great Western terminus is George-street, within five minutes' walk of the Castle, and the South Western terminus in Thames-street, ten minutes' walk from the Castle. Crossing the Bridge, which, spanning the Thames, connects ETON with Windsor, we may glance at the celebrated college, founded in 1442 by Henry VI., console ourselves with a passing quotation from Gray's ode on a distant prospect of its towers, for the bygone glories of its vanished "Montem", and then enter the royal town, that has been for centuries the chosen seat of the kings and queens of England. WINDSOR PARK AND WINDSOR CASTLE possess, with the surrounding scenery, inexhaustible attractions for the stranger, and lose none of their charms even after an acquaintance of several years. So long back as the days of the early Saxons, when WINDLESHORA was its name, from the windings of the Thames, a castle stood at old Windsor, appropriated to the crown as a palatial residence. William the Conqueror next built a far better structure on the present site, and laid the foundation of its future importance. Here Henry I. held his court, and having enlarged the castle with "many fair buildings," kept the festival of Whitsuntide with unusual solemnities in 1110. In the time of Stephen it was the second fortress in the kingdom, and sustained several changes of masters during the wars between the crown and the barons, in the turbulent reigns of John and Henry III. Edward III. was born here, and extended the structure, on a most expensive scale, in 1356. William of Wykeham was the architect, and it is recorded that in one year 360 workmen were impressed to be employed at the king's wages—no very liberal remuneration, we may be sure, when the architect himself had only a shilling a-day. The festivals of the Order of the Garter were here celebrated with great splendour. For the especial service of this order, Edward III. erected at Windsor a chapel dedicated to St. George, but the present beautiful chapel is of much later date. It was begun by Edward

IV., who found it necessary to take down the original fabric on account of its decayed state, and was not completed until the beginning of Henry VIII.'s reign. It was here that Richard II. heard the appeal of high treason brought by the Duke of Lancaster against Mowbray Duke of Norfolk, and which ended in the former becoming Henry IV. The Earl of Surrey, imprisoned for violating the canons of the church by eating flesh in Lent, here wooed the muse in his retirement; and here was the last prison of that unfortunate monarch, Charles I. Passing over the intermediate reigns, as presenting little of interest in connexion with the building, we may mention that George III. dwelt for many years in a whitewashed house, at the foot of his own palace, till he was persuaded at length to occupy the old castle. George IV., soon after his accession, commenced some extensive improvements, and, under the superintendence of Sir Jeffrey Wyatville, it was thoroughly renovated, and in many portions rebuilt. With this brief preparatory glance at its former history, we now proceed up Castle Street, and commence a rapid survey of its prominent features.

The usual entrance is under Henry VIII.'s gateway, leading to the lower ward, and close to that magnificent specimen of Gothic architecture, ST. GEORGE'S CHAPEL. Though this building and its decorations are pre-eminently beautiful, it is perfectly of a devotional character. The richly decorated roof, supported on clustered columns, the "storied windows, richly dight," the banners and escutcheons of the knights of the garter, and the massive floor of marble, all unite to produce a striking and impressive effect. As works of art, the monuments in the chapel are, perhaps, disappointing. Edward IV. is buried here, beneath that remarkable specimen of elaborate ingenuity, the iron tomb of Quintin Matsys, the artist-blacksmith of Antwerp; and in the opposite aisle, under a plain marble stone, his unhappy rival, Henry VI., is interred. Henry VIII. and Charles I. are entombed under the choir, without any memorial; and there is a cenotaph, by Wyatt, to the memory of the Princess Charlotte. At the foot of the altar is a subterraneous passage, communicating with the tomb-house, in which is the cemetery of the present race of monarchs, containing, amongst others, the remains of George III. and Queen Charlotte, George IV., William IV., the Duke of York, Duke of Kent, and the Princesses Amelia, Augusta, and Charlotte. From the east end of the lower ward we pass into the middle ward, bounded by a low battlement, enclosing a deep moat, cultivated as a garden. The CHAPEL may be viewed during the summer months between the intervals of divine service, which is celebrated daily at half-past ten in the morning, and half-past four in the afternoon, on application to the sextons, Mr. Wise and Mr. Winter, Horse-Shoe Cloisters, one of whom is usually in attendance. For full particulars of admission to the Castle, see page 242. The ROUND TOWER, with the royal standard floating from the summit, hence appears to great advantage, and twelve counties are within its ken. This "keep," as it is sometimes called, as it formed the prison of the castle till 1660, is not a perfect circle, for it is 192 feet in its greatest diameter, and 93 in its smallest; its height is 80 feet from the top of the mound; watch-tower, 25 more; and its entire height, from the level of the quadrangle, 148 feet. In the Great Quadrangle, at the base of the Round Tower, is a bronze statue of Charles II., erected in 1679 at the expense of one Tobias Rustat, described by Evelyn as "a very simple, ignorant, but honest and loyal creature," and who thus bestowed a thousand pounds. The pedestal, by Grinling Gibbons, is very fine. On the north side of this quadrangle is King John's Tower, and the space between this and the massive square tower beyond is occupied by the Queen's Audience Chamber, at which the suite of state apartments commences. The projecting doorway is the state entrance, on a line with which is the vestibule, continued through to George IV.'s Tower in the North Terrace, whence there is a magnificent vista of nearly three miles.

Within our prescribed limits it is manifestly impossible to give more than a mere enumeration of the State Apartments, which form a series unequalled in Europe for magnificence.

Approaching through the Gothic porch at the north-west angle of the upper ward, we are led by a fine staircase to the AUDIENCE CHAMBER, hung with Gobelin tapestry, and embellished with a painted ceiling by Verrio. The PRESENCE CHAMBER, or Ball-Room, for which purpose it is generally appropriated, is a spacious apartment, ninety feet long, thirty-two broad, and thirty-three feet high, opening at the southern end into St. George's Hall, and terminating at Cornwall Tower on the North Terrace. The decorations are in the *Louis Quatorze* style. The VANDYKE ROOM comprises a fine collection of the works of that eminent master, twenty-two in number. The "Five Children of Charles the First," over the chimney-piece, and a picture representing that unfortunate monarch on horseback, at the end of the room, are particularly admired. The GUARD CHAMBER is very attractive to visiters, and is seventy-eight feet long and thirty-one feet high. It contains Chantrey's colossal bust of Nelson, and part of the foremast of the Victory; the Blenheim white banner; a bust of the Duke of Marlborough; Cellini's silver shield, inlaid with gold, presented by Francis I. of France to Henry VIII.; and a bust, by Chantrey, of the Duke of Wellington, with the last annual banner presented on the Waterloo anniversary, in memory of the tenure by which Strathfieldsaye is held. The walls are decorated with arms. ST. GEORGE'S HALL, with its portraits of eleven of our latest sovereigns, and the Waterloo Gallery, pictorially presenting the most eminent statesmen and soldiers connected with that decisive battle, are sure to engage the visiter's attention. The other apartments are enriched with numerous paintings by the most distinguished masters; but the catalogues describing them are so cheap, and so complete, that it would be useless for us to encroach on pages that might be much better occupied than by giving a mere list of pictures, which space would not permit us to dwell upon as they deserve.

Beneath the North Terrace are the SLOPES, extending into the HOME (or LITTLE) PARK, which has been for a long period an appurtenance to the Castle. Near the avenue called "Queen Elizabeth's Walk," tradition still points out a withered tree as the identical oak of "Herne the Hunter," who, as the old tale goes,

" Sometime a keeper here in Windsor Forest,
  Both all the winter time, at still midnight,
  Walk round about the oak with great ragged horns."

The LONG WALK, affording perhaps the finest vista of the kind in the world, extends from the principal entrance of the castle to the top of a commanding hill in the Great Park, called Snow Hill, a distance of three miles. There is a splendid prospect at the end, affording a panoramic view of several memorable places, endeared by historical and poetic associations. A mile to the eastward, on the same hilly ridge where we stand, is "Cooper's Hill," the subject of a pleasant descriptive poem by Sir John Denham; Windsor Castle appears in all its massive grandeur beneath us; to the right is the Thames, seen beyond Charter Island, and the little plain of Runnymede, where the turbulent barons extorted "Magna Charta" from King John; whilst far beyond, in the blue distance, are the hills of Harrow and Hampstead. On the summit of this hill, where the avenue terminates, was placed, in the summer of 1832, a colossal bronze equestrian statue of George III., by Westmacott. The total elevation is more than fifty feet; the statue, without the pedestal, being twenty-six feet high. The likeness is very striking; but the Roman costume, adopted as being more manageable in art than a square-cut coat and military jack-boots, will convey an odd notion, a thousand years hence, of the King of England's dress in the nineteenth century.

Of course, those who can afford the time will not leave Windsor Park without seeing VIRGINIA WATER, which was planted and the lake formed by Paul Sandby, when the Duke of Cumberland, the hero of Culloden, resided at the lodge, which still bears his name, about three miles from Windsor. The lake is the largest piece of artificial water in the kingdom, if that can be called artificial where man has only collected the streams of the district into a natural basin. The surrounding scenery is exceedingly pleasing and picturesque. After passing through a woody dell, we come to some serpentine walks, which lead in different directions; those to the right conducting us to a somewhat steep hill, on the summit of which stands a handsome Gothic battlemented building, called the BELVIDERE; and those to the left leading to the margin of the lake. At the head of the lake is a cascade, descending some twenty feet, over massive fragments of stone, into a dark glen or ravine. Near it is an obelisk standing on a small mount, and bearing the following inscription, added by William IV.:—"This obelisk was raised by the command of George II., after the battle of Culloden, in commemoration of the services of his son William, Duke of Cumberland, the success of his arms, and the gratitude of his father." There is a road hence to the banks of the lake, where we can reach a rustic bridge, and get a fine view of the waterfall and its cavern adjacent, formed of stones brought from Bagshot Heath, where they indicated the ruins of a Saxon cromlech. At the point where the lake is widest, a fishing temple was erected by George IV.

A bold arch carries the public road to BLACKNEST, over a portion of the grounds, and adjoining is an ornamental ruin, called the "Temple of the Gods," manufactured from some really antique fragments of Greek columns and pediments, that used to lie in the court-yard of the British Museum. The effect is striking, and much more so if the spectator will for a moment let fancy delude him into the belief that he is gazing on a real temple of ancient Athens. The tall trees, clustering round in one part, and in another opening on to glades of truly sylvan aspect, impart a romantic beauty to the landscape from this point which utterly defies description. It is worth while to cross the little bridge above alluded to, and, passing one of the streams that feed the lake, pursue its windings among the underwood, or strike into the path which leads to

BISHOPSGATE, a beautiful village, environed by all the charms of wood and water diversity. Here resided for some time Shelley, who has consecrated the allurements of this spot by some of his finest poems, written in the vicinity. There are several ways of approaching Virginia Water, each so attractive that it is difficult to decide upon the best; but, by whichever route the excursionist comes, we would suggest the adoption of another road for the return. About two miles beyond the town of Egham is a neat wayside inn, called the "Wheatsheaf," from the garden of which there is direct access to the lake. From Egham Hill a road diverges through Windsor Park to Reading, nineteen miles distant. A few hundred yards above the inn is a branch road to the right, leading to Blacknest, where there is also an entrance through the keeper's lodge. Besides this, there is a delightful drive of five miles to Virginia Water from Chertsey.

Stoke Pogis, two miles from Slough, is hallowed ground, from containing the churchyard which suggested Gray's well-known "Elegy," as well as the remains of the pensive poet himself. Gray died on the 30th of July 1771, in the 55th year of his age, and was buried, according to his own affectionate wish, by the side of his mother; thus adding another poetical association to this beautiful and classic region. BURNHAM is a small but most picturesque village, four miles from Slough, with a marvellous miniature forest, called "Burnham Beeches,"—the finest spot in the world for a pic-nic, and absolutely unrivalled for the romantic character of its sylvan scenery. There are the ruins of an Augustine nunnery close by, which, though now partly fashioned into a farmhouse, had the honour of having been built by an expatriated king of the Romans, in 1228.

A pedestrian of congenial temperament, who rambles down here in the dawn of a summer's morning, would find it no easy matter to tear himself away before twilight. The Great Western Railway is again our connecting link with town, and hence the train will bear us back to those gas-lit streets, which, in their noisy bustle and confusion, will contrast so strangely with the sylvan glades and tranquil solitudes from which we have just departed.

RICHMOND,

WHERE either train or steamboat will enable us to stop, is just the pleasant point for an excursionist to reach bent upon exercise and enjoyment. The walks by the margin of the river, the leafy luxuriance of the park, the famed view from the hill, and the varied scenery of its environs, through which wind the prettiest green lanes imaginable, all tend to make this "region of loveliness" attractive beyond the day. Monarchs and monks had a wonderful knack long ago of discovering the prettiest places for a summer retreat round London, and accordingly we find it was a royal residence at a very early period. At Richmond Green, where the only remains of the "aun-ciente Palace of Sheen" is to be found, in a gateway at the north-east angle, Kings Edward I. and II. lived, and the third King Edward died—broken-hearted, it is said, for the loss of his heroic son, "The Black Prince." Here, too, died Anne, Richard II.'s queen, who first introduced the side-saddle for the benefit of succeeding female equestrians. In 1492, Henry VII. gave a grand tournament, and here, in 1509, he died. Queen Elizabeth also breathed her last in this regal abode, which, after minor changes connected with royalty, was finally demolished by George III. in 1769. Passing through the town, which contains on its outskirts several elegant villas of the nobility, we proceed up the hill to the park, which embraces an area of about 2,300 acres, and is nearly nine miles in circumference. It was enclosed by Charles I. with a brick wall, and this became one of the articles of his impeachment. An attempted exclusion of the public, in the reign of George III., caused a spirited resistance from a brewer named Lewis, who, by an action at law, established the right of footway, and since then no further encroachment upon the privileges of the public has been essayed. The umbrageous solitudes of this fine park, and the comprehensive and beautiful views from its summit, extending over the fertile valley of the Thames, and even including the distant turrets of Windsor Castle, have long been the theme of eulogy in book and ballad. At sunset, when the far-off masses of foliage are sobered down by twilight, and the river, catching the last beams of the sinking orb, gleams through the leafy landscape like a fairy lake, in which every ripple yields a golden sparkle, the scene is truly enchanting. In Richmond Church, a neat structure, partly ancient and partly modern, there are several interesting memorials of the departed great. The first that arrests attention is a marble tablet on the well, with a medallion head sculptured on it, beneath which is the following inscription,—"Edmund Kean—died May, 1833, aged 46—a memorial erected by

his son Charles John Kean, 1839." Here, too, is the grave of the poet James Thomson, with the Earl of Buchan's copper tablet, the inscription on which time has almost made illegible. He was buried without the wall; but the church having been enlarged to make room for the organ, the wall now passes right across his coffin, cutting the body, as it were, in twain. Near the communion table lies Mary Ann Yates, a celebrated tragic actress, and once the Mrs. Siddons of her day, but now her very name appears forgotten. In a whimsical epitaph to a Welsh lawyer, one Robert Lewes, it is recorded to his honour, that he "was such a great lover of peace and quietness, that when a contention began in his body between Life and Death, he immediately gave up the ghost to end the dispute." Among the rest may be mentioned, tombs to the memory of Joseph Taylor, the original "Hamlet;" Dr. Moore, the author, and father of the Corunna-renowned general, Sir John Moore; Gilbert Wakefield, the critic; Viscount Fitzwilliam, who founded the Museum at Cambridge; and Edward Gibson, an artist of repute. Richmond has a theatre, first opened in 1719 by the facetious Will Penkethman, and carried on for some time by Cibber; it was the scene of many of Kean's triumphs in the mimic art; latterly it has been badly managed and worse frequented; but the Prince

O

of Wales having taken up his residence at Richmond as Ranger of the Park the fortunes of the theatre even may be revived. Near it is "Rosedale House," where Thomson lived and died (August 22, 1748), and having lately become the residence of the Countess of Shaftesbury, it is known as "Thomson's Villa." Many relics of the poet, and some manuscript portions of "The Seasons," in his own handwriting, are here carefully preserved. The summer-house, his poetic study, still exists.

Petersham, reached by a pleasant rural lane leading from the hill, is delightfully situated in the valley beneath, and has some fine springs of water, which are duly taken advantage of by a hydropathic establishment recently formed. Ham House was once a royal domain, where James I., Charles I., Charles II., and James II., the latter by compulsion, occasionally resided. About a mile west from Richmond is TWICKENHAM, near which is TWICKENHAM AIT, or Eel-pie Island, consecrated from time immemorial to the votaries of that esteemed delicacy. Pope's Villa, now demolished, and having a number of villas on its site, has long associated the poet's name with the place. In the village church may be seen his tomb, with a Latin inscription written by his friend Warburton, Bishop of Gloucester, and a more characteristic one beneath, written by the bard himself. The once celebrated actress, "Kitty Clive," is also buried in this sequestered church; she died in 1785, aged 75. The almshouses of the Carpenters' Company occupy a prominent situation beyond. Nearly a mile farther is STRAWBERRY HILL, where the celebrated Horace Walpole collected the famous assortment of valuables and curiosities, which, under the direction of the late Earl of Waldegrave, were consigned to the hammer of George Robins, and dispersed among those private individuals who were wealthy enough to become possessed of the varied contents of this Gothic hall.

Teddington, two miles further, is well known to the angling fraternity, and here the first "lock" is encountered in the upward progress along the Thames. It is worth while to turn aside from the road, and have a look at the old church, which, though recently modernised, presents in its south aisle a specimen of architectural stability of 800 years back. "Peg Woffington," the clever actress and beautiful woman, whose history is of itself a romance, was here buried in 1720, and there are other monuments of remunerative interest and antiquity.

HAMPTON COURT,

To which another two miles from Richmond will bring us, requires a volume exclusively devoted to its attractions to render them due justice; but in default of a professed "Guide," our account —though necessarily compressed—will be found sufficient to prevent any of its "Lions" being overlooked from a want of their being enumerated. The situation of Hampton Court, which stands on the north bank of the Thames, about twelve miles from London, is so happily described by Pope, that we cannot resist quoting the favourite passage:—

" Close by those meads for ever crown'd with flowers,
  Where Thames with pride surveys his rising towers,
  There stands a structure of majestic frame,
  Which from the neighbouring Hampton takes its
    name
  Here Britain's statesmen oft the fall foredoom
  Of foreign tyrants and of nymphs at home;
  Here thou great Anna, whom three realms obey,
  Dost sometimes counsel take, and sometimes—tea."

In summing up the points of its early history, we may briefly state, that in the thirteenth century the manor of Hampden was vested in the Knights of St. John of Jerusalem. Cardinal Wolsey, its illustrious founder, was the last of the enlightened churchmen of old, whose munificence patronised that style of building; which, originating with the ecclesiastics, seemed to end in his fall. He is supposed to have furnished the designs, and having been commenced in 1515, the building, when finished, was in so magnificent a style, that it created great envy at court. The banquets and masques, so prevalent in the age of Henry VIII., were nowhere more magnificently ordered than here; and, however vast the establishment of the Cardinal, it could not have been more than sufficient for the accommodation of his train of guests. Numerous sovereigns since that time made it their temporary abode; and the last who resided here were George II. and his Queen, since which period various members of the court have occupied the apartments, the Crown reserving the right of resuming possession. At present, about 700 decayed gentlemen and gentlewomen, with their servants, occupy offices connected with the establishment, to which they are recommended by the Lord Chamberlain. The Lion gate, which fronts the entrance to the magnificent drives and promenades of Bushy Park, is the chief avenue; and continuing through the Wilderness, by a path overshadowed with lofty trees, we find ourselves by the side of the palace, in front of which extends a long walk, ornamented with parterres, an exotic shrubbery, and a spacious fountain in the centre. The grand east front extends 330 feet, and the grand south front 328 feet, from the designs of Sir Christopher Wren. The grand staircase and the guard-chamber lead to the picture galleries, to which so many cheap catalogues furnish descriptive guides, that our enumeration of their magnificent contents is unnecessary. Suffice it to say, the paintings are about 1,000 in number. Retracing our steps to the middle court, we may observe, under the archway, the flight of steps leading to Wolsey's Hall. It is 106 feet long, forty feet wide, and illuminated by thirteen windows, each fifteen feet from the ground. On one of the panes of the bay window at the end, extending nearly to the floor, the young Earl of Surrey wrote his lines to the fair Geraldine. On each side the walls are hung with tapestry of the most costly material and rarest workmanship, said to have formed a portion of the gifts interchanged between Henry and Francis, at the celebrated "Field of the Cloth of Gold." In the centre of the dais there is a doorway leading to the withdrawal room. The beautiful gardens in front of the palace have been repeatedly the admiration of all visiters. They were laid out by William III. in the Dutch style, with canal and watercourses, and the compass and shears were industriously employed in making birds, beasts, and reptiles, out of yew, holly, and privet. The private gardens extend from the sides of the palace to the banks of the river, and contain, besides some remarkably fine orange-trees, many of them in full bearing, a fine oak nearly forty feet in circumference, and an ancient elm called "King Charles's swing." The large space of ground on the opposite side of the palace is called "THE WILDERNESS," and was planted with shrubs by order of William and Mary. Most of the walks are completely overshadowed, and on a hot summer day a stroll through these umbrageous paths is exceedingly inviting. In this portion of the grounds is situated the MAZE, so constructed that all the paths apparently leading to the centre turn off to a more distant part, and involve the inquisitive adventurer in constant perplexity. Though we are not quite sure that the revelation does not spoil the chief sport, the secret of success in threading this miniature labyrinth is, that after the first turning to the left the right hand should be kept towards the fence the whole of the remaining way. The greatest curiosity, however, is perhaps the famous Vine, which, sheltered and nurtured in a hothouse, is 110 feet long, and, at three feet from the root, is twenty-seven inches in circumference. It bears from two to three thousand bunches of the black Hamburg grape in the season. We may now mention the arrangements made for the reception of visiters.

The State Apartments, Public Gardens, and Picture Galleries, are open daily (Friday excepted) throughout the year, from ten till dusk; and on Sundays after two P.M. The Public Gardens have generally a military band in attendance, and a small fee is expected by the gardener for exhibiting the orangery and the vine.

The Chestnut Avenue of Bushy is world-famous. "Look across the road," says a pleasant companion to the spot, "upon those dark masses of a single tree with thousands of spiral flowers, each flower a study, powdering over the rich green from the lowest branch to the topmost twig. Now you shall have a real reward for your three hours' toil under a lustrous sun. Look up and down this wondrous avenue. Its mile length seems a span; but from one gate to the other there is a double line of unbroken green, with flowers rich as the richest of the tropics contending for the mastery of colour. Saw you ever such a gorgeous sight? Fashionable London even comes to see it; but in theWhitsun week, and during the some twenty days of the glories of the chestnut, thousands come here to rejoice in the exceeding beauty of this marvel of nature, which the art of the Dutch gardeners, whom William of Nassau brought to teach us, have left as a proud relic of their taste."

We hence recommend the excursionist to proceed across Kingston Bridge, erected in 1827, to KINGSTON, a distance of not much more than two miles, and take a train homeward by the South Western Railway. Kingston Church was the scene of the coronation of many of our Saxon kings, who here held their court, and the stone on which the ceremony took place is still preserved near the Courts of Assize. A striking illustration of the creative powers of a railroad is manifested by the rise of a new town by the station, called Surbiton, or Kingston-on-Railway. Although this was, only a few years back, a mere piece of waste ground, it is now a populous and thriving settlement, with a fashionable assemblage of shops continued along one wide street, from the "Railway Hotel" to a considerable distance down the Kingston road. Near this spot took place the last struggle of the Royalists in favour of Charles I., who was then a prisoner in Carisbrooke Castle; but, with that fatality which seemed to attend all their efforts, the cavaliers were repulsed with great slaughter, Lord Francis Villiers slain, and the Earl of Holland captured, with others of the nobility. Selecting an easy seat in the compartment of a comfortable carriage, we shall now be borne back in an hour to the terminus at Waterloo Road, whence we started; and this rapid progression, after our agreeable sauntering through the meadows and by paths, will, to our thinking and experience, be a very pleasant mode of terminating a very pleasant pilgrimage, during which we trust you have found in us a very communicative companion.

EPSOM

ENJOYS a world-wide celebrity, for two very different things—its RACE-COURSE and its SALTS. Whilst the former, however, still flourishes in unabated attraction, the latter has been long superseded by an artificial preparation of the same nature, and bearing the same name. In the seventeenth century this was the fashionable Spa of England, and the newspapers at the time advertised, "that the post will go every day to and fro, between London and Epsom, during the season for drinking the waters." In the time of Charles I., these salts were so celebrated that they were sold at 5s. the ounce, and from 1690 to 1720, the wells were in their zenith of prosperity. As chemical science improved, cheaper and more abundant sources were discovered, and even sea-water was found to yield it by evaporation. It is simply a sulphate of magnesia, and is generally prepared for commerce by subjecting magnesian limestone to the action of muriatic and sulphuric acids. The old bath room was pulled down in 1804. The race-course, on the Downs south-east of the town, with its noble "Grand Stand," and the annual attractions of the "Derby" day, form a combination of attractive features too familiar to need more than a brief mention. Epsom Races— the most truly national festival of which we can boast—have been held annually on the same spot since 1730; the two great races, "The Derby" and the "Oaks," deriving their names, one from the title of the nobleman by whom it was instituted, and the other from the fine seat of the Earl of Derby, near Sutton, called "The Oaks."

THE CRYSTAL PALACE.

The Crystal Palace stands upon the heights of Penge, the most remarkable work of its kind the world has ever witnessed, appealing to appreciation of the wonderful with a force unknown in this country, and unrivalled in any other.

Versailles is not nearly so marvellous a sight as that brilliant fabric which rears its glittering hulk upon the Surrey hills, within view of the metropolis. It is a work fit to take rank with the noblest and greatest in the world.

The building, the park, the waterworks, the garden inside and out, the fine art collection—all, more or less, surpass what could be hoped for or desired.

This marvellous work of commercial enterprise and human ingenuity has now so far reached perfection as to realise all the anticipations that had been formed during its progress. What was said of it on its first pillar being raised has become a demonstrated truth, as the structure has grown into maturity, and we here behold a building which, for the excellence of its objects, the magnitude of its design, and the triumph of its execution has no equal in the world. Former ages, it is true, have raised palaces enough, and many of them of surpassing magnificence. We have heard of the Hanging Gardens of Babylon, the colossal temples of Egypt, and the gorgeous structures of Nineveh and Persepolis; many have seen the scattered fragments of Nero's Golden Palace on the Palatine Hill, and the vast ruins which still speak so eloquently of the grandeur of Imperial Rome; but these were but raised by the spoils of captive nations and the forced labour of myriads of slaves, to gratify the caprice or vanity of some solitary despot. It is to our own age that the privilege has been reserved of raising a palace for the people—the production of their own unaided and independent enterprise. We find here the greatest amount of instruction, combined with the largest amount of amusement, the highest utility blended with the highest refinement, and, as an educational institute, as well as an enchanting recreative resort, the Crystal Palace will every year strengthen its claims upon the patronage of the public, and more triumphantly attest the genius and indefatigable energy of its founders.

The origin of that peculiarly appropriate style of architecture, which has now become so familiar to the eye, is worth remembering. A few years ago, a party of naturalists proceeding in a boat up some unexplored river in South America came suddenly upon a floral specimen which filled them with amazement and delight. They beheld peacefully floating on the waters a lily of such gigantic proportions that its petals could not be embraced by the outstretched arms, and whose boat-like leaves were able to support the full weight of a man. Extraordinary as this discovery was considered at the time, no one could imagine the train of events to which it was destined to give rise; that the sudden surprisal of that Brobdignagian flower in its native wilds, where for thousands of years it had bloomed unseen by man, would be the immediate cause of a crystalline structure —yet so it proved.

When the Victoria Regia Lily was brought to this country and removed to the princely grounds of Chatsworth, it was found necessary to build a conservatory purposely for its accommodation. This conservatory was constructed by Mr. Paxton, of glass and iron—the first of its kind ever erected, and this little house of glass was the first fruits of that mother-thought which reared the gleaming arch, and stretched the vast arcades upon the emerald sod in Hyde Park, and which has since ornamented all the important capitals in Europe and America with palaces of crystal such as we only read of in old fairy tales.

The Crystal Palace estate was originally called Penge Park, and is situated in the parish of Battersea, partly in Surrey and partly in Kent. A finer site could not possibly have been chosen. Standing on the brow of a hill rising some two hundred feet above the valley through which the railroad passes, the Crystal Palace is visible for miles away in every direction. The grounds form an irregular parallelogram, about half way between the Sydenham and Annerley stations, having a frontage towards the railway of 1,300 feet, and facing the New Road, Dulwich Wood, a frontage of 3,000 feet, giving a magnificent panoramic view of London, and the high grounds of Middlesex from the galleries on the Dulwich side, and of the beautiful undulating scenery of Kent on the Penge side. The entire area consists of about 289 acres, and the carriage drive round the park and grounds is nearly two miles. The building covers a space of 20 acres, and is, from end to end of the nave, 1,608 feet, and from side to side, 384

CHELSEA HOSPITAL

WESTMINSTER ABBEY

THE ARMY AND NAVY CLUB HOUSE

HUNGERFORD SUSPENSION BRIDGE

HAMPTON COURT

KEW GARDENS

GREENWICH HOSPITAL

TEMPLE BAR

THE TREASURY WHITEHALL

VIEWS IN LONDON AND ITS ENVIRONS

feet. It is intersected by three transepts, the central one being 384 feet long and 120 feet wide. The two end transepts are each 336 feet in length and 72 feet in width, and the whole length of the palace, from end to end of the wings, is 2,000 feet. These wings are each 600 feet long, and terminate in towers 100 feet in height. The chief transept is about 200 feet in height, and has five tiers of galleries; the end transepts, three tiers. Five hundred tons weight of glass have been consumed in the roof and sides, and the cubic contents of the building are estimated at 40,000,000 feet—about one-fourth more than that in Hyde Park, and forty times more than Westminster Hall, the largest hall in England.

With reference to the distinctive dimensions of the Palace at Sydenham and the one in Hyde Park a few figures will assist us in drawing a comparison between them. The length is 1,608 feet, or less by 240 feet than the building of 1851. It is broken by three transepts instead of one, of which two are 136 feet in height from the garden, with a span of 72 feet, and the third 200 feet, with a span of 120 feet. The extreme breadth of the building is 384 feet at the transept, or 72 feet less than the Palace in Hyde Park, and this breadth is apparently further diminished by the arched roof which now runs the full length of the whole building. The diminution of the length and breadth is in some measure compensated by the capacity of the two wings, which stretch on either extremity 567 feet. These extend into, and as it were, enclose the Italian terrace garden. There is also an additional basement story, which goes by the appellation of Sir Joseph Paxton's tunnel.

This basement story or tunnel contains apparatus for warming the building by rows of furnaces and boilers, and an iron network forming fifty miles of steam pipes. It extends from end to end of the building—a distance of 1,608 feet, and is 24 feet wide. There are about thirty boilers arranged in pairs along the tunnel at regular distances.

Conveyances to the Palace.— No undertaking, however wonderful, will be largely visited for pleasure which demands a sacrifice of some three hours to reach or to leave. The noble site, the unrivalled view, the splendid gardens and fountains will spread their attractions in vain on the heights of Penge unless the bulk of the people of London can get there as quickly, as cheaply, and as pleasantly as they can get up or down the river. The Company have done all they possibly can to facilitate the passage of visitors at a distance to and from the palace, the new west-end railway materially aiding those residing west of London. The trains start punctually from the London Bridge and Victoria Stations at the times advertised in the official bills; but special trains are put on always as occasion may require.

The shortest route from London, by carriage, is by the Elephant and Castle, Camberwell, Denmark Hill, Herne Hill, and Dulwich. The ordinary entrances from the road are at the South and Central Transepts. Entrances are also provided opposite Sydenham Church, and at the bottom of the Park, below the Grand Lake and Extinct Animals.

Omnibuses leave Gracechurch Street for the Crystal Palace at intervals from 10 in the morning. An omnibus also loaves the Paddington Station at a quarter to 11 A.M. Also one from the Kings and Key, Elect Street, at 12 o'clock, and one from the Green Man, Oxford Street, at the same time. Omnibuses leave the City for Camberwell every ten minutes. Conveyance can also be procured from Peckham and Clapham. On fête days omnibuses run at frequent intervals, at times according to the season.

ORDER OF INSPECTION.—The plan of arrangement adopted in the following description supposes the visitor to have arrived at the Crystal Palace by railway, and to have proceeded at once by the covered way into the South Wing, where he will find the Screen of the Kings and Queens, and the well-known Crystal Fountain from Hyde Park. Here he may commence his journey of inspection, beginning with the Pompeain Court, on the left hand, and continuing the series in the order indicated. Before he does so a familiar object will have now caught the visitor's attention in this part of the Southern Transept, for amidst beautiful trees, plants, and evergreens of all descriptions, will be recognised the equestrian statue of Charles I., taken from that at Charing Cross. Here also are prepared birds and animals, placed upon and surrounded by the trees, which would be their favourite haunt in a state of nature. The best view is attainable from the galleries above.

As a general guide to the visitors, it will be convenient to remember that one half of the building is devoted to ancient art, architecture, and sculpture, and that the other half, that facing the garden, is appropriated to all the various forms of modern art, architecture, inventions, improvements, and manufactures, together with a well-arranged Picture Gallery, which now contains nearly 1,000 pictures, by ancient and modern artists. There are some exceptions to the rule, where exigencies of space have modified the arrangements, but this will serve as some clue to guide the stranger through the beautiful labyrinth, in the apparent intricacies of which he will find himself at first bewildered. The very brilliant and fairy-like aspect of the place, as it reveals itself suddenly to the eye, will produce an impression, of itself calculated to absorb the utmost attention a visitor can bestow on his first becoming acquainted with the interior, and the multitude of objects around him will seem to baffle all attempts to discover the nature of their arrangements. So admirably, however, have the different compartments been designed, that a very little consideration will soon enable the public to reach that in which they may be especially interested, and the multiplicity of claims upon our notice will only serve to elicit from us additional tributes of admiration. It is emphatically the triumph of artistic design as well as of artistic construction.

The Great Transept, where the Handel Orchestra, capable of holding 4,000 performers, and the organ built by Gray and Davidson are conspicuous, divides the nave into two equal parts, the northern division dedicated to art, and the southern to commerce, and both presenting all the embellishments of fountains, flowering shrubs and rare trees. The South wing connects the railway with the palace, by means of a covered way. The North Wing was blown down during the gales of last winter; fortunately, at the time, this part of the building was but little used.

The Pompeian House, which begins the series, is the fac-simile of a building discovered when excavating the ruins of Pompeii, and from the character of the ornamental decoration, has been named the house of the Nereids and the tragic poets. As he enters, the visitor steps, as it were, into the first century of the Christian era, with all the associations of Tacitus and Pliny around him. The building is formed of an open court, with smaller apartments on each side, and the centre is occupied by a fountain, the roof above which is supported by Fames or winged angelic figures, the four above the Tablinum, or state room, leading to the inner court, being gilt. Against the walls of the outer court, stands, in a niche, like that of an Italian Madonna, the altars of the guardian LARES, to whom incense was burned and offerings made on certain days. The quadrangle is paved with mosaic, and passing on through an open room on its side passages, we reach the inner quadrangle, with its garden also open to the sun, and with its roof supported by sixteen pillars. Round these are disposed the dining rooms, baths, and kitchen. The walls of the Pompeian Court are divided into compartments by pilasters, and each compartment is painted, for half the height of the room, a deep red or deep brilliant blue.

These colours form a sort of frame, within which mythological subjects are painted, such as the "Release of Andromache by Perseus," "Ceres, sitting on a throne," &c., pictures possessing not so much artistic merit in themselves, as presenting a faithful copy of the paintings found in the Pompeian dwellings. In compartments towards the ceiling, are figures of dolphins, centaurs, dragons, birds, and cars drawn by leopards. The pilasters are coloured green, red, and yellow, at their base; the rest are white, with ornaments in yellow, except the capitals, which are adorned with a white and blue acanthus on yellow and red; above the pilasters, all along the apartments, is a very beautiful toothed beading in yellow, blue, and red. A series of gilt figures support the roof, which is white, picked out with ornaments of red. The floor is mosaic, and a marble basin is sunk in the centre. Signer Abbate has exactly reproduced the forms and colours, as well as the proportions of the rooms in the buried city, which it should be borne in mind were adapted for a climate in which a greater part of the day was spent in the open air.

The Sheffield Court, constructed of glass and iron, with specimens of hardware and manufactures.

The Birmingham Court, erected by Mr. Tite, M.P., containing a collection of its well-known manufactures.

The Stationery Court, designed and decorated by Mr. Grace, where the articles themselves enhance the beauty of this department.

The Industrial Court, where amidst eight specimens of the mechanical arts, the collossal head of "Bavaria" and Halbig's large statue of "Franconia" are placed, next demand our notice, and will conduct us by the back of the orchestra, through the collection of CLASSICAL SCULPTURE to

The Egyptian Court, which is sufficiently indicated by six recumbent lions (cast from a pair brought from Egypt by the present Duke of Northumberland) ranged along the entrance, and the massive pillars that present every kind of Egyptian architectural device, and which form the corridors through which we pass. On the right hand side of this court is reproduced on a scale a little more than one-third of the original size, the entrance hall of the palace of Karnac, the ruins of which are the most ancient, and at the same time the most gigantic and spendid in the world. They stand on a portion of the site, and formed a part of the ancient city of Thebes, and date from at least fifteen hundred years before the Christian era. The columns, as well as the walls, are profusely covered with hieroglyphics, also reduced to the same scale, and coloured red, green, blue, yellow, and black, according to the original tints. Their form is polygonal, having sixteen sides of eight inches each, hollowed to the depth of half an inch. The most prominent figures on the columns are the god Ammon, which is bright cobalt blue, and his wife, who wears a red dress, covered with a sort of hexagonal pattern of the same colour. Other figures show the red flesh colour with a transparent dress over it. The ceiling at the sides is blue, with gold stars in relief, emblematic of futurity, and over the principal parts in the centre are a series of formidable vultures, with outspread wings, in black and red, on a blue ground. The façade and frieze of this court, supported by tall lotus-headed pillars, bears the following inscription, in hieroglyphics: "Victoria and Prince Albert. In the seventeenth year of the reign of Her Majesty, the ruler of the waves, the royal daughter Victoria, lady most gracious, her chiefs, architects, sculptors, and painters, erected this Palace and Gardens, with a thousand columns, a thousand decorations, a thousand flowers, a thousand birds and beasts, a thousand fountains, and a thousand vases. The architects and painters, and sculptors, built this palace as a book for the instruction of the men and women of all countries, regions, and districts. May it be prosperous." This inscription reads from right to left, as was the custom of the Egyptians and Hebrews. It is repeated, after the old fashion in Egypt, around the three sides of the outer court. The whole reproduction is highly suggestive of the grand, massive and permanent character of Egyptian architecture. The rock tombs of Aboosimbel, the columns from the Temple of Denderat, and numerous other restorations of ancient Egyptian art, will here invite the examination of the visitor.

The Greek Court presents sculptural attractions that are more familiar to the eye, from the collection that is in the British Museum. Beauty, grace, and simplicity are their chief features.

The portico of the Parthenon, and the noble frieze of that building, extending along the wall at the appropriate height, form striking objects. Around are the matchless sculptures from the pediments of the Parthenon, and a number of those unrivalled works of art which are faithful copies of the originals in the museums and galleries of Europe. It will be here sufficient to indicate the Theseus, Ceres and Proserpine, the Tlyssus, the famous horse's head, from the chariot of the goddess Nox, the Niobe group, the Farnese Hercules, and Flora, the Wrestlers, the Farnese Juno, the Dying Gladiator, the Laocoon, the Ariadne of the Vatican, and the Apollo. The ceilings of the vestibules are richly ornamented, and the architecture is strictly Doric.

The Roman Court, with its imitative pillars of porphyry, jasper, and malachite, is richly stored with specimens of Roman sculpture. Among the principal are the Young Hercules, Diana with the Fawn, the celebrated Apollo Belvidere, the Tortonia Hercules, and a number of fine colossal busts. Besides some admirably executed casts of the bassi-relievi from the Arch of Titus, representing the leading of the Jews into captivity, there is a complete model of the Roman Forum, 15 feet long, a restoration of the Coliseum, 12 feet long, a model of the celebrated Temple of Neptune, at Pœstum, and curious collection of gems from the antique.

The Alhambra Court, which follows next, is distinguished by its elaborate and magnificent combination of gold and colours, glittering in all the fantastic forms of Moorish architecture. On the walls and cornices, chequered with minute patterns of the brightest hues, are traced Arabic characters and devices. The portion here represented of the famous palace of the Moorish kings of Granada comprises the Court of Lions and the Hall of Justice; in the centre of the former is the celebrated fountain, with those leonine supporters from which the court derives its name. The amount of manual labour employed upon this marvellous fac-simile of Moorish grandeur must have been enormous. The floors are marble, with highly enriched entablatures of jasper and mosaic.

The Assyrian or Nineveh Court is the last in this direction, and occupies a considerable portion of the Northern Transept. The two colossal divinities *Rhea,* 90 feet high, and a double row of gigantic Sphynxes, each twenty feet long and ten feet high, form an appropriate avenue through the whole length of this transept, only broken by the foliage of the trees and the groups of rare plants that occupy the centre. The Assyrian Court, with its massive looking columns rising to double the height of the other courts, so that the character of the architecture may be more fully developed, presents the audience chamber of an Assyrian monarch, such as it appeared in all its bold and primitive grandeur three thousand five hundred years ago. Four columns, each fifty feet in height, support the roof of the largest room, which is flat, and ornamented with deeply sunk panels in differently shaped divisions. The eagle-winged and human-headed bulls that stand guardians over the entrance are exactly reproduced from the originals. The audience chamber is a hundred feet in length. Nineveh and its wonders are here revealed to us: its architecture and its sculptures, its social, political, warlike, and even domestic life is here made manifest, and with all its solemn and mysterious associations; a thousand visions of departed grandeur rise vividly before the eye until we become in imagination ourselves a portion of the past. We have here displayed upon the walls the history of the first empire, at the period when Sennacherib ruled, and Ezekiel prophesied; a history inscribed in pictures of stone, which, after having been entombed beneath the dust of some thirty centuries, are here to attest in the latter days of progress and civilization, the massive greatness of the world's youth, and to rebuke the caviller at the truth of Revelation.

Crossing the opposite side and returning along the garden front, the visitor will observe corridors along the entire length looking out upon the grounds, and commanding beautiful views of the surrounding scenery. The first court opposite the Assyrian is

The Byzantine and Romanesque Court, with all its richness and variety of details. Among other interesting objects will be noticed, restorations of the cloisters of St. Mary, in the Cathedral of Cologne; a portion of the cloister of St. John Lateran, with its gold mosaics; the fountain of Heislerback in the centre; and an archway, from Romsey; the Prior's Gate at Ely; and many of the most celebrated tombs and monuments of our kings and queens, from the Cathedrals of France and England. Some very interesting memorials of Irish sculpture, and crosses of ancient date are also found in this court.

The Mediaeval Court presents a series of *fac-similes* of early ecclesiastical architecture, in its most beautiful form, and comprises various compartments illustrative of the French, German, and Italian schools, all of which are characterised by their use of the pointed arch. In the centre of the court, facing the grounds, is the door-way of Rochester Cathedral, and on each side are two small fine rich canopies, and two tombs with rich foliage and groups of figures. The examples of German Gothic include the great Nuremburg door, and the effigies of the Archbishop Electors of Mayence. The French specimens are chiefly the bas-reliefs of the choir of Notre Dame, and this period of Italian art is represented by the celebrated work of Andrea Orcagna, the great altar of the church of San Michael.

The Renaissance Court has a façade representing the Hotel Bourgtheroulde, at Rouen, the upper portions being copies of the great frieze from the hospital for the poor at Pistoja, representing the seven acts of mercy; and upon the lower part is depicted the meeting of Francis the First and Henry the Eighth on the Field of the Cloth if Gold. The ceiling of the portico, which is divided into three compartments, exhibits copies of twelve signs found in the entrance to the Certosa, at Pavia. In the centre of the court are three fountains, the central one being reproduction in terra-cotta of the celebrated vase in the Louvre from the Chateau Guillon. The two others are from the court-yard of the Ducal Palace at Venice. Facing the entrance from the nave is the figure of a nymph reposing on a stag, enclosed in a semicircular pediment supported by Caryatides, the figure being by Benvenuto Cellini. A fountain from the Piazza di Tartarughi at Rome, at one end of which lie the two colossal figures of Light and Night, and at the others, those of Twilight and Dawn by Michael Angelo, from the Medici chapel, at Florence, will be found in the centre of the ITALIAN COURT, the exterior of the building being copied from the Farnese Palace, and the external right hand façade from the

Casa Taverna, Milan. A gate from the Campagnile, a crucifix from the Certosa, a Triton by Montroioli, and the Madonna Della Scorpia, may be especially mentioned among the contents of this court, which, with the exception of the Greek, is richest in its numerous treasures of Statuesque art.

The Elizabethan Court has its façade from Holland House, and within are choice collections of monuments, among which will be recognised some from Westminster Abbey: those of Queen Elizabeth, Mary Queen of Scots, the Countess of Richmond, and Sir John Cheney, are conspicuously prominent. Under the arch, in the centre, is the bust of Shakspeare, from his monument in Stratford-on-Avon church. The architecture of this court, with its scroll-work, medallions, and coloured marbles, is very remarkable.

The nave which divides this double row of courts is profusely adorned with groups of statuary and classic figures, arranged on each side, with beds of flowers and shrubs to heighten the effect and relieve the eye. Modern sculpture is well represented here in the works of the English, Italian, German, and French schools. In our own division we see the grace and purity of Gibson, the tenderness of Marshall, the force of Lough, the delicacy of Westmacott, and the dignity of Theed. Of the German school are beautiful works from the hands of Rauch and Schwanthaler, Danneker, Thorwaldsen, whose Venus is one of the finest works of modern continental art, and a fine collection from the studies of the French sculptures make up a most unprecedented exhibition, whilst the Italian school is adequately represented by Canova's Dancing Girl, Nymph and Cupid, Three Graces, Mars and Venus, Paris, Venus and Adonis, Hebe, Magdalen, &c.,

At the end of this series of courts, clever copies of the most famous Italian paintings, expressly executed for the Crystal Palace, will be found.

In speaking of the great works of sculpture that are to be found within the Crystal Palace, we may comprehensively affirm, that every work in ancient or modern art, of name and fame, will be found there. Hitherto we have been told to go to Naples, to see the FARNESIAN marbles; to Munich, to see the BAVARIA; to Berlin, to see Rauch's Frederick the Great; but here we have them all united under one roof; so that time and purse are both spared to the thousands who have little to spare of either one or the other. The colossal figure of Sesostris, 64 feet in height, forms a prominent object in the nave: the cap alone is 12 feet high. This and the "Bavaria" form the most striking features in the Palace for size; but comparison leads us no further; for the hard and stiff lines of the Egyptian king are in striking contrast to the soft and feminine beauty of the German sculptor's work. There is another work of colossal proportions, which is sure to arrest the eye of the visitor—a figure of Liberty, from the Befreiung's Halle, at Kelheim. Also, conspicuous, are colossal statues of Lessing, Rubens, Du Quesne, and others; Rauch's far-famed Frederick the Great; besides Milo and Satan, by Lough. Some hundreds of busts are ranged round the court, and will prove especially intersting to the students of phrenology and physiognomy, embracing some of the most celebrated poets, dramatists, musicians, painters, sculptors, and statesmen, handed down to us by the genius of the masters of the plastic art. Near the Elgin marbles are a fine collection of statues called the Niobe group, apparently from the pediment of some Grecian temple: the originals are at Florence. In this apartment are statues of Ceres, Proserpine, Venus, Apollo, &c., from the Louvre and other continental galleries; also a "Boar and Dogs," from Florence. The famous VELLETRE VENUS adjacent will also command attention. The view of these groups of sculpture from the galleries above (reached by winding staircases placed at regular intervals) is exceedingly beautiful. Osier's great Crystal Fountain will be recognised in the centre of the South Transept, and many of the pillars ranged along the nave will be seen to have handsome circular cages, filled with singing birds, whose notes fall agreeably upon the ear, amidst the cool splashing of waters and the genial hum of social converse. Crossing the central transept our attention is called to the Opera Concert Room, the FRENCH COURT, with its bronzes, &c.; the CERAMIC COURT, the CHINA AND GLASS COURT, and the BOHEMIAN GLASS COURT, all of which are filled with very beautiful and interesting works.

The Galleries.—The main galleries around the central transept are devoted to the exhibition of articles of industry. The NEW PICTURE GALLERY runs over the Stationery Court and the series on that side, and here are exhibited original British and Foreign water-colour pictures, and a copy of the celebrated Correggio in the National Gallery.

The Long Gallery, stretching from this point to the south end of the building, is fitted up for the exhibition of the pictures, which are well shown, the light falling on them from the roof. This gallery is 700 feet in length, and contains nearly 1,000 pictures, by British and Foreign artists. They are for sale in most instances, and the subject, prices, and artists' names arc affixed. Mr. C. W. Wass has the management of this new department.

On leaving the Central Transept the visitor descends a flight of granite steps

120 feet wide, which leads to the upper terrace. This magnificent terrace extends along the whole base of the building, and is 1,700 feet long and 50 feet wide. Fifteen feet lower lies the Terrace Garden, reached by six flights of steps, and bounded on the southern side by a stone balustrade, with numerous recesses. Besides the magnificent central circular basin, throwing out a lofty *jet d'eau*, there are numerous others of an elliptic shape, profusely intermingled with statues, vases, rich coloured flower beds, shrubs, and trees, on which the shadows of the projecting transepts fall. From the Terrace Gardens three flights of stone steps (the side balustrades adorned in like manner with statuary), conduct the visitor to a garden fifteen feet lower.

A central walk, 96 feet in breadth, leads from the centre of the Terrace Garden through the lower garden, where it divides, and, re-uniting on the other side of a basin, 200 feet in diameter, continues on more than 2,000 feet through parterres laid out in a graceful admixture of the Italian and English styles of ornamental gardening. Along the margin of this great walk flows the water of the upper basins in a series of cascades, until at the extremity they fall over an open colonnade 240 feet long and 15 feet high, and rush into a series of continuous basins extending on each side the walk,

more than half a mile in length, and sending forth from central groups hundreds of aqueous jets. The crystal towers, of which there are two, one at each end of the building, have been erected for the purpose of carrying the tanks that supply the fountains in the lower basin, and are, with the exception of the tank and stays, constructed of cast iron. On ordinary occasions the basins are filled with the gentle overflowings of the upper fountains; but on fête days vast streams of water are liberated, and rushing upwards in a thousand spire-like forms, and dashing downwards over their artificial boundaries, make the whole park and garden resonant with the tumultuous murmurings of a volume of water estimated to be only one-sixth less than that discharged by the mighty cataracts of Niagara. The extent of the ground in which these fountains are displayed is ingeniously made to appear greater than it really is, by the skilful mode in which it has been treated. Broken ground, mounds, artificially constructed, crowned with forest trees, and groves of rich evergreen shrubs, forming tortuous alleys of perpetual verdure, and intersecting each other in the most natural manner, impart the effect of size and distance to a space that is comprised in about two hundred acres. Years may elapse before the mature development of these trees will produce all the effects of which they are capable, but enough is now visible to attest the great taste and skill of the designer.

The south end of the Palace and the South Transept contain a selection of plants, consisting chiefly of Rhododendrons, Camellias, Azaleas, and other choice conservatory plants, most carefully selected; in the South Transept, especially, are arranged the finest specimens of these plants that can be seen. Opposite the Pompeian Court are placed two fine specimens of aloes, and, conspicuous opposite the Birmingham Industrial Court, are two Norfolk Island pines. Opposite the Stationery Court are two specimens of Moreton Bay pine, as well as several specimens of *Telopea speciosissima* from Australia. Under the first Transept may be noticed two remarkably fine Norfolk Island pines, presented by his Grace the Duke of Devonshire.

The garden facing the Egyptian Court is principally filled with palms; and on either side of its entrance are two curious plants (resembling blocks of wood) called "Elephant's Foot;" they are the largest specimens ever brought to Europe, and were imported from the Cape of Good Hope by the Crystal Palace Company. This plant is one of the longest lived of any vegetable product, the two specimens before the visitor being supposed to be three thousand years old. Before this Court will be noticed also two fine Indian-rubber plants—a plant that has latterly acquired considerable interest and value, on account of the variety and importance of the uses to which its sap is applied. Here will also be noticed an old conservatory favourite, though now not often met with, the *Sparmannia Africana*. Amongst the palms will be remarked many of very elegant and beautiful foliage, including the *Seaforthia elegans*, one of the most handsome plants of New Holland, and the *Chamædorea elegans* of Mexico. On the left of the entrance to the Egyptian Court will be seen perhaps the largest specimen in Europe of the *Rhipidodendron plicatile* from the Cape of Good Hope. Opposite the central entrance to the Greek Court, and in front of the beds, are two variegated American aloes. The beds are filled with a variety of conservatory plants, and have a border of olive plants. In front of the Roman Court will be observed, first, on either side of the second opening, two large Norfolk Island pines, presented by Her Most Gracious Majesty and His Royal Highness Prince Albert. The beds, like those before the Greek Court, are principally filled with Camellias and Rhododendrons, and are also bordered by several small specimens of the olive plant. Between the two foremost statues, at the angles of the pathway leading to the second opening, are placed two specimens of the very rare and small plant which produces the Winter bark of commerce, and which is called *Drymus Winterii*. The garden in front of the Alhambra is devoted to fine specimens of the pomegranate. Having passed the Alhambra, we find the garden of the whole of this end of the building devoted to tropical plants, including a most magnificent collection of different varieties of palms.

Between the sphynxes are placed seven Egyptian date-palms *(Phoenix dactylifera)*, recently imported from Egypt; out of the sixteen originally imported, nine were killed, owing to the delay that took place in their transmission, the steamer in which they were conveyed having been engaged, on her homeward passage, for the transport of troops. Amongst the different varieties of palms, the following may be noted, either for their large growth or their beautiful foliage: an immense specimen of the *Sabal palmetta*, from Florida, and a fine *Sabal Blackburniana*; also several fine specimens of the cocos, amongst which is the *Cocos plumosa*, reaching the height of thirty-five feet; numerous specimens of the wax-palm *(Ceroxyl n andricola)*, natives of Columbia, and the curious *Calamus maximus*, which, in the damp forests of Java, grows along the ground to an immense length, and forms with its sharp prickles an almost impenetrable underwood, are also here. The *Sanguerus saccharifera* of India, noted for its saccharine properties, and the vegetable ivory-palm *(Phytelephas macrocarpa)*, deserve attention. The specimen of *Pandanus odoratissimus*, from Tahiti, is also remarkable, on account of its sweet smell.

Opposite the Bryzantine Court, the garden is filled with different varieties of palms brought from South America, Australia, and the Isle of Bourbon. Before the Mediaeval Court may be noticed two Norfolk Island pines, and close to the monuments at the entrance of the English Mediaeval Court are two funereal cypresses, brought from the Vale of Tombs, in North China. Close to the Norfolk Island Pine, on the right, facing the Court, is a small specimen of the graceful and beautiful Moreton Bay pine. The *Mammoth Tree of California* is a most interesting addition to the wonders of the Palace. The portion of the tree which has been erected reaches to the roof of the transept, and furnishes a very good idea of the gigantic proportions of these trees in their native clime.

The Tropical End of the Building.—Our further progress towards the end of the building is barred during a great part of the year by a gigantic curtain, which, falling from the roof completely cuts off the north transept; the visitor has only to open one of the double doors of this partition to know at once the reason of its erection. From a temperature of about 55 in the winter mouths, which pervades the part of the building he is leaving, he steps at once into a tropical climate of some 85 degrees. It was found that the valuable collection of palms, and other Eastern specimens of vegetation, could only be kept healthy by isolating the department devoted to them, and heating it to a degree which would not be pleasant in all parts of the building. The temperature suits so well the plants, that many which, on their arrival, appeared to be dead have suddenly revived — the Egyptian palms, for instance, now wear a crown of verdure, in place of the dead brown leaves which they exhibited formerly.

The Aviaries.—The visitor should not omit to inspect the small wire Aviaries, of which there are three, in this end of the building. These contain Weaver Birds, Grenadiers, Grosbeaks, Mocking Birds, and Paroquets, most of them inhabitants of warm climates. The Weaver Birds, in the spring, may be seen constructing their curiously-woven nests of grass, which hang from the branches like so many stockings; others of the feathered tribe build their habitations fearlessly in the presence of the visitor, with all the art of a basket-maker; here, indeed, bird-architecture of the most unique kind may be studied by the naturalist with delight and advantage.

Traversing the Avenue of Sphynxes —to be noticed on our return down the garden side, from which point a better view of the whole Transept is gained—we pass a variety of Palms, Bananas, and other tropical plants, continued throughout this part of the Nave, and rendered more agreeable to the eye by the addition of an artificial soil and rock work.

On a natural knoll near the railway has been erected an ornamental colonnade, where climbing roses and other plants of a similar tendency will form umbrageous avenues, teeming with all the efflorescing beauties of the floral kingdom. By one of these paths the visitor is conducted to a collection of those hardy trees and shrubs that can be successfully cultivated in this climate *al fresco*, and thence to a lake about six acres in extent, which receives, by open and subterranean channels, the water from the larger basins. Islands of irregular shape, covered with luxuriant vegetation, here arise from the glassy surface, studded with the animals and reptiles of the antediluvian world. To increase the illusion, the waters of the pool rise and fall at intervals (partially submerging the amphibious inmates) from three to eight feet alternately, after the appearance of an actual tidal influx and efflux. Here we behold, pausing among the rushes, the Iguanodon, or monstrous lizard, thirty feet high, and a hundred feet from the snout to tip of tail; the Megatherium, or monster sloth, climbing an antediluvian tree; huge Chelonians, basking upon the tanks; the Plesiosaurus, with its reptile form and bird-like neck, wallowing in the mud; and gigantic crocodiles and tortoises, apparently crawling about as they did in those early periods of our infant world when air, sea, and land must have been so strangely tenanted.

This department is sure to prove one of the most interesting of which the Palace can boast. The Inland lakes, 250 feet each in length, 60 feet wide, and five in depth, form beautiful aquariums, stocked with gold and silver fish, and other marine marvels, besides being bordered by the rarest and most ornamental aquatic plants. A spacious bower, called the Temple of Roses, occupies an elevated position in the grounds; and exhibits a display of floral beauty such as the most excursive poetic imagination has only yet conceived. The artesian well which supplies the great reservoir, is 245 feet deep, and is computed to discharge 400 gallons a minute. The supply, which is obtained by three powerful engines, will be sufficiently ample to feed the lakes and reservoirs; and it is again pumped by intermediate engines from the lakes to feed the basins and fountains. The basin of the grand fountain has a circumference of 1,200 feet. The panorama of natural scenery beheld from the ground, extends in clear weather, over a circumference of fifty miles; and from the summit of the Water Towers (which may be ascended by visitors) it is even said that the sea at Sussex coast becomes visible.

The Penny Reading and News Rooms.—Pleasantly overlooking the ground, and near the Byzantine Court, are to be found the Reading and News Rooms, to which is attached a free library. All the morning, weekly, and country papers are to be found here, and can be consulted at any time. The very latest news by telegraph is exhibited immediately upon its receipt; there is a postage-box upon the reading table, from which letters are collected several times in the course of the day, and paper, envelopes, and postage stamps can always be obtained from the attendants at a moderate charge. The nucleus of a very valuable library has been already formed by the purchases of the Company, and the free gifts of individuals; and it will, we doubt not, develop in time into a goodly collection. To this library subscribers to the News-room are admitted free of charge. The terms of subscription are: Yearly, 10s.; Quarterly, 2s. 6d.; Monthly, 1s. Admission to non-subscribers 1d. each time. Mr. Shenton, Superintendent.

Railway Trains.—These being subject to frequent change, parties would do well to consult "Bradshaw's Monthly Guide," which will furnish full particulars as to trains and fares.

Days and Hours of Opening.—The Palace is opened on Mondays at 9 0 a.m.; on Tuesdays, Wednesdays, Thursdays, and Fridays, at 10 0 a.m.; and on Saturdays at noon; and is closed daily at sunset.

Visitors should remember that it takes from ten minutes to a quarter of an hour to walk leisurely from the middle transept to the Railway, by way of the Colonnade. Those in haste to catch a train had better take the short cut down the Central Transept stairs, and across the grounds to the last Tower in the right-hand wing.

The Citizen and Iron Companies' Steam Boats run from their several piers to the Surrey side pier at London Bridge, at least every ten minutes during the day; and at those hours, when increased numbers require it, every five minutes. Tickets to the Palace, including conveyance by railway, can be obtained at these piers.

Rates of Admission, Season Tickets, &c.—The following are the arrangements for the season, ending on April 30th, 1862:—

The prices of season tickets are two guineas, which are available on all occasions, and one guinea; children at half-price. The one guinea ticket does not admit to the opera concerts, nor on the extraordinary special fêtes, which the directors reserve themselves power to give during the season, and when the price of admission is 5s. and upwards, at which time, however, the guinea ticket holders will have the privilege of entrance on payment of half-a-crown.

The Tickets may be obtained at the following Offices: The Crystal Palace, Central Transept Entrance; at the Offices of the London and Brighton Railway Company, London Bridge; Victoria Station, and Regent Circus, Piccadilly; the Central Ticket Office, 2, Exeter Hall; Cramer, Beale, & Co., 201, Regent Street; Dando, Todhunter, & Smith, 22, Gresham Street, Bank; M. Hammond and Nephew, 27, Lombard Street; Keith, Prowes, and Co., 48, Cheapside; Letts, Son, and Co., 8, Royal Exchange; Mead and Powell, Railway Arcade, London Bridge; J. Mitchell, 33, Old Bond Street; W. R, Sams, 1, St. James's Street; W. R. Stephens, 36, Throgmorton Street; and of Charles Westerton, 20, St. George's Place, Knightsbridge.

Remittances to the Crystal Palace for Season Tickets to be by Post-office Order-payable to GEORGE GROVE.

The Ordinary Rates of Admission are, on Mondays, Tuesdays, Wednesdays, Thursdays, and Fridays (excepting special occasions), 1s. On Saturdays; (excepting special occasions), 2s. 6d.

Note.—During the months of August, September, and October, the ordinary rate of admission on Saturdays will be 1s.

Books of Admissions.—Books containing 25 Admissions for ordinary occasions may be obtained at any of the above-named offices at the following rates:—Shilling Days, Book of 25 for £1 2s. 6d. Half-Crown Days, of 25 for £2 10s.

A Wind Band for performing occasionally with the String Band in the building, and in the evenings at various chosen positions in the grounds, for open air promenades.

Lectures, of a popular character, on the various Courts and Departments, are delivered during the season, on appointed occasions.

A Crystal Palace Art Union has been formed, the particulars of which may be obtained at the proper offices. Benevolent Societies, Schools, and other large bodies are admitted by arrangements, at a reduced tariff.

Wheel and Lifting Chairs, for Invalids, may be hired within the Palace, for use therein, or for conveying the visitor to any hotel or residence in Sydenham or Norwood.

Shareholders are now admitted to the Palace on Sundays, during certain defined hours.

Daily Tickets, including conveyance by railway, are issued at *Bradshaw's Guide Office*, 59, Fleet Street.

Summary of Attractions and Objects of Interest.—We may here, in the limited space at our command, summarise the permanent attractions and objects of interest which will be found at the Crystal Palace.—There are Ethnological and Zoological Collections in the South Wing, illustrated in various forms.—The student of botany, within and without the building, will always find the best specimens he requires.—The lover of art, whether sculptural or architectural, will enjoy the unique advantage of being surrounded by works, all of them above mediocrity, and most of them masterpieces. If the visitor is of an inventive or mechanical turn of mind, there is the Court of New Inventions and Industrial Court to suggest speculation and approval; or if he is interested in India and the colonies, there are collections of the greatest value to the emigrant and colonist. Does he linger over sweet sounds, he may come here and listen to the finest voices and the most perfect instrumentation, and on special occasions the organ and amphitheatre of 3,000 or 4,000 performers will suprise and delight his senses with a choral march or a nation's hymn. To utilise the wealth around, schools of art, science, and literature, conducted by celebrated masters, impart privately, or through lectures, the stores of knowledge the student seeks. Are you an antiquary, the monuments of Christian art are here for inspection, and doubtless will support the pet theories you have formed about Irish round pillars and other mysteries. Should you have decided to set up a carriage, here you can see, in a long line, those of the best makers. Exercise and pastimes of all sorts may here be enjoyed—a boat on the lakes, cricket, quoits, rifle shooting at the butt, or the lounge over the grass from flower-bed to parterre. Naturalist or Geologist, extinct animals and strata of the natural size are here to assist you in your favourite study. And, oh visitors! are you single, maid or bachelor? if you wish to remain so, do not come to the Crystal Palace, which we may mention is a popular place for wedding breakfasts. For married folks, here is a wilderness of toys beloved by children. If you want to boy a good picture, there are more than a thousand to choose from. For the news of the day, to write a letter, to read a book, there are library and reading rooms overlooking a green landscape rich with sweet smelling flowers. During the season, once a week or a fortnight, as the daily papers will remind you, the oratorios of the Sacred Harmonic Society are performed by an orchestra of 700. Have you a conservatory or poultry yard? The annual Flower and Poultry Shows offer you a prize, or what is the same thing, a prize for the best specimens, to whomsoever sends them, and of course, you desire nothing better than that desert shall be rewarded, and you have learnt something, and will try again. And here, at the end of this summary, you exclaim, "Under such a beautiful building, so many attractions and objects of interest cannot elsewhere be found," so that, when you can on rainy days and fine, you elect to visit the Crystal Palace as we do. In this frame of mind, we beg to take leave of you at the

Refreshment Department.— The various saloons and dining rooms for the Refreshment Department are situated at the South End of the Palace, but branch stations for light refreshments will be found in various convenient positions throughout the building, and on special occasions requiring it, in the grounds.

THE SALOON is entered at the right hand corner of the extreme South End of the Palace, and is richly carpeted and decorated, and fitted with every elegant convenience. The very highest class of entertainment is served here to due notice and order.

Hot Dinners—Soups, Fish, Entrées, &c., &c., to order at a few minutes' notice. Price as per detailed Carte.

The authorised charge for attendance is 3d. each person.

The DINING ROOM is on the left of the Saloon.

The TERRACE DINING ROOM is entered from the garden end of the South Transept, near to the entrance from the Railways. The front, towards the garden, in glass, giving a view of the terraces and grounds. Cold Dinners only are served in this room; 1s. 8d., including attendance.

	s.	d.
Cold Meat or Veal Pie, with Cheese and Bread	1	6
Chicken with Ham and Tongue, and ditto	2	6
Lobster Salad, per dish	2	6
Jelly or Pudding	0	6
Ice (Nesselrode) Pudding	1	0
The authorised charge for attendance, each person, is	0	2

The THIRD CLASS ROOMS are situate near the Railway Colonnade, in the lower story of the South Wing, and near the staircase at the end of the Machinery Department.

		s.	d.
Plate of Meat		0	6
Bread		0	1
Bread and Cheese		0	3
Porter	(per Quart)	0	4
Ale	"	0	6
"	"	0	8
Coffee or Tea	per Cup	0	3
Roll and Butter		0	2
Biscuit		0	1

	s.	d.
Bun	0	1
Bath Bun	0	2
Soda Water, &c.	0	3

GENERAL TARIFE.

	s.	d.
Ices, Cream or Water	0	6
Coffee or Tea per Cup .... per Cup	0	4
French Chocolate (Chocolat-Ibled)	0	6
Sandwich	0	6
Pork Pie	1	0
Pale Ale or Double Stout (Tankard)	0	6
(Glass)	0	3
Soda Water, Lemonade, &c.	0	4
Glass of Iced water	0	1
Carafe of Iced Water (Eau frappée)	0	1

Confectionery at the usual prices.

No charge for attendance is authorised on light refreshments.

Note.—The Full Wine List will be found on all the tables, and at all the Stations.

THE PUBLIC AND PRIVATE DINING ROOMS.—These are at the extreme end of the South Wing, and are only opened daring the Summer season, commencing on the 1st of May. Properly they may

be termed the "Crystal Hotel," for here the same class of dinner may be had as at the Star and Garter, Richmond, or at Quartermaine's famous Greenwich Tavern. The kitchen arrangements are on the largest scale, whilst the fitting up of the suites of rooms is of the most tasteful and *recherché* order. The Coffee Room, nearly 50 feet high, with a gallery at one end for either ladies or an orchestra, is a suitable room for a public banquet, where room is required for 500 guests. About a dozen smaller rooms, richly furnished, are for the use of private dinner parties and wedding breakfasts. Nearly all the rooms are, from the construction of the wing, pleasant corner rooms, affording a view of the fountains and grounds, and of the unrivalled landscape beyond. A list of the best sorts of wine imported is near for consultation, and the prices of the entertainment will be on a moderate hotel scale.

First class Music and Refreshment Hall—special entertainments as advertised in daily papers.

*** In case of any complaint against waiters, visitors are requested to report the circumstance, together with the number of the Waiter, at the office of Mr. F. Strange. Waiters are not allowed to receive any gratuity.

PLACES WORTH SEEING, AND AMUSEMENTS OF LONDON.

Abney Park Cemetery, Stoke Newington, open by application at the entrance lodge.

Alhambra Palace, Leicester Square.

Ancient Masters, 49, Pall Mall, 10 to 5, 1s. Masterpieces by the Caracci, Murillo, Rubens, Raphael, and Correggio.

Antiquarian Society, Somerset House. Antiquities, admission by an order from any of the members.

Antiquarian Museum, Guildhall, open daily, gratis.

Armourers' Hall, 81, Coleman Street.

Armour, admission by an order from any of the Livery.

Artillery Company, City Road. Armoury, admission granted by any of the Volunteers.

Asiatic Museum, Grafton Street, per ticket, Monday, Wednesday, and Friday.

Bank of England, on introduction, free.

Barbers' Hall, 33, Monkwell Street, Cripplegate. Picture Gallery, admission by order from Members of the Court.

Barclay & Perkins's Brewery, Bankside, Southwark. A visit to this stupendous establishment will amply repay the visitor. Admission is readily obtained by application at the Counting-house Park Street, Southwark, or by a note from any of their customers.

Bethlehem Hospital, Lambeth, for the Insane. Visitors admitted first Thursday in each month, or daily, by special order from any of the City Aldermen.

Blind (School for), St. George's Fields, admittance granted to visitors on application.

Botanic Gardens, Regent's Park, daily, by Member's Ticket.

British Museum, Great Russell Street, Bloomsbury, Mondays, Wednesdays, and Fridays, May 8th to August 31st, 10 to 7; September 1st to May 7th, 10 to 4, free. Closed on the first seven days of January, May, and September, also on Ash Wednesday, Good Friday, and Christmas Day. Unequalled collection of Greek, Roman, and Egyptian Antiquities, Minerals, Fossils, Zoology, Statuary, and Coins; also a most extensive collection of Books, Manuscripts, Prints, and Drawings. For admission to the Library apply to the Chief Librarian; a letter of recommendation by a person of known respectability is required.

Bridewell Hospital, 14, Kew Bridge Street, Blackfriars. Picture Gallery, open to strangers upon application.

British Institution, 52, Pall Mall, Exhibition of British Artists, 10 to 5, admission 1s., February, March, and April; Ancient Masters, June, July, and August, 10 to 6, admission, 1s.

Buckingham Palace Picture Gallery, order granted by application by letter to the Lord Chamberlain of Her Majesty's Household, at Buckingham Palace.

Royal Mews, Pimlico. The Stables and Stud may be seen, by tickets from Mr. Lewis, Clerk of the Stables, at the Mews.

Burlington Arcade Piccadilly, a pleasing lounge.

Canterbury Hall, Westminster Road. Performance of operatic and other music, every evening; admission, 6d. A really good collection of paintings on view. Refreshments may be obtained.

Catholic Cathedral, St. George's Fields, Lambeth, opposite Bethlehem Hospital. Admission to body of Chapel, 1s.

Catholic Church, Moorfields. High Mass on Christmas Day, Easter, and most of the Church Festivals. Mass every Sunday, 7, 8, 9, 10, and 11. Admission to the body of the Chapel, 1s.

Chiswick Horticultural Gardens, 9 to 6,

free. Cards of admission obtained only from Subscribers.

Christ's Hospital, Newgate Street, a noble establishment, for clothing and educating 1,300 children. Here is a fine collection of paintings, and a refectory, in which the sholars sup in public every Sunday evening during Lent. Tickets to be obtained by application to any of the Governors.

Colloseum, Regent's Park. The large picture of London, and also a view of Paris by moonlight, on a most gigantic scale, are the chief attractions of tins celebrated place of amusement. Concerts and scientific lectures, on the plan of the Royal Polytechnic Institution, have been lately introduced.

Commercial Docks. Shipping, free.

Cremorne Gardens. Admission, 1s. Open daily, at 3 p.m. The gigantic Stereorama shows the various points of interest of the route across the Alps into Italy. Public dancing, vocal concerts, rope walking, celebrated dogs and monkeys, balloon ascents, fireworks, bowls, and rifle shooting, may be named as among the popular entertainments which take place in different parts of the grounds. These ornamental gardens are planned to obtain the best and largest scenic effects, to which Messrs. Grieve and Telbin contribute their beautiful landscape paintings, and which are reproduced by the numerous reflectors and mirrors about the place. Ample hotel arrangements accommodate the visitors' requirements.

Crosby Hall, Bishopsgate Street, an interesting and ancient building, recently restored, and occupied as a Literary Institution; hall shown on application, free.

Custom House, Lower Thames Street; 9 to 3, free. Celebrated for its long room of nearly 200 feet.

Deaf and Dumb Asylum, Old Kent Road, admission on personal application.

Deptford Dockyard, Deptford, 10 to 3, free. Shipbuilding in all stages.

Drapers' Hall, Throgmorton Street. Portrait of Fitz-Alwyn, first Lord Mayor.

Duke of York's Column, St. James's Park, 12 to 3, 6d. A granite column, 150 feet high.

Dulwich Gallery, Dulwich College, April to November, 10 to 5; November to April, 11 to 3; except Fridays. Tickets to view the gallery are not required under the new regulations.

Earl's Court Cemetery, Brompton. Admission by signing book at porter's lodge.

East and West India Docks, Blackwall, admission free.

East India Company's Museum, in Middle Scotland Yard, Whitehall. Exhibition closed during a re-arrangement of the curiosities, trophies, &c., &c.

East Country Dock. Shipping, admission free.

Electric Telegraph. Electric Telegraph Office, Lothbury, Great Western Paddington Stations, admission 1s.; a series of communications during the whole day.

Entomological Society, Bond Street, Tuesday, per card of admission.

Eton, near Windsor, School and College, admission free, upon application to attendant. Valuable collection of drawings, paintings, and Oriental MSS. The chapel is a very fine structure.

Exeter Hall, near Southampton Street, Strand. A noble Hall, with magnificent organ; here are held meetings of most of the religious societies, also the concerts of the Sacred Harmonic Society.

Female Orphan Asylum, Westminster Bridge Road, Tuesday, Wednesday, and Friday. Admission on personal application.

Fishmongers' Hall, London Bridge. Curious statue of Sir Wm. Walworth, and the mace with which he struck Wat Tyler to the ground.

Foundling Hospital, Guildford Street. Admission Sunday and Monday, midday; the morning and evening church services on Sunday are chanted, as in Cathedrals. Visitors are expected to give silver at the door.

Gallery of Illustration, Regent Street. Mr. and Mrs. German Reed, with Mr John Parry's Entertainment. Open every evening at 8, except Saturday. On Thursday and Saturday, at 3 o'clock.

Geological Museum, 28 to 30, Jermyn Street, 10 to 4, free. British specimens of the strata of the earth in the order of their deposit, and a valuable collection of ores.

Geological Society, Somerset House Geology. Admission on application.

Great Globe, Leicester Square. Dioramas and Lectures. Open from 10 till 10. Admission, 1s.

Greenwich Hospital, Greenwich, 10 to dusk. Painted Hall, 3d., Chapel, 2d., but on Mondays and Fridays free, from 10 to 4. Appropriated to decayed seamen of Her Majesty's service. Indoor pensioners, 2,500; out-door pensioners, 3,000.

Greenwich Park, a most beautiful summer day's ramble. Blackheath and surrounding scenery will be found delightful excursions.

Gresham Lectures, on Philosophy and Science, Gresham Hall, Gresham Street, City, held during each Term time, on days and hours of which due notice is always given by advertisement.

Guildhall, King Street, Cheapside, 10 to 3. Collection of paintings. Great Hall, 150 feet long, contains several monuments of great interest; 10 to 3, free.

Guy's Hospital, St. Thomas's Street, Borough, Medical Museum. Introduction to be obtained by any of the Students.

Hampton Court Palace, Hampton Court, every day, except Friday, free.

Hanover Square Rooms, Hanover Square. See daily advertisements for programme.

Highgate Cemetery, Highgate. Admission by signing a book on entering.

Hunterian Museum, see College of Surgeons.

Institution of Civil Engineers, 25, Great George Street, Westminster. Mechanical Museum, order from member.

Kensal Green Cemetery, Kilburn, free on signing a book at entrance gate.

Kensington Gardens, West of Hyde Park. A delightful and fashionable promenade.

Kew, Surrey, Botanical Garden, open from 1 to 6 every day, free. Palace Gardens, Thursday and Saturday, free,

King Street Bazaar, Portman Square, a pleasant lounge.

King's College, Somerset House, Anatomy and Curiosities, introduction by member or student.

Ladye Chapel, St. Saviour's, Southwark, a beautifully renovated structure, with tomb of Gower the poet, and other ancient tombs of the most elaborate description; optional fee to sexton.

Lambeth Palace, a valuable collection of Pictures, open upon application.

Lincoln's Inn Hall and Library. Lincoln's Inn Fields, free.

Linnœan Society, 22, Soho Square, Wednesday and Friday, Natural History, order from member.

London Docks, East Smithfield, open free. A glance at the extent of business carried on here may give faint idea of the magnitude of British commerce.

London Hospital, Whitechapel Road, Medical Museum.

London Mechanics' Institution, 29, Southampton Buildings, Geological Museum; Members only, Lectures, 6d. each.

Lowther Arcade, West Strand. A Lounge. It has much architectural beauty, and is worthy a visit.

Mansion House, connecting Cornhill with Poultry, 11 to 3. The residence of the Lord Mayor of London. The Egyptian Hall and state apartments will well repay a visit. The attendant expects a fee.

Mercers' Hall, Cheapside. Richly sculptured façade. Contains some interesting relics of the celebrated Whittington, "thrice Lord Mayor of London."

Middlesex Hospital, Charles Street, Cavendish Square, admission daily.

Mint, Tower Hill, 11 to 3, free. Here all the coin of the realm is manufactured with powerful machinery. Previous application for admission must be made to the Deputy Masters, accompanied by a letter of recommendation from a Member of Parliament, or one of the City Aldermen, or by any of the Officers of the Mint.

Missionary Museum, 8, Bloomfield Street, Finsbury, 10 to dusk, Tuesdays, Thursdays, and Saturdays, free. Specimens of Zoology, Idols, War Implements, and native produce, obtained in course of Missionary labours.

Monument, Fish Street Hill, 9 to dusk, 6*d.* A column 202 feet high, raised to commemorate the Fire of London.

Museum of Asiatic Society, Grafton Street, Tuesday, Wednesday, and Thursday. Order from any of the members.

Museum of London Antiquities, 5, Liverpool Street, Bishopsgate. A collection of Coins and other Antiquities discovered within the precincts of Roman London. Collected by Mr. C. R. Smith, F.S.A., free.

Music Hall, Store Street. See advertisements in the daily papers.

National Gallery, Trafalgar Square, Mondays, Tuesdays, Wednesdays, Thursdays, May 1st to September 1st, 10 to 6; November 1st to April 30th, 10 to 6; closed six weeks from middle of September. A collection of the most celebrated Paintings; free.

National Portrait Gallery, at the Temporary Rooms, 29, Great George Street, Westminster. This collection, consisting of Portraits of British Worthies and historical celebrities, is open to the public by tickets (gratis), on Wednesdays and Saturdays, from 12 to 4. Tickets may be obtained on application at Messrs. Colnaghi, Pall Mall, East; Messrs. Graves, Pall Mall; and Mr. J. Smith, 137, New Bond Street.

Newgate Prison, order from Visiting Magistrates, any day between 11 and 4, free.

Norwood Cemetery, Norwood, open to visitors.

Nunhead, Peckham, ditto, ditto.

Ordnance Office, 86, Pall Mall. Mechanical Museum, admission upon application.

Oxford, the (Oxford Street).—A well conducted musical entertainment, by an excellent orchestra and good vocalists every evening at eight o'clock. Admission to hall, 6*d.*; to stalls and balcony, 1*s.* Refreshments served to visitors.

Painters' and Stainers' Hall, 9, Little Trinity Lane, City. A valuable collection of paintings, to be seen by an introduction from any of the Livery.

Pantechnicon, Pimlico, a Lounge and Bazaar, Free.

Pantheon, Oxford Street Conservatory, Aviary, Paintings, and Bazaar, free. A very agreeable lounge.

Parliament, Houses of, Admission on application, but a fee is expected. The now House of Lords is always open, free, when their lordships sit to hear appeals, for which see the daily papers, and on application at the Lord Chamberlain's Office during sitting of Parliament.

Polygraphic Hall, King William Street, Charing Cross. Mr. W. S. Woodin gives his well known entertainment every evening at eight o'clock, excepting Saturday, when it begins at three o'clock.

Polytechnic Institution, 309, Regent

Street, 12 to 5, 7 to 10, 1s. Popular Lectures on the Sciences, by Professors.

Private Picture Galleries, only accessible by special introduction:—Marquis of Westminster, Upper Grosvenor Street; Lord F. Egerton, Belgrave Square; Duke of Sutherland, St. James's; Lord Ashburton, Piccadilly; Sir Robert Peel, Whitehall Gardens; Duke of Devonshire, Piccadilly; Joseph Neeld, Esq., 6, Grosvenor Square; Mr. Hope's Collection, &c.

Richmond, a most pleasant summer trip by steam vessel.

Rosherville Gardens, Gravesend. Admission, 6d.

Royal Academy, Trafalgar Square, 8 to 7, 1s. Open only in May, June, and July. For exhibitions of new Paintings to encourage the Fine Arts.

Royal Asiatic Society, 14, Grafton Street, Asiatic Antiquities and Natural History, member's introduction.

Royal Exchange, Cornhill, the Temple of British Commerce; open every day till 4 P.M. Lloyd's Rooms only to be seen by the introduction of a subscriber.

Royal Society, Somerset House. A valuable collection of Paintings, admission by trifling fee to attendant.

Royal Institute of British Architects, 16, Grosvenor Street, Architectural, member's introduction.

Royal Institution Museum, Albemarle Street, 10 to 4, by Member's order. Specimens of Minerals.

Saull's Museum of Geology, 15, Aldersgate Street. Admission, Thursdays, at 11 o'clock, free.

St. James's Gallery of Paintings, 58, Pall Mall. Admission, 1s.

Sir John Soane's Museum, 13, Lincoln's Inn Fields, to Strangers Artists, and others making special application, every Tuesday, from the first in February to the last in August, and to the general public on Tuesdays, Thursdays, and Fridays in April, May, and June, from 10 to 4 free. Cards of admission to be obtained of the Curator at the Museum, either by personal application, or by letter. Statuary, Antiquities, Models, Paintings, Drawings, &c. Here is the celebrated Egyptian Alabaster Sarcophagus, discovered at Gournou by the late G. Belzoni, in 1816.

Society of Arts, John Street, Adelphi, daily, except Wednesdays, 10 to 3, admission by member's order, Museum of Arts and Science, Models, Machines, and Paintings.

Society of Painters in Water Colours (New), 53, Pall Mall, 9 to dusk, 1s. April, May, June, July. Water Colour Drawings only.

Society of British Artists, Suffolk Street, Charing Cross. 1s. April, May, June, July.

Soho Bazaar, Soho Square. A very agreeable and fashionable lounge.

South Kensington Museum, containing works of Decorative Art, Modern

Pictures, Sculpture and Engravings, Architectural Illustrations, Building Materials, Educational Apparatus and Books, Illustrations of Food and Animal Products. Open on Mondays, Monday evenings, Tuesdays, Tuesday evenings, and Saturdays, free; and on Wednesdays, Wednesday evenings, Thursdays, and Fridays (Students' days), on payment of 6d. each person. From 10 to 4, 5, or 6 in the daytime, according to the season, and from 7 to 10 in the evening.

Somerset House, Navy Department, Naval Models, free upon application.

St. Luke's, Old Street, for the insane open daily to see patients.

St. Bartholomew's Hospital, West Smithfield, Picture Gallery and Medical Museum.

St. George's Hospital, Hyde Park Corner, Medical Student's order.

St. Katharine's Docks, East Smithfield. Shipping, open free.

St. Thomas's Hospital, Wellington Street, Southwark, Medical Museum, free upon a member's introduction.

St. Paul's Cathedral, Ludgate Hill, open daily from 10 till dusk. Admission free; whispering and two outside galleries 6d., vaults 6d., clock and belfry 1d., library, model hall, and geometrical staircase, 6d., ball, 1s. 6d. It is hoped the Dean and Chapter will not long persist in exacting these disgraceful charges. The Annual Service on be-

half of the Sons of the Clergy is performed in May, and the interesting meeting of the children from the various Charity Schools of London takes place in June, both very interesting ceremonies.

Suffolk Street Gallery, Suffolk Street, Pall Mall, 9 to dusk, 1s. Open only April, May, June, July. For Oil and Water Colour Paintings.

Surgeons' Halt (Hunterian Museum), Royal College of Surgeons, Lincoln's Inn Fields, opens Monday, Tuesday, Wednesday and Thursday, from 12 till 4, closed in September, free. This celebrated Anatomical Museum was chiefly collected by John Hunter, and purchased by the government for this Institution, which is very liberally conducted.

Surrey (Royal) Gardens, Penton place, Walworth. Open occasionally in the summer months, with Concerts, Music and Fireworks. Panorama on the Lake, admission, 1s.

Thames Tunnel, Rotherhithe and Wapping, open day and night, 1d. A most wonderful undertaking, being an excavation under the bed of the Thames, 76 feet below high watermark, and 1,200 feet long, cost £614,000.

Tower of London, Tower Hill, 10 to 4. Armouries, 6d. Jewel Office, 6d. The oldest national fortress in England, with a most extensive collection of Arms and Armour of ancient usage, and a great store ready for instant warfare.

Trinity House, Tower Hill. Curiosities.

Tussaud's Wax Exhibition, Baker Street Bazaar, Portman Square, in Summer, 11 to 10; in Winter, 11 to dusk, and 7 to 10, 1s.; principal room, 6d. Napoleon, &c. Faithful models in wax of important personages, both living and dead.

University College, Gower Street, Medical Student's order.

United Service Museum, Scotland Yard, Whitehall, open January to September, 11 to 5; rest of the year, 11 to 4, member's order. Valuable collection from all parts of the known world, chiefly presented by British Officers.

Vernon and Turner Collection of Pictures, removed from Marlborough House, and temporarily lodged in the museum at South Kensington, to which refer.

Veterinary College, Camden Town, School and Museum of Veterinary Science, Anatomical Preparations; student's or member's introduction.

Water Colours, Old Society of Painters in. Exhibition of Water Colour Drawings, 5, Pall Mall, East, 9, to dusk, 1s., May, June, and July.

Water Colours, Exhibition of the New Society of Painters in, 53, Pall Mall, 9 to dusk, 1s., May, June, and July.

Westminster Abbey, Palace Yard, Westminster, daily, from 9 to dusk, 6d.

Wesleyan Centenary Hall, Bishopsgate Street, on application.

Windsor Castle.—The state apartments are open to the public gratuitously on Mondays, Tuesdays, Thursdays, and Fridays. Visitors arriving at Windsor unprovided with tickets to view the state apartments must apply to John Roberts, Esq., at the Lord Chamberlain's Office, near the Winchester Tower. From April to October inclusive, from 1 to 3: from November to March inclusive, from 12 to 2. These tickets can only be used previous to the closing of the apartments on the day they are issued. Tickets procured in London are available for one week, and admit the visitor at 11 o'clock, and may be obtained of Mr. Moon, 20, Threadneedle-street; Mr. Mitchell, 33, Old Bond-street; Messrs. Colnaghi, 14, Pall Mall East; Ackerman and Co., 96, Strand; and Mr. Wright, 60, Pall Mall. Admittance to the Round Tower on the same days as the state apartments. The Queen's private apartments are shown only when the court are residing elsewhere. To view them it is necessary to obtain a special order from the Lord Chamberlain. The royal stables and riding school may be viewed by a ticket from J. Cocum, Esq., Clerk of the Stables, between the hours of 1 and half-past 2 o'clock.

Wyld's Model of the Earth, Leicester Square, daily; admission 1s.

Zoological Gardens, Regent's Park, 10 to dusk. Mondays, 6d.; on Tuesdays and every other day, 1s. Children, at all times, 6d.

Places of Amusement, &c., in the Metropolis and Environs.

OPEN ON CERTAIN DAYS, AS UNDER.

1	Asiatic Museum, Grafton Street	Monday, Wednesday, and Friday.
2	British Museum, Great Russell Street	Monday, Wednesday, and Friday.
	Chelsea Military Academy	Friday.
1	College of Surgeons' Museum	Monday, Tuesday, Wed. & Thursday.
1	Dulwich Gallery.................................	Monday, Tuesday, Wed., Thurs., & Sat.
2	East India Company's Museum	Saturday.
1	Entomological Museum, Bond Street	Tuesday.
	Faraday's Lectures, Royal Institution	Tuesday, Thursday, and Saturday.
	Greenwich Hospital..........................	Monday and Friday.
2	Gresham Lectures	Wednesday, Thursday, and Friday.
2	Hampton Court.................................	Monday, Tuesday, Wed., Thurs., & Sat.
	Hullah's Singing Classes.................	Tuesday and Friday.
1	Linnaean Collection, Soho Square ...	Wednesday and Friday.
	National Gallery...............................	Monday, Tuesday, Wed., and Thurs.
	Society of Arts, Adelphi....................	Mon., Tues., Wed., Thurs., Fri., & Sat
1	Sir John Soane's Museum	Tuesday and Friday.
1	Windsor Castle	Tuesday, Thursday, and Friday.

Tickets to be obtained from London Stationery

OPEN DAILY.

1 Antiquarian Museum, Guildhall.
1 Ashburton Collection, Piccadilly
1 Botanic Gardens, Chelsea.
  Botanical Gardens, Gravesend.
1 Botanic Gardens, Regent's Park.
  British Institution, Pall Mall.
  Chelsea Hospital.
  Christ's Hospital, Newgate Street.
  Colosseum, Regent's Park.
1 Geological Museum, Jermyn Street,
  St. James's.
1 Grosvenor Gallery, Upper Grosvenor Street.
1 Horticultural Gardens, Chiswick.
1 Hunterian Museum, College of Surgeons.

1 House of Lords.
2 Kew Gardens.
2 London Missionary Museum, Bloom-
  field Street, Finsbury.
  Madame Tussaud and Son's, Baker
  Street, from 11 a.m. till 10 p.m.
  Monument.
2 Pantheon, Oxford Street.
  Panorama (Burford's), Leicester Sq.
  Polytechnic Institution, Regent St.
  St. Paul's.
  Thames Tunnel, Rotherhithe.
  The Tower.
  Westminster Abbey.
  Woolwich Arsenal.
  Zoological Gardens, Regent's Park.

1 Require Tickets.   2 Are Free.   The others to be paid for.

Theatres.

Her Majesty's Theatre, Haymarket, —Established for the performance of Italian Opera. Open from February to August. Admission: Stalls, £1 1s; Pit, 8s.; Gallery, 5s.

Royal Italian Opera, Covent Garden.

Drury Lane Theatre, Brydges Street. —Admission: Boxes, 4s.; Pit, 2s.; Gallery, 1s.; Upper Gallery, 6d.

Haymarket Theatre, in the Hay-market.—Admission: Boxes, 5s.; Pit, 3s.; Gallery, 2s.

Lyceum Theatre, Wellington Street, Strand.—Admission: Dress Circle, 5s.; Upper Boxes, 4s.; Pit, 2s.; Gallery, 1s.

Adelphi Theatre, Strand.—Admission: Dress Boxes, 5s.; Boxes, 4s.; Pit, 2s.; Gallery, 1s.

St. James's Theatre, King Street, St. James's.—Admission: Stalls, 10s. 6d.; Pit, 3s.; Gallery, 2s.

Princess's Theatre, Oxford Street.—Admission: Boxes, 4s.; Pit, 2s.; Gallery, 1s.

Strand Theatre, Strand.—Admission: Stalls, 4s.; Boxes, 3s.; Pit, 1s. 6d.; Gallery, 6d.

Sadler's Wells Theatre, Islington.—Admission: Boxes, 2s.; Pit, 1s.; Gallery, 6d.

Royal Surrey Theatre, Blackfriars Road.—Admission: Boxes, 2s.; Pit, 1s.; Gallery, 6d.

Victoria Theatre, New Cut, Lambeth.—Boxes, 2s.; Pit, 1s.; Gallery, 3d.

City of London Theatre.—Admission: Boxes, 2s.; Pit, 1s.; Gallery, 3d.

Astley's Royal Amphitheatre, Westminster Bridge Road.—Admission: Boxes, 4s.; Pit, 2s.; Gallery, 1s.; Upper Gallery, 6d.

Marylebone Theatre, Church Street, Paddington.—Admission: Boxes, 2s. 6d.; Pit, 1s.; Gallery, 6d.

Queen's Theatre, Tottenham Street, Tottenham Court Road.—Admission: Boxes, 2s.; Pit, 1s.; Gallery, 6d.

Royal Standard Theatre, Shoreditch.—Admission: Boxes, 1s.; Pit, 6d.; Gallery, 4d.

Olympic Theatre, Wych Street.—Admission: Boxes, 3s.; Pit, 2s. Gallery, 1s.

Commercial Coffee-Houses.

Lloyd's Coffee-House, Royal Exchange, established for information relative to shipping. The rooms are three in number; viz. the Subscribers', the Merchants', and the Captains' rooms. Lloyd's books give daily accounts of the arrival of vessels, wrecks, or accidents at sea.

North and South American Coffee-Houses, Threadneedle Street.—The headquarters for American intelligence.

The Baltic, Threadneedle Street.—The rendezvous for merchants in the Russian trade.

Garraway's, Change Alley, Cornhill,—for the sale of estates by auction. It is also the resort of merchants who speculate after Change hours, and known in the City as "late men".

The Jerusalem, Cowper's Court, Cornhill.—The resort of Merchants and Captains connected with the East India trade.

The Jamaica, Michael's Alley, Cornhill, frequented by Merchants engaged in the Madeira and West India trade.

The Auction Mart, Bartholomew Lane, Bank, for the sale of estates.

Peel's, Fleet Street, and *Deacon's*, Walbrook, as well as the Public News Rooms, 154, Leadenhall Street, are celebrated for keeping hundreds of files of newspapers. A small fee is payable to the waiter for the examination of files.

Excursions round the Environs of London.

The Omnibuses upon these Roads will furnish a ready and economical conveyance.

To Finchley and Crouch End—through Islington, Holloway, over Highgate Hill, Barnet Road; turn down by the wood houses, to Muswell Hill, taking any of the several lanes leading to Hurnsey, and return by Newington, Islington, etc.

To Enfeld—A beautiful drive of 10 miles, and back.

To Hampstead.—The rides about this neighbourhood can be easily varied, the lanes being pretty and numerous. We may drive through Regent's Park, by Camden Town, pass the Brecknock Arms, and take the lane to Highgate; pass to the left on the hill to Hampstead, where we shall find many lanes diverging from the Heath.

Harrow Road.—A most beautiful drive as far as the fifth milestone. The way to Harrow Road is by Paddington, Westbourne Green, and Kensal Cemetery; and the drive to Harrow (10 miles) will well repay the excursionist. About seven miles from town on the road is a turning to the right, leading to Whimbley Hill, where provender can be had for the horse. From the hill, a most beautiful view may be commanded.

A pleasant Two Hours' Ride can be had through and round Hyde Park, out at the Bayswater end; or to Bayswater through Kensington Lane to Knightsbridge.

The Kilburn Road is very cheerful and countrified; the lanes branching off from the right to Hampstead, Hendon, and Finchley, have all the appearance of the country a hundred miles from town. The lanes on the left, of which there are many, lead to Willesden and numerous villages.

To Acton (4½ miles) and *Ealing* (6½ miles from Hyde Park corner), or by Southall (nine miles) through Bayswater, down Notting Hill, a very pleasant drive. It may be extended on to Uxbridge (15 miles.)

Kew (seven miles). The Botanical Gardens are well worth a visit; open all the year round to the public gratuitously. There are also steamboats from London Bridge; there are various routes to Kew. One through Kensington and Fulham (over the bridge); another through Hammersmith (over the bridge), or on to Kew bridge, which must be crossed. From Kew the drive may be extended to Richmond and its neighbourhood. The walks about Richmond are very beautiful, especially those along the side of the river. The Park is open to equestrians.

Surrey Excursions.—The Wandsworth Road is a delightful ride to Richmond: the route is through Wandsworth, across the Common (over the railroad) on to Tooting, or continue on to Wimbledon. The lanes are most countrified. There are plenty of signposts to direct the passenger. There are turnings before we reach Wandsworth, on the right hand side of the road, exceedingly pretty, leading to the Thames, the banks of which are traversible. Putney may be reached over Battersea Bridge, or from Wandsworth, which affords a very agreeable ride. The Clapham Road, leading to Balham, Tooting, Merton, and Mitcham, and the intersecting lanes, five or six miles from town, are very romantic and retired. There are many pretty lanes also from Tooting across the Common to Streatham. The road to Croydon over Mitcham Common, affords excellent ground for riding or driving.

The Brixton Road is one of the most charming outlets from London. From it, on the right, we have Clapham New Park, and by-lanes to Tooting Common; on the left, Tulse Hill, leading to Norwood, and lanes leading to Camberwell—is a beautiful ride as far as Thornton Heath, Mitcham Common, or to Carshalton (about 10 miles); the lanes leading to Norwood Hill are numerous and pretty.

Streatham Common by the "Greyhound," a bridle-road to Mitcham, over the Common, to Norwood.

From the end of the Common is a road leading to Brixton. On certain eminences of this road lovely views are to be obtained.

The Camberwell Road leads to Norwood and its hills (about eight miles); also, to Dulwich (about five miles); and these neighbourhoods are truly delightful.

To Penge Wood, from Dulwich to Norwood, round the Norwood Hills, and down Streatham Common, to the "Jolly Sailors," taking the circuit of the Norwood Hills, and return by Croydon or Thornton Heath, through Streatham, Brixton, etc.

Dulwich to Lewisham, Beckenham, and Sydenham, for beauty of scenery cannot be surpassed.

Bromley, in Kent (about 10 miles); a most charming ride through Lewisham and Southend.

Hayes, in Kent (about 11 miles), a sweet spot, retired, healthy, and adapted for a summer residence for a young family or an invalid. The route through Dulwich and Bromley, or by the direct high-road through Lewisham, Blackheath, Greenwich, Charlton, and Shooter's Hill, are all delightful neighbourhoods. There are numerous communicating lanes and turnings about these places to Woolwich, Eltham, Lee, etc.

Eastern Excursions,—From the east end of the town, there are many agreeable drives and rides. The "Barge House" is about six or seven miles distant. Barking (about seven miles) down the Whitechapel Road, through Ilford (green lanes). The church is an object of interest.

Wanstead (six miles) may be reached through Ilford, Snaresbrook, or Barking. This neighbourhood, though flat, abounds in pleasant roads, and is remarkably beautiful.

Epping Forest.—Fairlop fair is hold the first Friday in July. A day should be devoted to it. A ride and a stroll about when there, will afford pleasant recollections for many a future time.

Woodford (about eight miles), over Lee Bridge, through Islington Lower Road, Ball's Pond, Hackney, and Clapton. On arriving at Woodford, the ride may be extended through the Forest, High Beach, Chingford, Walthamstow, or Epping. From Woodford the Forest may be traversed in every direction.

Chief Statues, &c.

Charles I., Charing Cross.
Charles II., Soho Square.
James II., back of Whitehall,
William III., St. James's Square.
Queen Anne, Queen Square.
George I., Grosvenor Square.
George III., Cockspurs Street.
George III., Court of Somerset House.
George IV., Trafalgar Square.
"William IV., King William Street, City-
Queen Victoria, Royal Exchange.
Pitt, Hanover Square.
Fox, Bloomsbury Square.
Duke of Bedford, Russell Square.
Duke of Kent, Portland Place.
Canning, Palace Yard.

Achilles, Hyde Park.
Nelson, Trafalgar Square.
Duke of Wellington, Royal Exchange.
General Sir Charles Napier, Trafalgar Square.
Jenner (the Discover of Vaccination), Trafalgar Square.
Sir Henry Havelock, Trafalgar Square.
Sir Robert Peel, Cheapside.
The Guards' Memorial, Waterloo Place, Pall Mall.
The Pillar Memorial to Lord Raglan and other of the Westminster scholars who fell in the Crimea, near Westminster Abbey.
Richard the First, Cœur de Lion, Palace Yard, Westminster.

Bazaars.—Visitors to the above will be gratified with a view of an infinite variety of fancy articles. The Bazaar in Soho Square was the first established in London, and, as a place of fashionable resort, has ever ranked very high in public estimation. It is remarkable for taste, neatness, and good order.

The Pantheon in Oxford Street, is splendidly fitted up, and contains a conservatory, many paintings, and an aviary. Lowther Arcade, in the Strand, Burlington Arcade, Piccadilly, and a new Oxford Street arcade, are also worth a visit.

Hackney Carriage Fares and Regulations.

Fares by Distance.—Sixpence for every mile, or fractional part of a mile, within a circle of four miles from Charing Cross. If required to drive beyond the circle and there discharged, the fare is one shilling a mile for any distance beyond such circle, no back fare being allowed. If a carriage be detained in the whole for 15 minutes the hirer must pay sixpence, in addition to the fare of sixpence per mile for every 15 minutes completed, but no charge can be made for any time under 15 minutes, but several stoppages added together making 15 minutes completed, is charged sixpence.

Fares by Time.—For any time not exceeding one hour, two shillings, and beyond the hour sixpence for every 15 minutes, or any part of 15 minutes. If driven beyond the four mile circle and there discharged, the fare beyond the circle to be charged by distance one shilling per mile. Fares to be paid by time must be so expressed by the hirer at the time of hiring; if not so expressed the fare to be charged by distance. No driver can be compelled to hire his carriage by time after 8 in the evening, or before 6 in the morning. When more than two persons are conveyed, sixpence for each person, for the whole distance, in addition to the fare of sixpence per mile must be paid. Two children under 10 years of age to be considered as one adult person. Every hackney carriage found standing in the street having on it the Stamp Office plate to be deemed as plying for hire, unless actually hired. Evidence of being hired must be produced by the driver.

Luggage.—The driver is bound to carry a reasonable quantity of luggage, either inside or outside his carriage, without any additional charge; but when more than two persons are carried with more luggage than can be carried inside, twopence additional for each package carried outside must be paid.

Speed and Distance—When hired

by distance the driver is bound to drive at a proper speed, not less than six miles an hour, except requested by the hirer to drive at a slower pace, or in cases of unavoidable delay. When hired by time to drive at the rate of four miles an hour, or if desired to drive at a greater speed, the driver shall be entitled to an additional fare of sixpence per mile over and above the four miles per hour; the driver must drive to any place not exceeding six miles from the place of hiring, or for any time not exceeding one hour.

Tickets to be given to hirer.—Every driver of a hackney carriage shall, when hired, deliver to the hirer a card, whereon is printed the number of the Stamp Office plate fixed on his carriage. The utility of this ticket will be readily seen in the case of loss of luggage or cause of complaint.

The number of persons licensed to be carried, and the fare per mile, to be distinctly painted inside and outside every hackney carriage, and the driver shall have with him when plying for hire a book of fares, and produce the same for inspection when required.

Disputes.— In case of any dispute between the hirer and driver, the hirer may require the driver to drive to the nearest Police Court, when the Magistrate then sitting will hear and decide the dispute without the formality of a summons; if the dispute should occur after the closing of the Police Courts,

then the driver to drive to the nearest Police station, when the complaint will be entered and decided by the Magistrate at his next sitting.

Property left in hackney carriages to be delivered by the driver within twenty-four hours at the nearest Police station, if not sooner claimed by the owner; such owner must prove his title to it to the Commissioner of Police, when it will be delivered up to him on payment of expenses incurred, and a recompence to the driver as the Commissioner shall award. All inquiries for lost property to be made at the Office of the Commissioner of Police in Great Scotland Yard.

Any driver of a hackney carriage refusing to comply to any of the foregoing regulations, is liable to a penalty not exceeding forty shillings, or one month's imprisonment.

Regulations respecting Stage Carriages, including Omnibuses.

No stage carriage is to carry passengers otherwise than upon proper seats, allowing sixteen inches in breadth for each passenger; children under five years of age, sitting in the lap, not to be reckoned. The number of passengers is to be painted conspicuously in the inside of every carriage, and on the back outside, under a penalty of £10 against the proprietor. No more than the proper number of passengers are to be carried, under a penalty of

£5 each against the driver and conductor respectively. Any constable, peace-officer, or passenger, may measure the seats, under a penalty of £5 against any person refusing or obstructing such measurement. N.B. Rules are laid down respecting the number of outside passengers, limiting it according to the height and size of the carriage, independently of the limitation resulting from the length of the seats. See 5 and 6 Victoria, c. 79, ss. 13—17; and 6 and 7 Victoria, c. 86, adds that a printed Table of Fares shall be placed inside; imposes a penalty of £5 for acting as driver, conductor, &c., without a license; and £10 on the proprietor knowing or permitting such act; also a penalty of £3 for furious driving or wilful misbehaviour; £2 for causing obstructions by loitering, deceiving as to route, stopping at crossings, &c.

Cab Stands in the Metropolis.

By virtue of the authority conferred upon the Commissioners of the Metropolitan Police by an act of last session, they have proceeded to make various alterations with respect to the old stands for hackney carriages, and to appoint others in different localities where the neighbourhood appeared to require such accommodation. Standings for hackney carriages have been appointed, which provide room for 1815 carriages. The chief objects kept in view have been to place them in the immediate neighbourhood where they are wanted, without causing obstruction by their being in the great leading thoroughfares. Regulations are made to prevent the drivers and others standing together on the footways, smoking, drinking, or by any improper behaviour causing obstruction or annoyance there.

The various cab stands, under this new regulation, are as follows:—

Whitehall Division.—Trafalgar square, one on the east side and another on the west side; Whitehall.

Westminster Division.—Buckingham-gate; Cadogan-place; Carey-street, Westminster; Commercial-road, Pimlico; Franklin's-row, Chelsea College; Fulham-road; Grosvenor-street; Knightsbridge-green; Knightsbridge-road; Milbank; Milton-row, Vauxhall-bridge road; Palace-yard, Shaftesbury-terrace, Vauxhall-bridge road, Sloane-square.

St. James' Division.—Broad-street, Golden-square; Conduit-street, Regent-street; Davies-street, Berkeley-square; Dean-street, Soho; two in the Haymarket; Leicester-square; Park-lane, Piccadilly; three in Piccadilly; two in St. James'-street; Woodstock-street, Oxford-street.

Marylebone Division.—Adam-street West, Upper Berkeley-street; Boston-street, Park-road; Great Marylebone-street; Great Quebec-street, New-road; Harrow-road; London-street, Paddington; Maida-hill; Marylebone-lane, Oxford-street; Old Cavendish-street; Oxford-street; Paddington-street; Praed-street, Edgeware-road; three in the Uxbridge-road; Winchester-place, New-road.

Holborn Division.—Berners-street, Oxford-street; Bloomsbury-street, New Oxford-street; Bury-place, Bloomsbury; Castle-street East, Berners-street; Compton-street, Brunswick-square; Duke's-road, New-road; Foley-street, Portland-place; Goodge-street, Tottenham-court road; Guildford-street, Foundling Hospital; John-street, Oxford-street; King's-road, Gray's-inn; two in the Portland-road; Southampton-row, Bloomsbury; three in Tottenham-court road.

Covent-garden Division.—Agar-street, Strand; Bedford-street, Strand; Broad-street, St.Giles; Burleigh-street, Strand; Duncannon-street, Strand; two in Holborn; two in the Strand; Upper Wellington-street; Wellington-street, Strand.

Finsbury Division.—Clerkenwell-green; Cobham-row, Clerkenwell; Goswell-road; Goswell-street; Gray's-inn road, King's-cross; Old-street, St. Luke's; St. John-street road; two in Shoreditch.

Whitechapel Division.—Dock-street, Whitechapel; High-street, White-chapel; Little Thames-street, St. Catherine; Tower-hill (east side); Tower-hill (west-side).

Stepney Division.—Epping-place, Mile-end gate; High-street, Shadwell; St. George-street, St. George's in the East; White Horse-street, Ratcliff.

Lambeth Division.—Blackfriars' road; Kennington-cross; Kennington-green; Lambeth-road; Mount-street; New Bridge-street; Vauxhall; Palace New-road; St. George's road; Water-loo-road.

Southwark Division.—Blackfriars'-road; Borough-road East; Borough-road West; Dover-road; High-street, Southwark; Old Kent-road; Wellington-street, Southwark.

Islington Division.—Belinda-Terrace, Canonbury-square, Islington; Canonbury-place, Islington; City-road; Clapton-square, Hackney; Clark's-place, High-street, Islington; two in the Holloway-road; Islington-green; Kingsland-road; London-lane, Hackney; Penton-street, Pentonville; Pit-field-street (near the church) Hoxton; Richmond-road, Islington; Rotherfield Street, Islington; Great William-street, Maiden-lane, Islington.

Camberwell Division.—Camberwell-lane; High-street, Camberwell; Kennington Church; Manor-place, Walworth-road; Stockwell-place, Brixton.

Greenwich Division.—Blackheath-village; six in Greenwich; High-street, Woolwich.

Hampstead Division.—Charles-street East, Hampstead-road; College-street, Camden-town; Cumberland-market (centre road); Edgeware-road; Hampstead-road; High-street, Camden-town; North-street, Portman-market; Ordnance-road, St. John's-Wood; Park-road, St. John's-Wood; Seymour-street, Euston-square; Wellington-road, St. John's-Wood; Wilstead-street, Somers-town.

Kensington Division.—Broadway, Hammersmith; four in the Great Western-road, Kensington; Great Western-road, Hammersmith; Uxbridge-road, Notting-hill.

Wandsworth Division.—Great George-street, Richmond; Kew-road, Richmond; two in the King's-road, Chelsea; New-road, water-side, Chelsea; Richmond-green; Richmond-hill.

Porterage.

The Rates of Porterage are regulated by Act of 39 Geo. IV., cap. 58.

For any parcel not weighing more than 50 lbs., and when the distance does not exceed a quarter of a mile, 3*d.*; half a mile, 4*d.*; a mile, 6*d.*; a mile and a half, 8*d.*; two miles, 10*d.*; and 3*d.* for every additional half-mile. Porters exacting more, to be fined not exceeding 20*s.*; misbehaving, 20*s.* to 10*s.* A ticket to be sent with every parcel; charge for carriage and porterage marked on it, under a penalty of 40*s.*, or not less than 5*s.* Parcels are to be delivered at any place within half a mile of the carriage pavement in six hours after arrival, under a penalty of 20*s.*, or not less than 10*s.* Parcels arriving between four in the evening and seven in the morning to be delivered in six hours from the latter period, under the like penalty. Informations under Act to be laid within fourteen days, with appeal to Quarter Sessions.

The business of the London and Metropolitan Parcels Conveyance Company, on the plan of the London local post, continues to be conducted with cheapness and punctuality, and to be successful and useful. Chief Station, Rolls Buildings, Fetter-lane, and there are upwards of 700 receiving-houses.

CARRIERS are not responsible for loss of parcel containing property where exceeding value of £10, unless same delivered as such and accordingly insured, for which insurance a receipt to be given. Any one coach proprietor or carrier may be sued. The Act does not relieve carrier, or proprietor, or mail contractor, from liability for loss occasioned by servants' acts, or his own neglect or misconduct.

Limits of the Metropolis.

The limits of the metropolis, as defined by 1 and 2 William IV., are comprised within a circle, the radius of which is three miles from the General Post Office :—

Bayswater Road, St.-George's Burial Ground; Edgware Road, Burwood Place; New Road, Homer Street; Blandford Square; Park Road, Regent's Park, Kent Terrace; Regent's Park, Hanover Terrace; Hampstead Road, Harwood Street; Kentish Town, Trafalgar Place; Holloway, King's Head; Highbury College; Stoke Newington, Paradise Row; Hackney Church; Mile End Road, Coborn Road; Commercial Road, Limehouse Church; Deptford Lower Road, 2 fur. beyond Plough Lane; Kent Road, the Asylum Road; Peckham, Camden Chapel; Camberwell Green, the Tiger; Brixton, Russell Street; Clapham Road, Augusta Place; South Lambeth, Montpellier Row; Wandsworth Road, Cavendish Road; Chelsea, S. W. End of Ebury Street; King's Road, Coleshill Street; Sloane Street, Hans Street; Knightsbridge Green.

Omnibus Routes.

The routes of the various metropolitan omnibuses are manifold. The principal lie north and south, east and west, through the central parts of London, to and from the extreme suburbs. Between the beginning and the end of the journey, the omnibuses make many deviations from the direct road, in order to accommodate all the chief thoroughfares, and to collect all the passengers the different streets may supply. The greater part of them commence running at nine in the morning, and continue without intermission until twelve at night. Within a few months it is likely tram carriages on rails will accommodate passengers on many of the following routes, where nearly a level road will permit of their introduction. At present only two lines are open, from Westminster Abbey down Victoria Street to the New Pimlico Station, and from the Marble Arch for a mile along the Bayswater Road. Both the common omnibuses and the new railway carriages will offer advantages respectively, which the public will soon discover, and support accordingly.

Any attempt at extortion or incivility should be at once reported to Mr. A. Church, the Secretary, at the office of the Company, 454, West Strand, and Moorgate Street, City.

Northern and Southern Routes.

☛ The places given in Italics are on or near the routes specified.

The Atlas Omnibuses

Start from Camberwell Gate, and pass along the Walworth Road (*Amelia Street, the Surrey Zoological Gardens*), and through, by, or over, Elephant and Castle, London Road (*Philanthropic Institution, School for the Blind*), Westminster Road (Orphan Asylum), Westminster Bridge Road (*Astley's Amphitheatre*), Westminster Bridge (*fine view of the New Houses of Parliament*), Bridge Street (*near Westminster Abbey, Westminster Hall, and New Houses of Parliament*), Whitehall (*Treasury, Whitehall Chapel, Horse Guards, and Admiralty*), Charing Cross (*Statue of Charles I., Nelson's Monument, National Gallery, Fountains, &c.*) Cockspur Street (*Equestrian Statue of George III.*), Pall-mall (*Her Majesty's Theatre and Haymarket Theatre*), Waterloo Place (*Duke of York's Column*), Regent Street Quadrant, Regent Street (*209, Cosmorama*), Oxford Street (*near the Polytechnic Institution*), Orchard St., Portman Square, Baker Street (*58, Madame Tussaud's, Christmas Prize Cattle Show*), Upper Baker Street, Park Road, Wellington Road, Eyre Arms, St. John's Wood.

The Waterloo Omnibuses

Have the same starting-point as the preceding, thence taking Walworth Road (*Amelia Street, Surrey Zoological Gardens*), Elephant and Castle, London Road (*Philanthropic Institution, Blind School*), Waterloo Road (*Royal Victoria Theatre*), Waterloo Bridge (*from this Bridge fine views of London*), Wellington Street, Strand (*Lyceum Theatre, Exeter Hall, Adelphi Theatre*), Charing Cross West (*Lowther Arcade, near Hungerford Market, Suspension Bridge, &c.*), Charing Cross (*Northumberland Home, National Gallery, Nelson's Monument, Fountains*), Cockspur Street (*Equestrian Statue of George III.*), Pall-mall (*Her Majesty's Theatre and Haymarket Theatre*), Waterloo Place (*Duke of York's Column, entrance to St. James's Park*), Regent Street Quadrant, Regent Street (209, *Cosmorama*), Oxford Street (*Close by the Polytechnic Institution*), John Street, Portland St., Portland Road, Albany Street (*Colosseum, Diorama*), Clarence Street, York and Albany Tavern (*near Regent's Park, Zoological Gardens, and North Western Railway*).

King's Cross Omnibuses

Start from Kennington Gate, and take the course of Kennington Road (*New Street, Penton Place, Surrey Zoological Gardens*), High Street (*Almshouses*), Elephant and Castle, London Road (*Philanthropic Institution, Blind School, Obelisk*), Great Surrey Street (*Royal Surrey Theatre, Magdalen Hospital, Rowland Hill's Chapel*), Blackfriars Bridge (*fine view of London*), Bridge Street (*Bridewell*), Fleet Street (*St. Bride's Church, St. Dunstan's Church, the Temple, Temple Bar*), Chancery Lane (*Lincoln's Inn, and Inns of Court*), Holborn, Gray's Inn Lane (*Gray's Inn and Garden, the Royal Free Hospital*), King's Cross, New Road, Euston Square (*North Western Railway Terminus*).

Islington Omnibuses

Have their starting-point at Kennington Gate, thence taking Kennington Road (*New Street and Penton Place, Surrey Musis Hall*), High Street (*Almshouses*), Elephant and Castle, London Road (*Philanthropic Institution, Blind School, Obelisk*), Great Surrey Street (*Royal Surrey Theatre, Rowland Hill's Chapel*), Blackfriars Bridge (*fine view of London*), Bridge Street (*Bridewell*), Ludgate Hill, Ludgate Street, St. Paul's Churchyard (*St. Paul's Cathedral, St. Paul's School*), Cheapside, St. Martin's-le-Grand (*General Post Office*), Aldersgate Street (*the General Post Money Order Office, Charter House Gardens*), Goswell Street Road, Islington (*the Angel*), White Lion Street, Penton Street (*White Conduit House*), Thornhill Road, Barnsbury Park.

Kingsland Gate to Camberwell, *via* Bishopsgate Street and the Borough; Camden Town to Pimlico, Victoria Railway Station; Holloway and Islington to Westminster Abbey; Stoke Newington and Kingsland, *via* Shoreditch, to Bank; Clapton and Hackney, *via* Hackney Road and Shoreditch, to Bank.

Eastern and Western Routes.

The omnibuses proceeding on these are too numerous to particularize. Their course, however, may be readily ascertained by observing whether the principal places mentioned in this Guide are written on the outside.

First Route.

Mile End (*London Hospital*), Whitechapel Road (*Whitechapel Church*), Whitechapel, Aldgate High Street (*the far-famed Aldgate pump*), Leadenhall Street (*India House*), Cornhill (*Royal Exchange, Bank of England, and many other large establishments*), Mansion House Street (*Mansion House*), Poultry, Cheapside (*near Guildhall, Bow Church, near General Post-Office*), St. Paul's Churchyard (*St. Paul's Cathedral, St. Paul's School*), Ludgate Street, Ludgate Hill, Fleet Street (*St. Bride's Church, St. Dunstan's Church, the Temple and Inns of Court, Temple Bar*), Strand (*St. Clement's Church, Strand Theatre, New Church, King's College, Somerset House, Lyceum Theatre, Exeter Hall, Adelphi Theatre*), Charing Cross West (*Lowther Arcade, near Hungerford Market, Suspension Bridge across the Thames, Northumberland House*), Charing Cross (*National Gallery, Nelson's Monument, Fountains, &c.*), Cockspur Street (*Equestrian Statue of George III.*). Pall-mall (*Her Majesty's Theatre, Haymarket Theatre*), Waterloo Place (*Duke of York's Column, entrance to St. James's Park*), Regent Street, Piccadilly (*New Branch Post-Office; St. James's Church, Burlington House, Devonshire House, Hyde Park Corner, Apsley House, Triumphal Arch, Colossal Statue of the Duke of Wellington, entrance to Hyde Park, St. George's Hospital*), Knightsbridge, Sloane Street, thence to Chelsea (*Chelsea Hospital*), Victoria Station, Putney, Brompton, and Hammersmith.

Second Route.

From Mile End by Cheapside, proceed through Newgate Street (*near General Post Office, Christ's Hospital, Jail of Newgate*), Giltspur Street, Old Bailey, Skinner Street (*St. Sepulchre's Church*), Holborn Hill (*St. Andrew's Church, Inns of Court*), High Holborn (*near Soane's Museum*), New Oxford Street (*near British Museum*), Oxford Street (*near Soho Bazaar, Princess's Theatre, Pantheon Bazaar*), Regent Circus (*near Polytechnic Institution*), Oxford Street (*entrance to Hyde Park*), Edgeware Road, Praed Street, to the Great Western Railway Terminus at Paddington, and Kilburn Gate from Hyde Park Corner, *via* Bayswater, Notting Hill to Starch Green and Shepherd's Bush.

R

General Directions for Railway Travellers.

Time—Greenwich time is now universally kept at all the railways in England, and partially in Scotland; the doors of the booking-offices are closed at the time specified in the tables, after which no person can possibly get admission.

Single Tickets.—These must, on all occasions, be produced when demanded by the Company's servants. Parties losing their tickets are liable to be charged the fare from the most distant station from which the train starts; they are only available on the day of issue. Parties cannot re-book at any intermediate station by the same train.

Return Tickets.—The rate of reduction in these tickets varies from one-third to one-sixth in the double journey; they are issued for the accommodation of first and second class passengers, and may be obtained at almost any station on the leading lines of railway, but only at the principal stations on most of the branches or more subordinate lines. They are not transferable, and are only available on the day and to the place for which they are issued, except such as are granted on the Saturday and Sunday, which are, in most cases, useable till the Monday evening following. On returning, the ticket must be re-stamped before starting, or other wise it will not be allowed. Passengers with return tickets can travel neither by the express, fast, nor government trains.

Season Tickets are issued for periods of not less than two months, at prices specially agreed for.

Smoking is strictly prohibited in the carriages or at any of the stations; persons found so doing are subject to a penalty of 40s.

Children under 12 years of age are charged half fare. Infants in arms are carried free.

Luggage.—Passengers are allowed to take with them, free, a certain quantity of personal luggage (*a table showing the amount allowed to each person by the various railways is given below*). Passengers should be very careful to have their names and destinations legibly marked upon their luggage, and see it properly disposed of in the train, and take the number of the porter, and the carriage in which he deposits it, as the companies are not responsible for the safety thereof, unless booked and paid for according to value, and a receipt granted accordingly. It may be advisable for the passenger, should he have any light luggage, to stow it under his seat.

Carriages and Horses are not taken

by the express, fast, or mail trains. Gentlemen riding in their own carriages are charged first class fare, and their servants second class fare. Carriages and horses must be at the stations fifteen minutes before the time of starting. Carriage-trucks and horse-boxes are only kept at the principal stations; and, to prevent disappointment, notice of such requirement should be given the day previous. The companies are not responsible for the loss of or damage to any horse above the value of £40, unless a declaration of its value, signed by the owner or his agent, shall be delivered to them at the time of booking, and an extra charge paid, amounting to about 2½ per cent, on the declared value above £40.

Dogs are on no account allowed to travel in the carriages; a proper place is assigned for them. They are charged for any distance not exceeding 12 miles, 6*d*., above that distance ½*d*. per mile.

Railway Assurance—We know of no more important direction or rather advice we could furnish the traveller by railway with, than that, before he commences his journey, TO INSURE HIS LIFE. There is a Company now in existence, called the RAILWAY PASSENGERS' ASSURANCE COMPANY, for this express purpose, and the traveller may, at the time of taking his journey ticket, if he be a first class passenger, by paying the clerk 3*d*. extra, insure himself for £1000; if a second class passenger, 2*d*. will insure him for £500; and if a third class passenger, 1*d*. will insure him for £200; the whole amount to be paid in cases of fatal accident, and a proportionate compensation in cases of non-fatal injury; we therefore think that no person who has occasion to travel, will, on reflection, refuse to spend the small amount required as premium to provide, not only such relief to themselves or their families if they should meet with an accident, but to maintain an institution designed to afford relief to those on whom the burden actually falls, as it must be remembered that the railway companies are not legally answerable for accidents that cannot be proved to arise from negligence on the part of their servants.

The Railway Stations.

The London and North-Western Railway, from Euston Square—for Aylesbury, Dunstable, Bedford, Northampton, Peterborough, Stamford, Rugby, Coventry, Leamington, Birmingham, Wolverhampton, Lichfield, Stafford, Crewe, Chester, Birkenhead, Conway, Bangor, Holyhead, and Dublin; also to Warrington, Liverpool, Manchester, Preston, Lancaster, Kendal, Carlisle, Edinburgh, Glasgow, Stirling, Perth, Dundee, and Montrose; likewise to Leicester, Nottingham, Lincoln, Derby, Sheffield, Leeds, York, Hull, Darlington, Newcastle, Berwick, Edinburgh, and Glasgow.

The Great Western Railway, from Paddington—for Berks, Oxfordshire, Wilts, Somerset, Devon, and Gloucestershire, Windsor, Reading, Oxford, Cheltenham, Gloucester, Bath, Bristol, Bridgewater, Taunton, and Exeter; and the steamers to Swansea and South Wales, Cork, Waterford, Dublin, and New York.

The Great Northern Railway, from King's Cross—for Barnet, Hatfield, Hitchen, Biggleswade, St. Neots, Huntingdon, Peterborough, Spalding, Boston, Tattershall, Kirkstead, Bardney, Lincoln, Retford, Bawtry, Doncaster, Knottingly, Harrowgate, York, Darlington, Durham, Newcastle, Berwick, Dunbar, and Edinburgh, and all parts of the north; also to Sheffield, Leeds, Manchester, Liverpool, Bolton, Fleetwood, &c.

Eastern Counties Railway, from Shoreditch—for Chelmsford, Colchester, Ipswich, and Bury St. Edmunds; also for Ware, Hertford, Bishop-Stortford, Newmarket, Cambridge, St. Ivea, Huntingdon, Ely, Norwich, Yarmouth, Lowestoft, Dereham, Lynn; also to Peterborough and Stamford.

London and South Western Railway, from Waterloo Bridge Road—for Surrey, Sussex, Hampton Court, Windsor, Winchester, Southampton, Dorchester, Weymouth, Exeter, Gosport, Portsmouth; and Steamers to Isle of Wight, Guernsey, Jersey, and Havre, St. Malo, Grandville, Exmouth, Plymouth, Falmouth, Waterford, Cork, Dublin, Spain, Portugal, Mediterranean, East Indies, West Indies, Mexico, &c., &c.

Brighton, Dover, Croydon, & Greenwich Railway, from London Bridge (Southwark side) or Newcross stations—for Croydon, Tunbridge, Maidstone, Folkestone, Dover, Brighton, Shoreham; and all parts of Kent and Sussex, and the Steamers to Havre, Dieppe, Boulogne.

Blackwall Railway, from Fenchurch Street and Minories—for Blackwall, Gravesend, Margate, and the Foreign Steamers.

Table showing the Amount of Luggage allowed to each Passenger, free of Charge, by the respective Companies.

NAMES OF RAILWAYS.	1st clss.	2nd clss.	3rd clss.	TERMS OF EXCESS.
	lbs.	lbs.	lbs.	
Birkenhead, Lancashire, and Cheshire Junction, and Shrewsbury & Chester	100	100	56	2s. per cwt. to Chester.
Chester and Holyhead	100	80	56	Under 40 miles, ¼d. per lb.; above, ½d.
Eastern Counties and Norfolk, and Eastern Counties and Eastern Union	112	84	56	¾d. per cwt. per mile, and not less than 12 miles being charged.
East Lancashire	112	60	56	1d. per cwt. per mile.
Edinburgh and Clasgow, Edinburgh, Perth, & Dundee & Scottish Central	112	100	56	Above this changed parcel rates.
Glasgow and South Western	100	60	40	Charged by weight.
Great Northern	112	100	56	Over these weights changed.
Great Western	112	56	56	According to distance.
Lancashire and Yorkshire	112	100	56	According to distance.
Lancaster and Preston, and Lancaster and Carlisle	100	100	56	¼d. per lb. for every additional 30 miles.
London, Brighton, and South Coast	100	60	56	Under 40 miles, ¼d. per lb.; above, ½d.
London and North Western	100	100	56	According to distance.
London and South Western	112	84	56	Under 40 miles, ¼d. per lb.; above, ½d.
Manchester, Sheffield, and Lincolnshire	100	100	56	Under 20 miles, ⅛d. per lb.; under 45, ¼d. per lb.; under 80, ½d. per lb.; under 160, 1d. per lb.; under 210, 1½d.
Midland	112	100	56	According to distance.
North Eastern	112	100	56	According to distance.
Oxford, Worcester, and Wolverhampton	112	100	56	According to distance.
South Devon	112	60	60	¼d. per lb.
South Eastern, or London and Dover	112	60	56	Under 40 miles, ¼d. per lb.; above, ½d.
South Wales	112	56	56	According to distance.

Metropolitan Omnibuses Departures, prior to the starting of Trains from the respective Stations, as below.—Fare, 6d. each.

DEPARTURES FROM	L. & N. Western, Euston Sq.	Great Western, Paddington.	Great Northern, King's Cross.	Brighton and S. Eastern, L. Bridge	South Western, Waterloo Rd.	Eastern Counties, Shoreditch.
	H. M.	H. M.	H. M.	H. M.	H. M.	H. M.
* Gresham Street Office, to	0 40	1 5	...	0 20	0 45	...
Griffin's Green Man and Still, Oxford Street, to	0 17	0 30	...	1 0	‡0 35	1 0
Spread Eagle, Gracechurch Street, to	0 45	1 10	...	0 15	0 30	0 20
Cross Keys, Wood Street, Cheapside, to	0 38	1 5	...	0 25	0 45	0 30
White Horse, Fetter Lane, to	0 30	...	...	...	0 25	...
Golden Cross, Charing Cross, to	0 30	0 40	...	0 45	0 20	0 50
Spread Eagle, 33, Regent Circus	0 23	0 35	...	1 0	0 30	1 * 0
George and Blue Boar, Holborn, to	0 25	†0 45	...	0 40	0 30	0 40
Bolt-in-Tun, Fleet Street, to	0 32	0 58	...	0 35	0 20	0 40
Bull and Mouth, Aldersgate Street, to	...	1 0	...	...	...	...

LUGGAGE.—The London and North Western allows 100lbs. of Luggage free by these Omnibuses; the Great Western charges 6d. above 25lbs.; 56lbs., 1s.; 112lbs., 1s. 6d.

* The Omnibuses from the Great Western Office, call at the Peacock, Islington; George and Blue Boar, Holborn; Green Man and Still, Oxford Street; Golden Cross, Charing Cross; Chaplin's Universal Office, and Bull and Mouth; Regent Circus; and Gloucester Warehouse, Oxford Street.

† Leaves 5 minutes earlier for every Train except the 6 50 a.m.

‡ For the 10 and 11 a.m., and & p.m. trains only.

Thames Steamers.

The Steam Packet Service on the Thames is very complete, forming, as it does, communication between London, Greenwich, Southend, Sheerness, Gravesend, &c, down the river, and Chelsea, Richmond, &c., up the river, frequently throughout the day.—For times, fares, &c., see *Bradshaw's Railway Guide*.

Residences of Foreign Ambassadors and Consuls.

America.—United States Ambassador, The Hon. Charles Francis Adams, 24, Portland Place.

Austria.—Ambassador, Count Rudolph Apponyi, Chandos House, Chandos Street; Consul-General, Baron Rothschild, No. 29, St. Swithin's Lane.

Baden.—Consul, John Simson, Riches Court, Lime Street.

Bavaria.—Ambassador, Baron de Cetto, 3, Hill Street, Berkeley Square; Consul, A. Brandt, No. 33½, Great St. Helen's, Bishopsgate.

Belgium.—Ambassador, M. S. Van de Weyer, 50, Portland Place; Consul's office, 52, Gracechurch Street.

Brazil.—Ambassador, Commandeur Francisco Ignacio de Carvalho Moreira, No. 9, Cavendish Square; Consul's office, 14, Cooper's Row, Crutchedfriars.

Denmark.—Ambassador, M. de Bille, 13A, Upper Brook Street; Consul's office, 6, Warnford Court, Throgmorton Street.

Frankfort.—Consul, B. Hebeler, 106, Fenchurch Street.

France.—Ambassador, Count Flahault, 1, Albert Gate, Hyde Park; Consular office, No. 5, Scott's Yard, Cannon Street.

Hanover.—Ambassador, Count Von Keilmansegge, 44, Grosvenor Place; Consulate, No. 31, Lombard Street.

Italy.— Ambassador, Marquis D' Azeglio, No. 23, Park Lane; Consul, 31, Old Jewry.

Netherlands.— Ambassador, Baron Bentick, No. 20, Lowndes Square; Consul General, No. 20½, Great Saint Helen's, Bishopsgate Street.

Peru.—Ambassador, I. Y. de Osma, 31, South Street, Grosvenor Square; Consul's office, No. 11, New Broad Street.

Portugal.—Ambassador, Count de Lavradio, No. 12, Gloucester Place, Portman Square; Consul's Office, 5, Jeffrey Square.

Prussia.—Ambassador, Count von Bernstorff, No. 9, Cavlton House Terrace; Consul General, 106, Fenchurch Street.

Russia.—Ambassador, Baron de Brunow, Chesham House, Chesham Place, Belgrave Square; Consulate office, No. 33, Great Winchester Street, City.

Saxony.—Ambassador, Count Charles Vitztham d'Eckstaedt, No. 3, Hobart Place, Eaton Square.

Spain,—Ambassador, Don Javier Ysturitz, No. 3, Hobart Place, Eaton Square.

Sweden and Norway.—Ambassador, Count Platen, 49, Grosvenor Place; Consul General, No. 2, Alderman's Walk, New Broad Street.

Wurtemburg.—Consul's, No. 106, Fenchurch Street.

Term Table.

Hilary Term begins January 11, ends Trinity 31.

Easter Term begins May 26, ends May 12.

Trinity Term begin May 26, ends June 16.

Michaelmas Term begins November 2, ends November 25.

Her Majesty Judges.

Court of Chancery.—*Lord Channellor*—Lord Westbury; *Lords Justices of Court of Appeal*—Sir J. L. Knight Bruce, Sir G. J. Turner (£6,000 e.); *Master of the Rolls*—Sir John Romilly (£6,000); *Vice Chancellors* — Sir R. T. Kindersley, Sir J. Stuart, Sir W. Rage Wood, (£5,000 e.)

Court of Queen's Bench.—*Lord Chief Justice*—Right Hon. Sir A. I. E. Cockburn (£8,000), Sir W. Wightman, Sir C. Crompton, Sir Hugh Hill, Sir Colin Blackburn, (£5,000 e.)

Common Pleas—*Lord Chief Justice*—Sir William Erle (£7,000), Sir E. V. Williams, Sir J. S. Willes, Sir J. B. Byles, Sir H. S. Keating, (£5,000 e)

Court of Exchequer—*Lord Chief Baron*—Sir F. Pollock (£7,000); Sir S. Martin, Sir G. Bramwell, Sir J. P. Wilde, Sir W. F. Channell (£5,000 e.).

Admiralty Court.—Sir S. Lushington, D.C.L.

Ecclesiastical Courts.—*Consistorial Court*—Sir S. Lushington; *Court of Probate*—Rt. Hon. Sir Cresswell Cresswell, Judge.

Bankruptcy Court.—*Lords Justices*—Sir J. L. Knight Bruce, and Sir G. J. Turner. *London Commissioners*—Joshua Evans, J. S. M. Fonblanque, R. G. C. Fane, E. Holroyd, E. Goulburn, Esquires.

Insolvent Debtors' Court.—*Chief Commissioner*—W. J. Law, Esq.; *Commissioner*—William Nicholls, Esq.

Probate and Divorce Court.—*Judge*—Sir Cresswell Cresswell.

POST OFFICE REGULATIONS.

Rated of Postage.— All letters from one part of Great Britain to another (including the Local Penny Posts and the London Twopenny Post), are charged, if prepaid, and not

Exceeding half an ounce   ... 1*d.*

Ditto and not an ounce   ... 2*d.*

and so on, at the rate of 2*d.* for every additional ounce or fraction of an ounce. Unpaid and unstamped letters are charged double postage on delivery.

Hours of Posting for the Evening Mails.—The Receiving-houses close at 5 30 p.m.; but letters are received for the evening's dispatch until 6 p.m., if an extra penny stamp is affixed. The Branch Post-offices at Charing Cross, Old Cavendish Street, and Stone's End, Southwark, receive letters until 6 p.m., and until ¼ to 7 p.m. by affixing an additional penny stamp. At the Branch Post Office in Lombard Street, the box remains open without additional fee until 6 p.m., and until 7 p.m. by affixing a penny stamp. At the General Post Office in St. Martin's-le-Grand until 6, free; and until 7, by payment of the extra charge as at Lombard Street. From 7 to ½ past 7 p.m., letters may be posted at the General Post Office upon payment of a fee of sixpence each, which must, as well as the postage, be prepaid. Letters intended to pass by outward mails to foreign parts must be posted at the above hours.—N.B. Newspapers for the evening mails must be put into the Receiving Houses before 5 p.m., the Branch offices before 5 30 p.m., or General Post Office before 6 p.m. From 6 p.m. to 7 30, on payment of one halfpenny late fee; except newspapers for foreign parts, which must be posted at the General Post Office and Branch Offices before 6 p.m., and at the Receiving Houses before 5 p.m.

Morning Mails must be posted at the Receiving Houses before 10 p.m. the previous evening, and at the Branch Offices, Charing Cross, Old Cavendish Street, and the Borough, before 7 15 a.m., and at Lombard Street and the Chief Offices before 7 45 a.m.

Transmission of Periodical Publications by Post within the United Kingdom.—Periodical Publications, including newspapers, published in the United Kingdom at intervals not exceeding thirty-one days, and which shall bear a stamp or stamps denoting the stamp duty, of the kind hitherto confined chiefly to News-papers, may be transmitted and re-transmitted through the Post within the United Kingdom free from postage. The publication must be folded in such a manner, that the stamps shall be exposed on the outside. It must be posted within fifteen days from the date of publication. It must either have no cover or a cover open at the ends. It must contain no en-closure. It must have no writing or other mark thereon but the name and address of the person to whom it is sent, nor anything on the cover but such name and address, the printed title of the publication, and the printed name and address of the publisher or vendor who sends it. If the publica-tion be addressed to any person with-in the free delivery of the place where it is posted, it will be liable to a postage of 1d., which must be prepaid by affixing a postage stamp. The free delivery of London, so far as applies to this rule, extends to such places only as are within three miles of the General Post Office. Unstamped pub-lications, or stamped publications which have been issued more than fifteen days, can be forwarded within the United Kingdom, and to most of the Colonies, under the regulation of the Book Post.

Books, Periodicals, &c.—*Inland Book Post.*—For a packet not exceed-ing 4oz., 1d. exceeding 4oz. and not exceeding 8oz., 2d.; exceeding 8oz. and not exceeding 16oz., 4d.; exceeding 1lb. and not exceeding 1½lb., 6d.; and so on, 2d. being charged for every additional ½lb. or any less weight. The postage must be prepaid in full by means of postage stamps affixed outside the packet or cover. Every packet must be sent either without a cover, or in a cover open at the ends or sides. If the postage paid on the packet amount to 4d., it may contain any number of separate books or other publications, prints, or maps, and any quantity of paper, parchment, or vellum (to the exclusion of letters whether sealed or open); and the books, &c., may be either printed, written, or plain, or any mixture of the three. All legitimate binding, mounting, or covering of a book, &c., will be allowed, whether it be loose or attached; also rollers in the case of prints or maps, markers (whether of paper or other-wise) in the case of books, and what-ever is necessary for the safe trans-mission of literary or artistic matter, or usually appertains thereto. But, if the postage paid be less than 4d., the packet must consist exclusively of printed matter, without restriction, however, either as to the number of publications or separate sheets, or as to whether they are bound or unbound. A packet must not contain any letter, or any enclosure, sealed or otherwise closed against inspection, nor any letter, or communication of the nature of a letter, written or printed, in any packet or on its cover. No book packet can be received, if it exceeds two feet in length, width, or depth. Any packet which shall not be open at the ends or sides, or shall have any letter, or any communication of the nature of a letter, written or printed in it or upon its cover, will be charged with the "unpaid" or double letter postage. If a packet contain any letter, closed or open, or any other unauthorised enclosure, the letter or enclosure will be taken out and forwarded to the address on the packet, charged as an unpaid letter, together with an additional rate of 4d.; and the remainder of the packet, if duly prepaid with stamps, will then be forwarded to its address. If a packet be not sufficiently prepaid with stamps, but nevertheless bear a stamp of the value of 1d., it will be forwarded, charged with the deficient book postage, together with an additional rate of 4d.; but any packet which shall bear no postage stamp, will be charged with the "unpaid" or double letter postage, according to its weight. In every case in which the postage charged upon a packet under these regulations would be greater than the letter rate, the latter postage must be substituted. These regulations will not interfere with votes and proceedings of parliament, or newspapers and other periodical publications, when duly stamped, and posted in accordance with the regulations applicable to publications. Any officer of the Post Office may detain a book packet for 24 hours. The head postmaster, who first receives a book packet must, whenever he has ground for suspecting an infringement of any of the above conditions, open and examine the packet; and every book packet, which shall not be open at the ends or sides, or shall exceed two feet in length, width, or depth, or shall have any letter, or any communication of the nature of a letter, written or printed in it or upon its cover, or shall bear no postage stamp, must be sent up to the Dead Letter Offices, in London, Edinburgh, or Dublin, as the case may be; but in the event of any other infringement, the packet must be dealt with by the Postmaster himself, as laid down in the previous observations thereon.

Printed Books, Magazines, Pamphlets, Maps, Music, Paper, Parchment, and Vellum, (to the exclusion of letters) whether British, Colonial, or Foreign, may be transmitted by the Post between the United Kingdom and the British West Indies, Bermuda, Canada, Nova Scotia, New Brunswick, Prince Edward's Island, Newfoundland, Gold Coast, Sierra Leone, New South Wales, South Australia, per packet, at the following reduced rates of postage, viz.: not exceeding ½lb. in weight, 6d.; not exceeding 1lb., 1s.; and for every additional lb. or fraction of a lb., 1s., provided they are made up the same as newspapers, in a cover open at both ends; but they must not exceed 24 in. any way; also Cape Town, New Zealand, and St. Helena, per *private ship*; and Malta, Gibraltar, and Ionian Islands (*via* Southampton) at the same charge, subject to the same restrictions as the above.

Money Orders are granted and paid at every Post Town in the United Kingdom, the commission for which is 3*d.* for sums not exceeding £2, and 6*d.*, for not exceeding £5, the highest sum for which a single Order is granted— Money Orders drawn on London are payable at the Chief Office, Aldersgate Street, between 10 and 4. Should this be inconvenient, they should be drawn on the nearest office to which the payee resides whose signature, with one Christian name, will be sufficient. The Hours for transacting Money Order business in London and its district, are between 10 and 4, and beyond, from 9 till 6 daily.

Money Orders are subject to the following rules:—1. Every money order issued on or after the fifth October, 1848, must be presented for payment before the end of the second calendar month after that in which it was issued (for instance, if issued in October, it must be presented for payment before the end of December), otherwise a new order will be necessary, for which a second commission must be paid. 2. As already notified to the public, if an order be not presented for payment before the end of the twelfth calendar month after that in which it was issued (for instance, if issued in October, and not presented before the end of the next October), the money will not be paid at all. 3. As, after once paying a money order, by whomsoever presented, the office will not be liable to any further claim, the public are strictly cautioned, *a.* To take all means to prevent the loss of the money order, *b.* Never to send a money order in the same letter with the information required on payment thereof, *c.* To be careful, on taking out a money order, to state correctly the Christian name as well as the surname of the person in whose favour it is to be drawn, *d.* To see that the name, address, and occupation of the person taking out the money order are correctly known to the person in whose favour it is drawn. 4. Neglect of those instructions will lead to delay and trouble in obtaining payment, and even risk the loss of the money.— These instructions, together with some others of more importance, will be found printed in every money order.

Letters and Newspapers.— Foreign Letters, insufficiently stamped, will be returned, in cases where the payment is compulsory. Letters cannot partly be paid in stamps and partly in money. Late letters must be posted pre-paid with stamps, both postage and late fee; and late newspapers, with stamps for the late fee, or they cannot be forwarded. Newspapers for Foreign Mails, which are made up in the morning, must be posted the previous evening at the same hours as newspapers for the Evening Mails. No letter, when once posted, can be given up to any one but the person to whom it is addressed, upon any pretence whatever.

Articles which may not be sent by Post.—Any glass, or glass bottle, any razor, scissors, knife, fork, or other sharp or pointed instrument; any leeches, game, fish, flesh, fruit, vegetable, or other perishable substance; any bladder, or other vessel containing liquid, or any other article, matter, or thing whatsoever which might, by pressure or otherwise, be rendered injurious to the contents of the Mail bags, or to the officers of the Post Office. Letters to, or passing through warm climates, should be sealed with wafers, or with hard wax made expressly for this purpose, as the *ordinary* wax softens in warm countries.

Stamps can be used to pay the postage on Foreign, Colonial, and Ship Letters and Newspapers, or they will be sent forward, charged with the deficiency. Inland letters insufficiently stamped are charged double the deficiency.

Fare from all the Coach Stands to the Theatres,

Hackney Coach and Cabriolet Stands. *Note.*—The Fares are calculated for Cabriolets with *one* horse, and to carry two persons.	Theatre Royal, Italian Opera.		Adelphi.		Astley's (Cooke).		Drury Lane.		Haymarket.		Lyceum.		Olympic.		St. James's.		Princess's.		Sadler's Wells.		Strand.		Surrey.		Victoria.		British Museum.		Colosseum and Diorama.	
	s.	d.	s.	d.	s.	d.	s.	d.	s.	d.	s.	d.	s.	d.	s.	d.	s.	d.	s.	d.	s.	d.	s.	d.	s.	d.	s.	d.	s.	d.
Acacia Road, St. John's Wood ...	2	0	2	0	2	6	2	0	1	6	2	0	2	0	1	6	1	6	2	0	2	0	2	6	2	6	0	6	1	0
Adm St. Wst, Upp. Berkeley St..	1	0	1	6	1	6	1	6	1	0	1	6	1	6	1	0	1	0	2	0	1	6	2	0	1	6	1	0	0	6
Adelaide Wharf, London Brdg.	1	6	1	0	1	0	1	0	1	0	1	0	1	0	1	6	1	6	1	0	1	0	1	0	1	0	1	6	2	0
Agar Street, Strand	0	6	0	6	1	0	0	6	0	6	0	6	0	6	0	6	0	6	1	0	0	6	1	0	1	0	0	0	1	0
Bank, Threadneedle Street	1	6	1	0	1	6	1	0	1	6	1	0	1	0	1	6	1	6	1	0	1	0	1	0	1	0	1	6	2	0
Berners Street	0	6	0	6	1	0	0	6	0	6	0	6	0	6	0	6	0	6	1	6	1	0	1	6	1	0	0	6	0	6
Blackfriars Rd., Christ Church	1	0	1	0	0	6	1	0	1	0	0	6	1	0	1	0	1	0	1	0	1	0	0	6	0	6	1	0	1	6
Black Lion, Bayswater	1	6	2	0	2	0	2	0	1	6	2	0	2	0	1	6	1	6	2	0	2	6	2	0	2	6	1	6	1	6
Broad Street, St. Giles'	0	6	0	6	1	0	0	6	0	6	0	6	0	6	0	6	0	6	1	0	0	6	1	0	1	0	0	6	1	0
Brydges St., Covent Garden	0	6	0	6	0	6	0	6	0	6	0	6	0	6	0	6	...		0	6	1	0	0	6	1	0	0	6	1	0
Buckingham Gate	1	0	1	0	1	0	1	0	1	0	1	0	1	0	1	0	1	0	2	0	1	0	1	0	1	0	1	0	1	6
Cadogan Place, Pond Street	1	0	1	6	1	0	1	6	1	0	1	6	1	6	1	0	1	0	1	0	2	0	1	6	1	6	1	6	1	6
City Road	1	6	1	6	1	6	1	6	1	6	1	6	1	6	1	6	2	0	1	6	0	6	1	6	1	0	1	6	1	6
Chelsea, King's Road	2	0	2	0	2	0	2	0	2	0	2	0	2	0	2	0	2	0	2	0	0	3	0	2	0	2	0	2	2	6
Cobham Row, Clerkenwell	1	0	1	0	1	6	1	0	1	0	1	0	1	0	1	0	1	6	1	0	0	6	1	0	1	0	1	0	0	6
Compton St., Brunswick Sq. ...	0	6	1	6	1	6	1	0	1	0	1	6	2	0	1	0	1	0	1	0	1	0	1	6	1	0	0	6	1	0
Conduit Street, Regent Street ..	0	6	1	0	1	0	0	6	0	6	1	0	1	0	0	0	6	0	6	1	6	1	0	1	6	1	0	0	6	1	0
Cumberland Gate, Uxbdg. Rd.,	1	0	1	0	1	6	1	0	1	0	1	0	1	6	1	0	1	0	1	0	2	0	1	6	2	0	1	6	1	0
Davies Street, Berkeley Square	1	0	1	0	1	0	1	0	0	6	1	0	1	0	0	6	0	6	1	6	1	0	1	6	1	0	1	0	1	0
Dover Road	1	6	1	0	1	0	1	0	1	6	1	0	1	0	1	0	1	6	1	6	1	0	0	6	0	6	1	6	2	0
Edgeware Rd., Aberdeen Place	1	6	1	6	2	0	1	6	1	6	2	0	2	0	1	0	1	6	2	0	2	0	2	6	2	0	1	6	1 ·	0
Epping Place, Mile End	2	0	2	0	2	0	1	0	2	0	2	0	1	6	2	0	2	0	2	0	1	6	1	6	1	6	2	0	2	6
Franklin's Row, Chelsea Col	1	6	1	6	1	6	1	6	1	6	1	6	1	6	1	6	1	6	1	6	2	6	1	6	1	6	1	6	2	0
Fulham Rd., Pelham Crescent	1 ·	6	1	6	1	6	1	6	1	0	1	6	1	6	1	6	1	6	1	6	2	6	2	0	2	0	1	6	2	0
Founding Hosp. Guildford St	1	0	1	6	1	6	1	0	1	0	1	0	1	0	1	0	1	0	0	6	1	0	1	6	1	0	0	6	1	0
Great Marylebone Street	1	0	1	0	1	6	1	0	1	0	1	0	1	0	1	6	1	6	1	6	1	0	1	6	1	0	0	0	0	6
Goswell Street	1	0	1	0	1	6	1	0	1	0	1	0	1	0	1	0	1	6	1	0	0	6	1	0	1	0	1	0	0	6
Gt. Western Rd. Holland Arms	2	0	2	0	2	6	0	0	2	0	2	0	2	0	2	0	2	0	2	0	0	3	0	2	6	2	0	3	2	6
Gt. Western Rd. Victoria Rd....	1	6	1	6	2	0	2	0	1	6	2	0	2	0	1	6	1	6	2	0	2	6	2	0	2	0	2	0	1	6
Grosvenor Street, West	1	0	1	0	1	0	1	0	1	0	1	0	1	0	1	6	1	0	1	0	2	0	1	6	1	0	1	6	1	6
Harrow Road	1	6	2	0	2	0	2	0	2	0	1	6	2	0	2	0	2	0	1	6	2	0	2	0	2	6	2	6	1	6
Haymarket, Lower End	...		0	6	0	6	0	6	0	6	...		0	6	0	6	0	6	1	6	1	0	1	6	0	6	1	0	1	0
Holborn, Dean Street	1	0	0	6	1	0	0	6	1	0	0	6	0	6	1	0	1	0	0	6	1	0	0	6	1	0	0	6	1	0
Holborn, Chancery Lane	1	0	0	6	1	0	0	6	1	0	0	6	0	6	1	0	1	0	1	0	0	6	1	0	1	0	0	6	1	0
Holloway Rd, Steyman's Row	2	0	2	0	2	0	1	6	2	0	2	0	1	6	2	0	2	0	1	0	1	6	2	0	2	0	1	6	2	0
High Street, Camberwell	2	0	2	0	1	6	2	0	2	0	2	0	2	0	2	0	2	0	2	0	0	6	2	0	1	0	1	6	2	6
High Street, Camden Town	1	6	1	6	2	0	1	6	1	6	1	6	1	6	1	6	1	6	1	0	1	6	1	6	2	0	1	0	1	0
Islington, Clark's Place	1	6	1	6	1	6	1	6	1	6	1	6	1	6	1	6	1	6	1	0	0	6	1	0	1	6	1	0	1	6
John Street, Oxford Street	0	6	1	0	1	0	1	0	0	6	1	0	1	0	0	0	6	0	6	1	6	1	0	1	6	1	0	0	0	6
Kennington Church	1	6	1	6	1	0	1	0	1	6	1	6	1	6	1	6	1	6	2	0	2	0	1	0	1	0	1	6	2	6
Kennington Cross	1	0	1	0	0	6	1	0	1	6	1	0	1	0	1	6	1	6	2	0	1	0	0	6	0	6	1	6	2	0
Kingsland Road	2	6	2	0	2	6	2	0	2	6	2	0	2	0	2	6	2	0	1	6	2	0	2	6	2	0	2	0	2	0
King's Road, Gray's Inn	1	0	1	0	1	0	0	6	1	0	1	0	0	6	1	0	1	0	0	6	0	6	1	0	1	0	0	6	1	0
Knightsbridge Green	1	0	1	0	1	6	1	6	1	0	1	6	1	6	1	0	1	0	2	0	1	6	1	6	1	6	1	6	1	6
Lambeth Road	1	0	1	0	0	6	1	0	1	0	1	0	1	0	1	0	1	6	1	6	1	0	0	0	6	0	6	1	0	2	0

Places of Amusement, and Railway Stations.

Houses of Parliament.	Charing Cross. The Statue	Leicester Square, N.W.	Polytechnic.	Bank of England.	St. Paul's Ch. Yd. Paul's Chain.	London Bridge. Adelaide Place.	London Docks.	Tower of London.	Tussaud, Madame	Lyceum.	Kensington Grdns Hopwood's Gate.	Zoolog. Gardens Regent's Park	Surrey Zoological Gardens.	Blackwall.	Brighton, Dover, Greenwich, &c.	Eastern Counties.	Great Northern.	Great Western.	North Western.	South Western.
s. d	s. d	s. d	s. d	s. d	s. d	s. d	s. d	s. d	s. d	s. d	s. d	s. d	s. d	s. d	s. d	s. d	s. d	s. d	s. d	s. d
2 0	2 0	1 6	1 6	2 6	2 6	3 6	3 0	3 0	1 0	2 6	1 6	0 6	3 0	3 0	3 0	3 0	3 0	1 6	1 0	1 6
1 6	1 0	1 0	0 0	6 2	0 2	0 2	0 2	0 2	6 1	0 2	0 0	6 1	0 2	6 2	0 2	6 2	6 1	6 1	6 1	0 1
1 6	1 6	1 6	1 6	0 6	0 6	…	1 0	0 6	2 0	1 6	0 6	1 6	1 6	1 6	2 6	3 0	1 0	1 0	1 0	1 6
0 6	0 6	0 6	1 0	1 0	1 6	1 0	1 6	1 0	1 6	1 0	1 6	1 6	1 6	1 6	1 6	1 6	1 6	1 6	1 6	1 0
1 6	1 0	1 6	1 6	…	0 6	0 0	6 2	0 2	0 2	6 2	0 2	0 1	6 0	6 0	6 0	6 0	6 1	6 2	6 1	6 1
1 0	0 6	0 6	0 6	1 0	1 0	1 0	6 2	0 1	6 1	0 1	6 1	0 1	6 1	6 1	6 1	6 1	0 1	0 1	6 1	0 1
1 0	1 0	1 0	1 6	1 0	0 6	1 0	1 6	1 0	2 0	1 0	2 0	2 0	1 0	1 0	1 0	1 0	1 6	2 0	1 6	0 6
2 0	1 6	1 6	2 6	2 6	2 6	3 0	3 0	1 0	2 6	0 6	1 6	3 0	3 0	3 0	2 0	1 6	1 6	2 0	—	—
1 0	0 6	0 6	0 6	1 0	1 0	1 6	1 0	1 6	1 6	1 6	1 6	1 6	1 6	1 6	1 6	1 0	1 6	1 0	1 0	—
1 0	0 6	0 6	0 6	1 0	1 0	1 6	1 0	1 6	1 6	1 6	1 6	1 6	1 6	1 6	1 6	1 6	1 0	1 6	1 0	1 0
0 6	1 0	1 0	1 6	2 0	1 6	2 0	1 6	2 0	2 6	1 6	1 0	1 6	2 0	1 6	2 0	2 0	1 6	1 0	1 6	1 0
1 0	1 0	1 0	1 0	0 2	0 2	0 2	0 2	6 2	6 1	0 1	0 1	6 2	0 2	0 2	6 2	0 2	6 2	0 1	6 2	0 1
2 0	1 6	1 6	1 0	1 0	1 0	1 6	1 0	2 0	2 0	2 0	2 0	0 1	0 1	0 1	1 6	1 0	1 6	1 6	1 6	1 6
2 0	2 0	2 0	2 0	3 0	2 6	2 6	3 6	3 6	3 0	2 0	2 0	2 0	3 0	2 6	3 0	3 6	3 0	2 0	2 0	2 0
1 6	1 0	1 0	1 0	1 0	0 2	0 1	6 1	6 1	6 2	2 0	2 0	1 6	1 6	1 0	1 6	1 0	1 0	1 6	1 0	1 0
1 6	1 0	1 0	1 0	1 0	1 6	2 0	1 6	2 0	1 6	2 0	2 0	1 6	2 0	1 6	1 6	1 6	0 6	1 6	0 6	1 6
1 0	0 6	0 6	0 6	1 6	1 6	2 0	2 0	0 1	6 1	0 1	0 2	2 0	0 2	0 2	2 0	2 0	1 6	1 0	1 0	—
1 6	1 0	1 0	0 6	2 0	1 6	2 0	2 6	0 0	6 1	6 0	6 2	6 2	2 0	2 0	1 6	1 6	1 0	1 6	1 0	1 6
1 0	1 0	0 0	6 0	0 6	1 6	1 6	2 0	2 0	0 2	0 0	6 1	6 1	0 1	6 2	0 2	0 2	2 0	1 6	1 0	1 6
1 0	1 6	1 6	1 6	0 1	0 0	6 1	0 1	0 2	0 1	0 2	6 2	6 1	0 1	0 0	6 1	0 2	0 2	6 2	0 1	6
2 0	1 6	1 6	1 0	2 0	2 6	2 0	2 6	2 6	0 2	6 1	0 1	0 3	0 2	6 2	6 3	0 1	6 1	0 1	6 2	0
2 0	2 0	2 0	2 0	6 1	0 1	6 1	0 1	0 1	0 2	6 2	6 3	0 3	0 2	0 1	0 1	0 1	0 2	0 3	0 2	6
1 0	1 6	1 6	1 6	2 0	2 0	2 0	2 6	1 6	0 1	0 2	6 1	6 2	6 2	0 3	0 2	6 2	0 2	6 2	0 1	6
1 6	1 0	1 0	1 6	1 6	2 0	2 0	2 6	3 0	3 6	1 6	1 6	1 6	2 0	2 0	2 0	2 0	2 6	3 0	2 0	2 0
1 6	1 0	1 0	1 0	1 0	1 0	1 0	1 6	1 6	1 6	1 0	2 0	1 0	1 6	1 0	2 0	2 0	1 0	1 0	1 0	—
1 6	1 0	1 0	1 6	2 0	1 6	2 0	0 0	6 2	0 0	1 0	1 0	2 0	2 0	2 0	2 0	2 0	1 0	1 0	1 0	—
1 6	1 0	1 6	1 6	0 6	0 0	6 1	0 1	0 1	0 2	0 2	0 2	0 2	0 1	6 1	0 1	0 1	0 1	0 2	6 1	0
2 0	2 0	2 0	2 0	3 0	2 6	2 6	3 0	3 0	3 0	3 6	2 6	2 6	2 0	2 0	2 0	2 6	3 0	2 6	2 6	2 0
1 6	1 6	1 6	1 6	2 6	2 6	2 6	3 0	3 0	1 6	2 0	1 0	1 0	1 6	2 0	1 6	2 0	1 6	2 0	2 0	—
1 0	1 0	1 0	1 6	2 0	1 6	2 0	2 6	2 0	1 0	1 0	1 6	2 0	2 0	0 0	6 2	0 1	6 2	0 1	0	—
2 0	2 0	1 6	1 6	1 6	1 0	1 6	1 6	1 0	2 0	2 0	2 0	1 6	2 0	2 6	0 0	6 2	0 1	0 1	0	—
0 6	0 6	0 6	1 0	1 6	1 6	1 0	1 6	1 0	1 6	1 0	1 6	1 6	1 6	1 6	1 6	1 6	1 0	1 6	1 0	—
1 0	0 6	0 6	1 0	1 0	1 0	1 0	1 6	2 0	1 0	2 0	1 6	1 6	1 6	1 6	1 0	1 0	1 0	2 0	1 6	1 0
2 0	2 0	1 6	2 0	1 6	1 6	2 0	2 0	0 2	6 2	6 2	0 2	6 2	0 1	6 1	0 2	6 1	6 2	0	—	—
1 6	2 0	2 0	2 6	2 0	1 0	1 6	2 0	0 2	6 2	0 3	0 3	0 1	0 1	6 2	0 2	0 1	0 1	6 0	6 1	6
1 6	1 6	1 6	1 0	1 6	1 6	1 0	2 0	1 6	1 6	1 6	0 1	6 1	0 2	0 0	6 2	0 1	0 1	0	—	—
1 0	1 6	1 6	1 6	1 6	1 0	2 0	0 6	1 6	2 0	0 0	6 2	6 3	0 0	6 1	6 1	0 2	6 2	6 1	0	—
1 0	1 0	1 6	1 6	1 6	1 6	1 6	1 6	2 0	1 6	2 0	0 0	6 2	6 2	6 1	0 1	6 1	0 2	0 1	6	—
2 6	2 0	2 6	2 6	1 6	1 6	1 6	2 0	1 6	2 0	0 2	6 3	0 2	6 2	6 1	6 1	0 1	0 1	6 3	0 2	0
1 0	1 0	1 0	0 1	0 1	0 1	0 1	6 1	0 1	6 2	0 1	6 1	6 1	0 1	0 1	6 0	6 2	0 1	0 1	0	—
1 0	1 0	1 0	0 2	0 1	6 2	0 2	6 2	6 1	0 1	6 1	6 2	0 2	0 2	6 2	0 2	6 2	0 1	6 1	6 1	6
0 6	1 0	1 0	1 6	1 0	1 0	1 6	1 6	6 2	0 1	0 2	0 2	0 1	0 1	0 1	0 1	6 2	0 2	6 1	6 0	0

Fare from all the Coach Stands to the Theatres, Places

Hackney Coach and Cabriolet Stands.

Note.—The Fares are calculated for Cabriolets with *one* horse, and to carry two persons.

Stand	Theatre Royal, Italian Opera	Adelphi	Astley's (Cooke's)	Drury Lane	Haymarket	Lyceum	Olympic	St. James's	Princess's	Sadler's Wells	Strand	Surrey	Victoria	British Museum	Colosseum and Diorama
Leicester Square, West Side	0 6	0 6	1 0	0 6	0 6	0 6	0 6	0 6	0 6	1 0	0 6	1 0	1 0	0 6	1 0
Manor Place, Walworth	1 6	1 6	1 0	1 6	1 6	1 0	1 6	1 6	1 6	2 0	1 6	0 6	1 0	1 6	2 0
Milton Row, Vauxhall Bdg. Rd.	1 0	1 0	1 0	1 0	1 0	1 0	1 0	1 0	1 0	1 6	2 0	1 0	1 0	1 0	1 6
North Street, Portman Market	1 6	1 6	2 0	1 6	1 6	1 6	1 6	1 6	1 6	1 6	2 0	2 0	2 0	0 6	1 0
Old Kent Rd., Bricklayers Arms	1 6	1 6	1 0	1 6	1 6	1 6	1 6	1 6	1 6	2 0	2 0	1 6	1 0	1 0	2 0
Palace New Road, Lambeth	1 0	1 0	0 6	1 0	1 0	0 6	1 0	1 0	1 0	1 6	1 0	0 6	0 6	1 0	1 6
Palace Yd., Houses Parliament	0 6	0 6	0 6	0 6	1 0	0 6	0 6	0 6	1 0	1 0	0 6	1 0	1 0	1 0	1 0
Park Lane, Grosvenor Gate	1 0	1 0	1 0	1 6	0 6	1 0	1 0	0 6	1 0	1 0	0 6	1 6	1 6	1 0	1 0
Park Lane, Stanhope Gate	1 0	1 0	1 0	1 6	0 6	1 0	1 0	6 2	0 0	1 0	1 0	1 6	1 0	1 0	1 0
Park Road. St. John's Wood	1 6	1 6	2 0	1 6	1 6	1 6	1 6	1 6	1 6	1 6	2 0	2 0	2 0	0 6	1 0
Penton Street, Pentonville	1 6	1 6	1 6	1 6	1 6	1 6	1 0	1 0	1 0	0 6	1 0	1 6	1 6	1 0	1 0
Piccadilly, Albany	0 6	0 6	1 0	0 6	0 6	0 6	0 6	0 6	1 0	1 0	0 6	1 0	1 0	0 6	1 0
Piccadilly, Apsley House	1 0	1 0	0 2	1 0	0 6	1 0	0 6	1 0	0 0	1 0	0 6	1 0	1 0	1 0	1 0
Piccadilly, Devonshire House	0 6	1 0	1 0	0 6	0 6	1 0	0 6	0 6	1 0	1 0	0 6	1 0	1 0	0 6	1 0
Pickering Place, Bayswater	1 6	2 0	2 0	2 0	2 0	1 6	2 0	2 0	1 6	1 6	2 0	2 0	2 0	2 0	1 6
Portland Road	1 0	1 0	1 6	1 0	1 0	1 0	1 0	1 0	0 0	1 0	1 0	1 6	1 6	0 0	0 6
Portland Road, Carburton St.	1 6	1 0	1 6	1 0	1 6	1 0	1 0	1 0	1 0	0 6	1 0	1 6	1 6	0 0	0 6
Praed Street, Edgeware Road	1 6	1 6	2 0	1 6	1 6	1 6	1 6	1 6	1 6	1 0	2 0	1 6	2 0	1 0	1 0
Richmond Road, Islington	1 6	1 6	1 0	1 6	1 6	1 6	1 6	1 6	2 0	1 6	0 6	1 6	2 0	1 0	1 6
Rotherfield Street, Islington	2 0	2 0	2 0	2 0	1 6	2 0	1 6	1 6	2 0	2 0	0 1	1 6	2 0	1 0	1 6
St. Clement's, Strand	0 6	0 6	1 0	0 6	0 6	0 6	0 6	0 6	1 0	1 0	0 0	1 0	0 6	1 0	1 0
St. George's Rd., Newington	1 0	1 0	0 6	1 0	1 0	1 0	1 0	1 0	1 6	1 6	1 0	0 6	0 6	1 6	2 0
St. James's Street	0 6	0 6	1 0	0 6	0 0	0 6	1 0	0 6	0 6	1 0	0 6	1 0	1 0	0 6	1 0
St. Luke's, Old Street	1 6	1 6	1 6	1 6	1 6	1 6	1 6	1 0	2 0	0 6	1 0	1 6	1 6	0 2	0 0
St. Paul's Church Yard, East	1 0	1 0	1 0	1 0	1 0	1 0	1 0	0 0	0 6	1 0	0 6	1 0	1 0	0 6	1 6
Shaftsbury Ter., Vauxhall Bdg.	1 0	1 0	1 0	1 0	1 0	1 0	1 0	1 0	1 0	1 6	2 0	1 0	1 0	1 0	1 6
Sloane Square [Road]	1 6	1 6	1 0	1 6	1 6	1 6	1 6	1 6	1 0	1 6	2 0	1 6	1 6	1 6	2 0
Southampton Row, Bloomsbury	1 0	0 0	0 6	1 0	0 0	0 6	1 0	0 0	0 6	1 0	0 0	0 6	1 0	0 0	0 6
Stockwell Place, Brixton	1 6	2 0	1 6	2 0	1 6	2 0	2 0	2 0	2 0	2 0	2 0	0 6	1 6	2 0	2 0
Tottenham Crt. Road, Percy St.	0 6	0 6	1 0	0 6	0 6	0 6	0 6	0 6	1 0	0 6	1 0	0 6	1 0	0 6	0 6
Tottenham Crt. Rd., Francis St.	1 0	1 0	1 0	1 0	0 6	1 0	1 0	1 0	1 0	0 6	1 0	1 6	1 0	0 6	0 6
Tower Hill, East Side	2 0	1 6	1 6	1 6	1 6	2 0	1 6	1 6	2 0	2 0	1 6	1 6	1 6	1 6	2 6
Tower Hill, West Side	1 6	1 6	1 6	1 6	1 6	1 6	1 6	1 0	1 0	1 6	1 6	1 6	1 0	1 0	2 0
Uxbridge road, Notting Hill	2 0	2 0	2 0	2 0	2 0	2 0	2 0	2 0	2 0	0 3	0 2	2 6	3 0	2 6	2 0
Whitechapel, Dock Street	2 0	1 6	1 6	1 6	1 6	2 0	1 6	1 6	2 0	2 0	1 6	1 6	1 6	1 6	2 6
Whitechapel, High Street	1 6	1 6	1 6	1 6	1 6	1 6	1 6	1 6	2 0	2 0	1 6	1 6	1 6	1 6	2 0
Whitehall	0 6	0 6	0 6	0 6	0 6	0 6	0 6	0 6	0 6	1 0	0 6	1 0	1 0	0 6	1 0
York and Albany, Albert Rd.	1 6	1 6	2 0	1 6	1 6	1 6	1 6	1 6	1 6	1 0	1 6	2 0	2 0	0 0	0 6
Railways, Blackwall	1 6	1 6	1 6	1 6	1 6	1 6	1 0	1 0	1 6	1 6	1 0	1 0	1 0	1 6	2 0
,, Eastern Counties	2 0	1 6	1 6	1 6	1 6	2 0	1 6	1 6	2 0	1 6	1 0	1 6	1 6	1 6	2 0
,, Great Northern	1 6	1 6	1 6	1 0	1 6	1 0	1 0	1 0	1 0	0 6	1 0	1 6	1 6	0 6	1 0
,, Great Western	1 6	1 6	2 0	1 6	1 6	2 0	1 6	1 6	2 0	2 0	2 0	2 0	1 6	1 0	1 0
,, North Western	1 0	1 0	1 6	1 0	1 0	1 0	1 0	1 0	1 0	1 0	1 0	1 6	1 6	0 0	0 6
,, South Eastern	1 6	1 6	1 0	1 6	1 6	1 6	1 0	1 0	1 6	1 6	1 0	1 0	1 0	1 6	2 0
,, South Western	1 0	1 0	0 0	0 6	1 0	0 0	6 0	0 1	0 1	0 1	0 6	0 6	0 6	1 0	1 6

of Amusement, and Railway Stations, &c., &c—*continued.*

Houses of Parliament.	Charing Cross. The Statue.	Leicester Square, N.W.	Polytechnic.	Bank of England.	St. Paul's Ch. Yd. Paul's Chain.	London Bridge. Adelaide Place.	London Docks.	Tower of London.	Tussaud, Madame	Lyceum.	Kensington Grdns Hopwood's Gate.	Zoolog. Gardens Regent's Park	Surrey Zoological Gardens.	Blackwall.	Brighton, Dover, Greenwich, &c.	Eastern Counties.	Great Northern.	Great Western.	North Western.	South Western.
0 6	0 6	...	0 6	1 6	1 0	1 6	2 0	1 6	1 0	1 6	1 6	1 6	1 6	1 6	1 6	1 6	1 6	1 6	1 0	1 0
1 0	1 6	2 0	1 0	1 6	1 0	1 6	1 6	2 0	1 0	2 6	2 0	1 0	1 6	1 0	1 6	2 0	2 0	2 0	2 0	1 0
0 6	1 0	1 0	1 6	2 0	1 6	1 6	2 0	2 0	1 0	1 6	1 6	2 0	1 0	1 0	1 6	2 0	2 0	2 0	2 0	1 0
2 0	1 6	1 6	1 0	2 6	2 0	0 2	2 6	3 0	2 6	1 0	2 6	1 0	2 6	2 6	2 6	2 6	1 6	1 6	2 0	2 0
1 6	1 6	1 6	2 0	1 0	1 0	0 1	0 1	1 6	1 0	2 6	1 0	2 6	1 0	1 0	0 1	1 6	2 0	3 0	2 0	1 0
0 6	0 6	1 0	1 0	1 6	1 0	1 0	1 0	1 6	1 6	1 0	2 0	0 2	1 0	1 6	1 0	1 6	2 0	1 0	6 0	6 0
...	0 6	0 6	1 6	1 0	1 6	1 0	1 6	2 0	1 6	1 0	2 0	0 2	1 0	1 6	2 0	1 0	6 2	2 0	1 0	6 0
1 6	1 0	1 0	0 0	6 2	0 1	6 2	0 1	0 2	0 0	6 1	6 1	0 1	6 2	0 2	0 2	0 2	0 1	6 1	1 0	1 6
1 0	1 0	1 0	1 0	0 2	6 2	2 0	6 2	3 0	2 6	0 0	6 1	6 1	0 1	6 2	0 2	6 2	6 2	6 1	6 1	6 2
1 6	1 6	1 6	1 6	0 1	0 1	6 1	6 1	6 1	6 2	6 2	0 1	6 2	0 1	6 1	6 1	0 0	6 2	0 1	0 1	6
1 0	0 6	6 0	0 6	1 6	1 0	1 6	0 1	6 1	0 1	6 1	6 1	6 1	6 1	6 1	6 2	0 1	6 1	6 1	0 1	6
1 0	1 0	0 0	6 1	0 2	0 1	6 2	0 2	6 2	0 1	0 1	0 1	0 1	6 2	0 2	0 2	0 2	0 1	6 1	6 1	6
1 0	0 6	6 0	6 0	6 1	6 1	6 1	6 2	0 2	0 1	0 1	6 1	0 1	6 2	0 2	0 2	0 2	0 1	6 1	6 1	0
2 0	2 0	6 1	6 2	6 1	6 2	6 2	6 3	0 3	0 1	0 2	6 0	6 1	6 3	0 3	0 3	0 3	0 2	0 0	6 1	6 2
1 6	1 0	1 0	0 0	6 1	6 2	0 2	0 2	0 2	0 0	6 2	0 1	0 2	0 2	0 2	0 2	0 1	0 1	0 0	6 1	6
1 0	1 0	1 0	0 0	6 1	6 2	6 2	0 2	0 2	0 2	0 0	6 2	0 1	0 2	0 2	6 2	6 2	6 1	6 0	6 1	0
2 0	1 6	1 6	1 6	1 6	0 2	0 1	6 1	6 2	0 1	6 1	6 2	6 2	0 1	6 1	6 1	6 1	0 2	0 1	0 2	0
2 0	2 0	2 0	0 1	6 1	6 1	6 1	6 1	6 2	0 2	0 2	6 2	0 2	6 1	6 1	0 1	6 2	6 1	6 2	0 1	6
1 0	1 0	0 0	6 1	0 0	6 1	0 1	6 1	0 1	6 2	0 2	0 1	6 1	0 1	6 2	0 2	0 1	0 1	0 1	0 1	0
1 0	1 0	1 0	1 6	1 0	1 0	0 1	6 1	0 2	0 1	0 2	6 2	6 0	6 1	0 1	0 1	6 2	0 2	6 2	0 0	6
1 0	0 6	6 0	6 1	6 1	0 1	6 2	0 1	6 1	0 1	6 1	6 1	6 1	6 2	0 1	6 1	6 1	6 1	0 1	6 1	0
2 0	1 6	1 6	1 6	0 0	6 1	0 1	0 1	0 0	6 1	0 2	0 2	6 2	0 1	6 1	0 0	6 1	0 0	6 1	6 1	0
1 6	1 0	1 0	1 0	6 0	6	...	0 6	1 0	0 6	1 0	6 2	0 2	0 1	6 1	0 1	0 1	0 2	0 1	6 1	0
0 6	1 0	1 0	0 2	0 1	6 1	6 2	6 2	0 1	0 1	0 1	6 2	0 1	6 2	0 1	6 2	6 2	0 1	6 2	0 1	0
1 0	1 0	1 6	1 6	2 0	2 0	0 2	0 2	0 2	6 2	6 1	6 1	0 1	6 2	0 2	0 2	6 2	0 2	6 2	0 2	0 1 6
1 0	1 0	0 0	0 1	0 1	0 1	0 1	6 1	6 1	6 1	0 1	6 1	6 1	6 1	6 1	6 1	0 1	0 1	6 1	0 1	0
1 6	1 6	2 0	2 0	2 0	2 0	2 0	2 0	2 0	6 1	0 1	0 2	6 1	6 2	6 2	6 2	6 2	6 1	6 1	0
1 0	0 6	0 6	0 6	1 6	1 0	1 6	2 0	1 6	1 0	1 6	1 0	1 6	1 6	1 0	1 6	1 0	1 0	6 0	6 1	0
1 0	1 0	0 0	6 1	6 1	0 1	0 1	0 1	6 1	0 1	6 1	0 2	0 1	6 1	0 1	6 2	0 1	6 0	6 1	0
2 0	1 6	2 0	2 0	2 0	0 1	0 1	0 0	6 0	6 2	2 0	3 0	2 6	1 6	0 0	6 1	0 1	0 2	0 3	0 2	0 1 6
1 6	1 6	1 6	2 0	0 0	6 0	6 0	6 0	6 0	6	...	2 0	1 6	2 6	2 6	2 6	1 6	0 0	6 1	6 2	0 1 6
2 6	2 0	3 0	3 0	2 6	3 0	3 0	6 3	0 3	6 3	0 1	6 2	6 1	0 2	0 3	6 3	0 3	3 6	2 6	1 0	2 0 6
2 0	2 0	2 0	2 0	2 0	0 1	0 1	0 1	0	...	0 6	2 6	2 6	2 0	3 0	3 0	1 6	0 6	1 0	1 0	2 0 1 6
2 0	1 6	2 0	0 0	6 1	0 0	6 0	6 0	6 0	6 2	0 2	6 2	6 1	6 0	6 1	0 0	6 2	0 3	0 2	0 1 6
0 6	0 6	0 6	0 6	1 0	1 0	1 6	1 0	1 6	2 0	2 6	1 0	1 6	1 6	1 6	1 6	1 6	1 6	2 0	1 0	1 0
1 6	1 6	1 6	1 0	0 2	0 2	0 2	0 2	6 2	−1	0 2	6 1	6 0	6 2	6 2	0 2	6 2	0 1	0 1	6 2	0
1 6	1 6	1 6	2 0	0 6	0 6	0 6	0 6	0 6	0 6	2 0	1 6	2 6	2 6	1 6	...	0 6	1 0	1 6	2 6	2 0 1 6
2 0	1 6	1 6	2 0	0 0	6 1	0 1	0 1	0 4	0 2	0 2	6 2	0 2	6 2	6 1	6 1	0 1	0	...	1 6 3	0 2 0 1 6
1 6	1 6	1 6	1 0	6 1	0 1	6 2	0 1	6 1	6 2	0 2	0 1	0 2	0 1	6 1	6 1	6	...	1 6 2	0
2 0	1 6	1 6	1 0	0 2	6 2	0 2	6 3	0 2	6 1	0 2	6 0	6 1	6 3	0 2	6 2	6 3	0 1	6	...	1 6 2 0
1 6	1 0	0 1	0 1	0 1	6 1	6 2	0 2	0 2	0 1	0 2	0 1	6 1	0 2	0 2	0 2	0 0	6 1	6	...	1 6
1 6	1 6	1 6	2 0	0 0	6 1	0 0	6 1	0 0	6 2	0 1	6 2	6 2	6 1	0 0	6	...	1 0	6 2	0 1 0
1 * 0	1 0	0 1	0 1	6 1	0 1	0 1	0 1	6 1	6 1	6 1	0 2	0 2	0 1	0 1	6 1	0 1	6 2	0 1	6	...

S

* If by Westminster Bridge, and York Street, 6d.

TABLE OF MONEY OF ALL NATIONS,
COMPUTED INTO ENGLISH FOR THIS WORK,
(Varying according to the Exchanges.)
BY MESSRS. ADAM SPIELMANN & CO.
Exchange, Bullion, and Foreign Banking Office, 10, Lombard Street, London

Name of Coin and Country.	Divis Parts.	From (£ s. d.)	To (£ s. d.)
America, U.S.			
GOLD.			
Double Eagle	20 dols.	4 2 0	4 2 6
Eagle	10 ,,	2 1 0	2 1 3
Half do	5 ,,	1 0 6	1 0 6
Quarter do.	2¼ ,,	0 10 3	0 10 3½
SILVER.			
Dollar	100 cts.	0 4 2	0 4 3
Halves, Qrs., Tenths, Twentieths	in pro.		
Austria.			
GOLD.			
Double Sovereign		1 7 0	1 7 8
Sovereign		0 13 6	0 13 10
Ducat		0 9 2	0 9 4
SILVER.			
Crown ...... piece of	2 florins	0 3 11	0 4 0
Florin	60 kr.	0 1 11	0 2 0
Swanziger	20 ,,	0 0 7½	0 0 8
NOTES.			
For every Florin		0 1 6	0 1 8
Belgium.			
GOLD.			
Leopold	25 francs	0 19 9	1 0 0
10 Franc piece	10 ,,	0 7 9	0 8 0
SILVER.			
5 Franc piece		0 3 11	0 4 0
2½ Ditto		0 1 11	0 2 0
1 Ditto	100 cts.	0 0 9¾	0 0 9½
China.			
IN ZINC & COPPER.			
Le, 800, equal to		0 4 0	0 4 4
Dollars and European coins are current			
Denmark.			
GOLD.			
Double Christian d'Or		1 12 4	1 12 8
Christian d'Or		0 16 2	0 16 4
Ducat		0 9 2	0 9 3
SILVER.			
Specie Dollar		0 4 2	0 4 4
Rigsbank Dollar		0 2	0 2 2

Name of Coin and Country.	Divis Parts.	From (£ s. d.)	To (£ s. d.)
East India.			
GOLD.			
Mohur	15 rups.	1 8 0	1 9 0
Thirds do.	5 ,,	0 9 4	0 9 8
Quarters do.	3¾ ,,	0 7 0	0 7 3
SILVER.			
Rupees		0 1 10	0 1 11
Halves, Qrs., & Eighths	in pro.		
Egypt.			
GOLD.			
Double Sequin		1 0 4	1 0 5
Double Sequin		0 10 2	0 10 4
Sequin		0 2 0	0 2 2
SILVER,			
Piastres		0 3 4	0 3 5
Halves and Quarters	in pro.		
France.			
GOLD.			
Double Napoleon	40 francs	1 11 8	1 12 0
Napoleon	20 ,,	0 15 10	0 16 0
Half	in pro.		
SILVER.			
5 Franc piece	180 sons.	0 3 11	0 4 0
1 Ditto	20 ,,	0 0 9¾	0 0 9½
German States.			
GOLD.			
Double Louis d'Or ...... fl		1 12 4	1 12 8
Louis d'Or		0 16 2	0 16 4
10 Gulden piece		0 16 7	0 16 10
Ducat		0 9 3	0 9 4
SILVER.			
Crown Dollar .... fl	2 42	0 4 4	0 4 6
Convention Ditto	2 24	0 3 11	0 4 0
Florin	60 kr. 8	0 1 7¾	0 1
Greece.			
GOLD.			
40 Drachma piece		1 8 6	1 8 9
20 Ditto		0 14 3	0 14 4
SILVER.			
5 Drachma	100 septe	0 3 6	0 3 7
1 Ditto		0 0 8	0 0 9½

NAME OF COIN AND COUNTRY.	DIVIS PARTS.	FROM £ s. d.	TO £ s. d.
Hamburg.			
GOLD.			
Ducat		0 9 3	0 9 4
SILVER.			
Hamburg Thaler	48 sh.	0 2 6	0 3 7
Marc Courant	16 sh.	0 1 2	0 1 3
Holland.			
GOLD.			
10 Florin piece	not curt.	0 16 4	0 16 6
Ducat		0 9 2	0 9 3
SILVER.			
2½ Guilder piece		0 4 1	0 4 2
1 Guilder	100 cts.	0 1 7¾	0 1 8
Italy.			
GOLD.			
10 Lire piece		1 11 3	1 12 0
20 Ditto		0 16 10	0 16 0
10 Scudi piece		2 2 4	2 2 7
SILVER.			
1 Scudi piece	100 bl.	0 4 2	0 4 3
5 Lire do.		0 3 11	0 4 0
Lire do.	20 sold	0 0 9	0 0 9¼
Sicillan Dollar	2 flories	0 3 11	0 4 0
Mexico.			
(Including all the South American Republics.)			
GOLD.			
Doubloon	16 dols.	3 5 0	3 7 0
Half do.	8 ,,	1 12 6	1 13 6
Quarter do.	4 ,,	0 16 3	0 16 9
Eighths and Sixteenths	in pro.		
SILVER.			
Dollars	8 reals.	0 4 2	0 4 3
Halves and Quarters	in pro.		
Norway.			
GOLD.			
Ducat		0 9 2	0 9 3
SILVER.			
Specie Dollar		0 4 3	0 4 4
Porsla.			
GOLD.			
Mahomet Shable		0 16 6	0 11 0
Brache		0 9 0	0 9 6
SILVER.			
Europe coin and Spanish dollars are current.			

NAME OF COIN AND COUNTRY.	DIVIS PARTS.	FROM £ s. d.	TO £ s. d.
Portugal.			
GOLD.			
Johannes		1 13 6	1 16 0
SILVER.			
Crown		0 4 7	0 4 9
Prussia.			
GOLD.	thal agr.		
Double Frederic d'Or	11 10	1 13 3	1 14 0
Single Ditto	5 20	0 16 7	0 17 9
SILVER,			
Thaler	30 agr.	0 2 11	0 3 0
One-third, One-sixth, & One-twelfth	in pro.		
1 Silver Groschen		0 0 1	0 0 1½
Russia,			
GOLD.	rbl. kmp.		
Half Imperial	5 15	0 16 2	0 16 3
Ducat		0 9 2	0 9 3
SILVER.			
Rouble	100 kops.	0 3 0	0 3 1
Fractional parts	in pro.		
Spain.			
GOLD.			
Doubloon	16 dols.	3 7 0	3 7 6
Pistole	4 ,,	0 16 6	0 16 9
SILVER.			
Dollar	20 reals	0 4 2	0 4 3
Halves Quarters	in pro.		
Sweden.			
GOLD.			
Ducats		0 9 2	0 9 3
SILVER.			
Specie Dollar		0 4 3	0 4 4 —
Fractional parts	in pro.		
Switzerland.			
GOLD.			
32 Franc piece	47 F. fr.	1 17 6	1 18 0
Double Pistele	,,	1 17 0	1 17 6
SILVER.			
4 Franken piece	40 batz.	0 4 8	0 4 9
1 Swiss franc	10 ,,	0 1 2	0 1 2
Turkey.			
GOLD.			
Double Sequin		0 18 0	0 18 8
Sequin		0 9 0	0 9 1
Quarters, &c	in pro.		

LIST OF PARISH CHURCHES IN LONDON,

WITH THE NAMES OF THEIR MINISTERS.

———

WITHIN THE CITY.

PARISH	MINISTER
Allhallows, Thames-street	G. Mansfield.
Allhallows Staining, Mark-lne.	F. J. Stainforth
Allhallows Barking, Tower-st.	J. Thomas
Allhallows, Bread-street..........	Joshua Dix
Allhallows, London Wall	Charles Lacy
Allhallows, Lombard-street	Thomas Jones
Bridewell Precinct	F. Poynder
Christ Church, Newgate-street	Michael Gibbs
St. Alban, Wood-street	H. J. Cummins
St. Alphage, Sion College	G. Kemp
St. Andrew, Holborn	J. J. Toogood
St. Andrew Undershaft, St. Mary Axe	F. G. Bloomfield
St. Andrew Wardrobe, Doctors' Commons..................	C. F. Chase
St. Ann, Aldersgate	J. V. Poyah
St. Antholin's, Watling-street	W. Calvert
St. Austin's, St. Paul's	W. H. Milman
St. Bartholomew, Cripplegate	W. Denton
St. Bartholomew the Great.....	John Abbiss
St. Bartholomew the Less	Samuel Wix
St. Benedict, Gracechurch-st ..	C. Mackenzie
St. Benedict, Paul's Wharf	J. H. Coward
St. Botolph, Aldersgate	W. C. F. Webber
St. Botolph, Aldgate.................	R. P. Baker
St. Botolph, Bishopsgate	John Russell
St. Bride, Fleet-street.............	C. Marshall
St. Catherine Coleman	W. H. Dickinson
St. Catherine Cree, Leadenhall-street	J. J. Gelling
St. Clement Eastcheap............	William Johnson
St. Dionis Backchurch, Fenchurch-street	W. H. Lyall
St. Dunstan-in-the-East, St. Dunstan's-hill..................	T. B. Murray
St. Dunstan-in-the-West, Fleet-street.......................	Edward Auriol
St. Edmund the King, Lombard-street........................	T. H. Horne
St. Ethelburga, Bishopsgate ...	J. M. Rodwell
St. George, Botolph-lane	A. D. Russell

PARISH	MINISTER
St. George, Queen-square	William Short
St. Giles, Cripplegate	P. P. Gilbert
St. Helen, Bishopsgate	J. E. Cox
St. James, Garlick-hithe	Thomas Burnet
St. Lawrence, Jewry	B. M. Cowie
St. Magnus, London-bridge ...	A. M'Caul
St. Margaret, Lothbury	William Goode
St. Margaret Patn., Rood-lane	H. J. Newbery
St. Mary Woolnoth, Lombard-street......................	Robert Dear
St. Mary Aldermary, Bow-lane	J. T. Bennett
St. Mary, Aldermanbury.........	C. C. Collins
St. Mary-at-Hill, Eastcheap ...	J. C. Crosthwaite
St. Mary, Abchurch.................	R. B. Gibson
St. Mary, Old Fish-street	R. S. Bower
St. Mary-le-bow, Cheapside ...	M. H. Vine
St. Mary Somerset, Thames-st	H. Stebbing
St. Martin, Ludgate.................	J. B. Bingham
St. Martin Outwich, Threadneedle-street.....................	J. B. Deane
St. Matthew, Friday-street	W. S. Simpson
St. Michael Basishaw, Basinghall-street...................	John Finlay
St. Michael, Cornhill	T. W. Wrench
St. Michael, Wood-street.........	C. Hume
St. Michael, Queenhithe..........	James Lupton
St. Michael, College-hill	Thomas Darling
St. Mildred, Bread-street	J. Charlesworth
St. Mildred, Poultry...............	J. C. Minchin
St. Nicholas Coleabby, Old Fish-street.......................	H. Kynaston
St. Olave, Hart-street.............	David Laing
St. Olave, Jewry......................	H. R. Roxby
St. Peter, Cornhill..................	Sir J. P. Wood
St. Peter-le-Poer, Bread-street	James W. Vivian
St. Sepulchre, Snow-hill..........	James Jackson
St. Stephen, Walbrook............	George Croly
St. Stephen, Coleman-street...	Joslah Pratt
St. Swithin, London Stone	E. Allfree
St. Thomas, Chancery-lane.....	T. R. Redwar
St. Vedast, Foster-lane............	T. P. Dale

WESTMINSTER, AND PARISHES WITHIN A CIRCUIT OF TEN MILES.

ALPHABETICALLY ARRANGED.

PARISH	MINISTER	PARISH	MINISTER
Acton	John Smith	St. Saviour's	William Niven
Barking	H. F. Seymour	Parish Chapel	R. H. Davies
Barnes	R. E. Copleston	St. Jude	S. M. Barkworth
Castelnau Chapel	A. Watt	St. John	A. G. Pemberton
Battersea	J. S. Jenkinson	Chigwell	W.S.H. Meadows
Christ Church	R. B. Mason	St. John	John Smith
St. George	H. B. Poer	Chingford	R. B. Heathcote
St. John, Pruge	David M' Anally	Chiswick	L. W. T. Dale
Beckenham	F. S. C. Chalmers	Turnham Green Chapel	J. N. Plieland
Beddington	Jas. Hamilton	St. Mary Magdalen	H. Stretton
Bermondsey	J. E. Gibson	Christ Church, Surrey	Joseph Brown
St. James	R. N. D. Brown	City-road, St. Matthew	J. Lawrell
Christ Church	R. M. Martin	Clapham ....W.	H. W. A. Bowyer
St. Paul's	W. D. Long	St. James	G. J. Collinson
Bethnal Green	Joshua King	St. Paul	H. Lewis
St. John	John Tagg	St. John	S. Reed Catley
Bethnal Green, Jews Chapel	J. B. Cartwright	Christ Church	B. Abbot
St. Peter	J. G. Packer	Clerkenwell, St. James's	R. Maguire
St. Andrew's	G. H. Parker	St. John	Hugh Hughes
St. Phillip's	Jas. Trevitt	St. Mark	F. M'Carthy
St. Bartholomew's	F. H. Vivian	St. Philip	W. R. Wroth
St. James the Great	E. F. Coke	St. James's, Pentonville } Chapel	A. L. Courtenay
St. James the Less	H. P. Haughton		
St. Matthias	J. Colbourne	Croydon	J. G. Hodgson
St. Jude	J. E. Keane	St. John, Shirley	M. T. Farrer
Bethnal Green, St. Simon	J. B. Anstead	Christ Church	O. B. Byers
St. Thomas	William Kerry	All Saints', Norwood	J. Watson
Bishopsgate, All Saints	R. H. Ruddock	St. James	G. Coles
Bloomsbury, St. George	Emillus Bayley	St. Peter	J. White
Bedford Chapel	C. W. Clarke	Deptford, St. Nicholas	A. E. Sketchley
Christ Church	G. Hamilton	St. Paul	B. S. Ffinch
Bow	G. T. Driffield	St. James, Hatcham	A K.B. Granville
Brentford, New	F. B. Briggs	St. John	C. F. S. Money
Old, St. George	F. E. Thompson	Duke's-Place, St. James's .... {	W. M. Whittemore
Bromley, Kent	J. E. Newall		
Bromley, Middlesex	A. G. How	Dulwich College Chapel	C. Howes
Brompton	John Sinclair	Eating	E. W. Relton
Camberwell	J. Williams	Christ Church	W. Lambert
St. George	Samuel Smith	East Ham	W. Streatfield
Christ Church Old Kent-road	R.P.Hutchison	Edgeware	Thos. Wall
St. Mary	J. G. Storie	Edmonton	Thos. Tate
Emmanuel Church	{ F. J. C. De Crespigny	St. James, Upper Edmonton	G. Phillips
		Winchmore Hill	J. D. Frost
Camden Church	D. Moore	Southgate	— Baird
St. Paul	M. Anderson	Eltham	C. G. Fryer
Peckham Church	E. Lilley	Enfield	J. M. Heath
East Dulwich Church	J. R. Oldham	St. James	J. Harman
Licensed Victuallers' Asylum	W. G. Martin	Jews Chapel	C. W. Bollaerts
Carshalton	W. A. B. Cator	Christ Church	C. Skrine
Charlton	A. Drummond	St. John	
St. Thomas	A. Delamare	Finchley	T. R. White
Blackheath Park Chapel	J. Ferm	St. John, Whetstone	H. L. Peutris
St. German's Chapel	H. Battiscombe	Trinity Church	F. S. Green
Chelsea	C. Kingsley	Fulham	R. G. Baker
(Upper)	Richard Burgess	St. John	W. Garratt
Christ Church	W. W. Robinson	St. Mary	S. B. Byers

PARISH	MINISTER
Gough Square, Trinity Church	Dennis Kelly
Greenwich, St. Mary	W. A. Soames
Trinity	L W. North
Christ Church	J. Y. Hughes
St. John, Charlton-road, Blackheath }	R. G. Lewis
Hackney	T. O. Goodchild
(West)	T. D. Lamb
(South,	G. P. Lockwood
St. Thomas, Upper Clapton	C. J. Heathcote
St. Philip, Dalston	T. P. Wright
St. James, Clapton	G. Powell
St. Barnabas, Homerton	J. Connell
Bain's Chapel	T. Griffith
St. Peter, West Hackney	{ Hon. F. S. Monckton
Hammersmith	E. F. Boyle
St. Peter's	T. A. Tagg
St. Stephen	W. L. Collett
Hampstead	T. Ainger
St. John	C. Dent Bell
Christ Church	E. H. Bickersteth
St. Saviour	J. P. Fletcher
St. Mary, Kilburn	G. B. Adam
Temporary Church, Avenue Road }	J. M. Farrar
Hanwell	{ Str C. Clarke, Bart.
Harrow	J. Cunningham
Weald	E. Monro
St. John, Wembley	W. F. Raws
Hendon	T. Williams
St. Paul, Mill Hill	B. Nicols
All Saints'	W. H. Shore
Heston	H. S. Trimmer
Hounslow	E. East
St. Mary, Spring Grove	J. N. Griffin
Highgate	C. B. Dalton
Holborn, Trinity Church	J. Worthington
St. Peter's, Saffron-hill	J. W. Laughlin
St. John's Chapel, Bedford-row }	J. B. Owen
St. Etheldreda, Ely-place	J. Evans
Hornsey	B. Harvey
St. James, Muswell-hill	J. Browell
Ilford, Great	H. W. Bertie
Aldbor Hatch	J. Budgen
Barkingside	J. Budgen
St. Mary	J. Reynolds
Ilford, Little	A. Hibbett
Isleworth,	H. W. P. Richards
St. John	J. Yarker
Islington, St. Mary	D. Wilson
Chapel of Ease Holloway	J. Hambleton
St. John's, Upper Hollo-way }	C. W. Edmonstone
St. Paul's, Ball's Pond	John Sandys
Trinity, Cloudesley-square	W. Vincent
St. Peter's	J. Haslegrave

PARISH	MINISTER
St. James's, Holloway	W. B. Mackenzie
All Saints	Theo. Saulez
St. Stephen's	Henry Deck
Christ Church, Highbury	M. A. Collinson
St. Matthew	E. T. Alder
St. Andrew	S. J. Altmann
St. Mark	J. Lees
St. Jude	T. Pitman
St. Michael	L. R. Ayre
St. Philip	J. Sutherland
St. Luke	G. W. Rogen
St. Barnabas	
St. Silas	— James
St. Matthias	
Kensington, St. Mary }	
Christ Church Chapel	John Sinclair
St. Paul's Chapel }	
St. Barnabas	F. Hessey
St. John	J. P. Gell
St. James	T. P. Holdich
Trinity, Broughton	W. J. Irons
St. Mary, West Brompton	T. Pearson
Brompton Chapel	C. W. Doherty
All Saints'	
St. Peter, Notting Hill	F. H. Addams.
St. Philip	J. D. Claxton
Kew-cum-Petershaw	R. B. Byam
Kingsbury	H. Atcheson
King's College Chapel, Strand	R. W. Jelf
Kingston-on-Thames	H. P. Measor
St. Andrew, Ham	T. G. P. Hough
St. Peter, Norbiton	R Holberton
St. Mark, Surbiton	E. Phillips
St. Paul, Hook	T. Pyne
Lambeth Chapel	Robert Eden
St. Matthew, Dunnark-hill	S.. Bridge
St. Mark	Charlton Lane
St. Michael, Stockwell	Charles Kemblo
St. Luke	Charles Turner
St. John, near Brixton	M. Vaughan
Trinity Chapel	Jas. Gilman
South Lambert Chapel	C. P. Shepherd
Stockwell Chapel	H. Clissold
St. James, Kennington	H. Woodward
Holland Chapel	F. G. Grossman
Verulam Chapel	C. Green
All Saints	Whitmore Carr
St. Mary, Prince's-road	R. Gregory
St. John, Waterloo	T A. Johnston
St. Thomas	J. R. Starey
St. Andrew	A. C. Canney
Christ Church, N. Brixton	J. M. Hussey
St. Barnabas, Kensington	W. Harker
St. Matthew, Brixton	N. A. Garland
St. John, N. Brixton	M. Vaughan
Trinity, Tulse Hill	J. W. Watson
Lambeth, St. Mazy	J. F. Lkigham
Lee	G. Lewis
Christ Church	W. Sims

PARISH	MINISTER	PARISH	MINISTER
Lewisham	Hon. H. Legge	St. Saviour	T. M. Hopkins
Southend	S. E. Forster	Pancras (St.) Middlesex	Thomas Dale
Dartmouth-place	G. Butler	Parish Chapel	C. Hart
St. Bartholomew, Sydenham	C. English	Kentish Town	W. Milne
Christ Church, Forest Hill	J. M. Clarke	Camden Town	J. Fitzgerald
Leyton	J. Parcloe	St. Paul's	A. R. G. Thomas
St. John	H. H. Evans	Regent's-square	G. A. Rogers
Limehouse	E. R. Jones	Somers' Town	T. J. Judkin
St. James	E. H. Atherton	Christ Church	H. W. Burrow
St. John	C. H. Carr	All Saints	Thos. Bennett
St. Paul		St. John	W. Gill
Luke (St.) Old-street	John Saunders	Fitzroy Chapel	W. G. Rooker
St. Barnabas, King-square	R. L. Hill	Gray's Inn-lane Chapel	T. Mortimer
St. Paul, Old-street-road	L. Marcus	St. Mary Magdalene	E. Stuart
St. Mark	W. Hinson	St. Mark	W. B. Galloway
Marylebone (St.)		St. Anne, Highgate	T. P. Stocks
St. Mary	C. J. P. Eyre	St. Bartholomew	E. Garbett
All Souls' {	E. R. Eardley Wilmott	Percy Chapel	S. Minton
		Trinity	E. Spooner
Trinity	T. Garnier	St. Luke	H. C. Radclyffe
Christ Church	J. L. Davies	St. Thomas, Agar-terrace	K. P. Clemenger
St. John's Wood	E. H. Carr	St. Jude	J. S. Wilkins
Parochial Chapel	W. H. Charlton	St. Matthew	C. Phillips
St. Peter's Chapel	Edward Scobell	Woburn Chapel	C. T. Woods
St. Paul's Chapel	George Pocock	St. James, Hampstead	
St. Paul's, Lisson-grove	J. Keeling	Free Chapel, Burton-street	T. Dale
St. James's Chapel	G. Evezard	Foundling Hospital Chapel {	J. W. Gleadall, J. M'C. Hussey
Portman Chapel	J. W. Reeve		
Christ Chapel	E. H. Carr	St. Andrew	H. J. C. Smith
Brunswick Chapel	B. R. Maitland	Perrivale	J. F. Lateward
Quebec Chapel	E. M. Goulburn	Plumstead	W. Acworth
All Saints, (S. & W.)	H. W. Maddock	Shooter's Hill	W. C. Ridley
St. Thomas	H. S. Lumsden	Poplar	T. T. Bazeley
St. Mary	R. F. Spencer	Putney	C. T. Robinson
St. Andrew	J. Murray	Roehampton	G. E. Biber
All Saints	W. U. Richards	Queen-square, St. George	William Short
St. Mark	A. B. Haslewood	Richmond	H. Dupuis
St. Stephen	E. H. Nelson	St. John	J. D. Hales
St. Luke	S. C. H. Hausard	Rotherhithe, (St. Paul's)	Edward Blick
Merton	W. Edelman	Christ Church	F. Perry
Minories, Trinity	Thos. Hill	Trinity	J. R. Turing
Mitcham	J. Whartou	All Saints	Robert Jones
Morden	R. Tritton	Shadwell, (St. Paul's)	B. Cox Sanger
Mortlake	J. T. Manley	Shoreditch, St. Leonard	T. S. Evans
Newington, St. Mary	A. C. Onslow	Christ Church	Wlliam Scott
Norwood	E. J. Smith	St. James	J. W. Markwell
Trinity	D. A. Moullin	St. John	A. P. Kelly
Newington		St. Mary	T. Clerk
St. Peter's, Walworth	F. F. Statham	Southall, St. John	W. F. Lanfear
Beresford Chapel	W. T. Maudson	Southwark, St. George	W. Cadman
St. Paul's	T. Mitchell	St. John, Horsleydown	H. Vachall
Paddington	A. M. Campbell,	St. Olave	G. P. T. Sproule
St. John	J. S. Boone	St. Saviour (chaplains) {	S. Benson, W. Curling
St. Mary	J. W. Buckley		
Bayswater Chapel	C. Smalley	St. Thomas	W. Deey
Holy Trinity	John Miles	St. Peter's	W. Mungeam
St. Stephens	H. W. Brooks	St. Stephens's	J. H. Simpson
All Saints'	E. H. Steventon	St. Jude	F. Cruse
Christ Church	H. Wood	St. Mary Magdalen	A. W. Snape

PARISH	MINISTER
St. John's Chapel	W. Lincoln
St. George's Chapel	J. Popham
St. Michael's Chapel	F. P. Le Maitre
St. Mark	G. F. Galaher
Spitalfields, Christchurch	J. Patteson
Spital-square, St. Mary	R. S. Clifford
St. George-in-the-East	Bryan King
Christ Church	G. H. McGill
St. Mary	W. M'Call
St. Giles	A. W. Thorold
Trinity Church	Saml. Garratt
Christ Church	J. Swayne
St. Matthews,	Tenison Cuffe
West-Street Chapel	R. W. Dibdin
St. Thomas, Charter House	W. Rogers
Stanmore, Great	R. G. Gorton
Stanmore, Little	G. B. Tuson
Stepney, St. Dunstan's	R. Lee
Trinity	F. S. Lea
St. Philip	James Bonwell
St. Peter's	T. J. Rowsell
St. Thomas	W. Valentine
All Saints	J. Harris
Stoke Newington	T. Jackson
St. Matthias	S. W. Mangin
Streathara	J. R. Nicholl
Christ Church	W. Raven
St. Mary	R. Bellamy
Trinity	E. D. Cree
Emmanuel	S. Eardley
Tooting	R. W. Greaves
Tottenham, and St. Michael's, Wood Green	W. J. Hall
Holy Trinity	G. B. Twining
St. Paul	D. J. Harrison
Tower, St. Peter ad Vincula	Henry Melvill
Twickenham	Chas. Proby
Trinity	James Twining
Montpelier Chapel	H. Parish
Walthamstow, St. Mary	T. Parry
St. John	C. J. S. Russell
St. Peter	F. Quarrington
Ht. James	R. Heap
Wandsworth	Henry Holmes
All Saints'	J. Buckmaster
StMary, Summer-terrace	R. F. Chambers
Wanstead	W. P. Wigram
Wapping	T. W. Nowell
West Ham	Abel John Ram
St. John, Stratford	W. Holloway
St. Mary, Plaistow	R. W. B. Marsh
Christ Church	T. J. Ram
Emanuel, Forest Gate	T. L. Ramsden
Westminster, St. Anne's	Nugent Wade
St. Clement Danes	S. C. Mason
St. George, Hanover-square	H. Howarth
Grosvenor Chapel	Evan Nepean
Hanover Chapel	T. G. James
St. Mark, North Audley-st.	J. W. Eyre

PARISH	MINISTER
St. Peter, Pimlico	Thomas Fuller
St. Paul's, Knightsbridge	Hon. R. Liddel
St. Michael, Chester, 59	J. H. Hamillton
St. George, Albemarle-st	W. W. Ellis
St. Mary's, Park-street	J. D. Glennie
Charlotte Chapel	F. T. Pearson
Trinity Chapel	H. H. Beamish
Berkeley Chapel	F. Tate
Belgrave Chapel	W. Thorpe
Curzon Chapel, May Fair	E. Hawkins
Eaton Chapel, Eaton, 19	J. Rashdall
St. Mary	J. C. Chambers
St. Gabriel, Pimlico	B. Belcher
St. Matthew, Gt Peter-st.	R. Malone
Holy Trinity	C. F. Secretau
St. Andrew	H. Walker
All Saint's, Knightsbridge	W. Harness
St. John, Broad-court	R. G. Maul
St. Mark	C. J. D'Oyly
St. James	J. E. Kempe
St. Philip, Regent-street	Edward Repton
St. Luke, Berwick Street	S. Arnott
Archbishop Tenison's Chapl	J. G. Cowan
York-street	T. T. Haverfield
St. James's Chapel	
St. John's	J. Jennings
St. Mary's, Tothill-fields	A. Borradaile
St. Margaret's	W. Cureton
Broadway	C. W. Pase
Christ Church	
St. Stephen's	W. Tennant
St. Martin-in-the-Fields	W. G. Humphry
St. Michael	A. G. Edouart
Spring-gardens Chapel	S. Flood Jones
St. Mary-le-Strand	J. F. Denham
St. Paul, Covent-garden	H. Hutton
Savoy Precinct	John Forster
Whitechapel, St. Mary	W. W. Champneys
St. Mark	D. J. Vaughan
St. Jude	Hugh Allen
Willesden	H. W. G. Armstrong
Kilburn	J. J. Bolton
Wimbledon	R. L. Adams
Woodford	W. P. Philips
St. Paul	C. B. Waller
Woolwich	H. Brown
Trinity	T. Reynolds
St. John	F. Cameron

FRENCH PROTESTANT CHURCH.
St. Martin's-le-Grand, opposite the General Post
Office—Minister, A. T. Marzials.

SWEDISH PROTESTANT CHURCH.
Swedish Protestant Church, Princes-square.
Ratcliffe—Minister, F. T. Carlson.

UNITARIAN CHAPELS IN AND NEAR LONDON.

NAME AND LOCALITY.	MINISTER
Brixton, Effra-road, Brixton, ..	Dr. Harrison.
Carter-lane, adjoining No. 12, Little Carter-lane, Doctor's Commons	H. Jerson, (temporarily).
Deptford (General Baptlst), Church-street, Deptford	M. C. Gascoigne.
Dockhead (General Baptist), Arnold's-place...................	Jas. Humphries.
Essex-street, Strand (adjoining No. 1)...................	Thos. Madge.
Hackney, New Gravel-pit.......	R.Brook Aspland.
Hampstead, Rosslyn-street....	Dr. Sadler.
Kentish Town (Free Christian Church), Clarence-rd.	W. Forster.

NAME AND LOCALITY.	MINISTER
Mill-yard, Goodman's Field (Seventh Day Baptist).....	W. H. Black.
Portland-street (Little Regent-street)........................	E. Tagart.
Stamford-street, Blackfriars (adjoining No. 26).............	Thos. L. Marshall.
Stoke Newington Green, near Ball's Pond...............	Dr. Cromwell.
Stratford (Christian Association).............................	T. Rix.
Worship-st. (General Baptist), Shoreditch, adjoining No. 63	J. C. Means

ROMAN CATHOLIC CHAPELS IN AND NEAR LONDON.

Bavarian, 12, Warwick-street, Golden-square.
Brompton-road, Church of the Immaculate Heart of Mary (the Oratory).
Holloway, 19, Cornwall-place, Holloway-road.
Deptford, High-street.
Berkeley-square, between 8 and 9, Farm-street.
French, Little George-street, Portman-square.
Great Saffron-hill, Hatton-garden.
Kensington, Upper Holland-street.
Dockhead, Most Holy Trinity, Parker's-row.
Oratory of Loreto, Johnson-street, Sun Tavern-fields.
Our Lady's, Grove-road, St. John's Wood.
St. Aloysius, Clarendon-square.
St. Ann's, Spicer-street, Spitalfields.
St. George, Lambeth-road.
St. John Evangelist, Duncan-terrace, City-road.

St. John's, Mare-street, Hackney.
St. Mary's, Cadogan-terrace, Sloane-street, Chelsea.
St. Mary (and College), Park-road, Clapham.
St. Mary of the Angels, Westmoreland-place, Bayswater.
St. Mary's, Moorfields, Finsbury.
St. Mary's, next Romney-terrace, Westminster.
St. Mary and St. Joseph, Gate-street, Poplar.
St. Mary and St. Michael, Lucas-place (West), Commercial Road (East).
St. Patrick, Sutton-street, Soho.
St. Patrick, Stratford, Essex.
St. Peter and St. Paul, Upper Rosoman-street, Clerkenwell.
Sardinian, 32, Duke-street, Lincoln's Inn Fields.
Spanish, 7, Spanish-place, Manchester-square.

JEWS' SYNAGOGUES.

Aldgate (Great Synagogue), St. James's-place.
Bevis Marks (Spanish and Portugese), between Nos. 10 and 11.
Cavendish-square, 49, Margaret-street, and 4, Wigmore-street
Covent Garden, 21, Maiden-lane.
Fenchurch-street (Hambro Synagogue), Church-row.

Great Portland-street, No. 120.
Haymarket (Western Synagogue), 12, St. Alban's-Plane's-place.
Great St. Helen's (New Synagogue), between 4, Crosby-square, and 21, Great St. Helen's.
Southwark, between 91 and 92, St. George's-road, Southwark.

SOCIETY OF FRIENDS' MEETING HOUSES.

Borough, Redcross-street.
Houndsditch, No. 86.
Lombard-street, 4, White Hart-court.
Ratcliffe-highway, Brook-street.

Peckham Rye.
Peel-court, St. John-street, Smithfield,
St. Martin's-lane, West-Strand.

LIST OF DISSENTING CHAPELS,

WITH THE NAMES OF THE MINISTER.

INDEPENDENT CHAPELS IN OR NEAR LONDON.

*** The Chapels are alphabetically arranged (for the most part) not according to their names, but to the locality in which they are situated.

CHAPEL	MINISTER
Acton	Supplied
Aldersgate-street (Welsh)	John Roberts
Anerley	Vacant
Artillery Chapel, Spitalfields.	J. F. Glass
Barbican	R. M. Macbrair
Barnet	J. C. Beadle
Battle-bridge	Vacant
Bayswater (Craven-hill)	E. Cornwall
Bedford Chapel, Charring-ton-road, St. Pancras	A. Reed
Bermondsey, Jamaica-row	G. Rose
Bermondsey, Neckinger-road,	J. Bodington
Bethnal-green-road	Vacant
Bethnal-green, Gibraltar Ch	J. Brown
Bethnal-green, Zion Chapel	T. G. Williams
Bothnal-green, Park Chapel	J. P. Mummery
Bothnal-green, Sidney-st. Ch.	T. J. R. Temple
Bethnal-green, Virginia Ch. Bishopsgate-street	E. Mannering
Blackheath, Congregational Church	J. Sheerman
Bow, Harley-street	S, Davis
Bow-road, Latimer Chapel	R Saunders
Brentford, Albany	E. Morley
Brentford, Boston-road	W. C. Yonge
Brixton-hill, Trinity	S. Eldridge
Brixton-hill, Union	J. Hall
Bromley, Kent	G. Verrall
Brompton, Trevor	Dr. Merrison / W. M. Stitham
Boxley, New	Vacant
Broad-street, New	W. O'Neill
Camberwell-green	J. Burnett
Camberwell, New-road	J. Tiddy
Camberwell, Albany-road	G. Rogers
Camberwell, Mansion-house	Vacant
Camden Town, Ebenezer	T. W. Gittens
Camden Town, Park Chapel,..	J. C. Harrison
Carey-street, New-court	Vacant
Chelsea, King's-road	J. C. Hooper
Chiswick	
City-road	W. S. Edwards

CHAPEL	MINISTER
Caledonian-road Chapel	Ebenezer Davies
Caledonian-road, Offord-road,	E. Paxton Hood
Clapham	John Hill
Clapham, Park-road	B. Price
Clapham-road, Clayland's Chapel	J. B. Brown
Clapton, Upper	J. H. Gamble
Clapton, Lower, Pembury	F. Soden
Commercial-rd., Wycliffe Ch	Dr. Reed
Commercial-rd., Bloomsbnry..	G. Bayfield
Craven Chapel, Golden-square	J. Graham
Dalston	C. Dukes
Deptford	J. Pulling
Deptford, (Welsh)	Job Thomas
Drury-lane, Whitfield Chapel.	D. Martin
Ealing	W. Isaac
Edgware	Supplied
Edgware-road, Trinity Chapel	R. H. Herschell
Enfield, Baker-street	S. J. Smith
Enfield, Chase-side	Supplied
Enfield, Highway	
Enfield, Countess of Hun-tingdon	J. Stribbling
Falcon-square	Dr. Bennett / J. Bartlett
Fetter-lane	S. March
Fetter-lane, (Welsh)	Owen Evans
Finchley	O. R. Howell
Finsbury Chapel	A. Fletcher, D. D.
Grafton-street	T. T. Lynch
Greenwich, Maize-hill	G. C. Bellowes
Greenwich-road	W. Lucy
Hackney, Hampden	H. Hooper
Hackney, Old Gravel-pit	J. Davies
Hackney-road, Adelphi Chapel	W. Woodhouse
Hackney, St. Thomas'-square	W. Kirkus
Hammersmith, Broadway	R. Macbeth
Hammersmith, Ebenezer Church	R. B. Isaac
Hanwell	J. Fitt
Haverstock-hill	J. Nunn
Hendon	T. Fison

CHAPEL	MINISTER
Highgate	J. Viney
Holloway	A. J. Morris
Horsleydown, Union Chapel	J. Adey
Hounslow	J. Callow
Hoxton	G. L. Herman
Hornsey Park Chapel	J. Corbin
Isleworth	R. Ann
Islington, Darasbury	Vacant
Islington, Upper-street	B. S. Hollis
Islington, Lower-street	Charles Brake
Islington, Union-street	H. Allon
Islington, Canonbury	Vacant
Jewry-street	F. Silver
Kennington-lane, Esher-street	Job Marchant
Kensington, Hornton-street	J. Stoughton
Kentish Town	J. Fleming
Kilburn (temporary)	J. C. Gallaway
Kingsland	T. Aveling
Kingsland, Maberley Chapel	E. M. Davis
Lambeth, York-road	R. Robinson
Lewisham, Union Chapel	H. Baker
Lewisham-road, St. Unvid's	D. J. Evans
Lewisham, Trinity Chapel	Vacant
Limehouse, Coverdale Chapel	J. E. Richards
Merton	J. G. Roberts
Mile End, Brunswick-street	J. B. Talbot
Mile End, Bedford-square	D. Davies
Mile End, Congregational Ch.	S. Eastmam
Mile End, New Town	W. Tyler
Millwall	Vacant
Mitcham	Geo. Stewart
Mortlake	Supplied
New North-road, Pavement Ch.	L. Herschell
New North-road, Salem Chapel	
New-road Tonbridge Chapel	H. Madgin
Norwood	B. Kent
Notting Hill, Horbury Chapel	W. Roberts
Old Ford, Bow	J. Hooper
Old Kent-road, Arthur-street,	D. Nimmo
Old Kent-road, Marlbro' Chapel	J. G. Pigg
Orange-street	E. Jukes
Paddington Chapel	J. Stratten
Peckham, Hanover Chapel	K. W. Betts
Peckham Rye Chapel	Vacant
Pentpnville, Claremont Chapel	A. M. Henderson
Pimlico, Buckingham	Vacant
Pimlico, Eccleston Chapel	J. S. Pearsall
Plaistow	J. Curwen
Ponder's End	J. Lockyer
Poplar, Trinity Chapel	G. Smith
Poultry	J. Spence

CHAPEL	MINISTER
Putney	T. Davies
Ratcliffe, Queen-street	James Frame
Regent's Park, Albany Chapel	
Richmond	
Richmond, Vineyard Chapel	J. B. French
Robert-street, Grosvenor-sq	A. Johnson.
Rotherhithe, Russell-street	T. Muscutt
St. John's Wood	H.Christopherson
St. John's Wood, Portland Ch.	Vacant
Shadwell, Ebenezer Chapel	J. Bowrey
Sloane-street, Union Chapel	Jas. Brake
Soho, Wardour Chapel	J. Basley
Southgate-road, De Beauvoir Town	J. Spong
Southgate, 1, Chase-side	{ W. Culverwell / W. M. Robinson
Southwark, Guildford-street (Welsh)	D. Davies
Southwark (temporary), 39, Bridge House-place, New-ington Causeway	J. Waddington
Southwark, Cole-street	R. Littler
Spa Fields	T. E. Thoresby
Stepney Meeting	J. Kennedy
Stockwell Green	D. Thomas
Stoke Newington, Abney Ch.	J. Jefferson
Stratford	T. E. Stallybrass
Surrey Ch., Blackfriars-rd	{ N. Hall / E. Cecil
Tabernacle, Moorfields	J. Campbell
Tabernacle, New, Old-street	J. Vaughan
Tottenham Court-road	J. W. Richardson
Tooting	F. F. Thomas
Totteridge	W.L.Brown,M.A.
Twickenham	G. S. Ingram
Walthamstow, Marsh-street	S. S. England
Walthamstow, Wood-street	Vacant
Walworth, Lock's Fields	P. J. Turquand
Walworth, Sutherland	E. Bewlay
Wandsworth	P. H. Davison
Wapping, Gravel-lane	Vacant
Weigh House, Fish-street-hill.	T. Binney
Westminster, James-street	S. Martin
Whitechapel, Sion Chapel	J. Thomas, B. A.
Willesden	Supplied
Winchmore Hill	J. H. Richards
Woodford Wells	Vacant
Woolwich, Ebenezer Chapel	W. Gill
Woolwich, Salem Chapel	Dr. Carlile
Woolwich, Union Chapel	W. Woodland
Woolwich, Welsh Chapel	Job Thomas

BAPTIST CHAPELS IN AND NEAR LONDON.

*** The Chapels are alphabetically arranged (for the most part), not according to their names, but according to the localities in which they are situated.

CHAPEL	MINISTER
Aldersgate-street	
Alie-street, Little, Whitechapel	P. Dickerson
Alie-street, Great, Zoar	Various
Artillery-lane...........................	
Bayswater, Westbourne-grove	W. G. Lewis
Brompton.................................	J. Bigwood
Blandford-street......................	W. B. Bowes
Bloomsbury-street	W Brock
Brick-lane, St. Luke's	J. A. Jones
Bunhill-row, BlueAnchor-alley	R. Morris
Brentford, New	
Brentford, Old	C. H. Coles
Bethnal-green, Heart's-lane....	D.Smither
Bethnal-green, Peel-grove.......	J. Sneath
Bethnal-green, Squirries-street	T. S. Tanner
Bethnal-green, Twig Folly.......	T. B. Parker
Blackheath, Dacre-park	C. Boxer
Battersea	J. M. Soule
Borough, High-street...............	T. Gunner
Borough-road	J. Harcourt
Borough Surrey Tabernacle	J. Wells
Borough Trinity-street	
Borough, Crosby-row	S. Ward
Blackfriars-road, Church-st. ...	W. Barker
Bow	W. P. Balfern
Bedford Chapel, Charington-street, St. Pancras .... }	Andrew Reed
Butterland-street, City-road ...	S. Green
Bermondsey, Jamaica-row......	Various
Bermondsey, New Church-st..	J. L. Meeres
Bermondsey Road	T. Chivers
Chelsea, Cooks-green, King's Road .... }	J. Nichols
Clapham, Cranmer-court........	R. S. Bird
Clapham Common	R. Hoe
Clapham, Courland-grove.......	S. Ponsford
Clapham, New park-road........	J. Hironz
Clapham, Wirtemberg-place...	
Camberwell, Cottage-green	B. Lewis
Camberwell, Denmark-place ..	E. Steane
Chadwell-street, Pentonville ..	C. J. Hezelton
Chelsea, College-street...........	G. Palliser
Chelsea, Paradise-walk.........	Supplied
Chelsea, King's-road................	J. Nichols
Commercial-st., Whitechapel..	C. Stovel
Commercial road, East, Wellesley-street .... }	W. Chamberlain
Commercial-rd. Devonshire-place .... }	G. W. Pegg
City-road, Nelson-place	J. Newborn
Dean-street, Soho, Meard's-ct.	G. E. Bloomfield
Deptford, Florence-place	
Deptford, Midway-place	R. R. Finch
Deptford, New Cross-road.......	G. Wyard
Devonshire-square...................	J. H. Hinton

CHAPEL	MINISTER
Dalston, Queen's-road	W. Miall
Dorset-square, Edward-street	J. Wise
Dorset-square, Hill-street	J. Foreman
Eldon-street, Finsbury	B. Williams
Edgeware-rd., New Church-st.	Dr. Burns
Edgeware-rd., Shouldham-st..	W. A. Blake
Enfield-highway.......................	J. Beavan
Euston-square, Gower-street...	
Gray's-inn-road, Henry-street	G. Horsley
Greenwich, Bridge-street	J. Wilkins
Greenwich, East-street............	W. Caunt
Greenwich, Stockwell-street ...	J. Gwinnell
Gower-street............................	
Holloway, Camden-road..........	F. Tucker
Holloway, John-street	
Homerton-row	W. Palmer
Hackney, Mare-street..............	D. Katterus
Hackney-road, West-street	
Hampstead-road, Aden-street	
Hampstead, Stanhope-street ..	R, Alldis
Hampstead, Hollybush-hill.....	J. Radbourne
Hampstead, New End	W. Cooper
Henrietta-st., Brunswick sq....	W. N. Vine
Hammersmith, West End	J. Leechman
Hammersmith, Second Church	
Hendon	
Highgate.................................	S. S. Hatch
Hoxton, Buttesland-street.......	J. Rothery
Hoxton, High-street.................	J. P. Searle
Islington, Cross-street	A. C. Thomas
Islington Green	J. C. Glaskin
John-street, Gray's Inn road...	B. W. Noel
Keppel-street..........................	S. Milner
Kent-road, Alfred-place	W. Young
Kennington, Charles-street	T. Attwood
Kennington, Ebenezer.............	
Kentish Town, Hawley Road ..	E. White
Kingston	T. W. Medhurst
Kingsgate-street, Holbom	F. Wills
Kensall Green	E. Harris
Lincoln's Inn Fields, Little Wild-street...................... }	C. Wollacott
Lewisham-road.........................	J. Russell
Lee, High-road	R. H. Marten
Lambeth, Waterloo-road	W. Bidder
Lambeth, Regent-street	Vacant
Lambeth, Kennington-road.....	J. Barfitt
London-road, Earl-street.........	P. H. Cornford
London-road, Garden-row.......	
Lisson-grove, St. John's-place	
Mile-end, Darling-place..........	
Macclesfield-place, St. Luke's	
Maze Pond	J. Malcolm
Moorfields (Little), White-st. ..	— Whitakor
Norwood Upper........................	J. H. Tipple

CHAPEL	MINISTER	CHAPEL	MINISTER
New Tabernacle, Kennington .	C. H. Spurgeon	Shadwell, Victoria-street........	T. Field
New Cross, Mason-street		Stratford Grove......................	G. W.Fishbourne
New North-road, Wilton-sq.....	R. Dunning	St. Luke's, Bunhill-row...........	R. Morris
Notting Hill, John-street........	P.W.Williamson	St. Luke's, Brick-lane.............	J. A. Jones
Old Ford-lane..........................	W. P. Balfern	St. Luke's, Ratcliffe-grove	
Old Pancras-road	J. Nunn	Salter's Hall, Cannon-street ...	
Poplar, Cotton-street...............	B. Preece	Shepherd's Bush (Baptist Independents) .... }	J. Stent
Poplar, High-street.................	T. Davies		
Poplar, East India-road, William-street ....}	R. Bowles	Shouldham-st., Bryanston-square ....}	W. A. Blake
Praed-street, Edgware-road....	Vacant	Soho Chapel, Oxford-street.....	
Pimlico, Princes-row...............	W. Freeman	Spencer-place, Goswell-road ...	J. H. Cooke
Pimlico, Westbourne-street.....		Tooley-street, Unicorn-yard	C. W. Banks
Peckham, Rye-lane	G. Moyle	Tottenham................................	R. Wallace
Peckham, Hill-street...............	T. J. Cole	Tottenham Church-road............	
Regent-st, Riding House-lane .	J. Wigmore	Vernon-square, Pentonville	J. Wills
Regent's-park..........................	W. Landells	Westminster, Princess-place...	
Rotherhithe, Lucas-street	J. Butterfield	Westminster, Romney-street ..	
Stockwell, Chapel-street	— Evans	Wilderness-row, Goswell-st.....	J. Shorter
Store-street.............................		Waltham Abbey	S. Murch
Shacklewell	J. Cox	Walworth, Arthur-street	J. George
Somers Town, Chapel-street...	S. Cozens	Walworth, East-street.............	J. Chislett
Shoreditch, Austin-street.........	J. Russell	Walworth, Lion-street	W. Howieson
Shoreditch, Mason's-court......	T. J. Messer	Wandsworth, Bridgefield	W. Ball
Shoreditch, Cumberland-street	C. Smith	Winchmore Hill........................	
Stoke Newington, Church-st....	W. Dovey	Woolwich, Bath Lecture Rooms ....}	H. Crasweller
Stoke Newington, Salem Chapel............................}	T. Pepper		
Stepney College.......................		Woolwich, High-street...........	C. Box
Stepney Old-road		Woolwich, Anglesea-road	H. Hanks
Shadwell, Devonport-street	J. Bowler	Woolwich, Queen-street	C. Hawson
		Woolwich, Charles-street	

SCOTTISH PLACES OF WORSHIP IN LONDON.

*** Those having N. C. attached belong to the National Church, and F. C. to the Free Church.

CHAPEL	MINISTER	CHAPEL	MINISTER
Regent-square, F.C.................	J.Hamilton, D.D.	Greenwich, F.C.	— Duncan
Crown-ct., Covent-gardn., N.C.	J.Cumming,D.D.	St. George's-rd., Southwrk, F.C.	J. Fisher
St. Andrew's, Philpot-street, Stepney, N.C. ....}	A. J. Black	John Knox Church, Green-street, Stepney, F.C.........}	W. Keeley
Halkin-st, Belgrave-sq., N.C.	J. Macbeth	Carlton-hill, St. John's-wood, F.C. ....}	
Swallow-st, Piccadilly, N.C. ..	R. M'Pherson		
Caledonian Church, Hollo-way, N.C. ....}	W. R. Pratt	Caledonian-rd., Islington. F.C.	
		Woolwich, Prospect-place, FC.	Wm. Thompson
George-street, Chelsea, F.C.	T. Alexander	River-terrace, Islington, F.C...	John Weir, D.D.
London-wall, F.C.	W. Ballantyne	Oxendon Chapel, Haymarket .	T. Archer, D.D.
George-st., Portman-sq., F.C.	W. Chalmers	Albion Chapel, Moorgate-st. ...	J. Macfarlan

WESLEYAN CHAPELS IN LONDON AND ITS SUBURBS.

FIRST LONDON CIRCUIT.— City-road; St. John's-square; Hackney-road; Jewin-street, City, Welsh Service; New North-road; Angel-Alley, Bishopsgate-street-without; Wilson-st.; Radnor-street; Chequer-alley.

SECOND LONDON CIRCUIT.—Great Queen-st.,

Lincoln's Inn Fields; King's Cross, Liverpool-street; Camden-town, King-street; Kentish-town, Gloucester-place; Harp-alley, Farringdon-street; Palace-yard, Palace-row, New-road; Finchley; Barnet; Whetstone.

THIRD LONDON CIRCUIT.—Spitalfields, Brick-lane; St. George's, Back-road; East India-road, Poplar; Brunswick, Limehouse; Globe-road; Stratford, Chapel-street; Old Gravel-lane; Mill-Wall.

THAMES MISSION—Seamen's, Commercial-road.

FOURTH LONDON CIRCUIT.— Long-lane, Southwark; Albion-street, Rotherhithe; Silver-street, Rotherhithe; Stafford-street, Peckham; The Grove, Guildford-Street; Union-street, Friar-street; Salisbury-terrace, Lock's-fields.

FIRST LONDON CIRCUIT.— China-terrace Lambeth; Walworth; Waterloo-road; South-ville, Clifton-street; Brixton Hill; Vauxhall, Lower Norwood; Lordship-lane, Dulwich; South Lambeth, Dorset-street; Upper-Sydenham.

SIXTH LONDON CIRCUIT.—Hinde-street, Manchester-square; Stanhope-street, Hampstead-rd, Brunswick. Milton-street, Dorset-square; Bayswater, Wellington-terrace: Victoria-terrace, Portland Town; Kensal Town; Norland-road; Harlesden Green.

SEVENTH LONDON CROWN.—Chelsea, Sloane terrace; Westminster, Romney-terrace; Justice-walk; Ranelagh-road; Battersea.

BRITISH & FOREIGN BIBLE SOCIETY,

7, KARL-ST, BLACKFRIARS, ESTABLISHED 1884.

Treasurer,—John Thornton, Esq.
Secretaries,—Rev. Robert Frost, M.A., and Rev. Samuel B. Bargne, *London.*

NAVAL & MILITARY BIBLE SOCIETY,

32, SACKVILLE-STREET, LONDON.

Its object is to encourage the circulation of the Scriptures among sailors, and soldiers, at home and abroad. It was originally formed by a small number of Wesleyan Methodists in the year 1779.

EDUCATIONAL STATISTICS FROM THE CENSUS OF 1851.

ENGLAND AND WALES.	Day Schools.	Day Scholars.	Sabbath Schools.	Sabbath Scholars.
Church of England	10,555	929,476	10,427	985,892
Church of Scotland	5	946	13	1,628
Presbyterian Church	28	2,723	64	8,244
United Presbyterian	3	217	58	6,590
Congregationalists	453	50,188	2,590	343,478
Baptists	131	9,390	1,767	186,510
Wesleyan Methodist	381	41,144	4,128	429,727
Romanist	339	41,382	232	33,254
Unitarian	39	4,309	140	15,279
British Schools	514	82,597	—	—
SCOTLAND.				
Wesleyan Methodist	—	—	58	5,124
Episcopal Church	36	2,658	57	3,700
Parochial and Burgh School	1,025	97,439	—	—
Church of Scotland	537	36,995	1,095	76,233
Free Church	712	62,663	1,243	91,328
United Presbyterian	61	5,807	568	54,324
Congregationalists and Baptists	5	591	221	15,229

LONDON BANKERS.

Agra and United Service, 27, Cannon-st., City,
Australasia, 4, Threadneedle-street
British North America, 7, St. Helen's place
Bank of England, Threadneedle-street, and Old Burlington-street
Bank of London, 52, Threadneedle-street
Bank of New South Wales, 37, Cannon-street
Bank of Egypt, 26, Old Broad-street
Barclay and Co., 54. Lombard-street
Barnett and Co., 62, Lombard-street
Biggerstaffs, 63, West Smithfield, and 6, Bank-buildings, Metropolitan Cattle Market
Bosanquet and Co, 731, Lombard-street
Brown, Janson, and Co., 32. Abchurch-lane
Brown, John, and Co., 25, Abchurch-lane
Call and Co., 25, Old Bond-street
Challis and Son, 16, West Smithfield, and 12, Bank-buildings, Metropolitan Cattle Market
Chartered of India, Australia, and China, 20, Threadneedle-street
Child and Co., Temple Bar
City Bank, Threadneedle-street
Cocks and Co., Charing Cross
Colonial, 13, Bishopsgate-street Within
Commercial Bank of India., 4, Princes-street, Bank
Coutts and Co., 59, Strand
Cunliffe Son, and Co., 24, Bucklersbury
Cunliffes and Co., 24, Lombard-street
Currie and Co, 29, Cornhill.

Dimsdale and Co., 50. Cornhill
Drummonds, 49, Charing-cross

English, Scottish, and Australian Chartered, 73, Cornhill
Exchange (Hogland, E. and Son), 113, Leaden-hall-street

Feltham and Co., 49, Lombard-street
Fullers and Co., 77, Lombard-street
General Bank of Switzerland, 2, Royal Ex-change-buildings
Glyn and Co., 67, Lombard-street
Goslings and Co, 19, Fleet-street
Hallett and Co., 14, Gt. George-street, West-minster

Hanburys and Co., 60, Lombard-street
Hankey and Co., 7, Fenchurch street
Herries and Co., 16, St. James's-street
Heywood and Co., 4, Lombard-street
Hill and Sons, 17, West Smithfield, and 2, Bank-buildings, Metropolitan Cattle Market
Hoares, 37, Fleet-street
Hopkinson and Co., 3 Regent-street
Ionian, 6, Great Winchester-street
Janvrin and Co., 14a. Austin Friars
Johnstone, H., J. and Co., 28, Cannon-street
Jones, Loyd, and Co., 43, Lothbury
Lacy and Son, 60, West Smithfield, and 11, Bank-buildings, Metropolitan Cattle Market
London and County Joint Stock Banking Company, 21, Lombard-street; Albert-gate, Knightsbridge, 6, Berkeley-place, Edgeware-road; 441, Oxford-street; 21, Hanover-square; and 201, High-street, Borough
London Chartered Bank of Australia, 17, Can-non-street
London Joint Stock, 5, Princes-street, Bank, and 69, Pall Mall
London and Westminster, Lothbury; St. James's-square; 214, High Holborn; Wel-lington-street, Borough; 87, High-street, Whitechapel; 4, Stratford-place, Oxford-street; and 217, Strand
Lubbock and Co., 11. Mansion-house-street
Martin and Co., 68, Lombard-street
Masterman and Co., 35, Nicholas-lane
Mercantile Bank of India, London, and China, 50, Old Broad-street
National Bank, 13, Old Broad-street
National Provincial, 112, Bishopsgate
Olding, Sharpe, and Co., 29, Clement's-lane
Oriental Bank Corporation, Threadneedle-street
Ottoman Bank, 26, Old Broad-street
Praeds and Co., 189, Fleet-street
Prescott and Co., 62, Threadneedle street
Price and Co., 3, King William-street
Provincial of Ireland, 42, Old Broad-street
Puget and Co., 12, St. Paul's-church-yard
Ransome and Co., 1. Pall Mall, East
Robarts and Co., 15, Lombard-street
Scott and Co., 1, Cavendish-squire

Samuel and Montagu, 21, Cornhill
Seale, Lowe, and Co., 7, Leicester-square
Shank, J., 4. Metropolitan Cattle Market
Smith and Co., 1, Lombard-street
South Australian, 54, Old Broad-street
Spielmann and Co., 79, Lombard-street
Spooner and Co, 27, Gracechurch-street
Stevenson and Co., 20, Lombard-street
Stride, 41, West Smithfield, and 8, Bank-buildings, Metropolitan Cattle Market
Twinings, 215, Strand

Union of Australia, 38, Old Broad-street
Union of London, 2, Princes-street, Bank; 14, Argyll-place; 4, Pall Mall East, and 13, Fleet-street
Unity Joint Stock Mutual Association, 10, Cannon-street, City; and 1, New Coventry-street, Leicester-square
Williams, Deacon, Labouchere, and Co., 20, Birchin-lane
Willis and Co., 76, Lombard-street

PUBLIC OFFICES IN LONDON,

WITH THE HOURS OF ATTENDANCE.

Accountant-General's Office, Chancery-lane, 9, to 2, and 4 to 7; and for delivery of drafts, 11 to 2

Admirality Court, College-square, Doctors'-commons

Admirality Court Office, 2, Paul's Bakehouse-court, 10 to 4

Advocates, College of, Doctors'-commons, 10 to 4

Affidavit Office, (Chancery), Symond's-inn, 11 to 4, in long vacation 11 to 1

Alien Office (at the Home Office), 11 to 4

Alienation Office, 7, King's Bench walk, 11 to 1, 3 to 5

Arches Court, College-square, Doctors'-commons

Arches Court, Registry Office, 20, Great Knight-rider-street, 10 to 4

Attorney-General's Office, 3, Stone-buildings, Lincoln's Inn, 10 to 4, and 6 to 10

Attorneys' Certificate Office, Stamp Office, Somerset-house, 10 to 4, but no money is received after 3

Attorneys' Register Office, Incorporated Law Society, Chancery-lane, 10 to 4

Bankruptcy, Court of, Basinghall-street, 10 to 4

Bankruptcy, Secretary of, 2, Quality-court, Chancery-lane, 10 to 4, and 6 to 8, except in long vacation and then 11 to 3

Bankruptcy, Court of Review in, Registrar of, 2, Quality-court, Chancery-lane

Bishop of London's Office, 3, Godliman-street 10 to 4

Bishop of Rochester's Registry, 19, Bennet's-hill, 9½ to 5

Bishop of Winchester's Office, 12, Knightrider-street, 10 to 5

Board of Health, Whitehall, 10 to 4

Central Criminal Court Office Sessions-house, Old Bailey, 10 to 5

Chancery Enrolment Office, Chancery-lane, 10 to 2, and 6 to 8 in Easter and Trinity Terms, and till the Second Seal after Hilary and the Last Seal after Michaelmas Terms; at other times from 10 to 3

Church Commission, 11, Whitehall-place

City of London Court of Requests, Guildhall-buildings, 10 to 1

City Police Commissioner, 26, Old Jewry, 9 to 5

City Remembrancer's Office, Guildhall yd. 9 to 8

City Solicitor's Office, Guildhall-yard, 9 to 7

Clerk of the Crown Office, Rolls-yard, Chancery-lane, during sitting of Parliament, 10 to 3, and (at House of Lords) 5 to 7, and at other times, 10 to 2

Clerk of the Escheats, Somerset-place

Clerks of the House of Commons, 43, Parliament-street

Clerk of Outlawries, executed by Attorney-General's Clerk

Clerkenwell Police Court, Bagnigge-wells-road

Commissary of London's Office, 16, Great Knight-rider-street, 9 to 4

Commissary of Surrey's Office, 12, Great Knightrider-street, 10 to 5

Commissioners for Affidavits in Chancery, Queen's Bench, Common Pleas, and Exchequer, and Bankruptcy Courts, Ireland, and for Proof and Registry of Deeds in Ireland, 10 Southampton-buildings. 10 to 4

Common Pleas, Sergeant's-inn, Chancery-lane, 11 to 5 in Term, in vacation 11 to 3, and long vacation 11 to 2, in Rule Department 11 to 3, and 6 to 8

Copyhold Commission, Somerset House, 9 to 6

Original Law Commission, 52, Lincoln's-inn-Bolds, 10 to 4

Crown Office (Queen's Bench), 2, King's-bench-walk, Temple, 11 to 5, in vacation 11 to 3

Crown Office in Chancery, Rolls-yard, Chancery-lane, 10 to 3 during sitting of Parliament, and (at House of Lords) 5 to 7, at other times 10 to 2

Cursitor's and Petty Bag Office, Rolls-yard, 10 to 6, in long vacation 10 to 4

Dean and Chapter of Westminster's Office, 19, Bennet's-hill, 9½ to 5

Dean and Chapter of St. Paul's, London Office, 5, Dean's Court, 9½ to 5

Duchy Court, Lancaster, Lancaster-place, 10 to 4

Duchy of Cornwall Office, Somerset-place, 10 to 4

Ecclesiastical Commissioners' for England and Wales, 5, Whitehall-place, 10 to 4

Examiners' Office. Rolls-yard, Chancery-lanc, 10 to 4 in Term, in vacation 11 to 3

Exchequer of Pleas' Office, 7, Stone-builings, Lincoln's-inn, hours the same as the Common Pleas

Faculty Office, 10, Knightrider-street, 9 to 7

Fee Farm Rent Office, 6, Lyons-inn, 11 to 3

Fen Office, 6, Serjeant's-inn, 10 to 2, Monday, Wednesday, and Friday

Fines Levied, Office for searching for, Rolls-garden, Serjeant's-inn. Chancery-lane, in term 11 to 7, vacation 11 to 5, long vacation 11 to 3

First Fruits' Office, Dean's Yard, Westminster, consolidated with Queen Anne's Bounty Office

Foreign Marriage, Baptism, and Burial Registry, at the Bishop of London's Office, 3, Godliman-street

Gazette Office, Cannon-row, Westminster, published Tuesdays, and Fridays; advertisements should never be taken later than 12 o'clock on the day previous to the publication

General Registry of Births, Deaths, and Marriages, Somerset House

Great Seal Patent Office, Quality-court, Chancery-lane, 10 to 4

Greenwich Police Court, Greenwich

Heralds' College Office, Bennet's-hill, Doctors'-commons, 10 to 4

Incorporated Law Society Channcery-lane

Insolvent Debtors' Court, 5, Portugal-St., 10 to 4

Joint Stock Company's Registration Office, Serjeant's-inn, Fleet-street, 10 to 4, created and regulated by 7 and 8 Vict., e. 110

Judge Advocate-General's Office, 35, Great George-street, Westminster, 10 to 4

Judges' Chambers, Queen's Bench. Common Pleas, and Exchequer, Rolls-gardens, Chancery-lane, in term 11 to 15, vacation 11 to 3, and long vacation 11 to 3

Kensington and Hammersmith Police Court, Brook-green-lane

Lambeth-street Police Court, Whitechapel

Legacy Duty Office, Somerset House, 10 to 4

Lincoln's-inn Library, at the north end of the New Hall, hours of attendance 10 to 4

Lincoln's-inn, Steward's Office, under the Library at the north end of the New Hall, in term 10 to 5, in vacation 10 to 4

Lord Mayor's Court and Office, 7, Old Jewry. 10 to 4

Lunacy Office, Masters of, 45, Lincoln's-inn-fields

Lunacy Office, Metropolitan Commissioners, 12, Abingdon-street, 10 to 4

Lunatic Office, &, Quality-court, Chancery-lane, 10 to 4

Marlborough-street Police Court, 21, Great Marlborough-street

Marshall's Office, Common Pleas, Chief Justice's Chambers, Rolls-gardens, term and sittings after 11 to 2, and 6 to 8

Marshall and Associate, Queen's Bench, and Clerk at Nisi Prius, Chief Justice's Chambers, Rolls-gardens, term and sittings after 11 to 2, and 6 to 8, vacation 11 to 2

Marshall and Associate's Office, Exchequer, 5, Child's Place, Temple-bar, term and sittings after 11 to 3, and 6 to 8, vacation 11 to 2

Masters in Chancery Office, Southampton-buildings, in term 10 till 4, in vacation 10 till 2, in long vacation 11 till 1

Master's Office in Queen's Bench, King's-bench-walk, Temple; in Common Pleas, at the Office, Serjeant's-inn, Chancery-lane; in Exchequer, at the Office, Stone-buildings, 11 to 5; in vacation 11 to 3; from 10th Aug. to 23rd Oct. uncertain

Metropltian Board of Works, 1, Greek-st., Soho

Metropolitan Police Office, 4, Whitehall-place, 10 to 4

Middle Temple Library, Garden-court, 11 to 4

Middle Temple Treasurer's Office, 1 Plowden buildings, 10 to 3

Middlesex Registry Office, Bell-yard, Temple-bar, 11 to 3 for searches, 11 to 2 for leaving deeds. Deeds are not to be called for between 1 and 2; generally kept 10 days

Patent Office, 13, Serle-st., Lincoln's-inn, 10 to 4

Patent Office. Great Seal, Quality-court, Chancery-lane, 10 to 4

Peculiar of Archbishop of Canterbury Office, Bell-yard, 9 to 7

Peel Office, Westminster-hall, 10 to 1

Petty Bag Office, Rolls-yard, 10 till 6, in vacation 10 till 4

Poor Law Commissioners' Offices, Gwydyr House, Whitehall, 10 to 4

Prerogative Court, College-square, Doctors Commons

Prerogative Office, Knightrider-street, 9 to 3 Oct. to Jan., 9 to 4, Feb. to Sep.

Presentation Offices, Quality-court, 10 to 4

Private Bill Office, 2, Parliament-street

Privy Council Office, Downing-street, 11 to 4

Privy Seal and Signet Office, 28, Abingdon-street, 10 to 3

Public Office in Chancery, Southampton-buildings, 10 to 4 in term, vacation 10 to 2, and in the long vacation 11 to 1 only. On Saturdays in vacation, no attendance

Public Record Office, Rolls House and Rolls Chapel, Rolls-yard, Chancery-lane; the Tower; Chapter-house, Poets'-corner; 3, Whitehall-yard; and Carlton-ride, Carlton Gardens; 10 to 4

Queen's Bench Office, King's Bench-walk, Temple; hours same as Common Pleas

Queen's Remembrancer's Office, 22, Duke-street, Westminster, 10 to 4

Record Office (Tower) Chancery, 10 to 4

Record Office, Rolls-chapel, 10 to 4

Record and Writ Clerks' Office, Chancery-lane, 10 to 4, except in the interval between the last seal after Trinity until the first seal before the following term, and then from 11 to 2

Register Office, Chancery-lane (C), open for general business from 11 to 3; for inspection of cause books and cause papers, from 9 to 3 in the forenoon, and between 5 and 6 in the forenoon; but it is particularly requested that the registrars and their clerks be not interrupted before 11 nor after 3

Register Office of Deeds (see Middlesex Register Office)

Register Office of the Dean and Chapter of St. Paul, 5, Dean's-court, Doctor's Commons, 9½ to 5

Registration Commission, Rolls-yard, Chancery-lane, 11 to 4

Registry Office of Judgement, &c., to bind lands, Rolls-gardens, Chancery-lane, 11 to 5 in term, 11 to 3 in vacation, 11 to 2 in long vacation.

Report Office, Chancery-lane, 10 to 1, and 4 to 8

Royal and Peculiar Jurisdiction of St. Catherine, Registry, Godliman-street, 9 to 8

Secondaries Office, 5, Basinghall-street, 10 to 7

Secretary's (Lord Chancellor's) Office, Quality-court, Chancery-lane, 10 to 4

Secretary's Office, Rolls, Chancery-lane, 10 till 3—in vacation 11 to 1

Sheriff's-Court Office, Whitecross-street Prison, 11 to 3, and 5 to 7

Sheriff of Middlesex Office, 24, Red Lion-square, Holborn, 11 to 5, 11 to 3 in the vacation, and 11 to 2 in long vacation

Signet Office, Somerset-place

Solicitor-General's Office, 1, Paper-building, Temple

Southwark Police Court, Blackman-street, Borough

Stamp Office, Somerset-house, 10 to 4

State Paper Office, 12, Duke-street, Westminster, 10 to 4

Subpœna Office (Chancery), Rolls-yard, 10 to 4 in term, and 11 to 1 in vacation

Tax Office, Somerset-place, 10 to 4

Taxing Master's Office (Chancery), Staple Inn, Holborn, 10 to 4, in vacation, 11 to 1

Thames Police Court, Arbour-street, East Stepney, 10 to 5

Tithe Commission Office, 3, St. James' Square

Vicar-General's Offices, Bell-yard, Doctor's commons, 9 to 7

Wandsworth Police Court, Love-lane, Wandsworth

Woolwich Police Court, Woolwich

Worship-street Police Court, Finsbury.

ARMY AGENTS IN LONDON.

Armstrong and Co., 2, Russell-street. St. James's

Barron and Smith, 6, Duke-street, Westminster

Codd and Co., 19, Fludyer-street. Westminster

Collyer, Geo. Sam., 9, Park-street. St. James's

Cox and Co., Craig's-court, Charing Cross

Culpeper, Mulcaster, and Co., 28A, Regent-st.

Downes and Son, 14, Warwick-street, Charing Cross

Hopkinson and Co., 3, Regent-street

Kirkland, Sir John and Co., 80, Pall Mall

Lawrie, A., 10, Charles-st., St. James's-square

Maynard and Harris, 126, Leadenhall-street

M'Grigor, C. R. and W., 17, Charles-street, St. James's-square

Price and Boustead, 34, Craven-street, Strand

Ridgeway and Son, 40, Leicester-square

Ross and Co., 35, Craven-street, Strand

Sandell, J. C, 2, Warwick-st., Charing Cross

Strequeler, J. H., 88, St. James's-street

Scarborough, J. R., 21 and 29, Crosby Hall Chambers, and 2, Crosby-square, Bishopsgate

Smith, T., Tavistock Chambers, 14, Southampton-street, Strand

Tear, L. W. (for Royal Marines), 44, Hatton Garden

Walker, Wm., 33, St. James's-square

Wilkinson, J. G., 95, Jermyn-street

General Agent for the Recruiting Service

Sir J. Kirkland and Co., 80, Pall Mall.

NAVY AGENTS IN LONDON.

Aaron, Joseph, 6, Watney-street, Commercial-road

Armstrong, II. and Co., 2, Russell-court, St. James's

Banton and Mackrell, 33, Abchurch-lane

Barwis, William H. B., 1, New Boswell-court, Lincoln's Inn

Burnett and Co., 17. Surrey-street, Strand

Case and Londonsack, 1. James-street, Adelphi

Chard, William and Edwd., 3, Clifford's Inn, Fleet-street

Chippendale. A., 10, John-street, Adelphi

Collier, Thomas and John Adolphus Snce, 6, New Inn, Strand

Dufaur, F., 13, Clement's Inn, Strand

Goode and Co., 15, Surrey-street, Strand

Hallett, Maude, and Hallett, 14, Great George-street, Westminster

Muspratt, John P., 33, Abchurch-lane

O' Byrne Brothers, 9, Adelphi-terrace

Ommaney, Messrs, 40, Charing Cross

Stillwell, John and Thomas, 22, Arundel-street Strand

Tear, L. W. (for R. Marines). 44, Hatton Garden

Tory and Hildreth, 41, Norfolk-street, Strand

Woodhead and Co., 1, James-street, Adelphi

Young, R. M., 1, James-street, Adelphi

METROPOLITAN COUNTY COURTS.

₊ There arc 10 Metropolitan Districts—8 in Middlesex, and 3 In Surrey.

Bloomsbury County Court, 11, Portland-road, Regent's Park

Bow, Fairfield-road, Bow-road

Brompton, Whitehead's Grove, Chelsea

Clerkenwell, 33, Duncan-terrace, Islington

Lambeth, Camberwell New-road

Marylebone, 179, Marylebone-road

Shoreditch, Old-street-road, and 12, Charter-square, Hoxton

Southwark, Swan-street, Trinity-street Borough

Westminster, 82, St. Martin's-lane

Whitechapel, 3, Osborn-street, Whitechapel

APPENDIX.

INTERNATIONAL EXHIBITION OF 1862.

On the 1st of May, 1862, there is to be a second Great International Exhibition. The backbone of the undertaking, the guarantee of a quarter of a million of money, was filled up by Her Majesty's subjects, at the rate of some ten thousand pounds per diem, until the quarter or a million has been exceeded by a trifling £100,000 or so, and now the Queen has guaranteed her part, by the promise to inaugurate the Exhibition with all the pomp and circumstance of a royal state ceremony, such as in 1851 auspiciously opened the Crystal Palace. We may therefore expect, on the 1st of May, 1862, a gathering of the people at Kensington, such as, since 1851, has not been witnessed. In that year, novelty, and the inherent merits of a great project, secured a splendid success, and justified a feeling of pride with which the promoters, and the exhibitors from all parts of the world, regarded the noble work they had attempted and achieved. Then, it may be said, the FIRST INDEX OF THE WORLD'S CIVILIZATION was taken in the British Metropolis, and, although Crystal Buildings and Palaces of Industry have since, in several countries, recorded the progress or Art, Science, and Manufactures, yet, there can be no question that the undertaking of next year, to take place in London, will really be the Second Great Exhibition, in which all the nations of the world will take part and be fairly represented. The size, appearance, and character of the present building, will best be described by comparison with the first Crystal Palace, so well known to all. Judging from the plans already published, it would seem that the brilliant experiment of 1851, which was also a brilliant success, was, in reality, a great mistake, as Captain Foukes's designs are as unlike those of Sir Joseph Paxton as they well can be. Cost being the simplest and most certain test, we may at first compare the two buildings under that head. The Palace of 1851 was erected for less than £100,000, whilst the contracts for the new one are £300,000 certain, and another £100,000 conditional on the Commissioners receiving a particular surplus. This difference in cost may be explained by stating that the new building will be, 1st, nearly double the size of the Crystal Palace; 2nd, bricks and mortar, more costly materials, will be the staple, instead of glass and iron; and 3rd, the present plans include two stupendous glass domes, which must require a large share of the outlay. The area in square feet covered in 1851 was nearly 800,000; the new building will cover 1,300,000 square feet, but will not lie so long, by 1,000 feet against 1,851 feet, the length of the nave in 1851. The increase of space is therefore gained in width, the new building being 700 feet wide instead of only 400 feet. So much for the dimensions of the block.

The situation decided upon by Her Majesty's Commissioners is but a little distance from the old site, and adjoins the gardens of the Royal Horticultural Society, whilst the principal front, a brick wall, some 60 feet high, will stretch along the Cromwell Road, Kensington, upon a portion of the ground purchased by the surplus resulting from the former Exhibition. As before noticed, the new building will be about one-third less in length than the old Exhibition, whilst the nave running north and south will be 100 feet high, instead of 72 feet high, and will be crossed by *two* transepts at either extreme ends, also of 100 feet high, in place of the central one, 80 familiar to thousands in 1851. In the centre of each transept will he a Polygonal Hall, of which the floor will be raised, and surmounting which will rise the dome of glass and iron, of the extraordinary dimensions of 135 feet diameter, and 250 feet in height.

These sublime proportions will be the more impressive, as they will be around and above the visitors on their first entrance into the building, as the two principal entrances will be at each end or the nave. To retain one of the pleasantest associations connected with the first Crystal Palace, under each dome, a fountain, surrounded with shrubs and flowers will be conspicuous.

Considered as a whole, and comparing the general appearance of the new building with the old, the comparison is certainly against Captain Foukes's plans. But, in truth, the difference in materials prevent any just estimate between the two. There was enchantment about the first Crystal Palace, which will not be found in any new combination of solid bricks and mortar; and when the stern decision of inexorable commissioners gave the fairy fabric over to destruction, to prove its fairy powers, the structure, as in one night disappeared, scarcely leaving a print on the sward in Hyde Park, but lo! on the next morning, amidst the sylvan landscapes of Sydenham, transformed and more beautiful, yet still the same, the Crystal Palace re-appeared to attract from all ends of the globe the offerings and admiration of art, science, and industry, and to which the hyperbole may be applied, with more justice than to a fair woman—

"Once being formed, the mould was broken. That never another such should be made."

Yet, comparing this new home for our works of art and industry, with other architectural buildings of similar materials, upon which a quarter of a million of money has been expended, the designs for the Exhibition exhibit a meanness and poverty, which only their magnitude can redeem from contempt and ridicule. Nor does the introduction of the magnificent, yet incongruous domes, probably on afterthought, make the matter better; they are so wide apart, that still the impression is that the building can only be regarded as a convenient show room, commodious, and unsightly, as the shelter provided for the treasures at South Kensington.

Failing in external beauty (the critic being naturally vexed to see so good an opportunity of display thrown away), the structure is likely to be as secure and convenient as can be desired, and there can be no doubt that as much light, as all the purposes of exhibition demand, whether to give cheerfulness to the interior, or a full and broad light on special objects, may be obtained, although the front and back be of bricks, and the roof of wood and felt, whilst such light as is obtained may be directed with more certainty than when crystal sides and roof let in the dazzling and uncontrollable sunshine. The Exhibitors will therefore be gainers in this respect, and probably the comfort of visitors will be increased. There are five entrances, but, excepting the two at either end, they are not made the conspicuous features they might have been with advantage to the general effect, and as opportunities of destroying the long monotony of wall-front, facing the Cromwell Road. The approaches to the two principal entrances under the domes, in the middle of the transepts, stretching out on either side like wings of some great bird, will doubtless afford the points to view the building with the most satisfaction, although *half the effect* will be lost, as the second dome will scarcely be seen at all, and with respect to the three front entrances, the two domes at one time will be out of the line of sight, except at a great distance from the building.

To turn to a more important subject than the appearance of the building, it is satisfactory, and fortunate, that the controlling authorities with whom the management of the undertaking will rest, possess entirely the public confidence. The following noblemen and gentlemen, the Earl of Granville, Mr. Wentworth Dilke, the Marquis of Chandos, Mr. Thomas Baring, M.P., and Mr. Thomas Fairbairn, are, under the patent of incorporation, the appointed and responsible body, on whom the success of the project, in a great measure, depends, and their names arc generally accepted as a guarantee for liberal and business-like administration of the power placed in their hands. The department to exhibit machinery in motion has been judiciously planned as a separate exhibition, and will be 800 feet long, 50 feet wide, and 45 feet in height, occupying the rear of the building, on the west side of the Horticultural Gardens, and between the transept wings, so that it will appear a portion of the entire block of building. By this arrangement many inconveniences will be avoided, and the unpleasant smell from machinery oil will be confined to the department where it is used, and not pervade, as in 1851, a great part of the Exhibition.

The Art Treasures Exhibition at Manchester furnished a precedent, of which the commissioners have not neglected to avail themselves, and consequently a superb picture gallery is included in the arrangements made for space and will form a most distinctive feature from the Crystal Palace of 1851. The collection of paintings which may be expected is likely to prove one of the most popular attractions of the new Exhibition, and afford some notion of the treasures on canvas which this country contains. Altogether, nearly 2,000 feet, more than a third of a mile, will be afforded by the first and second galleries, parallel, and close to each other, situated in the front of the building. It is proposed to light the pictures by a clerestory in the roof. To form a conception of the space provided in the new building we must remember that, between the picture galleries in front, and the nave in the centre, there will be a distance of 300 feet. And if we consider that the front wall is 60 feet high, it will be evident the appearance of the nave, 100 feet high and of the domes, 250 feet high, cannot, at such a distance, and behind such a wall, be anything like so impressive as at first might be supposed.

On all sides the undertaking appears exceedingly popular, and whether the architect has achieved a success, or only designed a plain, useful and secure building, there is a grandeur in the purposes for which it will be erected, that dwarfs every other consideration. And when we think these great purposes can be carried out to a successful result, after the noble support given by the spirited guarantors;

after the royal patronage has been extended; only by the cordial co-operation of exhibitors in all parts of the world and especially our own manufacturers, we have every satisfaction in feeling assured even the enormous extent of the new building will but be sufficient for the treasures of art and industry, and of raw produce, which that co-operation will supply as the index of the world's civilization, on the first day of May, 1862. Appended are some of the principal regulations to be observed, and we think, in conclusion, we may remark, that as the first exhibition was preceded by a long era of peace, and which that gathering of the nations was thought likely to perpetuate, so may the International Exhibition of next year, coming after the contentions of strife, battle, and mutiny, be followed by another era, in which the arts of civilization may progress fruitful and unchecked, and this hope is strengthened by witnessing the love and eagermess with which the people have returned to the arts of peace from the turmoils of war, with an appreciation of their relative value, which the former and present International Exhibition cannot fail to extend.

All works of industry to be exhibited should have been produced since 1860.

Subject to the necessary limitation of space, all persons, whether designers, inventors, manufacturers, or producers of articles, will be allowed to exhibit; but they must state the character in which they do so.

Her Majesty's Commissioners will communicate with foreign and colonial exhibitors only through the commission which the Government of each foreign country or colony may appoint for that purpose; and no article will be admitted from any foreign country or colony without the sanction of such commission.

No rent will be charged to Exhibitors.

Prizes, or rewards for merit, in the form of medals, will be given in the industrial department of the Exhibition.

Prices may be affixed to the articles exhibited.

Her Majesty's Commissioners will be prepared to receive all articles which may be sent to them on or after Wednesday, the 12th of

February, and will continue to receive goods until Monday, the 31st of March, 1862, inclusive.

Articles of great site and weight, the placing of which will require considerable labour, must be sent before Saturday, the 1st March, 1862; and manufacturers wishing to exhibit machinery or other objects that will require foundations or special constructions, must make a declaration to that effect on their demands for space.

Any exhibitor whose goods can properly be placed together, will be at liberty to arrange such goods in his own way, provided his arrangement is compatible with the general scheme of the exhibition, and the convenience of other exhibitors.

Where it is desired to exhibit the processes of manufacture, a sufficient number of articles, however dissimilar, will be admitted for the purpose of illustrating the process; but they must not exceed the number actually required.

Exhibitors will be required to deliver their goods at the building, and to unpack and arrange them, at their own charge and risk; and all articles must be delivered with the freight, carriage, porterage, and all charges and dues upon them paid.

Packing cases most be removed at the cost of the exhibitor or his agent, as soon as the goods are examined and deposited in charge of the Commissioners.

Exhibitors will be permitted, subject only to the necessary general regulations, to erect, according to their own taste, all the counters, stands, glass frames, brackets, awnings, hangings, or similar contrivances which they may consider best calculated for the display of their goods.

Exhibitors must be at the charge of insuring their own goods, should they desire this security. Every precaution will be taken to prevent fire, theft, or other losses, and her Majesty's Commissioners will give all the aid in their power for the legal prosecution of any persons guilty of robbery or willful injury in the Exhibition, but they will not be responsible for losses or damage of any kind which may be occasioned by fire or theft, or in any other manner.

Exhibitors may employ assistants to keep in order the articles they exhibit, or to explain them to visitors, after obtaining written permission from her Majesty's Commissioners; but such assistants will be forbidden to invite visitors to purchase the goods of their employers.

Her Majesty's Commissioners will provide shafting steam (not exceeding 30lbs. per inch), and water, at high pressure, for machines in motion.

Intending exhibitors, in the United Kingdom, are requested to apply, without delay, to the Secretary of her Majesty's Commissioners, at the offices, 454, West Strand, London. W.C., for a form of demand for space, stating in which of the four sections they wish to exhibit.

Foreign and colonial exhibitors should apply, to the commission, or other central authority, appointed by the Foreign or Colonial Government, as soon as notice has been given of its appointment.

Her Majesty's Commissioners having consulted a committee as to the organisation of the Fine Art Department of the exhibition, will publish the rules relating thereto at a future date.

By order,

F. R. SANDFORD, Secretary,

Offices of Her Majesty's Commissioners,
    454, West Strand, London, W.C.

INDEX.

Abney Park Cemetery, 234
Acton, 246
Adelphi Terrace, 80
Admiralty, The, 84
Admiralty Court, 44
Albemarle Street, 112
Aldermen, 25
Aldersgate Street, 58
Aldgate, 72
Almack's, 105
Ancient Concerts, Society of 116
Ancient Masters, Gallery of, 234
Ankerwyke, 177
Antiquarian Museum, 234
Antiquarian Society, 234
Apothecaries Hall, 60
APPENDIX :—
  International Exhibition of 1862, 292,
Apsley House, 108
Argyll Street, 118
Arlington Street, 112
Armourers' Hall, 234
Army Agents, 290
Artillery Walk, 154
Artillery Ground, 154
Artillery Company, 235
Asiatic Museum, 235
Ashburnham House, 111

Baker Street Bazaar, 118
Balham, 247
Bancroft's Almshouses, 74
Bankers, 287
Bank of England, 38, 235
Bankside, 168
Barbers' Hall, 235
Barclay and Perkin's Brewery, 168, 235
Barge House, The, 248
Barking, 248
Barnsbury Road, 152
Barnsbury Park, 152
Barnard's Inn, 131
Barnes, 173

Battersea, 173
Battersea Park, 173
Beaumont Literary and Philosophical Institution, 73
Beckenham, 247
Bedford Row, 131
Berkeley Street, 112
Berkeley Square, 112
Bethelem Hospital, 161, 235
Bethnal Green, 74
Billingsgate, 18, 185
Bishopsgate, 42
Bishop-gate (Berkshire), 207
Bishop's Walk, 167
Blackheath, 188
Blacknest, 207
Blackwall, 71, 182
Blackwall Pier, 182
Blind, School for the, 161, 235
Bloomsbury Square, 145
Board of Trade, 84
Bolt Court, 62
Bond Street, 116
Botanic Gardens, 147, 173, 235
Bow Bells, 35
Bow Street Police Office, 121
Bridewell, 61, 225
Bridgewater House, 107
BRIDGES :—
  Battersea, 173
  Blackfriars, 60, 171
  Chelsea, 101
  Chelsea, New, 173
  Chertsey, 177
  Hammersmith, 173
  Hampton Court, 176
  Hungerford, 80, 171
  Kew, 174
  Kingston, 176, 213
  London, 47, 170
  Putney, 173
  Richmond, 174
  Southwark, 4, 170
  Staines, 177

Bridges—continued
  Vauxhall, 160, 172
  Victoria Railway, 173
  Walton, 177
  Waterloo, 78, 171
  Westminster, 85, 171
British Museum, 132, 235
British and Foreign Bible Society, 286
British and Foreign School, 160
British Institution, 103, 235
Brixton, 217
Bromley (Kent), 248
Brunswick Square, 150
Brunswick Wharf, 72
Buckingham Palace, 107
Buckingham Palace, Picture Gallery, 235
Bunhill Row Cemetery, 154
Burlington Arcade, 113, 235, 249
Burlington House, 113
Burnham, 208
Burnham Beaches, 208
Burton Crescent, 150
Bushy Park, 211

Cab Stands in the Metropolis, 251
Cadogan Pier, 173
Caledonian Asylum, 153
Camberwell, 247
Camden Town, 151
Canonbury Tower, 53
Canterbury Hall, 235
Carshalton, 247
Catholic Cathedral, 23
Catholic Church, Moorfields, 235
Central Criminal Court, 56
Chancery Lane, 63
Chapel Royal, 101
Charter House, 57
Charter Island, 177

Charlton, 182, 190
Charing Cross, 83
Cheapside, 35, 43
Chelsea Hospital, 172
Cheyne Walk, 173
Chiswick, 174
Chiswick Horticultural Gardens, 235
Christ's Hospital, 55, 236
CHURCHES :—
  St. Anne's, Soho, 115
  St. Botolph's, 75
  St. Bride's, 62
  St. Clement's Danes, 76
  St. Dunstan's in the East, 49
  St. Dunstan's in the West, 62
  St. George's, Hanover Square, 116
  St. George's Martyr, 159
  St. Giles's in the Fields, 119
  St. James's, 113
  St. James's, Paddington, 149
  St. James's, Clerkenwell, 155
  St. John's, Paddington, 149
  St. John the Evangelist, 100
  St. John's, Waterloo Road, 164
  St. Lawrence, 36
  St. Luke's, 152
  St. Magnus, 47
  St. Martin's, 81
  St. Margaret's, 86
  St. Mark's, 148
  St. Mary's, 153
  St. Mary-le-Strand, 77
  St. Mary's, Lambeth, 166
  St. Mary-le-Bow, 35
  St. Michael's, Queenhithe, 45

Churches—continued
St. Michael's, Peter-noster Royal, 45
St. Olave's, 157
St. Paul's Cathedral, 27, 241
St. Paul's, Shadwell, 279
St. Paul's, Covent Garden, 123
St. Paul's, Bermond-sey, 158
St. Pancras, New, 150
St. Pancras, Old, 152
St. Peter's, 153
St. Saviour's, 156
St. Stephen's, Wal-brook, 38
St. Swithin's, 46
All Souls, 117
All Souls, Padding-ton, 149
Barnes, 174
Battersea, 173
Charlton, 182
Christ Church, 168
Cobham, 198
Dartford, 194
Erith, 183, 193
Fulham, 173
Greek, 75
Holy Trinity, Pad-dington, 149
Isleworth, 174
Kingston, 175
Lambeth, 165, 172
Marylebone, New, 150
National, Scottish, 150
Northfleet, 195
Richmond, 209
Shepperton, 177
Sunbury, 177
Temple, The, 66
Walton, 177
City Boundary Stone, 177
City Companies, 25
City Gas Works, 61, 171
City of London School, 36
City Road, 153, 154
City, The, 24
Clapham New Park, 247
Clare Market, 124
Clement's Inn, 76
Clerkenwell House of Detention, 155
Clerkenwell Green, 155
Clifford's Inn, 68

CLUBS :—
Army and Navy, 103
Arthur's, 105
Athenæum, 102
Boodle's, 105
Brooke's, 105
Carlton, 102
Garrick, 124
Military, Naval, and County, 105
New Conservative, 105
Oriental, 116
Reform, 102
The Park, 103
Travellers', 103
Union, 101
University, 102
White's, 105
Coal Exchange, 48, 179
Cobham, 197
Cobham Wood, 200
Cogers' Hall, 61
Coldbath Fields, 152
College of Arms, 44
College of Physicians, 54, 101
Colloseum, Regent's Park, 236
Colonial Office, 84
Copenhagen Fields, 153
Commercial Coffee Houses, 245
Commercial Docks, 236
Consistory Court, 44
Constitution Hill, 107, 108
Corn Exchange, 49
Cornhill, 42
Court of Probate, 44
Court of Arches, 44
Court of Chancery, 85
Court of Common Coun-cil, 25
Court of Common Pleas, 86
Court of Exchequer, 86
Court of Queen's Bench, 86
Covent Garden Market, 121
Crane Court, 62
Cremorne Gardens, 236
Crosby Hall, 42, 236
Crouch End, 246
Custom House, 48, 185, 236
Croydon, 247

CRYSTAL PALACE, 215:
Alhambra Court, 222
Assyrian or Nineveh Court, 222
Aviaries, 229
Birmingham Court, 220
Books of Admission, 231
Byzantine and Ro-manesque Court, 222
Ceramic Court, 225
Conveyances to the Palace, 217
Crystal Palace Art Union, 232
Days and Houses of opening, 231
Elizabethan Court, 224
English and German Sculpture Court, 224
Egyptian Court, 220
Fares, 231
Flower Shows, 233
Fountains, 226
French and Italian Sculpture, 224
Greek Court, 221
Handel Orchestra, 219
Industrial Court, 220
Italian Court, 223
Lakes, 230
Lectures, 232
Mediæval Court, 223
Modern Picture Gal-lery, 225
Nave Court, The, 224
Order of Inspection, 233
Penny Reading and News Room, 230
Pictury Gallery, 225
Pompeian House, 219
Poultry Shows, 233
Public and Private Dining Rooms, 234
Railway Trains, 230
Refreshment Depart-ment, 233
Renaissance Court, 223
Roman Court, 221
Season Tickets, 231
Sheffield Court, 220
South Transept, 227
South End of the Palace, 227

Crystal Palace—contind.
Stationery Court, 233
Summary of Attrac-tions, 232
Terrace Garden, 226
To the Crystal Palace by Road, 218
To the Crystal Palace by Omnibus, 218
Tropical End of the Building, 228
Dagenham Breach, 193
Dartford, 194
Deacon's Coffee House, 38
Deaf & Dumb Asylum, 236
Debtors' Prison, White-cross Street, 58
Deptford, 180, 186
Deptford Dock Yard, 237
Devonshire House, 112
Dissenting Chapels, 280
District Telegraph, 22
Dover Street, 112
DOCKS :—
Commercial 180, 186, 236
East India, 72, 182, 236
London, 68, 179, 186, 238
St. Katherine's, 53, 67, 179, 186, 241
West India, 71, 180, 186
Doctors' Commons, 33, 44
Downing Street, 85
Drapers' Hall, 236
Drinking Fountains, 22
Drury Lane, 120
Duke of York's Column, 238
Dulwich, 247
Dulwich Gallery, Dul-wich College, 286
Ealing, 216
East India House, 42
Earl's Court Cemetery, 236
East India Company's Museum, 236
East Country Dock, 236
East and West India Docks, 236
Educational Statistics, 286
Eel-pie Island, 175, 210

Egham, 207
Egham Hill, 207
Egyptian Hall, 113
Eltham, 189
Elephant and Castle, 160
Electric Telegraph Co., 42, 236
Enfield, 246
Entomological Society, 236
Epping Forest, 248
Epsom 214
Erith, 183, 193
Erith Pier, 193
Erith Arboretum, 193
Essex Street, 76
Eton, 202, 237
Euston Square, 150
Excursions round the Environs of London, 246
Exeter Hall, 79, 237
Exhibitions :—
  Burford's Panorama, 114
  Colloseum, 146
  Gallery of Illustration 237
  Polytechnic, 117, 239
  Suffolk Street Gallery, 241
  Tussaud's, 118, 242
  Wyld's Model of the Earth, 114, 237
Fares from all the Coach Stands to the Theatres, Places of Amusement, Railway Stations, &c., 270
Farringdon Market, 59
Female Orphan Asylum, 165, 237
Fenchurch Street, 49
Finchley, 246
Finsbury Square, 73
Finsbury Circus, 75
Fishmongers' Hall, 47, 237
Fishmongers' Almshouses, 160
Fitzroy Square, 150
Fleet Street, 62
Foreign Office, 84
Foreign Ambassadors and Consuls, 263
Foundling Hospital, 150, 237
French Protestant Church, 280

Fulham, 173
Furnival's Inn, 59

Gallion's Reach, 183
General Post Office, 33
General Directions for Railway Travellers, 258
Geological Museum, 237
Geological Society, 231
Golden Square, 115
Goldsmiths' Company, 26
Goldsmiths' Hall, 35
Goswell Street, 155
Gough Square, 63
Government Powder Magazine, 194
Gravesend, 184, 195
Grays, 195
Gray's Inn, 130
Gray's Inn Lane, 151
Gray's Pier, 195
Great Fire of London, 24
Great Russell Street, 132
Great Marlborough Street, 118
Green Park, 107
Grecian Saloon, 154
Greenwich, 181, 186
Greenwich Observatory, 181, 188
Greenwich Park, 181, 237
Greenwich Hospital, 182, 186, 237
Greenhithe, 183, 194
Gresham Lectures, 237
Grocers' Hall, 37
Grosvenor Street, 117
Grosvenor Square, 117
Guards' Memorial, 103
Guildhall, 36, 237

Hackney Carriage Fares and Regulations, 249
Hampstead, 246
Hampton Court, 176, 211
Hampton Court Palace, 237
Hampton Wick, 176
Hanover Chapel, 116
Hanover Square, 116
Hanover Square Rooms, 116, 237
Harrow Road, 246
Hayes, 248
Henry VII. Chapel, 90
Herald's College, 44

Her Majesty's Judges, 263
Highbury, 153
Highgate Cemetery, 237
Holborn Hill, 58
Holland House, 110
Horse Guards, 84
Horsemonger Lane Gaol, 160
Home Office, 84
Hospitals :—
  Bethlehem, 161, 235
  Bridewell, 235
  Charing Cross, 81
  Guy's, 157, 237
  King's College, 125
  London, 73, 238
  London Fever, 153
  Magdalen, 161
  Middlesex, 238
  Royal Free, 151
  Scottish, 62
  St. Bartholomew's, 57, 241
  St. George's, 109, 241
  St. Katharine's, 146
  St. Luke's, 154, 211
  St. Thomas's, 157, 241
  University College, 146
  Westminster, 96
Houses of Parliament, 97, 171, 240
Hungerford Market, 80
Hungerford Pier, 80
Hunterian Museum, 237
Hyde Park, 108
Hyde Park Corner, 108

Ilford, 248
Inner Temple Gate, 64
Insolvent Debtors' Court, 125
Institute of Civil Engineers, 238
Isle of Dogs, 112
Isle of Sheppey, 184
Islington, 153
Islington Cattle Market, 154

Jews' Synagogues, 281
Johnson's Court, 62

Kennington Common, 165
Kennington Road, 165
Kensal Green Cemetery, 238

Kensington Gardens, 110, 238
Kensington (South) Museum, 111, 241
Kensington Palace, 110
Kentish Town, 151
Kew Botanic Gardens, 174, 238, 246
Kilburn Road, 246
King Street 105
King Street Bazaar, 238
King William Street, 43, 46
King's College, 78, 238
King's Cross, 151
Kingston - on - Railway, 213
Kingston-on-Thames, 175, 213
Knightsbridge Barracks, 109

Ladye Chapel (St. Saviour's, Southwark) 238
Lambeth Palace, 167, 172, 238
Lamb's Conduit Street, 151
Leadenhall Market, 42
Leadenhall Street, 42
Lee, 188
Leicester Square, 114
Lewisham, 24, 248
Licensed Victuallers' School, 165
Limehouse, 71, 186
Limits of the Metropolis, 251
Lincoln's Inn Fields, 125
Lincoln's Inn Hall, 126, 238
Linnæan Society, 288
Lloyd's, 40
Lollards' Tower, 167, 172
London Bridge, 47
London Crystal Palace, 115
London Docks, 238
London Hospital, 238
London Institution, 75
London Mechanics Institution, 238
London Stone, 45
London University, 78
London University College, 146
Long Acre, 121

Lord's Cricket Ground, 149
Lord Mayor, 25
Lothbury, 42
Lowther Arcade, 80, 238, 249
Lyon's Inn, 77

Mansion House, 37, 238
Mark Lane, 49
Marlborough House, 104
Marylebone Baths and Washhouses, 150
Mechanics' Institution, 63
Mendicity Society, 131
Metropolitan Railway, 59
Mercers' Company, 32, 238
Mercers' Hall, 37, 238
Merchant Tailors' School, 46
Merton, 247
Middle Temple, 65
Middle Temple Hall, 65
Middlesex Hospital, 238
Middlesex House of Correction, 152
Middlesex Sessions House, 155
Millbank, 100
Millbank Penitentiary, 100, 172
Milton, 196
Minories, The, 73
Mint, The, 54, 238
Missionary Museum, 238
Mitcham, 247
Model Buildings, The, 152
Money Order Office, 34
Monument, The, 61, 239
Morden College, 189
Mortlake, 174
Museum of Asiatic Society, 239
Museum of London Antiquities, 239
Music Hall (Store St.) 239

National Gallery, 82, 239
National Portrait Gallery, 239
Naval and Military Bible Society, 286
Navy Agents, 291

New Bond Street, 116
New River Head and Reservoir, 152
New Road, 146, 153
Newgate, 56, 239
Newgate Market, 55
News Rooms in London, 38
Nine Elms, 172
Nore The, 184
Northfleet, 183, 195
Northumberland House, 81
Norwood, 247
Norwood Cemetery, 239
Nunhead Cemetery (Peckham), 239

Old Bailey, 56
Old Brentford, 174
Old London Bridge, 48
Old Windsor, 178
Omnibus Routes, 254
Ordnance Office, 239
Ornithological Society, 106
Oxford Street, 118
Oxford, The, 239

Paddington, 149
Painters' and Stainers' Hall, 239
Palace Yard, New, 85
Palace Yard, Old, 85
Pall Mall, 103
Pantheon, 118, 243, 239
Pantechnicon, 239
Parliament Street, 85
Parish Churches in London, 276
Parish Churches in Westminster, and within a circuit of ten miles, 277
Parcels Conveyance Company, 253
Paternoster Row, 33, 54
Paul's Cross, 27
Pentonville, 152
Pentonville, or Model Prison, 153
Petersham, 210
Philanthropic Society, 161
Philharmonic Society, 116
Piccadilly, 111
Poet's Corner, 86, 87
Polygraphic Hall, 239

Polytechnic Institution, 117, 239
Pool, The, 53
Porterage, 253
Portland Place, 117
Portland New Town, 149
Portman Square, 118
Portugal Street, 124
Post Office Regulations, 265
Privy Council Office, 84
Private Picture Galleries, 240
Public Offices, 288
Purfleet, 183, 194
Putney, 173, 247

Queenhithe, 45
Queen's Square, 146
Queen's Bench Prison, 160

Railway Passengers' Assurance Company, 259
RAILWAYS :—
Blackwall, 49, 72
Eastern Counties, 75
Great Northern, 151, 260
Great Western, 149, 260
London and North Western, 150, 260
London and South Western, 165, 260
London, Brighton, and South Coast, 157, 160
South Eastern, 157, 260
West India Docks and Birmingham Junction, 153
Reading, 207
Recorder, 25
Red Lion Square, 131
Red Lion Street, 151
Regent Street, 115
Regent Circus, 115
Regent's Canal, 71, 186
Regent's Park, 146
Regent Square, 150
Regulations respecting Stage Carriages, including Omnibuses, 260
Richmond, 208, 240, 247
Richmond Hill, 174

Richmond Park, 175, 208
Rolls, The, 63
Roman Catholic Chapels, in and near London, 281
Rosedale House, 210
Rosherville, 195
Rosherville Pier, 195
Rosherville Gardens, 195, 240
Rotherhithe, 186
Rowland Hill's Chapel, 164
Royal Academy, 82, 240
Royal Academy of Music, 116
Royal Asiatic Society, 240
Royal College of Surgeons, 126, 241
Royal Exchange, 39, 240
Royal Humane Society, 109
Royal Institution, 112
Royal Institute of British Architects, 241
Royal Institution Museum, 240
Royal Mews, Pimlico, 235
Royal Naval School, 188
Royal Society, 78, 240
Royal Society for Preservation of Life from Fire, 21
Runnimede, 117
Russell Institution, 145

Saddlers' Hall, 36
Saull's Museum of Geology, 240
Savoy Chapel, 79
School of Design, Government, 78, 238
Scotland Yard, 83
Scottish Places of Worship, 285
Serpentine, The, 109
Seven Dials, 119
Severndroog Castle, 189
Shadwell, 70
Sheerness, 184
Sheerness, 184
Shooter's Hill, 189, 190, 191
Shoreditch, 74
Snaresbrook, 248
Soane's Museum, 125, 240
Society of Arts, 80, 240

Society of Antiquaries, 78
Society of British Artists, 210
Society of Friends' Meeting Houses, 281
Society of Painters in Water Colours, 103, 240
Soho Bazaar, 119, 241, 249
Soho Square, 119
Somerset House, 77, 171, 241
Southall, 246
Southend, 248
South Kensington Museum, 241
South Sea House, 43
Southwark, 156
Spa Fields Chapel, 152
Springhead, 197
Stafford House, 105, 107
Staple's Inn, 59, 131
Stationers' Company, 26
Stationers' Hall, 54
STATUES :—
  Achilles, 108
  Canning, 85
  Charles I., 83
  Charles II., 172
  Charles II., (Windsor Castle) 204
  Charles James Fox, 145
  Duke of Bedford, 145
  Duke of Kent, 118
  Duke of Wellington, Royal Exchange 39
  Duke of Wellington Hyde Park Corner 108
  Duke of York, 103
  Edward VI., 157
  George I., 116
  George III., Pall Mall, 101
  George III., Somerset House, 77
  George III., Windsor Castle, 206
  George IV., 81
  James II., 84
  Jenner, the Discoverer of Vaccination, 82
  Napier, Sir C., 82, 248
  Nelson, 81

Statues–continued.
  Pillar Memorial to Lord Raglan, and other Westminster Scholars, 248
  Pitt, 116
  Queen Anne, St. Paul's Church Yard, 30
  Queen Anne, Queen's Square, 146
  Queen Victoria, 40
  Richard Cœur de Lion, 248
  Sir Robert Clayton 157
  Sir Henry Havelock, 248
  Sir Robert Peel, 35
  Thomas Guy, 158
  William IV., 43
Stock Exchange, 40
Stoke Pogis, 207
Strand, 76
Stratton Street., 112
Strawberry Hill, 210
Streatham, 217
Street Architecture, 23
Sunbury, 177
Surgeon's Hall, 241
Surrey Royal Gardens 160, 241
Sutherland Gallery, The 105
Suffolk Street Gallery, 241
Swanscombe Wood, 195
Swedish Protestant Church, 280
St. Clement's Reach, 195
St. George's Roman Catholic Cathedral, 161, 235
St. James's Gallery of Paintings, 240
St. James's Hall, 115
St. James's Palace, 104
St. James's Park, 105
St. James's Street, 105
St. James's Square, 105
St. John's Gate, 57
St. John's Lodge, 147
St. John's Wood, 148
St. Martin's Baths and Wash Houses, 114
St. Martin's Music Hall, 121
St. Paul's Church Yard, 83

St. Paul's School, 33
Tabernacle, 160
Table of Money of all Nations, 274
Teddington, 175, 210
Temple, The, 64
Temple Bar, 63
Temple Gardens, 66, 171
Tennison's, Archbishop, Chapel and School, 116
Term Table, 263
Thames Ditton, 176
Thames, The, below Bridge, 170
Thumps Steamers, 262
Thames Street, 45
Thames Tunnel, 70, 179, 186, 241
Thavies Inn, 59
THEATRES :—
  Adelphi, 79, 244
  Astley's, 167, 215
  City of London. 215
  Drury Lane, 121, 244,
  Olympic, 77, 120, 245
  Haymarket, 101, 244
  Her Majesty's, 101, 244
  Lyceum, 79, 244
  Marylebone 245
  Princess's, 118, 215
  Queen's, 245
  Royal Italian Opera, 123, 244
  Royal Standard, 245
  Sadler's Wells, 152, 245
  St. James's, 105, 244
  Surrey, 164, 245
  Strand, 76, 245
  Victoria, 164, 245
Thornton Heath, 247
Threadneedle Street, 43
Tilbury Fort, 184, 197
Times Printing Office. The, 59
Tobacco Warehouses, 69
Tooting, 217
Torrington Square, 146
Tottenham Court Road, 132
Tower of London, 49, 179, 185, 242
Toxopholite Society, 147
Trafalgar Square, 81
Treasury, The, 84
Trinity House, 53, 242
Turner Gallery, 104, 212
Twickenham, 175, 210

Unitarian Chapels in and near London, 281
United Service Museum, 84, 242
University College, 146 242
Uxbridge, 246

Vauxhall Gardens, 165, 172
Vernon Gallery, 104, 242
Victoria Park, 74
Victoria Railway Bdge, 173
Victoria Station, 101
Vintners' Hall, 45
Veterinary College, 212

Walthamstow, 248
Walton, 177
Wandsworth, 247
Wanstead, 248
Wapping, 70, 186
Water Colours Exhibition of the New Society of Painters in, 242
Water Colours, Old Society or Painters in, 242
Waterloo Road, 164
Watling Street, 44
Wellington Car, at Marlboro House, 104
Wellington Sarcophagus in St., Paul's 80
Wesleyan Centenary Hall, 242
Wesleyan Chapels in London and its suburbs, 285
Western Literary and Scientific Institution, Leicester Square, 114
Westminster Abbey, 86, 242
Westminster Bridge Road, 167
Westminster Hall, 85
Westminster Road, 165
Westminster School, 95
West Thurrock, 195
Whispering Gallery, 32
Whitechapel, 73
Whitehall, 84
Whittington Club, 76
Wilderness Row, 155
Willis's Rooms, 105
Wimbledon, 247

Winchester House, 169
Windmill Hill, 196
WINDSOR CASTLE, 178
  242
  Audience Chamber, 206
  Home Park, The, 205
  King John's Tower. 204
  Long Walk, The, 206
  North Terrace, 204

Windsor Castle-contnd
  Presence Chamber, 206
  Queen's Audience Chamber, 204
  Round Tower, 204
  Slopes, The, 205
  St. George's Chapel 203, 204
  St. George's Hall, 205
  Vandyke Room, 205

Windsor Castle-contind
  Virginia Water, 206, 207
  Waterloo Gallery, 205
Windsor Park 202
Woburn Square, 146
White Conduit House, 153
Woodford, 248
Woolwich, 182, 190, 193

Woolwich Reach, 182
Woolwich Common, 191
York and Albany, The, 113
Young Men's Christian Association, 58
Zion House, 174
Zoological Gardens, 243